DAILY LIFE IN PORTUGAL
IN THE LATE MIDDLE AGES

A. H. de Oliveira Marques

DAILY LIFE IN PORTUGAL
IN THE
LATE MIDDLE AGES

Translated by S. S. Wyatt
Drawings by Vítor André

THE UNIVERSITY OF WISCONSIN PRESS
Madison, Milwaukee, and London

1971

F 11-16 to Suso Brigilion   16-00

Published 1971
The University of Wisconsin Press
Box 1379, Madison, Wisconsin 53701

The University of Wisconsin Press, Ltd.
27-29 Whitfield Street, London, W.1

A Sociedade Medieval Portuguesa:
Aspectos de Vida Quotidiana originally published by
Livraria Sá da Costa Editora, Lisbon
Copyright © 1964 by Livraria Sá da Costa Editora

Printed in the United States of America
The William Byrd Press, Inc., Richmond, Virginia

ISBN 0-299-05580-9; LC 78-106040

To the memory of Jaime Cortesão

CONTENTS

ILLUSTRATIONS

Figures

Maps

PREFACE

THIS book seeks to bring something new to the area of Portuguese history. The subject focused upon—aspects of Portuguese medieval society in its daily actions—has never drawn the attention of historians, except for a few pages in Costa Lobo's *Historia da Sociedade em Portugal no Seculo XV* [History of society in Portugal in the fifteenth century] referring to personal incomes. This is consequently a pioneer study, exhibiting all the defects which the opening up of new paths always entails because of inexperience and indecision concerning unforeseen difficulties.

The originality of the theme diminishes somewhat in Chapters 5 and 7, and disappears altogether in Chapter 8, devoted to culture. Nevertheless, they were thought indispensable in a book on the most significant elements of daily life, even though they are limited to a synthesis, made inevitable by already existing studies on their subjects. Each chapter would justify a book, for the available material is extensive and the theme considered is complex in both time and space. Consequently, it was impossible to reduce the number of pages devoted to clothing, even though endangering the equilibrium of the work.

A primary aim was to avoid anecdotal elements, a pitfall of many similar studies detracting from the sobriety so necessary to books on history. But I have lightened the text as much as possible by reducing the scholarly notes to a minimum, by avoiding specialized terminology and even density of style, and by frequently resorting to picturesque examples from the chronicles of the period. The intent is to present genuine history to a wide audience, moderating the apparent contradiction between specialized science and general interest.

A bibliographic guide is supplied instead of the sterile listing of publications that is usually presented as a bibliography. It is necessarily longer, but much more useful.

The arrangement of the chapters was dictated by the life and necessities of each human being. Man needs, above all, to be fed, clothed, and provided with shelter. In order not to die, he is obliged to follow certain habits of cleanliness and to attempt to preserve his health. It is after these considerations are met that he loves, works, prays, is educated, and participates in amusements. Finally, he dies and is buried.

In the discussion of each subject the reader may note certain omissions, or what seem to be omissions. Chapter 2, for instance, does not discuss military apparel. I had to decide whether the wardrobe of a warrior should or should not be analyzed as an element of *daily* life. Certain omissions in Chapters 3 and 4 are mentioned in the text itself; they are the result of the scarcity of sources. A chapter on political and social life was omitted after being initially included; such a chapter would require a basis in a series of monographs on the figures and political events, and these have not yet been attempted. Here again, moreover, one may ask whether it is appropriate to include in a study of daily life an examination of phenomena which are far from common occurrences. Much the same can be said in regard to jurisprudence.

The customs of the Jewish and Morisco communities, which constituted only a small proportion of the total medieval Portuguese population, are omitted from this book. When Jew and Moor lived in the Christian manner—so far as type of home or hygienic practices, for example—nothing distinguished them from other Portuguese. When, on the contrary, they followed living practices of incontrovertible originality—and that was the usual case—analysis falls rather to a scholar of international Judaism and Islamic society.

I have not attempted to capture the totality of day-to-day existence. Only certain aspects, perhaps the most important ones, are studied. To cover all of them would take over a thousand pages. Such detail is also impossible until Portuguese historiography has progressed much farther than at present and is capable of furnishing basic scholarly studies on standard and cost of living, analysis of salaries, behavior of prices, and other topics. This book deals, in short, with what it was able to deal with.

The chronological limits are, with few exceptions, from the twelfth century to the end of the fifteenth century. Following a tendency which is becoming generalized, I have regarded the second half of the quattrocento as "medieval." Furthermore, this permitted the utilization of much more abundant sources than adopting the traditional delimitation of the Middle Ages would have. The reader will sometimes wonder, and rightfully so, if the sources of information on the fifteenth century allow one to draw conclusions for the twelfth century. He will see, however, that my preoccupation was always with soundly explaining the period to which the sources belong, and that some material is also collected for the preceding centuries.

The illustrations—taken from contemporary paintings, book illuminations, bas-reliefs, sculptures, and other contemporary works—always have a functional purpose: to explain the text and to make it more vivid. All the drawings are based on works of art from the medieval period, particularly Portuguese ones. When such art is rare for certain subjects—as in Chapter 4—illustrations were omitted in preference to supplying more or less hypothetical substitutes. Hence the obvious disequilibrium among the chapters. The profusion of drawings in Chapter 2, "Dress," arises from the obvious necessity of making intelligible concepts totally unknown to most readers. That necessity does not arise, at least with such urgency, in regard to other aspects of medieval life, as for example, the religious and emotional.

I must express my gratitude to several persons for the interest they demonstrated and the valuable assistance they gave during the preparation of this book. Dr. Vitorino de Magalhães Godinho patiently read the manuscript as each chapter was being written, expressing his opinion, both on the general contents and on the details, and helping with corrections and suggestions for improvement of the text.

My wife also patiently listened to the reading of each page, as a preview of a demanding and critical public.

Dr. Maria José de Mendonça, director of the Museu Nacional de Arte Antiga (National Museum of Ancient Art) of Lisbon, was kind enough to criticize Chapter 2 in her capacity as a specialist on textiles and an expert on problems relating to apparel.

To my friend Dr. Adriano de Gusmão fell the reading of Chapter 3, on which he gave me extremely useful material.

My late colleague at the University of Lisbon, Reverend Honorato Rosa, Ph.D., was kind enough to read Chapter 7, to its considerable benefit.

Miss Fernanda Eugénia de Castro Freire, professor in the Museu Ricardo Espírito Santo, Lisbon, and my distinguished former student, supplied useful information for revising Chapter 3 and even lent me books.

Miss Sharon Wyatt translated this book into English, a difficult task, particularly because of the medieval terminology. Yet I think she did it very well and am happy to discover in the English version that same easy and readable style I tried very hard to achieve in Portuguese.

My friend and colleague at the University of Florida, Dr. Richard Preto-Rodas, revised the English text of the poems, for which both the translator and the author wish to express their gratitude.

Last but not least, Dr. Vítor André gave this book character and movement and contributed to its better comprehension with his graceful drawings.

A. H. de Oliveira Marques

S. João do Estoril, August 1963
Gainesville, Florida, March 1969

DAILY LIFE IN PORTUGAL
IN THE LATE MIDDLE AGES

Map by the University of Wisconsin Cartographic Laboratory

Map 1. Modern Portugal.

INTRODUCTION

IF we view the more general geomorphological characteristics of the Hispanic peninsula as a whole, no peculiarity appears to warrant a political fragmentation within it," the historian Jaime Cortesão remarked. And in fact, it is impossible to speak of a unit of Portuguese territory with a basis in the accidents of nature, or of a Portuguese individuality within the Iberian whole.

The northwest (Minho, or better, Entre-Douro-e-Minho, as it was formerly called, extending from the Minho down to the Douro) is a continuation of Galicia in orography, in climate, and in forms of exploiting the soil. The northeast (Trás-os-Montes and northern Beira) is a continuation of the Iberian Meseta, while the central cordillera (Serra da Estrela, etc.) separates northern Portugal and southern Portugal, just as it does northern Castile and southern Castile, their neighbors. Beira Baixa and Alentejo share conditions resembling those of Spanish Extremadura. And the Algarve, the southernmost province in Portugal, does not differ in any way from maritime Andalucia. In each case we note resemblances not only in features of terrain and weather but also in way of life and general economic conditions. In fact, the most geographically unique regions in Portugal are a relatively narrow strip of the coastline (Beira Litoral and Portuguese Estremadura) and the flood plains of the Tagus basin (Ribatejo). This in its entirety, however, covers only a little less than 25 percent of the country.

The unusual length of the low plateaus does bestow a distinctive aspect to certain areas of Portugal if these are compared with the rest of the Iberian peninsula. But this conclusion is more the result of comparing Portugal as a political unit with Spain as a political unit, than of actually detaching from the peninsula, taken as a whole, a genuine geographic unit. The particular structural features found in Catalonia-Aragon, Murcia-Valencia, and Andalucia, to mention only the most obvious, are just as varied as those in Portugal. The truth is that in the large Iberian unit, several of its regions are distinctive. And Portugal—or better, a part of Portugal—is but one of them.

This fact, taken by itself, neither makes the independence of Portugal an absurdity nor justifies Iberian union. Throughout Europe, as in the rest of the world, geographical and political boundaries often are contradictory. For example, the northern European plateaus, a geomorphic unit, were and are crossed by frontiers manifestly as arbitrary as those of Portugal. Much the same is true of many areas in Africa and America.

Much more important than an alleged geographic individuality is the geographic *location* of Portugal. This can explain many of the characteristic features of its history and the very existence of Portugal as a nation. Lying on the farthest point of Europe, Portugal was for many centuries the end of the world. *Finisterre*, the name of a Galician cape, would be more appropriately applied to Cabo da Roca, the "tip of Europe." Beyond, there was nothing, not even islands. In fact, the Portuguese coastline, 527 miles long, does not contain any islands worthy of the name. Furthermore, there are few reentrants, despite the long beaches, which limits the number of good ports to three or four. Gulfs are not found, and even though the sea affects most of Portugal through the climate and vegetation, the economic life depending on it is secondary. Lashed by sea winds, which are frequently tempestuous, and possessing an extremely narrow continental shelf (averaging nineteen miles), the Portuguese coast does not seem favorable to maritime enterprises. On the contrary, the geographic conditions of the greater part of the country would indicate a limited living from the sea, restricted to local fisheries.

The end of the world, a place of destination rather than of passage, with little attraction to the sea, the physical location of Portugal did not seem designated to favor the development of progressive cultures, and would account, over the long centuries, for the backwardness of many of the national features. And in spite of all the changes in the world in the way of discovery and transportation, for part of which Portugal was responsible, this condition can be observed even today.

Although Atlantic in location, Portugal is Mediterranean in most of its distinctive traits. Weather, vegetation, the types of economy, the way of life, the characteristics of the soil are much closer to the Greek or Italian than to the Basque or Breton. Rainfall and temperature follow the typical Mediterranean pattern, with a dry, hot summer followed by a rainy but mild winter. Most of the country's vegetation shares in this Mediterranean appearance. Every visitor to Portugal is impressed with the diversity of the landscape in such a tiny area

(35,000 square miles, almost the size of the state of Indiana, a little more than that of Scotland). There are no true forests but, instead, dense woods of trees and shrubs, and thickets and other vegetation scattered here and there. Fruit trees play an important role in the landscape, whether by themselves or connected with tilled fields and other cultivation. Large vineyards and fields of cereals such as wheat, corn, rye, and barley can be seen everywhere. The soil, however, is generally light and poor, in large part mountainous and subject to constant erosion, and less than half the land is cultivated. The conditions of the terrain favor either the minifundia, the center of immensely individualistic methods of life and work, or the latifundia, ineffectively exploited and in large part abandoned to pasturage and uncultivated lands. Sheep, goats, mules, and swine are more numerous than cattle. Manual labor and primitive techniques have persisted everywhere. And in spite of all the advances of the twentieth century, malaria, characteristically Mediterranean, continues to exist, at least in an endemic state.

Obviously, the farther south one goes, the more one senses the Mediterranean presence. In fact, the general Mediterranean characteristics of the country aside, geographers usually divide Portugal into two large areas, north and south, divided roughly at the fortieth parallel or just a little below this line. North and south form a contrast in climate and soil; all the other differences—in economy, in psychology, and in history—are no more than the consequences of these. Of the plains lower than 656 feet in altitude, 61.5 percent are found in the south; 95.4 percent of the plateaus and the mountains above 1312 feet lie in the north. The greater part of the north is wet, with a much higher percentage not only in precipitation but also in humidity; in contrast, the south is dry, without rain for four to six months. It is not surprising that two patterns of life have resulted from such diversity. The humid valleys of the north have always favored isolation, sectionalism, and dense but scattered settlements. They have always retained more archaisms and withstood both invasions and innovations. On the other hand, the arid plains of the south contributed toward opening the intellect as well as the highways. They facilitated both invasions and communications. And they favored a less heavy population, concentrated in a few populous centers, with large, empty spaces between them.

After the great ethnic mixtures of prehistory and protohistory and the landings and the invasions of the Phoenicians, Greeks, and Carthaginians, the two major groups of peoples and cultures who came to shape the Portugal of the Middle Ages were the Romans and the Moslems. The Romans dominated and pacified the entire Iberian peninsula, civilized it in their image, created the administrative units from which emerged the Portuguese frontiers, and covered Spain with roads, monuments, and small-scale replicas of Rome. They established the bases of a harmonious economic system that brought prosperity to the people. They introduced forms of soil exploitation, and adapting them to the local conditions, originated the fragmentation of land holdings in the north (even though to a limited degree) and their concentration in the south. And, more than anything else, they brought their language, which diversified into popular dialects.

Afterwards came the Arabs and the Berbers from North Africa, who colonized vast sections of Portugal, especially in the south. The Islamic contribution is much more difficult to evaluate than the Roman, not only because the Christian Reconquest from the eighth century to the thirteenth endeavored to obliterate all traces of it, but also because this has received much less attention from historians. Nevertheless, Arabic weighed heavily upon the language spoken by the inhabitants of the peninsular west, especially during the Middle Ages. The percentage of Arabic words having to do with clothing, furniture, agriculture, scientific instruments, etc., was then quite pronounced (many of these terms have since become obsolete); and this fact well evidences the Islamic contribution to the improvement of rural techniques, to the development of the sciences, and to greater refinement and ease in daily life. The Moslem civilization persisted in many other ways: in artistic and architectural forms, such as interior decoration, the use of tiles (azulejos), elaborate ceilings, and city plans; in the impulse given to navigation and naval techniques, with the expansion of fishing areas to the coast of Morocco and the development of new types of ships capable of being maneuvered, fundamental factors in the future Portuguese expansion; in the customs of their daily life; in the very essence of being Portuguese—the fatalistic psychology, the love for poetry, the capacity for assimilation and adaptation. In the formation of Portugal, these two great elements—the Roman above all, the Moslem afterwards—need to be perfectly understood because they surpass all the others.

"A vast intertwined forest" is the way the historian Costa Lobo defined the Portugal of the fifteenth century. The same could be said of the preceding eras. Forests and dense thickets covered most of the country, making it an excellent refuge for wild and sometimes vicious animals.

Here and there one came across a clump of houses, a center surrounded by cleared fields which sustained its population.

It is true that Minho or certain coastal zones in the north and in the Algarve escaped this desolate panorama to a small extent. Here one would find a more dispersed settlement, in even smaller hamlets and little farms scattered along the valleys, the lower slopes of the mountains, and the few plains.

The population was scanty: a million inhabitants, perhaps a few more, distributed irregularly from the north to the south, with the maximums and minimums of density in the same areas where they are reached today, not exceeding an average of twenty-eight inhabitants per square mile (or eleven inhabitants per square kilometer). There were, it is true, rises and drops in population throughout the three centuries of medieval Portugal. There may have been more than a million between 1250 and 1350, when the peace and prosperity of the kingdom had succeeded the rigorous times of the Reconquest, but the number dropped below the million mark after the Black Death of 1348, or even before, to reach one million again only a century later.

Between the north and the south, the panorama of the populational groupings was strikingly different. Down to the line of the Tagus, with the exception of Braga, Guimarães, Oporto, Coimbra, and perhaps Bragança, almost no cities existed, and even the villages were small and poorly kept. The large nuclei of inhabitants were found in the south, heir of the Roman and Islamic traditions: Santarém, Lisbon, Montemor-o-Novo, Estremoz, Elvas, Vila Viçosa, Évora, Beja, Silves, Lagos, Faro, Tavira. Lisbon, where the court and the public administration were gradually established, gained prominence over all the other cities. As important as Guimarães, Coimbra, or Santarém in the twelfth century, Lisbon was clearly preeminent a hundred years later, and held six or eight times as many inhabitants as any of the others from the end of the fourteenth century on. The expression "Portugal is Lisbon" had already been coined by this time. And this in spite of the preference shown by many monarchs for various cities, villages, and hamlets, in which they sometimes spent more time than in the capital.

Communications between the various regions of the country were precarious and depended almost entirely upon the conditions of the land. If it was flat, suitable for the tracing of beaten paths, trails, or roads, or if there were navigable rivers or the coast nearby, transportation could be relatively rapid and regular. On the other hand, forests and thick woods, mountain ranges, and obstructed rivers almost completely isolated certain areas of the kingdom, as, for example, some villages and districts, forcing their inhabitants to live independently of others.

But ease of communication was not enough to dilute the localist attitudes and provincial spirit that reigned in all of the municipalities during the Middle Ages, helping to block the rise of a national consciousness, which only the unity of language and the necessity of defense against the Castilians would finally cement.

Portugal lived principally on agriculture: cereals, wine, olives where they would grow, made up the trilogy of the Portuguese farmer. Wine was almost the only export; at times some olive oil and, very rarely, wheat were exported, but as a rule, neither was sufficient to feed the population. In coastal zones, fishing and salt were particularly important, both in everyday nutrition and in commerce. Salt brought wealth to many a merchant of Lisbon, Setúbal, and Aveiro, who exported it at high profits to the Nordic countries. In Algarve the most lucrative activity was the sale of fruit—figs, grapes, and almonds—which, duly dried and prepared, was profitably shipped to Flanders and England.

There was no industry. Even artisanship was minimal and confined to the necessities of consumption; clothing and shoes were manufactured, and objects of iron, wood, and clay, utensils for home and farm, but little else. Good cloth, moreover, had to be imported from Flanders and Italy, as did also armor, munitions, and a multitude of manufactured articles.

Of interest to the foreigner, in addition to wine, fruit and salt, were leather and small red scales (kermes) which grew in the bark of the oaks—a precious raw material for the making of the best scarlet dye, used in the richest and most expensive fabrics. Foreign commerce particularly began to develop during the thirteenth century, when maritime exchange with Northern Europe began to replace the voyages of the Crusades. Internally, the building of a state involved a certain commercial activity, fomented and developed by means of trade fairs, but already heralded by mercantile relations between the entire territory of Entre-Douro-e-Minho and Beira with centers in Guimarães, Oporto, Braga, and Coimbra. The integration of the Muslim south, rich in important centers of population where a strong tradition of commerce and artisanship prevailed, was an outstanding factor in the creation of a Portuguese economy.

Monetary circulation was also stimulated in the 1200's. But the rudimentary forms that commerce had always taken in a good part of the national territory hindered the complete changeover from a natural to a monetary economy. Barter and payments for services in kind continued to nourish this interchange throughout the Middle Ages. The phenomenon is exemplified, in fact, in the few kinds of currency existent in the Portugal of the time: gold coin was rare and ceased to be minted after the middle of the thirteenth century; good silver coin did not exist until the mid-fourteenth century; only coin of silver alloy (*bilhão*), with about one gram of silver, and foreign currency had any significance, therefore, in the transactions. Except for a few years in the reign of Fernando I (1367–83), this situation was maintained without great changes until the first quarter of the fifteenth century.

In this Portugal lived a million people stratified in classes, subclasses, groups, and subgroups. There were the nobility, the clergy, and the people. But nobility did not signify a single social class: *ricos-homens* (grandees), *infanções* (a middle-class nobility), knights, and squires were clearly distinguished by their well-differentiated codes of behavior, rights, and duties. Soon the ranks of infanções were thinned out, the term "knight" was obliterated as a third degree in the higher class, and the original meaning of *rico-homem* was forgotten. Toward the end of the fourteenth century and in the fifteenth, there were vassals of the king, knights, and squires. The expression *fidalgo* (nobleman) appears in the texts, and lineage is based more on an authentic nobility than on feats of arms or on office held. The point is that a new danger, that of the infiltration of the bourgeoisie, was threatening the purity of the blood. The bourgeois, who was above all the great merchant, strove to free himself from the feudal bindings, and to ascend to knighthood, or at least, to assume a separate place all his own.

Nor was the clergy a homogeneous class. High and low clergy, regular clergy and secular clergy appeared in time with their distinctions, their rivalries, and their struggles. What distinguished both nobles and clergy—and this represents perhaps the authentic cleavage which separated them from the third estate—were their privileges. They paid no taxes, they received protection from above, they assumed rights over the masses.

The people, with no privileges and with the task of maintaining the other two orders by their work, were in turn split into many groups. I have mentioned the bourgeoisie, whose presence made itself especially felt after the fourteenth century. In the country resided the "goodmen," a higher caste of farmers, almost all of them rather well-to-do landowners, who owned a horse and the arms necessary for going to war and who for this reason were designated *cavaleiros-vilãos*. Below them was the peasantry, a group of tenants paying rents, quitrents, and services, upon whom fell the principal weight of taxation. Last of all were the serfs and the slaves, gradually disappearing, and a vast mass

Fig. 1. Panels of St. Vicente de Fora (1465–75): Panel of the Prince (Henry the Navigator). The artist and purpose of these panels remain a mystery. All classes of

the Portuguese people are supposed to be represented on the panels. *Left-hand page,* left and right panels; *right-hand page,* center panel.

Fig. 2. Panels of St. Vicente de Fora: Panel of the Archbishop. *Left-hand page,*

left and right panels; *right-hand page,* center panel.

of rural laborers, who began to become an indispensable labor force after the mid-fourteenth century. In the cities, below the merchant burghers, were the craftsmen, or artisans, and a rabble of day laborers, peddlers, and the poverty-stricken. Nor can the men of the sea be forgotten, especially the fishermen, who for all practical purposes were integrated into the category of the craftsmen.

Lastly, removed from the people, but also distinct from the clergy, the nobility, and the bourgeoisie, lived a class which was easily distinguishable, very homogeneous, and extremely conscious of its rights and its role within the state. These were the men of letters, the professors in the university, the notaries scattered about the country, the lawyers, the doctors, and the apothecaries. Drawn from the ranks of the people, but almost always privileged, these men were close to the nobility, the clergy (of which they were often members), and the mercantile bourgeoisie, although they are clearly distinguished from all of these.

All these people lived in a manner very different from ours. They ate, dressed, and were entertained according to other standards. They lived in different kinds of houses. They had a different level of life and other ways of spending their time. They did not even conceive of time, in fact, as we do today. Time was more vague, less a thing to be rigorously counted, less clear in its passage and its uses. Time was sun and darkness. There were no mechanical clocks. The basic divisions of day and night corresponded to about only a third of those which exist today: there were four hours of daytime (prime, tierce, sexte, and none) and three hours of night. Beyond these, there was no such thing as minutes or seconds, at least in daily use. Half hours and quarter hours could be counted, but without that rigorous, scientific precision which so concerns us today.

If the months were the same, the days were indicated in a different way, at least until the middle of the thirteenth century. The Roman system of calends, nones, and ides, with a backward count was used: the fourth of calends in January meant December 29, since the first day of the calends corresponded to the first day of the month. Again, dates were frequently designated in terms of religious feast days: the day of St. John the Baptist instead of June 24, the day of St. Michael instead of September 29, and so on.

Even in the counting of the years, differences can be seen. None of the great years which stand out in Portuguese medieval history and which are learned at school—1128, 1143, 1249, 1385, 1415—would have had any meaning at all for the Portuguese of those times. For they counted their years by the era of Caesar, thirty-eight years ahead in relation to the era of Christ (not until 1422 was the change made). Those numbers, therefore, are purely fictitious. The battle of St. Mamede really took place in 1166; the treaty of Zamora was signed in 1181; the Algarve was wrested from the Moors in 1287; the Interregnum and the crisis of the Independence occupied the years 1421 to 1423; and Ceuta was conquered in 1453. The years from 1422 to 1460 were lived and counted twice: the first, while the era of Caesar was still in force; the second, after the era of Christ became the standard.

We should like to know how these people behaved in the face of joy or sorrow; what their normal expression of sentiments was; what the possible social and economic differences that conditioned them were. Life and death, the dealings with the one and the prevention of the other, the attitude toward the supernatural, the concern for neighbor, individualism and collectivism, the moral code—all these are aspects of daily life, omitted as a rule by the historians of structures and events. Some of these aspects and their interrelated problems are studied in the pages which follow. In this way, we shall try to capture as much as possible a vision of the space and the time and of human life as it was really lived in the land the Portuguese inhabit today.

1 : THE TABLE

IT is not particularly easy to discuss the food consumed by the Portuguese during the Middle Ages. Few sources provide information on this subject: the first known book of culinary recipes dates only from the fifteenth century. Descriptions of banquets, collected in chronicles or in other narratives, generally contain scant information about the foods eaten: the picturesque outward appearance of the dishes is described, but their exact contents are ignored. It is true that a few legislative texts do help the historian. Nevertheless, an attempt at reconstruction must be based upon the sum of the most disparate elements, obtained from the greatest possible number of sources, of the most diverse origins.

Medieval diet was generally poor by comparison with modern standards. Much of the time quantity took the place of quality. Culinary techniques were still in an elementary state, and the refinements of Roman cooking had been lost. Seasoning conformed to extremely simple principles. Based on cereals, meat, fish, and wine, the medieval diet was greatly deficient in vitamin D and considerably so in vitamins A and C. The effects of these deficiencies were manifested in the weak resistence of people to infections, with the consequent easy progression of epidemics; in frequent afflictions of the bladder, the kidneys (resulting from the accumulation of stones), and the eyes (blindness, xerophthalmia), resulting from the lack of vitamin A; and in the very common occurrence of scurvy, due to the deficiency in vitamin C.[1]

The two principal meals of the day were dinner and supper. At the end of the fifteenth century, dinner was between ten and eleven o'clock in the morning; but in earlier centuries, it probably had been eaten at eight or nine o'clock. Supper was around six or seven o'clock at night. In *The Loyal Counselor (Leal Conselheiro)*, King Duarte (1433–38) recommends allowing seven to eight hours to elapse between the two meals, and also advises eating a light supper after a heavy dinner, and conversely, having a light dinner the morning after a heavy supper. With frugality in mind, he prescribed that there should be no other

16

meal during the day.[2] One presumes, however, that as the hour for dinner began to fall later and later, eating a "lunch" soon after waking in the morning would presently become necessary.

Dinner was the largest meal of the day. On the average, three courses were served, not counting soups, side dishes, and desserts. This, of course, refers to meals consumed by the king, the nobility, and the high clergy. Among those less privileged or less wealthy, the number of dishes for dinner might be but two or even one. For supper, there were usually only two courses, or one, depending on the conditions just pointed out.[3]

The staple of the diet was preeminently meat. There were the meats from the slaughterhouse—beef, pork, mutton, goat. In Coimbra in the twelfth century, the best prices were quoted for pork and fat mutton, followed by beef and goat; in Évora in 1280, as in 1384, the price of beef was twice that of pork and more than twice that of mutton and goat. Game and poultry were also eaten liberally. Medieval Portugal was a country of game preserves and uncultivated lands; hunting was included among the principal pastimes of the noble and represented an important source of subsistence for the peasant. In the marketplace prices were listed for the meat of fallow deer, zebro,* deer, roebuck, hare, and even bear, among the animal meats, besides an amazing variety of fowl: partridge, the great bustard, crane, wild duck, teal, heron, halcyon, redshank, collar duck, bald coot, calander lark, and many others. Poultry was not much different from that of today: chickens, ducks, geese, pigeons, pheasant, peacock, doves. The turkey alone is missing, for this bird came to Europe only after the discovery of America. A good part of the payments (rents, quitrents, and various other payments) which the peasant was obliged to make to his lord consisted of game and poultry. The noble received such an abundance of these kinds of meat that a law of 1340 expressly forbade him to purchase them in the market.[4]

Rabbits were also among the small livestock raised for food; and the people made various sausages, such as chouriços, a smoked kind, and linguiças, a thin variety.[5]

The most common method of cooking meat was to roast it on the spit (assado). But meat was also boiled (cozido), chopped into hash (desfeito), and stewed (estufado). The badulaque (a hash) was a kind of boiled mutton that existed at least in the fifteenth and sixteenth centuries.[6]

* A variety of cattle, now extinct.

Fig. 3.   Killing the pig. 15th century.

Let us look at some examples of recipes which, even though they date from the first half of the sixteenth century, cannot be very different from medieval ones, excluding, of course, the abundant use of spices.

Recipe for minced, dry-cooked beef

Take a pulpy, boneless piece of beef and not an outside cut because it is very tough. Mince it well and add herbs (cut in the same way as for a salad) and finely chopped onion. In place of butter, add very good olive oil without any rancidity. Once sautéed, season the meat with vinegar (add no water since it was washed before being minced). Then wash as before, since no more water will be added. After it begins to simmer, seasoned with vinegar, salt, and spices (cloves, saffron, pepper, and ginger), continue cooking until no liquid remains, or, if not done in this way (as you would lamprey eel), it may instead be done by placing slices of bread under the meat to absorb the liquid.

This is the recipe for boiled and fricasseed chicken

Take chicken and boil it with parsley, corianders, mint, and onion; then add a seasoning of vinegar and, once seasoned and boiled, pour off broth into a pot and bring the chicken to boil in another kettle; in this same kettle hard-boil a half dozen eggs. Take the yolks of four other eggs, beat them, then add to them the broth in which the chicken and hard-boiled eggs were cooked, thereby making a yellow sauce. Remove the chicken to a plate on which slices of bread have been laid; then arrange the hard-boiled eggs on the plate around the chicken. Pour the yellow sauce of the other eggs over the chicken and sprinkle with ground cinnamon.[7]

Goshawk

Turtledove

Heron

Cock

Swallow

Ostrich

Hoopoe

Rook

Fig. 4.   Birds in medieval Portugal. 12th century.

Peacock

Pelican

Dove

Crow

Pigeon

Stork

Vulture

Crane

Fig. 4 (cont.).   Birds in medieval Portugal.

Fish also formed a basic part of the Portuguese diet, particularly among the less well-to-do classes. The frequent consumption of fish by the nobility and clergy stemmed from their religious precepts: about sixty-eight days a year abstinence from meat was obligatory for Catholics. On those days dishes of fish or shellfish replaced meat courses at dinner and supper. The prohibitions were rigorous; in times of fasting there could be absolutely no meat, eggs, cheese, butter, lard, or even oily fish. Instead, peas, fruit, and small fish were commended by the Church.[8]

One of the fish most frequently eaten by the Portuguese in the Middle Ages seems to have been whiting (*peixota*), found in almost all the documentation that specifies varieties of fish. Sardines, conger eels, shad, surmullet, and lamprey eels were also frequently seen on the tables of every social class. Red mullet, snapper or porgy, tuna, trout, flounder, *bizugos,* shark, turbot, sea bream, and many other fish were objects of culinary art. Meat from the whale and the porpoise was also eaten. Shellfish (like tellin shell and mussels) and crustaceans (like lobsters and crabs) were common.[9]

An interesting "notebook of the amounts of money which the storekeeper spent on the fish for the king in the year 1474" has been preserved. Afonso V (1438–81) was living in Santarém, and almost every day fish, which the fishwives carried in by the hundreds, by the dozen, or even singly, were bought for the royal table. There is little variety in the types of fish: only flounder, sole, and surmullet, alternating with a single kind of shellfish—oysters. Santarém was not Lisbon: it offered less choice in fish; either that, or the king preferred these particular ones. The fish were served fried or in patties at the royal table. The little notebook mentions "griddles for frying," measures of flour for batter or for the dough used in pies, and as *adubos* (seasonings), only oranges (the bitter kind, it must be remembered), parsley, olive oil, and vinegar. The patties were not made in the royal kitchen but rather by a baker. The moneys paid to the "wife of Jorge Esteves Lula" or to Margarida Luís for the work of scaling and washing the fish are also noted in the book.[10]

The sixteenth-century "Treatise on Cooking" from which the meat recipes quoted above were taken includes only one recipe for fish:

Recipe for lamprey eel

Wash the eel in hot water and remove its entrails over a clean pan so as to catch the blood as it comes out; then roll the eel up in that same pan and add coriander, parsley and finely chopped onion. Add a little olive oil, cover with a wooden plate and place over heat. When it is well sautéed add a very small amount of water and vinegar, and sprinkle on cloves, pepper, saffron, and a little ginger.

Besides fresh fish, the people of the Middle Ages consumed a great deal of dried, salted, and smoked fish. In Northern Europe, the trade in salted and smoked herring filled many ships and set in motion large amounts of capital. If, in Portugal, piscatorial abundance and the small extent of the hinterland were less justification for the consumption of fish that was not fresh, nevertheless it would be wrong to think it nonexistent. Given the lack of refrigeration and the warm climate, recourse to drying fish by the sun facilitated their transportation over great distances and made possible storage over long periods of time. A written receipt given by Afonso III (1248–79) to his stewards in 1279 reveals the delivery to the royal pantry between 1257 and 1270 of some 7,687 dried fish ("640 dozen plus seven"), 317 dried conger eels ("26 dozen plus five"), 2,658 cuts (*talhos*) of whale, and 1,656 dried lamprey eels—all resulting from services and payments of fishing populations. In Lisbon at the end of the fourteenth century, sardines were smoked for export to Seville or Aragon. Dried whiting also were sent to Castile. And it is known that the Portuguese imported dried fish from northern Germany.[11]

Greens and vegetables were not particularly appreciated, at least among the upper classes. The common people, of course, made abundant use of the cabbage family (common cabbage, cauliflower, and other Portuguese varieties such as *couve murciana* and *couve tronchuda*) as well as of beans and broad beans, both of which were widespread in several varieties throughout the Islamic world. Broccoli, lettuce, cucumbers, radishes, mushrooms, carrots, turnips, asparagus, and other garden products were likewise eaten. Broad beans, peas, lentils, chickpeas, and chicklings also figured as substitutes for or complements of bread. When grain was scarce in the kingdom, which happened fairly frequently after the mid-fourteenth century, broad beans often were imported from abroad to meet the needs of the people. Breton ships then sailed for the Tagus with cargoes of broad beans and other vegetables which had been loaded at French or English ports. Ground into flour, or simply cooked, the bean warded off starvation until the return of good harvests.

But the Portuguese of the interior, especially those of Beira and Trás-os-Montes, did not need to resort to the broad bean. The chestnuts of the abundant chestnut trees which the soil and the climate favored met their needs. Half of the year, they ate chestnuts in place of bread. It does not appear, however, that this substitute spread throughout the country, for there is little evidence of a trade developing in chestnuts from the inland regions to the thickly populated centers of the seaboard and the south.[12]

In wealthy homes, where culinary art was highly perfected, fragrant spices and seasonings were indispensable ingredients in the preparation of appetizing foods. Coriander, parsley, and mint, besides various juices (of lemons and unripe grapes), vinegar, onion and pine nuts, contributed to the good taste of foods. Onion browned in olive oil was traditionally used in the preparation of certain dishes. The use of seasonings in the fourteenth century is illustrated by the wry anecdote in which Pedro I, ordering the death of Pero Coelho, one of the executioners of Inês de Castro,* called for "onion, vinegar, and olive oil for the rabbit (coelho)" and then had Coelho's heart torn out.[15]

The sixteenth-century "Treatise on Cooking" contains a recipe for roasted rabbit which uses butter instead of olive oil:

Recipe for rabbit

After the rabbit has been roasted, sauté finely minced onion in butter; once sautéed, season the onion with vinegar and sprinkle in cloves, saffron, pepper, and ginger. Cut the rabbit into pieces and put it in with the spice and onion mixture to simmer briefly. Lay some slices of bread on a plate and top with the rabbit pieces.

Cloves, saffron, pepper, and ginger, of course, were not very common in Portuguese recipes of the Middle Ages. Only after the establishment of commerce with the Orient were great quantities of spices imported into Portugal at comparatively moderate prices. Before long, the use (and abuse) of such seasonings was familiar in the preparation of food.

Nevertheless, from the twelfth century to the fifteenth, various spices were known and used in cooking. Catalan and Sevillian merchants brought them to Portugal, imported from the Orient. In the royal household there is evidence of the consumption of several ingredients in appreciable quantities, at least from the end of the thirteenth century. The bills of the royal pantry of King Dinis for 1278–82 show the purchase of sugar (which was then considered a spice), with such varieties as rose-colored and Alexandrine sugar. It was so expensive that it was worth more than fifty times the price of honey! The royal household also bought pepper, ginger, and other spices that are difficult to

* Inês de Castro was famous in Portuguese history for her love affair with Prince Pedro, later King Pedro I (1357–67). She was killed by order of Pedro's father, King Afonso IV (1325–57).

identify today.[14] Pepper must have been relatively common, though costly: it is mentioned in most of the borough charters of the twelfth and thirteenth centuries.

The Portuguese of the Middle Ages used a variety of fatty substances for seasoning. Undoubtedly, olive oil occupied first place, and its role in cooking increased as the cultivation of olive groves spread to the north. Nevertheless, the use of butter was also quite important, as is indicated by the numerous references to butter in surviving documents, and seems to have corresponded to a local industry that was quite extensive, perhaps even more so than that of cheese-making. Besides butter, other animal fats of ample consumption were bacon fat and lard. Given the fact that the number of swine was outstanding among the livestock raised, and that therefore pork abounded in the butcher shop, the role of pork fat in culinary seasoning by every social class is understandable. Less frequently, beef shortening also was used in the preparation of foods.

Naturally, salt cannot be forgotten, for it not only functioned as the basic condiment in almost all foods, but also was required for the preserving of meats, fish, and other food that had to be stored or transported.

Dairy products (known as *viandas de leite*) were frequently present among the medieval Portuguese provisions. They included cheese, cream, butter, and sweets made from dairy products, in addition, obviously, to milk itself. As a mater of fact, milk was not drunk in very large quantities. In the sources of information, references to milk are unusual. Most of it was converted into cheese and butter. It was also used as medicine. But it seems to have been little used to quench thirst or as food *per se*.

Dairy products usually were eaten as side dishes or as desserts. In the *Loyal Counselor,* however, King Duarte advised the reader neither to drink cream nor to eat other dairy products, as they were believed to be moist and consequently injurious to health; or if he did eat them, to do so in small quantities and always at the end of meals; and never to drink after consuming them.[15]

The "Treatise on Cooking" from the sixteenth century includes more than half a dozen recipes for milk delicacies: white custard, milk turnovers, boiled milk, milk pudding, rice crullers, milk pudding à la D. Isabel de Vilhena, and small milk cakes à la D. Isabel de Vilhena. All were served as desserts. Let us look at one at random:

Milk pudding
Combine four eggs, sugar, and five silver spoonsful of flour in a wooden porringer and beat. In a small earthenware bowl, melt a quantity of

butter equal to the size of a walnut for each dish of pudding to be made. After the butter has melted and been distributed among the several dishes, pour in the batter seasoned with salt. Then put it in the oven, and once the pudding has set, top it with a little butter. This recipe can also be made with boiled milk, and with soft cheese. Cooked-rice pudding with milk is also made this same way. If desired, the rice pudding can be topped with whole egg yolks.

Eggs were eaten in enormous quantities. Practically all the recipes written down called for them. The production of eggs was the natural consequence of the abundance of poultry (chickens, ducks, geese, and pigeons). In the *Loyal Counselor,* eggs are neither condemned nor prescribed; it seems their noxiousness or utility varied according to the ideas of the individual. The "Treatise on Cooking" mentions them boiled, poached, and scrambled.[16]

Fruit played an outstanding role in medieval diets, especially in countries such as Portugal where Mediterranean fruits were grown. Practically all the fruits that we eat today were known then. Many were native; others were introduced by the Arabs. Only the sweet orange remained to be introduced by Vasco da Gama. The bitter orange, a variety rarely produced today, was used like the lemon, which was also consumed. Certain fruits were considered unwholesome: King Duarte proscribed the consumption of cherries and peaches, as he thought them "moist" products. He also advised against the use of lemons, as they are "cold and sharp."[17] Usually fruit was eaten accompanied by wine, as a kind of refreshment, or as a light meal, most appropriate for evening. The chronicler Fernão Lopes, in narrating one of the famous evening balls of King Pedro I, relates that "the king . . . returned to the palace dancing, and requested wine and fruit." In the *Chronicle of King João I,* he mentions a similar event and notes that "on that day, at night, the king [asked] for wine and fruit."[18] In addition to fresh fruit, the people ate dried fruits, preserves, and sweets made from fruit. Dried figs, raisins, almonds, walnuts, carob beans, chestnuts, and olives were items of enormous domestic consumption, without even speaking of the lucrative commerce in them which was caried on with foreign countries. Preserves and sweets were made from citrons (candied citron rinds, such as *casquinhas* and *diacidrão),* peaches (*pessegada*), lemons, pears (both candied—*perinhas*— and in preserves—*perada*), squash, and quince (marmelade, a dried sweet called *bocados,* and another sweet called *almivar de marmelo*). From oranges was made the famous orange blossom (*flor de laranja*), seasoning and perfume at one and the same time. And even lettuce was made into a special preserve, known as *talos* (stalks):

Glacéed lettuce stalks

Pick the lettuce when the stalks are tall and firm. Keep the stalks in cold water to maintain firmness while trimming and deveining them well. Put a large pot of water on to boil. While trimming the stems, put on another pot and boil the sugar into syrup. Select the thickest stalks and cook them in the boiling water until a pin can go through them as if they were dough. When they are cooked, put them in a pan and pour the still bubbling sugar-syrup over them. Repeat the hot-syrup process each day for up to two weeks or until they are done.

The production of cakes was not very widespread. Before the fifteenth century, the high price of sugar necessitated the use of honey, the only sweetening within reach of all pocketbooks. Yet even afterwards, one does not find any indication that cake was consumed as frequently as it is today.

There were some exceptions: the people made cookies of orange blossom, milk turnovers, and sponge cake, besides what is known as *fartéis*, made with a base of honey, flour, and spices. They also made some sweets with eggs: *canudos* (long, thin sticks) and *ovos de laços* (cream eggs), for example.[19] Nevertheless, only after the Renaissance, and more particularly, from the seventeeth and eighteenth centuries on, did the famed national confectionery industry develop.

Nevertheless, the base of medieval nutrition, particularly for the commoners, lay in the cereals—flour and bread, made of wheat, millet, or rye, and also of barley and oats—and in wine. The modern traveler would find the panorama of the cultivated fields monotonous, so ubiquitous were grainfields and vineyards throughout Portugal.

Bread of the highest quality was of wheat, but even though wheat fields were numerous throughout the country, production was insufficient for consumption. They sowed grain everywhere, in soils that did not offer even minimally favorable conditions, and the result was a low yield per unit. Grain crises occurred frequently, especially in centers of dense population. A city like Lisbon or a province like the Algarve then had to import wheat from abroad. Shipments of grain came from France, England, Germany, Italy, and Castile. Bread rose in price, and many people died of hunger.

In the country, the situation for the common people was a little better. There were substitutes for bread: chestnuts or the acorn, for example. As a matter of fact, flour made from wheat was not the base of breadmaking here. Millet, rye, and even barley were used at times. Millet was grown in two varieties—*milho miúdo* (minute corn) and *milho painço* (millet corn)*— both of which were widespread in the most humid regions of Portugal, the same areas in which maize would later replace them. In Trás-os-Montes and the interior of Beira, rye provided the basis for the bread normally consumed. Wheat, however, was always present to some extent.

Bread was also made from combinations of various flours—wheat and millet, wheat and rye, wheat and barley, and so on. At times, flour made from three different grains was employed in making bread.

The greater part of the population made its own bread in the bread ovens about which references abound in the documents, although there were women bakers in the cities who baked and sold bread in their shops and homes. The bread was baked in large loaves, which were generally of a circular shape and which rose very little. These were used at one and the same time as food and as a simulated plate for the meal, as we shall see. Rolls were not used, as they are today. Price lists from the fifteenth century indicate that the loaves of bread normally eaten weighed from 150 to 750 grams (⅓ to 1⅔ pounds).[20] Slender loaves baked under ashes or hot cinders were called *fogaças*. By the late fifteenth century, the term *broa* appears in the *Cancioneiro Geral* [General songbook] to designate bread made from millet.

But flour had many other uses besides being made into bread. It was utilized to prepare turnovers and patties. It was used as batter for fish or meat. It was employed for baking biscuit for the armies or fleets. At other times, it was simply mixed with water, like gruel.[21] The sixteenth-century cookbook, to which we have already referred, is full of references to flour, used in preparing most of the tidbits.

The number of beverages in medieval Portugal was extremely limited. Coffee, tea, and chocolate were unknown. Thirst was quenched and meals were accompanied with wine or water.

Vineyards alternated with grain fields in covering the land. There is no indication of any crises in wine cultivation comparable to those occurring in grain production. The most varied types of wine, both white and red, were produced and were exported from Portugal throughout Northern Europe. Rosé wines were famous abroad. The wine from Azoia (a small village south of Lisbon and the area surrounding that village), which medieval documents seem to have equated

---

* The "corn" of medieval Portugal was the present millet (*milheto*). American maize was introduced into Europe only toward the beginning of the sixteenth century.

with the Greek malmsey wines, was known in England, the Nether-
lands, and the whole Hanseatic world.

Wine was consumed both in its natural state and mulled. Tem-
pered with water, it was considered the ideal beverage, even by such
champions of frugality and moderation at the table as King Duarte.
That ruler, however, recommended drinking no more than two or
three times during the course of dinner and supper and advised that
the beverage always be two parts water as well. After dinner, one
should drink very little, or even nothing, continues the *Loyal Counselor*. In the *Book on Hunting (Livro da Montaria)*, the same advice
can be found: wine should be diluted until it is either two-thirds, or at
least half, water, but never drunk in a pure state.[22] But this was
advice that did not go beyond the paper on which it was written, for
these were times when struggles were more violent and refreshments
less plentiful.

In the monasteries, the use of wine did not arouse criticism until
much later. The daily ration of wine given to the religious of the monastery of Vila do Conde by the will of Afonso Sanches, its founder,
amounted to at least a quart and a half per person.[23]

In Northern Europe, there was an enormous consumption of beer.
But in Portugal, although evidence of intermittent imports of this
product exists, it does not seem that its consumption ever was popular
during the Middle Ages.

In 1451, Lopo de Almeida, a favorite of King Afonso V, accompanied
Princess Leonor to Italy for her marriage to the emperor of Germany,
Frederick III. He wrote letters to his king along the way, in which he
described the details of the trip and the state of health of the princess.
Of these letters, extremely interesting because of their exact descriptions and the vivid panorama of daily life which they present, only
three have survived. In one of them, the ambassador of Portugal reports on a banquet offered in Italy for the emperor, his fiancée, and
the retinues. From his comments about the arrangement of the tables
and the local practices, it is possible to deduce what the approved
custom was in Portugal in the middle of the fifteenth century, at least
among the upper classes.

Lopo de Almeida is astonished that the tablecloths did not cover the
entire surface of the main table: "About two handspans of the table
remained uncovered." On the edge of the table were placed smaller
cloths for the guests, "on which to clean themselves," or as we would
say today, common napkins. Apparently, it was customary in Portugal
to place underneath the tablecloth a kind of carpet-like covering

called a *bancal* or a *mantel,* which was also used to cover the benches: at any rate, Lopo de Almeida is amazed at its absence, because only at the seat intended for the emperor was there "a cushion of velvety crimson." There were no rules governing seating arrangements: "At the other tables were seated bishops, counts, and prelates and all the other nobles, and all the other people, indiscriminately bunched together, as at a wedding." Moreover, comments Lopo de Almeida, the din and hullabaloo were frightful! [24]

It was customary to wash one's hands before meals. The very first article of the rule about meals in the monastery of Alcobaça establishes that the religious must always wash and wipe their hands before eating.[25] In wealthy households servants carried in water in *justas* (ewers) or *gomis* (pitchers) of silver or whatever metal was consonant with the wealth displayed on the table, and brought in large *bacias* (bowls) over which the guests held their hands while water was poured over them. At banquets of special refinement, rose water or some other perfumed water might be substituted for plain water. The hand-washing ceremony was concluded by the guests' wiping their hands on *napeiras* (napkins) or small towels.

On the table would be arranged gold and silver utensils that were at once decorative and utilitarian. In France, it was usual to place an object called the salt boat in front of the host with the articles intended for his use: knives, spoons, salt, spices, and so on.

Then the food was brought in tureens or basins. In Portugal, the custom was to precede each dish, as well as the wine, with servants bearing torches under the leadership of an usher. In Castile, as in

Fig. 5. Meal. 15th century.

Germany, huge tureens from which everyone ate in common were used, but the basins used in Portugal were smaller. King Dinis (1279–1325) had eleven silver ones, weighing from two to four pounds. Although the servants generally carried in the food in a procession, preceded by the usher and the torchbearers, the Cistercian rule ordered that the "dishes or foods eaten on bread be placed on the tables before ringing the bell"—that is, they should all be brought out together.[26]

The dread of poisoning, allied with the general superstition of the time, led to the use of some curious "utensils," intended for inspecting the food. These included "unicorn horns" (in reality birds' beaks or horns of other animals), provided with a gold or silver handle, and *lingueiros,* a sort of rod on which were suspended serpent tongues or a large number of rare stones (such as the agate and serpentine), to which were attributed magical virtues. People believed that when these and other such talismans came near contaminated food, they would change color, become spotted, or even begin to bleed. The "Inventory and Accounts of the Household of King Dinis" enumerates certain stones, some with very strange names, which must have been used for this very purpose. It also mentions such items as a "scorpion's tooth" and a "bone suspended in the head of a silver stick."

Plates were not used for a long time in the Middle Ages. Meat and fish were eaten over manchets, large slices of round bread placed in front of each guest. At the end of the meal in the wealthy homes, these pieces of bread, which by then were soaked in gravy or other more or less savory morsels, were distributed among the mob of beggars or thrown to the dogs that wandered around the table. The round slice of bread was later replaced by a wooden *talhador* (plate). Nevertheless, both methods coexisted for a long time. *Talhador* was also the word used to designate a tray or large platter on which meat was carved before being distributed among the guests.

Naturally, plates were used for soups and other liquid foods; they were called *escudelas* (porringers) if they were made of wood or silver and *tigelas* if of pottery. Later, these bowls also began to be used for solid foods. It must be emphasized, however, that each bowl or plate was always used by two guests, seated side by side. Perhaps from this practice was derived the Portuguese expression "comer com alguém no prato," literally, "to eat with someone on the plate," signifying to be very close to someone.

Spoons were known and used, though quite rarely, it is true. But there were no forks: these became known in the West much later. Hence the indispensable necessity of washing one's hands before and after meals. The utilization of forks actually led, in the last analysis, to reduced hygiene: because contact of hand and food was decreased, it became unnecessary to wash one's fingers before and after eating as before. The sharp pointed knife was the utensil par excellence. Knives rarely were distributed to the guests at a banquet, however, for the guests themselves normally brought with them the knives they were going to employ, just as a comb or mirror is carried today. After eating, they cleaned the implement on the tablecloth or napkins. One of the rules of conduct for the Cistercian monks ordered them not to wipe "their hands or knives on the tablecloth unless they had first cleaned them with bread."

The glasses used for drinking, called *vasos* (goblets), were somewhat larger and heavier than those of today ("He who drinks, must hold the goblet with both his hands," decrees the Alcobacense rule). Larger vessels were called *grais* (grails) and *tagras* (chalices). Hot liquids were often served in *copas* (goblets) covered with lids.[27] The pottery *púcaras* (mugs) and little pottery *pucarinhas* (cups) were furnished with handles.[28]

Even though data is scarce, we do know that a large number of rules governing good conduct at the table were in effect in medieval Portugal. We have seen some of them already. There were also rules about precedence in serving. "The cook will carry the spoons," says the Cistercian rule, "first to the right side, beginning with the prior; then to the left, beginning with the person next to the prior."[29] We are convinced that the monastic discipline, extending even to the smallest details of good conduct at the table, exercised a great deal of influence on the elaboration of a code of social deportment. But only at the close of the fourteenth century, or the beginning of the fifteenth, were seating arrangements established. As late as 1386, when King João I and the Duke of Lancaster met, "they disarmed there and both sat down to eat, without bothering about the right or left side, as this was not yet the custom, and those who came with the Duke sat down as they pleased in the same way" (Fig. 6).[30]

The excessive luxury flaunted by the nobles and the wealthy—including their lavishly supplied tables—occasionally became a matter of concern, especially just before or during periods of crisis, when sumptuousness became most flagrant. At such times the rulers attempted to curb excesses. In Portugal in 1340, for example, the king and his counselors believed that "greater expenditures than should be made for food were being paid out," and from this came a dictate which established a certain number of moderate rules. Dividing the population to which it pertained into nobles, gentry, and townsmen *(cidadãos)*, the dictate forbade the first group more than three courses of meat at

Fig. 6.   João I of Portugal meets the Duke of Lancaster, 1386. 15th century.

dinner and two at supper, and permitted the second and third groups no more than two such dishes at dinner and one at supper. They could eat all the fish, shellfish, game, poultry, and milk products they might wish, so long as they had gotten them from their own rents or by hunting.[31]

To conclude this chapter, let us look at descriptions of two festive banquets honoring the marriage of Prince Afonso with Princess Isabel, daughter of the Catholic Monarchs, both of which Garcia de Resende included in his *Chronicle of King João II.*

So the third day at night there was a supper banquet in the hall of wood, in which the King and the Queen, and the Prince and Princess ate, and with them the Duke and Lord Jorge, and Rodrigo de Ilhoa, ambassador, all at a great table, covered with brocade, which filled the whole room from one side to the other, and at the first table on the right-hand side ate the Marquis of Vila Real with the ladies, and at the first table on the left were the Archbishop of Braga and the Bishop of Évora, and other ladies and gentlemen were seated on both sides.

And the table of the King was attended by officials, all of whom were dressed in brocade, and served by richly dressed young boys from the nobility who carried torches and basins. And the other tables all had carvers and officials who were dressed in rich silks and brocades, very gallant in appearance, as were the young men of the chamber, dressed in black velvet, who attended each table. At that banquet there were innumerable dishes and foods of all kinds, everything of a singular harmony and wealth, and many signal ceremonies. And when they brought to the table of the King the principal dishes and the first fruits and last ones, and drank to him and the Queen, and to the Prince and Princess, there always went before the food and drink, two by two, many ushers with maces, kings at arms, heralds, and pursuivants, the head ushers, four grand masters, the chamberlain, and the superintendents of the treasury, and behind all of them, the majordomo; and all, carrying their caps, walked to the dais, where they made great bows, except the superintendents of the treasury, who wore their caps on their heads till they were in the middle of the room, where they doffed them and then carried them, and the majordomo, who wore his until bowing, which he did at the same time as removing it. And there was so much ceremony that it took a long time whenever they came to the table.

And the blare of trumpets, drums, shawms, and sackbuts, and of all the minstrels was so great that no one could hear over it; this happened every time the King, Queen, and the Princess drank and the principal dishes came to the table; and the meal was an astounding thing to see.

And then there came to the head of the table a large golden cart which seemed to be pulled by two huge roasted whole steers, with gilded horns and hooves; the cart was completely filled with a large number of roasted

whole sheep with gilded horns; the whole thing was on such a low con-
traption, with little wheels underneath where they could not be seen, that
the steers appeared to be alive and walking.

In front of them walked a young noble holding an ox goad in his hands,
goading the steers which seemed to walk and pull the cart; he was dressed
as a drayman with a jerkin and a cloak of white velvet lined with brocade, with a cap of similar material, so that from a distance he resembled
a real carter; in this manner he went to offer the steers and sheep to the
Princess, and having done this, made them turn with his goad and go
about the room and leave; then he gave the meat to the people, who tore
it apart with great shouting and pleasure, each person carrying away as
much as he could.

And then there came to all the tables many roasted peacocks along
with their entire tails and the heads and necks with all the feathers in-
tact, which looked beautiful because there were so many of them, and
many other kinds of birds and game, delicacies and fruits, all in very
great abundance and great perfection.[32]

Many great feasts were held every day and night until Sunday, the fifth
of December, at which time there was held another, second banquet in
the above-mentioned hall of wood, with many more devices, great abundance and courtesy, and with many more officials, and even better served
than the first.

And it was a beautiful thing to see the way the tables were arranged,
for on each one there were three large covered platters of food, and on
top of the two at either end of the table were tents of white and purple
damask, which were the colors of the Princess; the tents were embroidered
and very gallant, with many little golden streamers, and were each larger
than ten ells. And the center dish was a fortress with the appearance of
a water chestnut, made of delicate wood and cloth of golden taffeta,
which was a very beautiful thing, and very costly.

And on entering the hall, one saw that the tables were so beautiful and
so warlike, that there was much to rejoice in seeing; as it was a new thing,
the like of which had not been seen before; and in all there were thirty
tents, and fourteen castles. And the King and Queen, and the Prince and
Princess came, and everyone who was to be seated at the table, and with
them the Duke and Lord Jorge, and Rodrigo de Ilhoa as before, and in
the same way the same persons at the other tables who had come to the
other banquet.

As soon as everyone was seated, the youths of the chamber who had
charge of the tables removed the tents which they kept for themselves,
but the castles, because they were of such a size that they could not fit beneath the tables, were given to persons who requested them for monasteries and churches, in which they were hung for a long time and looked
very beautiful.

They began to eat, and because of the infinity of delicacies, foods,
perserves, fruits (as if it were Christmas eve supper), it lasted a very long

time. Once the meal was over, there were so many and rich mummeries and very singular plays, each one with more wealth, gracefulness, and better contrivances, that they lasted until nearly morning. . . .

And all the people from the court and the city who were standing on foot at the many gratings, all ate what was removed from the tables, for there was such abundance that what was left over was greater in quantity than what was eaten, and for this reason there was no one who laid hands on anything nor behaved badly; also undoubtedly because there were guards who took careful notice of this, and because of the punishment that they knew they would receive if they did so; besides there was more than enough for everyone, for certainly there was such abundance and such perfection, so much honor, such estate, as much as could ever be seen in the whole world.[33]

2 : DRESS

╺╾╼╾╼╾╼╾╼╾╼╾╼╾╼╾╼╾╼╾╼╾╼╾╼╾╼

THE style consciousness which so occupies the modern world did not appear until the thirteenth century. Although some alterations in apparel and in the styles of wearing hair and beards are recorded before that period, it would be difficult to interpret them as actually meaning new fashions, because the concept of style is directly related to the economic transformations which the western world experienced from the eleventh century on. These changes were characterized by an increase in commercial transactions, especially ones involving long-distance traveling. On the social plane, a new class was born—the bourgeoisie. Population becomes concentrated in the cities, which begin to constitute the principal nuclei of economic activity. Now living in the city, the burgher is in direct and daily contact with the other bourgeois. Emulation, characteristic of his professional activity, comes to be reflected in his dress. Leaving church, taking a seat in the administrative assembly, participating in the festivities of his city, the burgher always is desirous of outdoing his fellow citizen. He tries to call attention to himself by the quality of the cloth that he wears and the fashion in which it is cut. He wishes, in short, to appear distinctive, wealthier, and more handsome than the others. He is going to bedeck himself and his family, just as he beautifies his home with the furniture that he acquires and the tapestries which cover it.

But fashion, in the sense of variety, also arises from the new conditions of production. Before the eleventh century, there was a comparative uniformity in fabrics woven in Western Europe. Differences in quality existed, of course, but to a very small degree. Following the Roman tradition, the people did not even dye the materials spun from wool or linen, which were tailored and worn in their natural color.

Then the development of the textile industry, whose principal centers were in Flanders, Northern Italy, and a little later, England,* brought with it the manufacture of innumerable kinds of cloth. There

* Here I am referring especially to woolen cloth. The most important centers for the manufacture of silk fabrics were Italy and the Iberian Peninsula.

are dozens of different fabrics revealed by the documents of the thirteenth, fourteenth, and fifteenth centuries. Practically every city possessed its special type of cloth, for whose production it alone knew and guarded jealously the secret. Woolen cloth, coarse or more delicate, striped or simple, with adornments and embroideries, was produced, exported, and used to make various kinds of clothing.

Consequently, there were the simultaneous factors of emulation and industrial development. Other elements, however, must be considered. The increase in long-distance commerce involves contact among various peoples. The great international fairs appear. The French merchant goes to Italy and Germany, to Constantinople and Cordova. He observes the local social customs and carries home with him strange clothes and revolutionary ideas. He copies and imitates what he sees, especially in the advanced civilizations, where the concept of style has long existed, as in those of Byzantium and Islam.

The developments in the art of war had marked influence on the alterations in apparel beginning with the thirteenth century. Up to that time, the warrior wore a dress or coat of mail down to his knees, wide and loose-fitting around his body, to protect him against sword and arrow. But the invention of the crossbow—such a deadly weapon that the Second Lateran Council condemned it in 1139 (without success, it goes without saying)—made the simple coat of mail less effective. Therefore, the warrior began to adopt new defensive garments. The whole outfit formed what was called his armor. This type of protective apparel no longer could be made of a single piece covering the entire body, as in the case of mail. Armor was essentially composed of an upper part protecting the torso down to the waist, two lower pieces protecting the legs, and an intermediate piece protecting the hips. All of these pieces fit the body tightly, and the clothes worn by the warrior under his armor had to conform to this shape (Fig. 7). And so instead of the flowing vestments of the previous centuries, those of the fourteenth and fifteenth centuries are characterized by the sleekness of body lines, accentuating the figure. Here is one of the reasons why masculine dress develops so spectacularly toward the end of the Middle Ages, in contrast to the feminine, which remains tied to the traditional forms.

The transformations in houses are reflected equally in the manner of dress. Toward the end of the Middle Ages, homes (not those of the peasant, obviously) are more comfortable and more protected. The first window panes appear, making the house much warmer. The number of tapestries increases, for the new conditions in production make them cheaper. Compartmentation itself becomes specialized: houses

Fig. 7. *Left,* coat of mail, 12th century. *Right,* armor, 14th and 15th centuries.

have more rooms which are smaller and snugger. Voluminous mantles and tunics, which covered the body entirely and were used as protection against the rigors of winter, become unnecessary at home. As soon as a person comes in the door, he may now walk around in a "well-made dress," in a style of deshabille until then unthinkable.

There were also aesthetic and psychological reasons. The evolution of the wardrobe from the thirteenth through the fifteenth centuries accompanies the evolution of artistic styles. It changes just as the ornamental concepts and decorative language of the Gothic change. It mirrors, in a quite distinctive way, the preponderance of the vertical line over the horizontal line. More than in any other period, the apparel of the fifteenth century, when verticality attains its extreme development, causes short, fat individuals to become ridiculous, tall, thin ones elegant.

Style also accompanies the decline of a society. The taste for luxury asserts itself especially in the second half of the fourteenth century and in the fifteenth century. It is the age of extremes, the period during which man vacillates between the most profound mysticism and the most extravagant pleasure. There is a need to live life, to live it intensely, to live it in all its fullness, because death watches in secret and reaps his harvest every moment. This is the outlook of a society used to the most devastating epidemics that our civilization has ever known.

The Black Death in 1348–50 kills a third of the European population. There are other plagues, in 1359–60, in 1373–75, and throughout the whole of the fifteenth century. Wars are likewise more frequent and perhaps more deadly. Famines of an unprecedented severity and duration are familiar. And this period witnesses the rupture in the established social scene and its cherished values. It is the time of transition from a feudal and seigniorial society to a precapitalistic society when the bourgeoisie begin to assert themselves. It is the phase during which Renaissance individualism arises. It is the age of fermentation for the great heresies which foreshadow the Reformation.

If everything else is changing, how could apparel fail to be modified? If the changes are abrupt and unexpected, why would they not be attended by a rapid succession of the most diverse and the most absurd fads? Clothing accompanies the social fluctuation, it reflects the turmoil in souls, it mirrors the convulsions of a world that is dying.

Fashion in Portugal is essentially imitative during this period. The stylish French people of the court of Saint Louis and his successors are copied during the thirteenth and the fourteenth centuries. In the fourteenth century, the English and Italian styles probably contribute their share to Portuguese fashion. In the fifteenth century, Burgundy directs the alterations in the apparel. But the Portuguese dress is always conservative and for a long time reflects yet another influence, the Moslem, unknown beyond the Pyrenees. Textiles woven in the Islamic countries and pieces of apparel with a Moorish look are used in medieval Portugal and are mentioned in contemporary documents. The Leonese, Castilian, and Aragonese ways of dressing also stamp Portuguese styles with their distinctive features. A great majority of the queens of Portugal were Castilian and Aragonese, and the significance which their presence, and that of their retinues, had for fashion never can be overly stressed.

Twelfth century clothing remained faithful to the Roman tradition. Garments were full and disguised the shape of the body (Fig. 8). Elegance had to be sought in the pleating of the dress and in the wealth and ornamentation of the cloth. Between men and women, the difference in the clothing was minimal. But while the classical tradition allowed certain parts of the body, such as the arms and neck, to be exposed, Christian austerity, based on the Byzantine fashion, obliged total covering.

The Roman wore as his basic items of dress the tunic and the toga. The Byzantine maintained the tunic, already greatly changed, but replaced the toga with a mantle that had less material and was simpler to put on. This mantle was principally a Christian contribution: it was the pallium of Christ and of the apostles, known, moreover, for a long time throughout the Near East, and even in the Greco-Roman world, as clothing appropriate for the lower classes.

The German introduced the first long breeches, and thus, the first clear distinction between men's and women's apparel (Fig. 9). In the tenth and eleventh centuries, however, Byzantine styles regained their ascendancy in Western Europe, owing to the intensification of political and commercial relations between the two areas. The Crusades had a decisive importance in this respect. Constantinople performed, in

Fig. 8.   Twelfth-century garment.

Fig. 9.   *Left,* Roman dress; *center,* Byzantine dress; *right,* German dress.

the eleventh and the twelfth centuries, the role Paris was to play later. It was the capital of fashion, just as it was the capital of luxury, wealth, and pleasure. The widespread fashion among men of wearing ankle-length clothing, following the Byzantine mode, scandalized the critics of that period—particularly the clergy and sober persons—for in such long, flowing skirts and mantles, men looked more like women. But nothing hindered this style from becoming predominant.

The man of the twelfth century wore as his main articles of clothing a shirt, a tunic, and a large mantle over them. The shirt, worn underneath the other garments, was a long tunic (Fr. *chainse*) falling to the feet, with narrow sleeves and a high neckline, and could be made· of linen, wool, or silk. It was also found in the Mozarab wardrobe. When its length was inconvenient, it was usually tucked up at the waist, sometimes only in front, and fastened with a girdle in the Roman fashion. Some pictures from the famous "Commentary on the Apocalypse of Lorvão" ("Comentário ao Apocalipse de Lorvão") and from the "Book of the Birds" ("Livro das Aves") show this practice very well (Fig. 10).[1]

Over the shirt was worn a tunic called the *brial* or *saia,* a garment which had evolved from the dalmatic. The dalmatic was nothing more than an outer tunic with full sleeves, originally decorated down both sides with bands of different colors called the clavi. Lying flat, it resembled a cross (Fig. 11). The dalmatic of the twelfth century, however, relinquished the clavi to the exclusive use of the ecclesiastics and began to appear in a single color, usually blue, green, or red. The tunic sometimes permitted the shirt to be seen, either through its sleeves, which were shorter and fuller than those of the shirt, or by its length, as it was shorter than the undergarment. Some tunics in the "Apocalypse of Lorvão" have three-quarter-length sleeves, although they may only appear shorter than the shirt's, as they are wrinkled up. In contrast to the shirt, which was an undergarment and infrequently seen, the tunic was made with great care, of rich cloth, and with a great profusion of embroidery and other ornamentation. The 1181 borough charter of Melgaço mentions robes of a single color, striped ones, and some in fanciful prints.[2] Tight-fitting, sleeveless tunics of Mozarab use, at times possibly worn without the undershirt, were called *mudbages* (Fig. 12).[3]

Over the tunic was worn a mantle, performing the same function as the present overcoat or gabardine raincoat. There were various types of mantles—the mantle properly so called, the cape, and the *granaia,* among others. Mantles and other outer clothing of Mozarab origin were called *alifafes* and *çorames.* Pelisses, or a "cloak of pelts," sanc-

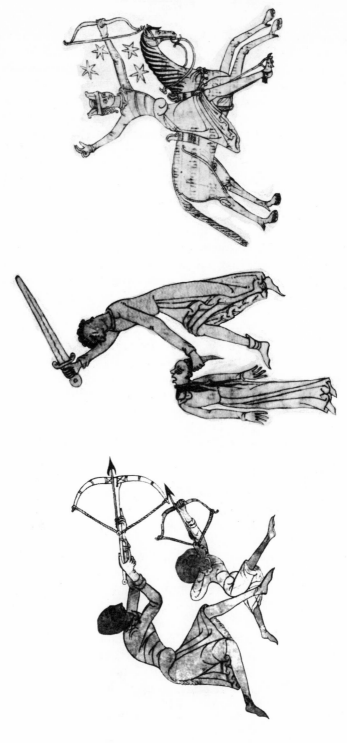

Fig. 10. Twelfth-century warriors (*left*), executor (*center*), and rider (*right*), showing practice of tucking shirt up at waist.

tioned by Portuguese borough charters, were also put on over the tunic for warmth. Shorter than the tunic, at times slit on the sides, it had large sleeves and a lining of rabbit fur, lambskin, or even ermine. Ribbons and scarves adorned it.

Directly connected to the Byzantine mantle, the medieval one also followed it in its cut. It could be tailored in a semicircle, or even in three-quarters of a circle, both with a small indentation for the neck (Fig. 13).[4] Mantles of scarlet, a superior quality of woolen cloth usually dyed in shades of red, were among the articles of apparel of greatest value in Portugal at that time. But the mantle could also be made, consonant with the occasion, of silk that was embroidered and interwoven with gold. The way it was worn also varied, either according to the taste of its owner or to the style of the times: it could be draped

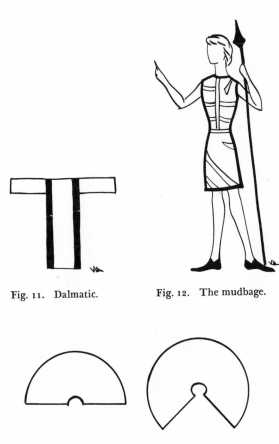

Fig. 11.   Dalmatic.   Fig. 12.   The mudbage.

Fig. 13.   Forms of mantle tailoring.

over the shoulders, falling along the arms; or in the classical and Byzantine style, fastened on the right shoulder by a brooch; or even arranged and clasped over the bosom with cords or brooches. The innovation of the twelfth century consisted in the mantle's being pinned on the left shoulder instead of on the right. (Fig. 14.)

The cape was shorter than the mantle and often had a hood. There were various kinds of capes; the Galician cape, for example, is mentioned in the 1181 charter of Melgaço.[5] They were cut from leather, woolen cloth, fur, and plain or patterned silk.

The meaning of the terms *garvaia* or *granaia* is still not perfectly clear. The more accurate spelling is probably the second, from Lat. *granum,* "cochineal," to denote a mantle dyed scarlet.[6] This kind of mantle had already appeared by the twelfth century and continued to be used until the fourteenth century. There is a beautiful poem written by Martim Soares toward the middle of the thirteenth century that refers to the scarlet mantle as a luxurious and expensive article of clothing:

> And Pai Moniz gets *you* as á gift
> And yet you would have me give you
> A scarlet cloak [*granaia*];
> But I, my lady, have never
> Received anything from you, not even
> The price of a leather thong.[7]

Fig. 14. Ways of wearing the mantle.

A variation of the mantle especially worn by travelers was the *balandrau,* a wide cape with sleeves, which protected a person from the rain (Fig. 15). Its origin was Moslem.

The twelfth-century man wore pointed shoes, a constant style during the Late Middle Ages. Nevertheless, there were various types of footgear. Inside a house, unsoled cloth shoes, molded to the shape of the foot, were used. They could assume the design of medium high boots, or else be cut away at the instep (*degolados* in the language of the period). (Fig. 16.)

But the rough, arduous life of those days required outdoor shoes of leather, almost in the modern style. These were made of well-oiled zebro hide or calfskin; those of better quality were of deerskin, sheepskin, or polished goatskin. There were red ones, of good cordovan leather, as well. And there were even boots, called *osas* (Fr. *heuses*) in Portuguese medieval texts, varying in size, in quality, and in price. The "Apocalypse of Lorvão" contains pictures of various kinds of boots.

Fig. 15. The balandrau.

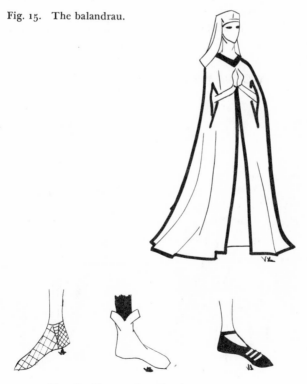

Fig. 16. Shoes, 12th and 13th centuries.

The junction of the sole with the shoe was unthinkable at that time: the sole was always a separate piece from the shoe, and every variety mentioned above lacked a sole. By the twelfth century, however, cowhide shoes were sold with good soles (called *sefiutas* or *sofiutas*) fastened onto them by means of leather straps. [8]

Head coverings did not reach the elaborations which are found in later centuries. The Portuguese in the time of King Afonso Henriques (1128–85) preferred to cover himself with a cowl, either loose or attached to a cape or mantle. He also wore caps of various shapes and small hoods molded to his head (Fig. 17). The cone-shaped bonnet like a Phrygian cap, for example, was very much in style. But the Roman tradition and Byzantine fashion prevailed. And in neither one nor the other did the "hat" ever play a role comparable to that of the tunic or the toga as symbols of elegance.

Whoever looks through the ingenuous illuminations of the "Apocalypse of Lorvão" will easily realize the differences between the noble's dress and the wardrobe of the peasant. Certainly the full, long apparel with which the nobleman bedecked himself was not practical for rural or artisan labor. Besides this, such clothing cost a great deal of money. The clothing of the peasant and the artisan, therefore, had to differ from that of the noble. The Germanic "mode," a reflection of less polished and more hardworking circumstances, was preferred. Conse-

Fig. 17. A form of the hood.

Fig. 18. Tunic (saio).

quently, the tenant farmer or the serf wore a tunic *(saio)* which fell to the middle of his leg and could still be tucked up into his girdle whenever uninhibited action was necessary. The tunic was provided with long, tight sleeves, and a small neck opening (Fig. 18). The peasant protected his legs with hose or with "trousers" of two separate legs that came up to his hips. He wore shoes or a tough kind of sandal with leather straps called *abarcas;* and he covered his head with a straw hat, or a broad-brimmed, cloth one, or simply with a hood.

During the thirteenth century, masculine apparel became complicated. The shirt *(camisa),* ordinarily of a coarse variety of linen known as *bragal,* became a simple undergarment, the first piece of underwear in the modern style (Fig. 19). Moslem textiles and styles exercised considerable influence on the Portuguese shirt of the thirteenth century. Moorish shirts, made of *alfola* (a fine cloth manufactured in Granada) or of *ascari* (another Moslem textile), are recorded as being found in the wardrobe of King Dinis, when he was still a prince (1278–82). The shirt could be embroidered (even with gold), or made from an imaginatively patterned textile.[9] Underneath the shirt, the Portuguese man slipped on his first drawers, the *bragas,* made, as the name suggests, from that same coarse linen. Here again, one notes the influence of the Islamic culture, in which that undergarment had already been used for a long time.

The shape of the tunic *(cotte* in the French of the thirteenth and fourteenth centuries) did not change in its essence. The sleeves appear

Fig. 19. Shirt (camisa), 13th century.

Fig. 20. Thirteenth-century garments. All three figures wear tunic, trousers, and pointed shoes; in addition, the man on the right wears a surcoat over the tunic and a toque.

to have become more close-fitting and invariably fell to the wrists. In length, the tunic varied according to the vogue at the moment. Now it fell almost to the feet, now it was angle-length, now it rose to mid-calf. In the second half of the thirteenth century, Alfonso IX of Leon ridicules the dandies who wore very tight-fitting gowns, with decoration of silken cords and enormous girdles:

> I should well like to know
> From these people who wear corded gowns,
> In which they squeeze themselves almost in half,
> Whether they do it to show off their bellies.
>
> .   .   .   .
>
> Oh, heavens! if someone could only tell me
> Why they wear these silken girdles,
> And so wide, too, the way pregnant women do.
>
> .   .   .   .
>
> Furthermore, I also see them wearing
> Very short sleeves artfully frayed at the edges.[10]

Another troubadour, Martim Soares, derides the excessively short tunics of the same period:

João Fernandes, how badly they cut
This tunic which you are wearing:
For never have I seen worse tailoring,
And they even cut it off very short.

    .   .   .   .

Such a short gown does not become you
Because you are not wearing a matching mantle
And so your backside often shows.

    .   .   .   .

And so the longer kind would look much better on you.[11]

Apparently, toward the end of the thirteenth century and the beginning of the fourteenth, the tunic tended to become shorter and shorter,
barely falling below the knees. The troubadours painted in the pages
of the *Cancioneiro da Ajuda* [Ajuda songbook], which is of this period,
almost all wear a tunic of this sort. Nevertheless, it is true that many of
the spectators, whether great lords or squires, appear to be wearing
longer tunics.[12]

Over the tunic, the man of the thirteenth century began to wear a
new item of clothing that had evolved from the mantle, but had become elongated and tended toward a sleeker body fit. The French
called this garment the *surcot* (hence, Eng. *surcoat*), because it was
worn over the *cotte*. In Portuguese, however, the comparable term—
sobressaia—rarely appears in the documents, the word *pelote* being
used instead.[13] The surcoats of the thirteenth century often did not
contain sleeves, allowing those of the tunic to be seen. Besides this,
they were provided with long armscyes that fell below the waistline
(Fig. 21). This type of surcoat can be clearly observed in the illuminations of the *Cancioneiro da Ajuda*. Other surcoats had sleeves, almost
always shorter than those of the tunic underneath. In length, the surcoat fell a little below the knee.

Mantles themselves become more complicated in this century. Besides the traditional flowing mantles, expensive and reserved for ceremonial dress, *guardacós* or *garnachas* were used. The first article, the
Portuguese adaptation of the French term *garde-corps*, enjoyed a great
vogue in the period of Saint Louis, King of France. The guardacós
filled the role of the present overcoat, inasmuch as it was relatively
close-fitting and provided with sleeves, a high collar and a hood. It
fell to the knee, leaving uncovered the lower border of the surcoat or
the tunic. The full sleeves had large slits from top to bottom, which
permitted freeing the arms whenever necessary, in which case the
sleeves hung along the body. The garnacha (Fr. *garnache*) seems to be
the same thing as the scarlet mantle which was mentioned above. Both

Fig. 21. Surcoat (pelote).

were a type of wool mantle, shorter and more form fitting than the traditional mantle, and open in front. The garnacha might or might not have sleeves (Fig. 22).

As in the twelfth century, so in the thirteenth, various types of capes were worn. The ordinary cape—in general rather long, with openings for the head and arms, either simple or double (that is, provided with a small overcape)—continued to be in style. There was also the *cerome,* or *cerame,* a Moorish cape to which the documents of the thirteenth century often refer. It was again a mantle that was worn over the tunic and the surcoat. The *capelo,* a small, hooded cape which gave Sancho II (1223–48) his nickname,* was worn with a leather trimming. The *clâmide,* a much rarer, more luxurious mantle, maintained the Roman tradition, being similar to the ancient toga and fastened like it on the right shoulder by a brooch. The *tabardo* (Fr. *tabart,* Eng. *tabard),* which was to experience such a great vogue, appeared about the middle of the century. It was slit on both sides, from the shoulders or the armscyes, in order to facilitate the movement of the arms. It could contain small sleeves (see Fig. 22).[14] For bad weather, tabards and *balandraus aguadeiros* (water-repellent cloaks) were worn over the tunic. João Baveca, one of the troubadours in the cancioneiros, directs a scornful song to a certain Bernaldo in this respect:

* "O capelo." Sancho was said to have worn the cape as a child because of a religious promise.

Fig. 22. Mantles and capes, 13th century. *Left,* garnacha; *center,* tabard; *right,* aljuba.

> Bernaldo, what you are wearing gives me sorrow:
> That cloak sheds water very badly,
> And here the bad weather lasts a long time,
> And you deceive yourself by not realizing this.
> I advise you to get some other cloak
> To cover the rather poor one you are wearing,
> So that you will not get so very wet.
>
> For if anyone saw your tunic soaked,
> He would think you were a stingy fellow,
> And yet you have always been so liberal.[15]

Another protective garment was the *aljuba,* a flowing Moorish dress with sleeves (Fig. 22).

Pointed shoes continued to be worn in this century and the next. Cut from leather—or from cordovan for the most valued and expensive —they were sold in white, black, blue, red, and even gold. There were also cloth shoes, including some of silk. In addition to shoes, sandals and boots in various shapes and heights were used. Soles continued to be sold separately. The trousers of that period were the equivalent of today's stockings, as they were divided and put on individually, but they were cut from cloth.[16]

On his head, the Portuguese of the thirteenth century could wear a toque, or coif, of cloth or silk in conformity with his means. That simple covering generally left the hair in front and back exposed. Twisted caps were also seen, and hats—the *sombreiros*—were much used for trips and pilgrimages (Fig. 23). A law of 1253 mentions hats with gold and silver ornamentation (gold or silver foil). Nevertheless, the hood *(eixarafa)* continued to be the favorite kind of headwear. Head coverings were not very expensive at that time, and they are almost completely omitted in the famous regulation of prices that Afonso III ordered in 1253.[17]

The girdle was greatly esteemed in the thirteenth century. In the regulation just referred to, approximately a dozen types are listed, with their prices equally varied. *Alfreses* were the most highly prized girdles. They were broad girdles of good foreign cloth, with adornments of gold or of silver (Fig. 24). One of these belts cost six pounds—as much as a saddle for a horse. Other belts were made in lighter fabrics, such as silk or linen.[18] Girdles and belts were used to clasp tunics, tabards, and garde-corps. The dandies of the early thirteenth century wore very large girdles. Alfonso IX of Leon had doubts about the military virtues of these items, as he reveals in a song:

> Whoever should bear the standard without dash
> And wear a broad girdle and a very high pompadour
> Does not come to the May campaign.[19]

The great vogue in fur, used to line clothing on the inside or to decorate it on the outside, continued into this century. Rabbit furnished the cheapest and most common fur in the thirteenth century. Articles of clothing were even made wholly of this fur, in the form of capes, mantles, and tabards. Prices varied according to whether it was the fur of a rabbit caught in the winter or in the summer (rabbit hunting was prohibited from Ash Wednesday to Saint Mary's in August). Squirrel provided some of the most-prized skins. In the summer, the pelt was chestnut brown; in the winter, more grayish. Thus, consonant with the season, skins were put on sale either as *penas veiras* ("reddish-

Fig. 23. Hats, 13th century. *Left,* toque or coif; *right,* pilgrim's hat (sombreiro).

Fig. 24. Broad girdle (alfrês).

brown pelts," from Fr. *vair*), or as *penas gris* ("gray pelts," from Fr. *gris*). Other skins (many of which were imported) for which prices were listed included those of the stone marten, sable, otter, ermine, weasel, genet, hare, and fox without speaking of the more ordinary skins of lamb and kid. Even the poor cat contributed its fur for the adornment of elegant persons, although cat fur was not highly valued: it was sold for one soldo per skin in 1253, the same as the price of over a yard of coarse linen for underclothes.[20] If the furs were dyed, their price evidently rose. The continued exploitation of furs in the fourteenth century provoked a sumptuary law from João I in 1391. According to it, no one except knights, doctors, prelates, clerics, and a few others could wear "brown or gray pelts, or ermine." Such prohibitions, however, never produced the desired results.[21]

There were also gloves, of course. Those of finest quality were of deerskin, worth three times as much as those made from sheepskin. Gloves were widely used in hunting and were sold particularly for the art of falconry, differing according to whether one wanted to hunt with goshawk or with sparrow-hawk.

Movable pouches which hung from the girdle took the place of pockets. In the thirteenth century, pouches of silk or ordinary cloth were sold for this purpose. It was also customary to hang similar receptacles, naturally larger and of greater strength. from the saddle of one's mount.[22]

The different pieces of apparel could be fastened by means of cords, brooches and other clasps, or buttons, which in the thirteenth century were beginning to become commonplace. King Dinis possessed some clothes which had buttons of patterned cloth, of silver with ornate golden carvings, of crystal, and of chalcedony.[23]

The great transformations in masculine apparel that led to the famous X-line of the fifteenth century began with the second decade of the fourteenth. This evolution was marked by the gradual shortening of men's clothing, which simultaneously became more form-fitting, revealing their figures. At the same time, the taste for voluminous mantles did not diminish, this fashion thus revealing one of the many inherent contradictions of the epoch. The elegant man ordered his tailor to make his tunics extremely short and body-clinging, put on hose which were molded to his thigh and leg, and wore shoes with abnormally long points. But, on the other hand, he also wore a voluminous houppelande which came to have a train that trailed on the ground, with sleeves reaching the floor, and covered his head with hats which were monuments of height and breadth. (Fig. 26.)

Fig. 25.   Fifteenth-century garments.

The pleasure in ornamentation, in variety and contrast of colors, in the richness of the fabrics, did not fail to worry the more timorous souls and the more puritanical consciences. Sumptuary laws against extravagances and laws of prohibition multiplied. Nevertheless, nothing had the power to obstruct the final evolution of a style which accompanied the changing of a society.

Fashion had been Byzantine throughout the whole of the twelfth century; in the hundred or hundred and fifty years following, the

Fig. 26. The well-dressed man,
14th and 15th centuries.

court of Paris defined elegance in raiment. That most of the thirteenth-century clothing terms mentioned above are French in origin is evidence of this. The same process occurred in the two centuries following. For, if the center of style moved from France to Burgundy after the mid-1300's, the language remained French.

In the middle of the fourteenth century—more exactly, in 1340—a sumptuary law concerning abuses in apparel and in food was issued from the Cortes of Santarém.[24] It is the first pragmatic against extravagance in Portugal. But here its moral character is less important than the wealth of information that it furnishes on the clothing of the period. Combined with the evidence of the numerous existing documents, it allows us to make an analysis of the dress and its evolution in the second half of the fourteenth, and in the fifteenth, century.

Every gentleman wore a shirt (camisa), or an *alcândora,** of linen or silk next to his skin. Although it was an undergarment, the wealthy man preferred to wear a shirt with embroidery or other decoration. As a rule, it was knee length, slit on the sides, and had long sleeves. At certain times, perhaps when the heat was oppressive, he might omit the shirt and substitute a shirt front, tied with cords or ribbons, called the *porta de Holanda.* This, at least, can be inferred from advice given in the late fifteenth century by the master of the royal stables, Fernão da

---

* The alcândora must have been slightly different from the shirt, using more cloth and needing more work; some had high collars (*gorjeiras*). See *Documentos Historicos da Cidade de Evora,* ed. Gabriel Pereira, pt. 1 (Évora, 1885), p. 140.

Silveira, to his nephew, Garcia de Melo de Serpa, on the art of dressing well for the court; the advice is recorded in the *Cancioneiro Geral:*

> Whoever wears a *porta d'Holanda*
> Does not have to worry about wearing a shirt,
> Only, tie the ribbons well
> So that it won't hang to one side.[25]

At night, the shirt was removed because medieval men were in the habit of sleeping completely nude.

The use of drawers continued throughout the whole of the fourteenth century and the fifteenth century. The terminology seems to have changed with the times, for a different word, *fraldilha* (Fr. *petits-draps*), now appears to designate those intimate garments. João Fogaça says in the *Cancioneiro:*

> *Dou fraldilhas, dou camisas,*
> *dou cotas, e dou mantilhas.*
>
> I give drawers, I give shirts,
> I give coats, and I give mantillas.[26]

The hose, *calças* (Fr. *chausses*), so typical of the end of the Middle Ages and the cause of so much scandal upon their appearance in plain view, were slipped on next. Always made of woolen fabrics,* the hose were long, completely form fitting, and of two separate pieces, one for each leg. There were two fundamental types: those with feet and underlying soles—the so-called soled leggings (*calças soladas;* Fr. *chausses semelées)*—and those without feet, stopping at the ankle. Both were fastened first at the waistline by means of laces, afterwards to the doublet by points (Fig. 28). In his discussion of the ideal dress of the hunter in the *Book on Hunting,* João I (1385–1433) recommends the use of boots and indicates that "by no means should they be soled leggings, nor shoes." [27]

The disclosure of the hose, converted into important pieces of masculine dress as tunics became shorter, took place in the second and third decades of the fourteenth century. Nobles and commoners began to appear publicly with their legs exposed, to the considerable scandal of "serious people." The pragmatic of 1340 found it best to restrict the use of hose to the greatest nobles, knights, squires, and rich bourgeoisie, expressly forbidding them to peasants.[28] Shortly, the hose came to be

* When Manuel de Noronha appeared in Saragossa in hose of fine camlet (a kind of satin), the astonishment and laughter were such that they inspired more than forty songs of scorn and derision! (*Cancioneiro Geral de Garcia de Resende,* ed. A. J. Gonçalves Guimarães [Coimbra, 1910–15], IV, 218–37.)

Fig. 27. Underwear, 15th century.

Fig. 28.   Soled leggings.

decorated with all kinds of ornaments, embroidery, pearls, and thread of gold or silver. A 1391 law prohibited everyone who was not a knight from wearing the style of hose that was "printed, painted, or striped in back."[29] In the diary of the journey that Afonso, Count of Ourém, made to the Council of Basel in 1437, one reads that in Tortosa, "the count removed his mourning clothes which he has been wearing, and in honor of Easter wore a blue tunic, very well dagged, and embroidered hose in which the threads were indistinguishable, so perfect was the work." When he arrived in Barcelona, Afonso wore "some hose embroidered with figures of thistles, in which no single thread was conspicuous."[30] Another extravagance consisted in wearing divided trousers, each of different color, called parti-colored or bi-colored, a characteristic style at the end of the fourteenth century and in the fifteenth (see Fig. 28). In the combination of tones, the good taste and elegance of the possessor became apparent.

In some fifteenth-century paintings existing in Lisbon, the so-called Panels of St. Vicente de Fora, the nobleman kneeling to the left of the saint on the Panel of the Prince (Henry the Navigator) wears dark blue hose, mostly covered by his high boots; the boy also wears dark blue hose (Fig. 1). On the Panel of the Archbishop, the knight in the foreground to the right of the saint wears scarlet hose. Those of the other knight to the left are of the same color (Fig. 2).

In the second half of the fifteenth century, a new item of dress was introduced to the masculine wardrobe: the breeches-hose, or *calças-bragas* (Fr. *haut-de-chausse* or *boulevard*). Made from woolen cloth or velvet and never longer than mid-thigh, these were slipped on over the hose. Usage of this garment never became generalized, however, and never even remotely was it worn daily. That is why Francisco da Silveira composed a song about Nuno Pereira, who "on Sundays..."

fastens on breeches-hose to his very doublet."[31] When the doublet, the tunic, and other clothes became so short that they did not fall below mid-hip, it was necessary to wear a codpiece (*braguilha;* Fr. *entre-jambe*) between the hose, fastened by buttons or trussing points to the hose (Fig. 29). When it became visible, the codpiece began to be made out of quality textiles. Some elegant fops carried exaggeration to the point of wearing codpieces of brocade, a practice which aroused the derision of the other courtiers.[32]

The pourpoint, or gipon, or doublet (*porponto, gibão,* or *jubão;* from Fr. *pourpoint, gipon,* and *joupon*), appears as courteous dress about the middle of the fourteenth century (Fig. 30). It corresponded, loosely speaking, to the modern shirt. The bodice was lined and padded throughout, with extra thickness over the chest for prominence, falling without a pleat or fold, as if it were full of air. It tightened at the waistline, then fell freely again down to the hips. A poet of the *Cancioneiro Geral* sings:

> The pourpoint may be of any cloth whatever,
> And loose over the belly.
> Around the chest it should be snug,
> So that its owner can show it off.[33]

Pourpoints were generally made of embroidered silk or velvet in vivid colors, whether in plain or patterned cloth. Count Andeiro, killed in 1385, "lay dressed and laced in a pourpoint of red satin," says Fernão Lopes.[34] The pourpoint in the portrait of João I (1385–1433), the collar of which is visible, is brocade (Fig. 31). The Count of Ourém appeared four times at the sessions of the Council of Basel, "and on the fourth, wore a decorated mantle with a brocade doublet." João Afonso de Aveiro describes his own pourpoint "of plain silk of very fine crimson" in the *Cancioneiro Geral* by Garcia de Resende.[35]

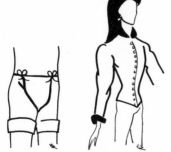

Fig. 30. Pourpoint, gipon, or doublet.

Fig. 29. Codpiece.

Fig. 31.   João I. Late 14th or early 15th century.

The pourpoint might or might not have a collar, although it appeared more frequently during the second half of the fifteenth century,
in particular the standing collar, which was quite high and fastened
tightly. Around 1465–70, the Burgundian style made fashionable
doublets with a V-opening to the waist, laced across with strings. Some
of the pourpoints, as can be seen in the St. Vicente panels (Figs. 1 and
2), have already developed in this fashion. For banquets and ceremonies,
as well as during warm weather, the doublet could be worn without
any other garment over it. Doublets worn for ceremonious occasions
were made of sumptuous textiles and displayed rich embroidery. The

doublet could also be shorter or longer, tighter or looser fitting, according to the occasion on which it was to be worn. In his *Book of Instruction on the Art of Riding Well (Livro da Ensinança de Bem Cavalgar
Toda Sela)*, King Duarte comments: "It should not be so large that the
body is swallowed up in it, or if by chance it is very tight, it should be
counterbalanced by the fit of the collar. And we ought to watch, if the
skirt is long, that the train does not hang below the rear bow of these
saddles from Brabant, unlacing it on one side if the pourpoint should
be open on the sides, or lacing it so tightly that its skirt cannot go
beyond the bows."[36]

Originally, the sleeves of pourpoints were long and tight, often buttoned from elbow to wrist. About 1460, the sleeves began to be
slashed, exposing the shirtsleeve. This can be seen on the figures of
the St. Vicente panels. Sleeves came to be extremely wide, variously
shaped, and of colors different from those of the rest of the garment.
Brocade doublets with half sleeves are mentioned in the songs of the
Cancioneiro Geral.[37] In the *Book on Hunting,* João I discourses on the
various types of sleeves suitable for hunting. One of them was a glove-
like sleeve, called *manga de luiva,* which fit the arm very sleekly.[38]

The tunic continued to be worn during the fourteenth and fifteenth
centuries, but with certain changes. In the middle of the fourteenth
century, it fell to the knees; afterwards, it was shortened more and
more until it barely reached the thigh; then it descended, about 1470,
again reaching the knees (Fig. 32). There were also several designs for
the sleeves of the tunic: they might be long, or caught a little below the

Fig. 32.   Tunic, 14th and 15th centuries.

elbows; full from shoulder to wrist, or gradually tightening down to the wrist; plain, or with long, narrow streamers called tippets which came to touch the ground; and so on. Terminology for the tunic varied: in 1340, the tunic was called a *saia;* a century later, the masculine form, *saio,* was preferred. The Gallicisms *jaca* and *jaque,* from Fr. *jaque* (Eng. *jacket*), are found concurrently in documents, although less frequently.[39] Corresponding to the modern jacket or vest, the tunic was usually cut from heavy silk or velvet, a cloth stronger than that of the doublet, and had paddings and linings. The Count of Ourém, entering Barcelona on his way to Basel in 1437, was "wearing a tunic of velvety satin lined with sable." On arriving in Florence, he wore a tunic of brocade, and his three pages, tunics of velvet and brocade. Throughout the mid-fifteenth century, however, tunics made of very fine cloth were also used in Portugal; these were called French tunics (*saios franceses*).[40] A little later, sleeveless tunics, which exposed the sleeves of the pourpoint, came into fashion. Several persons on the Panels of St. Vicente de Fora are wearing these. In the last quarter of the fifteenth century, the tunic seems to have disappeared from the history of Portuguese dress, in favor of other pieces to which we shall refer further on.

Dagged apparel—garments with scallops cut in, or bands added to, the edges—appeared in the second half of the fourteenth century, and the style lasted nearly a hundred years. Sleeves and hems of mantles, tunics, and other items in the male wardrobe were dagged. By the mid-fifteenth century, however, the style was confined to servants and squires. In 1451, the Marquis of Valença accompanied Princess Leonor to Italy. On that occasion, he gave each squire in his household "two French tunics, which were then made of very fine cloth, one dagged and the other in black fur [that is, lined with black pelts]." On another occasion, he had three pages who had gone along dress in dagged green French tunics with pendents on each dag (probably small bells), "which were made in Burgos, because there was no one who could have made such things in this Realm."[41] Dags also became characteristic of the clothing of scribes, who were required to wear them as symbols.[42]

The man of 1340—except for the peasant—still wore a pelote, or surcoat, over his tunic. Around the middle of the fourteenth century, when these two articles of clothing were still relatively long,* some

---

* The pragmatic of 1340, with the aim of putting an end to trains on masculine apparel, ordered that every item of clothing should be at least three fingers off the ground (A. H. de Oliveira Marques, "A Pragmática de 1340," offprint of *Revista da Faculdade de Letras* [Lisbon], 2nd ser., XXII [1956], 24).

7.2 yards were required to make both. Quite form fitting, the surcoat might or might not have sleeves. These were cut in various shapes, often not falling below the elbow. During the second half of the fourteenth century, surcoats were very tight, with low waists and padded shoulders. The pelote seems to disappear from male apparel toward the end of the fourteenth century, only to reappear around the middle of the following century as the Portuguese translation of the French *paletot*. This new surcoat (or paletot) began by being quite short, reaching about mid-hip. By the end of the century, however, much longer paletots were used, particularly by elegant dandies, who came to order them ankle length.

> Let the surcoat be worn
> Just a little above the ankle.
> It may be white or red,
> Which are proper colors for headgear.[43]

It was also stylish to wear slashed paletots, so that the clothes underneath could be seen, or paletots adorned with ribbons, fringe, or furs. At the beginning of the reign of João II (1481–95), long, full surcoats with embroidered trimmings were popular.

The *jórnea,* or *jorne* (Fr. *journade;* Eng. *cyclas*), was a loose, full surcoat used during the first half of the fifteenth century. King Duarte advises hunters that the clothing that they should wear "should be loose, such as mantles or cyclades." The young hunters who accompanied the Count of Ourém on a hunting trip in Milan wore crimson cyclades, and cyclades enter into the livery of the same nobleman.[44] Apparently, the cyclas was a garment appropriate for hunts and trips but otherwise reserved for persons of inferior social status.

One of the most typical items of dress at the end of the Middle Ages was surely the *opa* (Fr. *houppe* or *houppelande;* Eng. *houppelande*). The pragmatic of 1340 does not mention it, since the vogue in houppelandes began only about 1360; in masculine dress, it disappears or becomes relatively rare about the middle of the fifteenth century. The houppelande was a quite voluminous, long coat, with a skirt that trailed along the ground, and with large, long sleeves that were of varied shapes and were often slashed on the side. The garment was open in front and sometimes on the sides as well; it had a very high, upright collar which pushed up against the ears and back of the head (Fig. 33). The houppelande could be made of wool, silk, or brocade, with plain or patterned textiles, and could include every kind of ornamentation. Furs were used liberally in their decoration, especially as lining: "João Esteves came back very gay, with the houppelande which the

Master had given him, lined with gray pelts, with a golden scallop on his chest," narrates Fernão Lopes in the late fourteenth century.[45]

At times the houppelande was used as a large, warm overcoat, but it was more properly ceremonial in use. On being received by the Pope in Bologna in 1437, the Count of Ourém "wore a brocade houppelande trimmed in fine sable, which fell to his feet; and all of his retainers were very well dressed in the finest clothes each possessed." In 1428 Prince Duarte wore "a very richly embellished houppelande" as a wedding gown. By 1451, houppelandes were no longer seen in Italy, which is why the one displayed by the Marquis of Valença in Rome and Naples occasioned great surprise.[46]

The *anselim* (Fr. *haincelin*) was a type of houppelande, a shorter and sleeker fitting garment, frequently used for hunting. For instance, King João I in his *Book on Hunting* recommends that one's hunting outfit "should be as tight-fitting as an *anselim*." [47]

Competing with the houppelande, but used more for the outdoors, the *roupa* (*robe* in both French and English) could also be seen. The robe generally covered the body completely, being open in front, or only at the neck if it were slipped on over the head (Fig. 33). But the preoccupation of the 1300's and 1400's in shortening every item of male raiment led to the tailoring of clothing that fell only to the knee or was even shorter; and in this case, it is practically impossible to dis-

Fig. 33. Outer garments, 14th and 15th centuries. *Left,* houppelande; *center,* robe; *right,* tabard.

tinguish robes from tunics or surcoats. Velvet in the majority of cases but also woolen cloth and even silk were used to make robes; the usual furs, embroideries, ribbons, etc., are found as decoration. The shape of the sleeves ranged from the famous mahoitres to tight, long sleeves. Robes might be worn loose as well as belted, with the girdle at the waistline or lower down on the hips. In the *Art of Riding Well,* King Duarte orders that the robe used for riding should be quite short, with "not very large sleeves."[48]

The term *gona*—whether derived from the English *gown,* or from the *gorna* in the religious wardrobe—designated a type of long robe appropriate for grand ceremonies. That is why João I says that it is not becoming "for a man to wear, when hunting in the rainy season, a very long gown of silk trimmed with brown pelts."[49] Another variety of robe seems to have been the *mongi,* or *mongil,* to which some songs in the *Cancioneiro Geral* refer.[50]

In 1340, a "pair of clothes" (a man's suit, in modern idiom) was defined as an outfit composed of a mantle + surcoat + tunic, or else of a tabard + cowl + surcoat + tunic. In other words, the tabard with a hood could perfectly well be substituted for the mantle. The tabard (called a *tabardo* or *talabarte*) of the fourteenth and fifteenth centuries was a kind of cloak which fell to mid-calf,* with or without sleeves, with or without a hood, open on the sides from top to bottom, and put on over the head. It was frequently trimmed with furs or with a fine airy cloth (Fig. 33). It might be worn directly over the doublet, dispensing with intermediate pieces of clothing. When Count Andeiro was murdered in 1383, he was wearing a scarlet doublet "and a tabard of fine black cloth, with slashes and sleeves." In the last quarter of the fifteenth century, the phrase "large cloak open at the sides" seems to have been synonymous with "tabard." Those favored included buttons by which to fasten the sides:

> In addition he made a tabard
> With buttons on both sides.

The *tabardo aguadeiro* (water-repellent tabard) was apparently used to protect a person from the rain.[51]

The shape of the mantle did not change essentially in the fourteenth and fifteenth centuries. It remained a long, voluminous item of dress which was worn over all the other pieces of apparel and used primarily as protection against cold and rain. But, while the cloak of 1340 seems

---

* The *tabardeta* (little tabard), mentioned in the late fourteenth century, was probably shorter; see *Doc. Hist. Evora,* pt. 1, p. 139.

still to have been part of the normal dress, the cloak of the fifteenth
century was worn as ceremonial dress and as decoration of the cavalry,
besides that practical use mentioned above. The traditional capes,
short and lightweight, always remained fashionable. In addition,
there were capes known as *capas aguadeiras* for protection against the
rain.

In the middle of the fourteenth century, more than six yards of cloth
were needed to make the normal mantle; and another mantle, the
redondel, was even more voluminous, for it contained about eleven
yards. Toward the end of the century, round *mantelotes,* either long
or short, were used. Mantles and *redondéis* could be lined with various
materials, including furs. In the last quarter of the fourteenth century,
Lombard mantles, which were open on the right side, were fashionable.
João I owned one of these mantles; his was embroidered with gold
and lined with ermine.[52] Toward the end of the fourteenth century,
guardaventres—perhaps the same as the garde-corps that were described before—were coming into style.[53] The double mantle went out
of fashion in certain regions of Europe—as, for example, in Italy—
during the mid-fifteenth century. That is why Lopo de Almeida, who
accompanied Leonor on her journey, exhibits so much pride in telling
the king: "I swear to you, my Lord, that here in this city [Naples] they
are amazed at seeing my double mantle, because here there is not even
a single cape, and in Rome the two double mantles and a houppelande
of the marquis and his pages shone very much." [54]

The shoes of the fourteenth and fifteenth centuries continued the
medieval tradition of ending in a point. More or less accentuated, according to the dictates of the style of the moment, the sharp points
represented a constant in masculine shoes (Fig. 34). The famous *sapatos
de ponta,* or *pontilhas* (Fr. and Eng. *poulaines*), made their appearance
in the second half of the fourteenth century and remained in fashion
until the end of the following century, with ups and downs in elegant
vogue. The point might be worn loose or tied to the leg with laces.
During the reign of Fernando I, these points seem to have reached the
height of exaggeration. In 1382, during the war with Castile, "the
Portuguese cut the points off their shoes, for at that time these were
worn very long; and when all of them were laid in one place, it was
delightful to see such a mountain of points; for then they regarded
as a Jew whoever did not wear long points on his shoes." [55] The point
was proscribed only when it hampered movement in any way; that is
why Duarte, in the *Art of Riding Well,* forbids knights to wear them.[56]

The material par excellence for medieval footwear was cordovan
leather, made of goatskin that had been soaked but not tanned. Cordo-

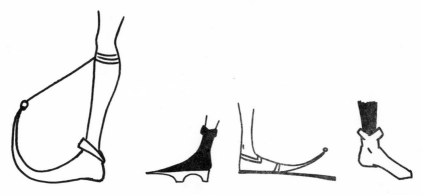

Fig. 34. Footwear, 14th and 15th centuries. *Left to right:* poulaine tied to leg with laces; poulaine with a sole tied beneath it; a third style of poulaine with a sole tied beneath; boot.

van could be dyed for the desired color. The most frequent colors for shoes in the fourteenth and fifteenth centuries were red and black; the poulaines worn by some figures in the Panels of St. Vicente de Fora are red. Shoes were also worn with all kinds of decorations, often of gold and silver. The term *gramaia* meant a type of shoe distinct from the poulaine, but just as expensive; we know nothing about its form. Cowhide shoes were worn for working, and peasants also used clogs (*socos*). More exquisite and expensive shoes and boots were of deerskin.[57] Buskins (*peúgas*) had appeared by the fifteenth century; they were worn over the hose, especially when these did not have feet, or simply in order to obtain more warmth.[58]

Boots (*osas*) or high-laced shoes (*botinas*) continued to be fashionable: height varied according to the occasion or the style. About the middle of the fifteenth century the boot came to be used as ceremonial and courtly footgear. Some persons in the St. Vicente panels wear high boots, although the poulaine had not quite yet fallen into disuse. Another kind of boot, the *borzeguim,* belongs rather more to the apparel of the sixteenth century than to the period under discussion, even though it had already appeared by the end of the fourteenth century: it was a low-cut boot, tight around the heel, then widening and rounding out toward the point. The master of the royal stables says in a song in the *Cancioneiro:*

> He who takes up horsemanship
> Prides himself for his short boots;
> But I hold as more genteel
> Boots with very fine folds . . . .

These I will praise, if I may,
Even if they be long.59

There is also evidence of the use of wide breeches called *safões,*
which João I recommends for the hunt. They were made of deerskin or
sheepskin and covered the legs and part of the shoes.60

In addition to shoes and boots, there were *servilhas,* a sort of leather
sandal corresponding to modern bedroom slippers. Fernão Lopes tells
how once João I, in an outburst of anger against his chamberlain
Fernando Afonso, arose "in the middle of his nap, just as he was, covered with a mantle, without hose, wearing slippers on his feet."61

The end of the Middle Ages saw a wide variety in head coverings.
Hoods or coifs constituted the habitual coverings of peasants and artisans: many book illuminations demonstrate this. Until the end of
the fourteenth century, the nobles and bourgeoisie also wore coifs. In
the following century, however, such people used them only as the first
covering, wearing a hat on top. The term *barrete* (skullcap) then appears to designate the coif. Hoods, or *enxarrafas,* continued to be
favored head coverings.

The noble or bourgeois of the mid-fourteenth century normally
used a chaperon (variously called a *capeirão, chapeirão,* or *capeirote*)
to cover his hair. The chaperon was originally a hood worn close about
the face with a long tail called a liripipe; below, the chaperon length-
ened into a very small cape reaching the shoulders.

The evolution of the chaperon into a hood-turban constitutes one of
the most fantastic transformations in medieval fashion. It began with
the enormous elongation of the liripipe of the hood, which the dandies
had already displayed by the middle of the thirteenth century. As the
fourteenth century came in, there also arose the style of putting the
face opening of the hood on the crown of the head. In this way, the
shoulder cape, which previously covered the neck and shoulders, came
to hang on one side of the head, while the long liripipe dangled down
the other. Finally, given a rotation of ninety degrees, the gorget of the
new hood-turban tumbled to the front, resembling a cock's comb, and
the liripipe to the back. The hood and hood-turban were worn in
these three positions throughout the fourteenth and fifteenth centuries, although the first two appear to be the most common (Fig. 35).
Nevertheless, for a long time, elegant men could be seen wearing the
hood in the third way, and at the same time, more sensible people
wearing it in the normal position.

As the length of the liripipe made it inconvenient to wear loose, it
began to be twisted either around the crown of the head or around

Fig. 35. The evolution of the chaperon.

the chin. Little by little, the reminders of the old hood were vanishing, leaving only a strange head covering, now resembling a turban, now looking like an enormous wheel or a plate resting on the head (Fig. 36, left). In the fifteenth century, especially in the second quarter of the century, the chaperons were arranged over foundations quite distinct from the older coiled turban. The famous chaperon of Prince Henry the Navigator is of this type, but the liripipe falls freely almost to his feet (Fig. 36, right; see Fig. 1). The chaperon was made of plain cloth; for feasts and ceremonies, silk and combinations of colors were also used. Different ornaments, such as jewels and embroideries, could be added.

The size and shape of the chaperon varied greatly, according to tastes and style, as has been said. The pinnacle in dimensions seems to have been attained between 1430 and 1440, if we may believe a poet in the *Cancioneiro Geral:*

> In the time of King Duarte
> It is said there were worn
> Huge chaperons —
> But never were they such as these.[62]

Although the chaperon had long endured the competition of other kinds of hats, only in the last quarter of the fifteenth century does it seem to have disappeared entirely from masculine apparel.

The sombreiro (hat) of the thirteenth century is transformed and included in the wardrobe of the elegant fop in the first quarter of the

Fig. 36. Chaperons.

fifteenth century. Hats appeared in extremely diverse forms, in certain cases even resembling the famous straw hats worn at the beginning of this century (Figs. 37–38). Materials also varied—including felt, fur, cloth, even straw or rushes, with adornments of plumes, embroidery, and jewels—and the diversity in form and material is reflected in the following verse from the *Cancioneiro:*

> This cap seems to me
> To have been sired
> By a huge chaperon
> Mated
> With a bushy-haired hat.[63]

Hats could be placed on top of small coifs which fit the shape of the head, as the following two verses illustrate:

> First of all, bring
> To the equestrian show
> A large felt hat
> Worn over a coif.

and

> Don't invest in a cloth hat,
> But rather one of very fine straw
> To wear over the coif.[64]

One of the most famous types of medieval hats was the beak-shaped one that was used in the fourteenth and fifteenth centuries, experiencing some fluctuation in style. The brim could be turned either up or down on the several versions. Around 1480, the Burgundian chronicler Olivier de la Marche refers to the introduction of the "Portuguese style" of round hats, encircled by dangling tassels.[65] At the end of the fourteenth century and the beginning of the fifteenth, large, high hats of a conical or roundish shape, pulled far down over the head, often covering the forehead almost down to the eyebrows, were worn in Portugal, as in the rest of Europe. João I wears one of these hats in the famous Vienna Museum painting, which has been returned to Portugal (Fig. 31).

About the middle of the fifteenth century, *craminholas* (Fr. *cramignolles*)—very high, sugarloaf hats, generally lacking brims—were very much in vogue (Fig. 38). In Castile, however (and perhaps also in Portugal), the term *carmañola* meant a round, small skull cap that fit the head exactly.[66]

Certain words which appear in medieval documents are often extremely difficult to interpret precisely. Thus the term *carapuça*, frequently employed, we believe denotes any kind of skull cap or even hat; the same is true of *capelo*. *Gorra* appears in the sense of *carapuça* or of skullcap but seems to have been rounded and to have had a double twist. *Chapéu* possibly meant "hat," as it does today.[67]

Almost all the masculine garments of the fourteenth and fifteenth centuries were girdled. The great vogue in girdles, beautifully embroidered and ornamented, seems to have reached its height as the fourteenth century wore on. Approximately between 1340 and 1430, the girdle was worn low, almost over the hips, although it was generally positioned a little higher when used over long clothing. After 1430, it

Fig. 37. Hats, 14th and 15th centuries. *Left,* sombreiro; *center,* beak-shaped hat; *right,* conical hat.

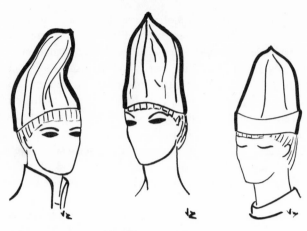

Fig. 38. Craminholas.

was again fastened at the waist. (Fig 39.) It was customary to load belts with massive decorations of gold, silver, and precious stones, to the point that the pragmatic of 1340 establishes rigorous rules against excessive display. Girdles also performed practical functions. Throughout the Middle Ages it was usual to carry knives and small daggers in the girdle, both for defense against attacks and as utensils for eating; knights even hung swords and larger daggers from their belts. The absence of pockets continued to necessitate pouches of varied forms and decorations, which were hung from belts, worn as often over the outer clothing as over the doublets themselves (Fig. 40).[68]

There were no great changes during either the fourteenth century or fifteenth in gloves, which were constantly used articles. Quality gloves were of extremely fine kidskin and fit the hand tightly. They had buttons sometimes. On the St. Vicente panels, some people are wearing gloves of such a fine fit that they can hardly be perceived. Elegant people of the late fifteenth century also wore gloves with a single finger, that of the thumb, to which songs in the *Cancioneiro Geral* refer.[69]

It has been said before that male apparel at the end of the Middle Ages followed the X-line. This fact is principally observed in the fifteenth century. Let us see how. All clothing sought to widen the shoulder line, even to the point of exaggeration. By means of padding and other methods of stuffing, men exhibited inordinately high shoulders and excessively broad backs. Mantles and capes also contributed to this enlargement. Then, girdles and broad belts pinched in the waist in such a way as to achieve the smallest possible perimeter. The belts of the dandies of the fifteenth century are so delicate that they

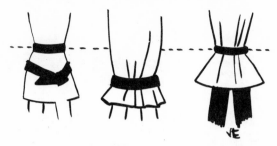

Fig. 39. Positions of the girdle in men's fashions, 14th and 15th centuries.

Fig. 40. Pouch hanging from the belt.

seem to imply the use of corsets. Immediately below, the clothing again widens, exaggerating the breadth of the hips and ending at the line where the legs begin. Thigh and leg are clothed with tight hose that appear molded to them. Finally, completely form-fitting shoes are prolonged in a never-ending point. The result is the famous X-line. A contemporary painting of King Afonso V (Fig. 41) provides an excellent illustration of the total effect, as do some charming fifteenth-century doodles discovered on the cover pages of the *Cancioneiro de Ajuda* (Fig. 42).

In summation, masculine dress in the fifteenth century accentuates, indeed exaggerates, all the horizontal and vertical lines of the body, with the exception of the waistline. Since the human being walks in a vertical position it is apparent that such a style became an absolute enhancement of verticality.

It must not be supposed, however, that the peasant or the artisan ever exhibited the X-line at harvest time or in labor at his craft. The attire of the "little people" was much less complicated and less subject to the caprices of fashion. Consequently, book illuminations of the fifteenth century differ little from those of the thirteenth when representing the peasant or even the small, itinerant bourgeois. On his head would be the toque or coif, sometimes a wide-brimmed hat as well to protect him from the sun. As clothing, there would be a tunic down to his knees, trousers, and shoes or boots. During cold weather or for protection against the rain, a mantle with a hood was thrown over his shoulders.

Afonso von gots genaden küng zu portgal vnd zalgarbe zher zu sept vnd zu algorro

Fig. 41.   The X-line: portrait of Afonso V, drawn between 1458 and 1471.

Fig. 42. Fifteenth-century dress: drawings made by a scribe representing noblemen of the mid-fifteenth century; also depicted is a court fool.

The pragmatic of 1340 designates for the peons in the city—"those men who live in towns who do not have enough wealth to possess horses"—a surcoat, tunic, and mantle, or cerome, besides the trousers. The mantle might be replaced by a tabard with a hood. The material that they were permitted to buy for making these garments, however, could not be worth more than thirty soldos an ell, less than half the price of the cloth permitted to the nobles. Moreover, the household servants could wear no more than tunics, surcoats, and capes or ceromes, all of a very low value. Furs and other ornaments, especially golden or silvered, were absolutely proscribed. João I legislated on this same subject in 1391; his laws were reaffirmed by his grandson fifty years later.[70]

The evolution of feminine apparel during the Portuguese Middle Ages was much less accentuated than that of the masculine and is much easier to describe. The reason for this is that while the silhouette of modern man has already been revealed by the fourteenth century, that of the lady remains rooted in an age-old tradition which hinders its rapid transformation. Religion, modesty, delicacy govern feminine dress until the dawning of the twentieth century, if we may exclude some truly exceptional periods. Long, full gowns, mantles, veils, and headdresses cloak the shape of her figure, substituting for its natural charm more or less elegant artificialities and more or less ridiculous principles.

In ancient Rome, the woman usually went about the house in a tunic with shoulder fastenings. To go out, she wore a stola over it, along with a flowing mantle with which to cover her head whenever necessary; a veil could also be used for this purpose. The girdle was worn high, just under the bosom. The lady's wardrobe in Byzantium remained loyal to the Roman tradition, although some changes should be noted. Thus, in certain cases the style of wearing two tunics is recorded, the one on top being shorter than the one underneath and having larger sleeves. The mantle also came to be worn in a different manner (Fig. 43).

The High Middle Ages preserved the double tunics, the mantle, and the veil for the head, but it added an undergarment: the chemise, made of linen or silk. In 1253, fine linen chemises cost as much as a pair of sheepskin shoes, and twice that of a chemise made of the coarse linen, bragal.[71]

Over the chemise, the matron and the maiden of the twelfth and thirteenth centuries wore the brial, or kirtle, which always had large sleeves and was decorated consonant with style. The kirtle was rela-

Fig. 43. Roman *(left)* and Byzantine *(right)* dress.

tively full over the bosom, then molded to the figure in the style of a corset down to the hips, where it immediately was cut wider to form a multi-pleated skirt (Fig. 44). The recumbent statue of Queen Beatriz, wife of Afonso III, exhibits an obvious example of the kirtle then worn.[72] In the thirteenth century, free sleeves, sewn on in the morning and unstitched every night, were fashionable. The term *brial* began to disappear around the middle of the fourteenth century and came to be used only in poetic language:

> *Fostes, filha, em o bailar*
> *e rompestes i o brial.*
>
> You went, my daughter, to the ball,
> And there ripped your kirtle.

sings Pero Meogo.[73] In 1253, *saia* (gown) was the Portuguese word used to denote the feminine dress worn over the chemise. But the gown did not differ essentially from the kirtle, even though it might vary in accordance with current vogues.

Between the middle and the end of the thirteenth century, the Portuguese lady began to wear another dress over the gown—the pelote (Fr. *surcot*, Eng. *surcoat*). The feminine equivalent of the man's surcoat, it was a very long garment, generally with a train which ladies had to carry when they walked (Fig. 45). Like the masculine version, the woman's surcoat could be open on the sides, without sleeves, and

Fig. 44. Kirtle, 12th and 13th centuries.

Fig. 45. Woman's surcoat, 13th century.

could have enormous armscyes which were extended below the hips, revealing the gown.[74] Over the surcoat was placed a cloak (or a double mantle), a granaia, or a cerome, identical to those of the men. In the fourteenth century, ladies also used the redondel, which was much fuller than the mantle, since it required six ells, or 4.59 yards, more to make (Fig. 46).

On her head, the lady of 1200 or 1300 wore a *crespina* (Fr. *crépine*), a kind of cloth toque, often rippled or pleated, of a circular shape, which was worn over a scarf or veil wrapped under the chin (Fig. 47).[75] The crespina assumed various forms with the passage of time. Further on, we shall see its fantastic evolution in the fourteenth and fifteenth centuries. In 1200 or 1300, however, the feminine headdress was less complicated. Sometimes a simple veil covered the heads of even the noblewomen. A kind of turban, of distinct Islamic influence, was worn from the end of the twelfth century until the fourteenth century.

On her feet, the lady wore shoes resembling the man's. Of black, red, or golden cordovan, the shoe was pointed, and of course, had no sole. It was actually seen very little, concealed as it was beneath a mass of skirts and cloaks, and consequently did not excite any concern about stylishness.

The taste for girdles is also marked in women's apparel. The girdles known as alfreses (see p. 52), of various widths and values, are men-

Fig. 46. Woman's redondel, 14th century.

Fig. 47. Crespina, 13th and 14th centuries.

tioned in the price schedule of 1253. The pragmatic of 1340 accepts them as lawful adornments for the dress of the nobility, besides ribbons (called *trenas*) and thick silken cords (*sirgo*) identical to those worn by men. The girdle was frequently worn low around the hips.

Furs trimmed the lady's gowns, surcoats, and cloaks. Buttons, brooches, and laces were used for fastening and clasping.

About the middle of the fourteenth century, feminine attire evolved more rapidly, although never as spectacularly as the masculine.

As an undergarment, the chemise (or *alcândora*), with a deep decolletage and slightly fitted sleeves, generally made of linen, continued to be worn. The trousseau of Beatriz, Duchess of Viseu and wife of Prince Fernando (mid-fifteenth century), included eighteen chemises of Holland cloth (a variety of very delicate cambric), three others embroidered with gold, and a large Moorish smock.[76] The noblewoman in the foreground of the St. Vicente panel of the Prince (Fig. 1) wears a very lowcut white chemise with a veil covering her throat and neck.

Over the chemise, ladies of superior social position sometimes wore small, quite tight pieces of cloth to support their breasts. They even placed padding underneath the chemise to round out their figures. Ladies' undergarments also included drawers (fraldilhas), made of very fine woolen cloth and probably similar to those worn by men.

The ladies of the fourteenth and fifteenth centuries wore hose of cloth or of mesh, resembling the hose used by men. They were fastened with garters below the knee.

The dress par excellence was called the *cota* (French and English *cotte*), a Gallicism that had been substituted for the traditional word, *saia*, although there does not seem to be any great difference between them. Fashioned out of various materials, including woolen cloth, velvet, and silk, the cotte generally contained long, narrow sleeves and was usually open down the sides, even below the waistline. Duchess Beatriz had three cottes of brocade, five of velvet, one of damask, and six of fine woolen cloth in her trousseau. Each lady-in-waiting in her retinue had a cotte of velvety satin, another of damask, and a third of woolen cloth.[77] The so-called corset, a type of cotte from France and Burgundy, had short sleeves, leaving those of the chemise exposed, and a skirt which was open in front or on the sides, fastened by laces. This is the kind of cotte which the lady portrayed on the Panel of the Prince is wearing (Fig. 48). The cotte could also be abbreviated to a simple skirt.

From about the middle or the end of the fourteenth century, an *opa* was worn over the cotte; this word was employed to designate either a surcoat or houppelande or even the French and Burgundian robe. The houppelande finally replaces the surcoat; at first it is open, just as the surcoat was, and sleeveless, allowing the upper part of the gown or cotte to be seen. Later, it is fastened, tight or wide sleeves are added, and it covers the dress underneath almost completely, so that sometimes this would be visible only at the wrists or through slits in the skirt. At other times the houppelande is buttoned on the sides up to the armholes. During the first quarter of the fifteenth century, the houppelande is fastened up to the throat and has a high collar; the sleeves are very large and long. Certain houppelandes have removable sleeves which are frequently changed. Beginning with the middle of the century or even before, the houppelande comes to be low-cut, at first only in front, but later both in front and back. The neckline is generally pointed, as if triangular. The skirt might be open in front to let the cotte be seen. It becomes fashionable to trim houppelandes with furs on the hem and along all the openings.

In the knowledge of color harmony and contrast between the cotte and the houppelande resided part of the secret of feminine elegance in that period. Naturally the shapes and colors of each article of clothing and the style of arranging them changed with each fashion. One of the favorite combinations of colors was the union of green and red: in 1437, while fording the Ebro on the way to Basel, the Count of Ourém met ten or twelve girls, "and they were wearing scarlet-red houppelandes trimmed with sable, and underneath were cottes of green velvet."[78] A lady in the Panels also wears a red houppelande over

Fig. 48. Cotte and houppe-
land, 14th and 15th centuries.

a green cotte. It is interesting to note some of the combinations of
houppelandes and cottes recorded as being in the trousseau of Duchess
Beatriz:

houppelande of rich scarlet brocade	cotte of rich scarlet brocade
houppelande of beautiful mulberry brocade	cotte of beautiful mulberry brocade
houppelande of luxurious green brocade	cotte of luxurious green brocade
houppelande of crimson velvet	cotte of purple velvet
houppelande of black velvet	cotte of black velvet
houppelande of purple velvet	cotte of orange velvet
houppelande of green velvet	cotte of green velvet
houppelande of grayish velvet	cotte of black velvet
houppelande of scarlet cloth	cotte of purple damask[79]

Lastly, the ladies of the fourteenth and fifteenth centuries wore
various kinds of capes and mantles to go outside during cold weather
or to display during ceremonial occasions. The garde-corps and the
guardaventre appear in feminine apparel as well as in the masculine.
Beatriz possessed a mantle of crimson brocade, another of black velvet,

a double mantle of Irish cloth, and one of cloth from Lille as well as a tabard of this same material. Each maiden in her household also had a double mantle in her wardrobe.[80] The *mongil*, a cowl worn by men, was also used as a lady's muffler.

It was customary during the fifteenth century to cover up the throat by wearing *teadas* or *gargantilhas*—small, almost transparent veils (although some were also of wool) which concealed the neckline of the chemise and the openings of the cotte and houppelande.[81]

Women's shoes essentially followed the masculine style: they were pointed and closely molded to the foot. They could be laced by means of ties or closed with buttons. They had heels of greater or lesser height. One style, almost always denoted by the generic term *sapato*, demanded shoes of a different color for each foot. In the fourteenth and fifteenth centuries, *chapim* indicated a lady's slipper, as it still does today. Duchess Beatriz carried six pairs of slippers in her trousseau.

The designs of feminine headdresses in the fourteenth and fifteenth centuries were as varied as those of today's hats, making it impossible to describe an average style. Although coifs and toques, with or without ribbons and clinging closely to the head, remained in continuous usage throughout these two centuries, the standards in feminine elegance began to require more and more elaborate head coverings. The first step in the direction of complexity consisted in covering the coif with a second headdress that was molded, in an exaggerated way, to the shape of the head. Since women wore their hair braided on each side of their heads, the coif showed two side protrusions. The hat placed on top thus had two enormous points. Even higher forms were achieved through stuffing the hat with cotton. The hat itself was made of cloth. Between 1370 and 1470, the mode called *coiffure à cornes* ("horned headdress") enjoyed a considerable vogue, arousing the most violent criticism and the most caustic sarcasm (Fig. 49). At other times, women pinned their hair in round or square shapes over their ears; on top of this hairstyle would be placed coifs with jewelled bosses known as *tauplas* (Fr. *templettes* or *tables*; Eng. *temples* or *templettes*) over each ear.

In the middle of the fifteenth century the hennin appeared; this was an extremely high, steeple-shaped headdress, which finally reached some thirty-five inches and from which veils were always draped (Fig. 50). The lady who is in the foreground of the Panel of the Prince wears one of these hennins, of a very curious pattern and without a counterpart in the book illuminations, paintings, or descriptions by foreigners. It is of a greenish-gray cloth, seemingly leaving free a wisp of hair to frame her face. An upper rigging of purplish-blue velvet burgeons on

Fig. 49. The "horned head-dress."

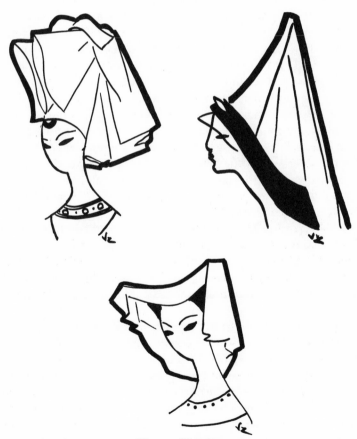

Fig. 50. Hennins.

top in an excrescence in the form of a tree, extending downwards in a long, rippling ribbon, half doubled when it reaches her legs. The portrait of Isabel of Portugal (Fig. 51) shows another elaborate hennin. Other hennins resembled unfurled sails of a ship, or the leaves of an open book, and so on.

It is possible that the *forcarete* (perhaps from Fr. *floquart,* or *flocart*) might also have been a type of hennin. Beatriz had seven of these, one of gold cloth and six velvet ones, all with ornamentation of gold, silver, and precious jewels.[82]

All these hats seem to have been known in Portugal under the generic name of *crespinas,* which was derived from the thirteenth century. For example, Lopo de Almeida says in describing to Afonso V the details of the marriage of Leonor to Frederick III of Germany: "The aforementioned lady, your sister, walked along in a lovely crespina with a veil over it."[83] The trousseau of Beatriz, in the middle of the fifteenth century, included nothing more or less than twenty-one! She had large and small ones, of wool, velvet, and silk, embroidered in gold and silver, with fancy handiwork in pearls or flowers, trimmed in velvet and furs, decorated with precious jewels, etc. Her ladies-in-waiting owned crespinas of twisted sewing silk. The veils which covered the crespinas and other medieval hats were called *rances,* or *ranges,* and could be delicately worked and embroidered. The crespina might be worn alone or over a toque. Beatriz carried with her forty-nine toques of various fabrics and sizes.[84] A simple type of crespina, which was related to a much older form of headdress, consisted of a kind of closed crown that allowed the head to be seen. This is the headdress which Princess Saint Joana is shown wearing about 1470 (Fig. 52), and was the kind generally used by maidens.

The high crespina ceased to be fashionable in the last quarter of the fifteenth century (in France, about 1470), to be replaced by the close-fitting coif, again covered by a veil.

The chaperon in its numerous shapes also had a place in the lady's wardrobe, its origin and development being identical to that worn by men.

Among other headdresses of the medieval lady, one particularly favored by elderly women and widows consisted of a hood with a gorget covered again by a veil, which gave the lady the countenance of a nun (Fig. 53). The hood could be replaced with a simple veil covering the head and wound underneath the chin; in the fourteenth century, women wore veils embroidered with gold, silver, and seed pearls.

The traditional hood—the *enxarrafa,* or *enxaravia*—also continued to be used. The list of the trousseau of the Duchess of Viseu included

Fig. 51. Isabel of Portugal, duchess of Burgundy (1430?).

Fig. 52.   Princess Saint Joana, daughter of Afonso V (1470?).

Fig. 53. Hood with a gorget.

sixty-seven *enxaravias*, six being doubled, twenty-four of a type called "Rui Sanches," and thirty-seven of silk and linen in various colors.

The girdle was worn low by women during the entire second half of the fourteenth century and the beginning of the fifteenth century. Then it rose and was worn high, a little below the bosom, until toward the end of the century. In certain periods it was also worn in the normal position (Fig. 54). The variety in girdles was enormous, for they could be seen in leather, wool, velvet, silk, and even of metal. Clasps also appeared in multiple shapes. The decoration of belts demanded large quantities of gold, silver, and precious gems, to the point of instigating official prohibitions.

Gloves also continued to be part of feminine style. Woolen gloves, however, were held in little esteem.

The famous X-line corresponds to the no less famous S-line in feminine clothing and posture. The elegant woman would assume a pose, bowing her head, retracting her bosom, protruding her stomach, and bringing her legs back a little (Fig. 55)—a posture exactly opposite to that commended by modern gymnasts. Her dress accentuated the voluntary line assumed by the body: wide pleats in front, girdle quite high cinching the bust, double skirts, and all kinds of effects to emphasize her abdomen. But it went even further: elegant ladies came to place stuffed pads of cotton under their cottes in order to intensify the roundness and protuberance of their stomachs! Beatriz, wife of Prince Fernando, had "a large amount of cotton," probably for this purpose, in her trousseau.[85] It could be said, as indeed contemporary critics did observe, that all the women looked as if they were perpetually pregnant. One may presume that many of the famous "Senhoras do Ó" ("Our Lady expecting her delivery") of Portuguese Gothic statuary are really statues of Mary in her normal condition, but positioned in the

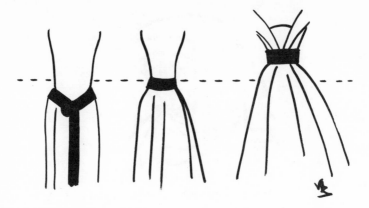

Fig. 54. Positions of the girdle in women's fashions, 14th and 15th centuries.

Fig. 55. The S-line.

elegant posture. The height of perfection in the pose went to the length of placing one hand over the projected stomach.

Ladies utilized perfumes and cosmetics in their beauty treatment. Beatriz carried with her ten glass jars of fine powders from Cyprus and a large amount of gum benzoin and perfumes.[86] In the thirteenth century, rose water, widely used in Moslem lands, was also known in Portugal; Alfonso X of Castile says in his songs to Holy Mary (mid-thirteenth century):

> ... she exhaled a scent lovelier
> Than lilies or violets or even rose water have.[87]

During this same period, the wardrobe for the common woman was infinitely simpler. Peasant women always used plain textiles of ordinary wool, fustian, or coarse linen. Over a chemise of coarse linen, they wore a kirtle with long sleeves, and over this, a shorter houppelande, generally sleeveless. They used aprons and wore coifs, hoods, and hats on their heads. In the "Book of Hours of King Duarte," which is preserved within the Arquivo Nacional da Torre do Tombo (Lisbon), there is an interesting illumination representing a woman of the people (Fig. 56). She wears a blue cotte with a wide neckline, a mauve houppelande slit in front, yellow shoes, and a white coif. From her belt hangs a pouch.

The use of ornaments of all kinds was very common among both sexes. Those who could afford it spent enormous sums on gold, silver, and jewels, which embellished their clothing, hats, and belts with brilliance and magnificence.

We have already seen how, from the first century of Portugal's independence, there are references to girdles and other large belts adorned with gold and silver. It was customary for kings and queens to leave girdles to their children and vassals in their wills. For example, Queen Beatriz, wife of Afonso IV, bequeathed a belt of gold and another of enameled silver.[88] The price list of 1253 mentions all sorts of belts embellished with gold and silver, the most costly of which reaches the price of six pounds—as much as one hundred and ten pounds of copper. One of the objectives of the pragmatic of 1340 was to restrain abuses in gold and silver ornaments. "Furthermore we order," Article 14 states in part, "that no noble or knight or squire nor any of their ladies may wear a gold or silver or enameled belt, or put more silver into a belt to girdle on than one mark of silver [230 grains]." But this prohibition was futile. Toward the end of the fourteenth century, João I legislated in the same vein, and with as little effect.[89] Ladies' girdles embroidered with gold and silver or plated with these metals appear in all the documents of the fifteenth century.

Besides ornaments of silver and gold, the Middle Ages preferred jewels. The numerous lists of precious gems in inventories, wills, trousseaus, and other rolls of jewels indicate the fondness of men and

Fig. 56.   Peasants' dress. 15th century.

women for this kind of adornment. Among the precious stones, perhaps
the most highly valued was the emerald. Dinis possessed such a stone, a
very large one, worn around his neck, and passed along from fathers
to sons within the royal family. Queen Beatriz, wife of Afonso IV,
owned several emerald rings. Rubies and sapphires were also prized.
The same lady owned a brooch, surely magnificent, made of a sapphire
mounted in gold, with two rubies and two grains of seed pearls. She
also owned, among many other gems, two sapphires, one cut in the

shape of an acorn and the other as an almond.[90] The diamond was equally highly esteemed. The future Duchess of Viseu counted among her jewels eight golden rings set with large diamonds. Other stones to which documents refer include *balais* (a variety of ruby), pearls, seed pearls, coral, amber, chalcedony, serpentine, crystal, and cameos. Any of these stones could be arranged (in any combination) in necklaces. Beatriz, wife of Prince Fernando, had a gold necklace set with one diamond, eleven rubies and eleven large pearls; another with two balais, three emeralds, two rubies, and nine large pearls. The inventory of her trousseau also mentions necklaces of amber beads and of coral.

Both men and women wore gold chains and cords over their clothing. Brooches or clasps were seen in abundance, and either used to pin mantles and other clothing, or utilized for purely decorative purposes. In the fourteenth century, very large round, polygonal, or heart-shaped brooches were worn. Then, combinations of enamel and jewels were very fashionable. Later on, they made pins only of precious stones and pearls.

Besides wearing necklaces and brooches, people wore rings profusely on all their fingers and even on all the joints of their fingers. Jeweled ties, or garters, came into vogue toward the end of the fourteenth century. Bracelets and armlets also began to be worn. The rosaries called paternosters are frequently found in lists of jewels and adornments at the end of the Middle Ages, as they were made of pearls, seed pearls, coral, amber, and other stones.[91] Crowns and diadems of various shapes adorned feminine heads and the hats of kings and the greatest nobles. On their ears, ladies wore large, round *arrecadas* and other kinds of earrings, although this ornament seemed to be considered more appropriate for common people than for those of higher degree. Other small objects which could be jeweled included combs, small mirrors and knives, and pins. Reliquaries were frequently used as pendants around the neck on cords and chains, as brooches, or as small domestic jewelry; reliquaries made of gold and jewels are present in almost all the last wills of rich persons.

The handkerchief, although known by the Romans, was not used during the Middle Ages. Only with the dawn of the Renaissance does the habit of drying perspiration or blowing one's nose with a small cloth begin to be introduced in Italy. The handkerchief becomes known outside of Italy only in the sixteenth century. But it is interesting to note that Portugal in the time of King Fernando I (1367–83) knew of sudaria (handkerchiefs for perspiration), although their use was far from generalized. In 1382 Count Gonçalo, brother of Queen Leonor Teles, and João Fernandes Andeiro, her favorite, "were sweating pro-

fusely and [the Queen], when she saw them coming toward her in this
condition, asked them if they did not have sudaria with which to wipe
away that perspiration, and they answered no; then the Queen took a
veil and tore it in two and gave a piece to each." 92

Fundamental to any detailed study of dress must be a knowledge of the
primary materials and of the standards of manufacture.

The material par excellence for the items of medieval apparel was
wool. Except for some velvets and silks, however, the textile "industry"
in Portugal generally produced cloth of inferior quality, such as *burel*,
a coarse cotton cloth, or estamene, a coarse woolen cloth, fit to be used
only by peasants or servants or for mourning. As these fabrics were
not usually dyed, the result was a whitish color, which led to the acceptance of white as the color for mourning until the end of the fifteenth century.

Consequently, it became necessary to import almost all of the materials meant for clothes. Of these, the most expensive and esteemed was
scarlet wool from Flanders or England, dyed in cochineal and produced
in tones closely related to red (red, violet, rose, blood red, mulberry,
crimson, etc.). The pragmatic of 1340 reserved the use of scarlet to the
king and other members of the royal family. After scarlet came a long
list of woolen fabrics, generally produced by the Fleming and English
shops (later also by Italian ones) and often named for the cities where
they were made. Thus there was *bifa* from Bruges and Malines, the
brou from Ypres, and the fabrics of Tournai, Abbeville (*abovila*),
Valenciennes (*valencina*), Arras (*arrás*), and Lille (*lila*). *Bruneta* was a
wool of inferior quality; one of its most important centers was at
Douai. There was also *frisa,* a thick wool cloth that was little used for
luxury garments but frequently for mantles in which to go out. The
fustians, of Portuguese manufacture, included cotton or even were of
cotton and linen alone. Serge was considered good enough for non-
ceremonial apparel. Other woolen fabrics without any special name
came from England or Castile.93

Besides woolen cloth, there were the precious silky materials, such as
damasks, velvets, and satins. When gold thread was interwoven in such
a way as to obliterate the textile base, the fabric is simply called cloth
of gold or cloth plated with gold. These fabrics were reserved for the
king and the royal family just as was scarlet.94 *Brocados* meant brocade,
as it does today. On the other hand, *damasco,* or *damasquim,* meant a
cloth of smooth silk. *Cendais* and *tafetás* were grades of very light silk.
Baldaquins, plain bolts of oriental silk, were used a great deal. *Cama-
lote,* or *chamalote,* resembled satin. *Grecisco,* or *crezisco,* a kind of

extremely costly silk, was imported from Byzantium. *Damis,** *ciclatons,* *ascaris,* and other silks were imported from Byzantium and the Islamic countries. Italy provided beautiful silks from Lucca.[95]

National production of linen was relatively high, especially of bragal, an inferior variety. But linen was also imported. From the Islamic countries came *mudbage,* a strong linen used for the clothing and capes of the clerics. *Lenço* and cambric, woven of very fine linen, were normally imported from Northern Europe.

There are few sources to inform us about fabric designs and colors fashionable in medieval Portugal. Portuguese museums possess limited collections, and few of these are elucidative of fabrics before the sixteenth century. Descriptions and pictures also reveal very little information regarding this subject.[96]

Generally, plain cloth—whether of wool, silk, or linen—was the kind most often used to make the various items of apparel. Easier to produce industrially, such cloth brought far lower prices at the market than printed fabrics. And, let us not forget, the high price of textiles was always a constant factor in medieval economy. In the middle of the fifteenth century, when the wool industry, particularly in Flanders and Italy, reached its maximum development, plain fabrics continue to predominate within the court itself. In the trousseau of Beatriz, the plain cottes and houppelandes seem to represent the great majority. Of the apparel seen in the Panels of St. Vicente de Fora, the plain doublets and tunics are clearly preferred.

This obviously does not exclude an abundance of printed cloths. Brocades, velvets, and silks were the fabrics most frequently decorated. The type of ornamentation varied in accordance with changes in artistic styles. In the twelfth and thirteenth centuries, the textile decorative grammar still complies to a great extent with Roman ornamentation when the oriental influence became marked. Animal motifs along with images and symbols of religion decorate the briais, the tunics, and the mantles of both gentlemen and ladies. In the fourteenth and fifteenth centuries these motifs change and draw closer to Gothic forms. Animal figures do not disappear, but their composition has a more naturalistic stamp, nearer reality: deer, eagles, dogs, and peacocks appear frequently. Floral and geometric themes are likewise used. A fabric exhibiting lines or streaks of a different color in the background was called *viado,* or streaked.

The decoration of some of the cloth portrayed in the Panels shows stylized motifs of botanical inspiration and Italian influence. Besides

* The singular is *dami* or *exami,* also assimilated into Portuguese as *eixamete:* it is the Fr. *samit.*

this, the border of the tunic of the knight kneeling in the Panel of the Prince is streaked vertically with gold. The two dalmatics of the Saint appear to be of silk with embroidery on a background of gold. The damask backgrounds of the Portuguese paintings of the famous "school of Nuno Gonçalves" reveal similar stylized motifs of a naturalistic base.

Color fashions would demand a monographic study in depth. In Burgundy between 1370 and 1400, greens, blues, and browns were fashionable. Later on, shades of reds, blacks, greens, and whites were preferred. A vogue in blacks, grays, and violets appeared during the time of Philip the Good (1419–67). In Portugal at the end of the third quarter of the fifteenth century, red and green were clearly in style, as is apparent from the St. Vicente panels.

In order to conclude this chapter, a few words about fashions in hair and beards over the four centuries of medieval Portugal are necessary.

At the beginning of the twelfth century, the Crusades brought the Byzantine and Moslem style of long hair, beard, and moustache to the West. Although it aroused the displeasure and even the anger of the Church, which saw in this hairy abundance a sinful approximation to the infidel, the fact remains that this fad prevailed and spread rapidly throughout all Christendom. The angels and other masculine figures in the "Apocalypse of Lorvão" exhibit long hair, parted in the middle, although they have neither beards nor moustaches (see Fig. 10). With the beginning of the following century the habit of completely shaving the face returned; at the same time, however, the hair was allowed to grow almost down to the shoulders and then curled in the feminine manner. The majority of Portuguese illuminated books, which had already appeared by this period, reveal this without a shadow of a doubt. The few recumbent statues also confirm it.[97]

In the first years of the fourteenth century, this style was retained. Almost all the figures in the *Cancioneiro da Ajuda* have shaved faces. Subsequently, men began to pull their hair back and catch it in a kind of a braid. The pragmatic of 1340 denounces wearing unbound hair. Even so, a little after 1340 the habit of growing a beard and moustache returned. Then large, curled beards were worn, which conferred on the men of the period that very characteristic "medieval" look to which we are accustomed. It is not positively known whether King Dinis (1279–1325) wore a beard.[98] Afonso IV (1325–57) probably had one, and there is proof for that of Pedro I (1357–67) in the magnificent portrait of him lying on the tomb in Alcobaça.

At the beginning of the last quarter of the fourteenth century, men again shaved off their beards and moustaches. According to tradition, King Fernando (1367–83) did this.[99] From then on, all the Portuguese monarchs, even including João II (1481–95), had clean-shaven faces. The chronicler tells of João I (1385–1433) ordering his servants to shave him just a short time before he died, since, "happening to rub his hands over the royal beard, and finding it had grown quite long, he gave orders for a shave, saying that it was not seemly for the king to be frightening and deformed after death because many people would look upon his corpse." [100] Both the portrait once in Vienna and his recumbent statue show him to be beardless. Duarte (1433–38) appears to have worn a moustache, a style which perhaps lasted a good many years, thus explaining the moustache of Henry the Navigator, his brother.[101] Still, he may have shaved it off before dying, as this is the way the recumbent statue on his tomb presents him. For Afonso V (1438–81) we have a drawing from the period (Fig. 41)[102] and possibly a portrait in the Panels of St. Vicente. In both he is smooth-shaven. And there is no reason whatever to believe that João II wore a beard, when throughout all Europe the fashion of clean-shaven faces was maintained until the first decade of the sixteenth century had passed.[103]

Men in Portugal began to wear their hair cut short (à chamorro, or "shorn") around the time of the Interregnum. With some variation, this remained the basic style until nearly 1465. Then long hair falling over the forehead down to the eye line and to the nape of the neck in back became fashionable, as certain figures on the Panels illustrate. About 1480, it was shoulder length and continued to be worn this way until the beginning of the sixteenth century.

Razors were utilized for shaving. Scissors exactly like the modern ones were used for cutting hair.

As far as women were concerned, there was no question of shearing off their hair. The problem lay solely in the way in which to comb it. Generally it was braided, and the braids were coiled and pinned cleverly under the headdresses. It was permissible, however, for maidens to wear their hair down and loose. At her wedding to Emperor Frederick III of Germany, reports Lopo de Almeida to Afonso V, Princess Leonor "wore the golden cord which you gave her in her hair; truly, my lord, she looked quite beautiful with her hair waved in the German style." [104] Female figures painted in the "Apocalypse of Lorvão" also have long, flowing hair.

From the middle of the fourteenth through the early fifteenth century, braids are arranged on either side of the head in rectangular shapes, or in compact coils. Then a new style appears: the ears are exposed, and foreheads are completely free of the shadow of a hair. Ladies went so far as to shave their foreheads in order to have them high and smooth. All their hair was pulled back under a coif which was covered with a crespina, although the Portuguese fashion some-times seems to reflect the Mediterranean tendency of allowing a halo of hair to frame the face. This was the mode in Spain (both in Castile and Aragon) and in Italy. Eyebrows were also plucked to achieve a delicate line, in the style of the makeup of the twenties and the thirties of the twentieth century.[105]

3 : THE HOUSE

THE study of "the house" in medieval Portugal has no particular meaning: what house, and whose, will be immediately asked. The royal palace, the nobleman's manor house, the habitation of the bourgeois, the hovel of the peasant are quite distinct and differentiated types of homes. On the other hand, almost all these forms changed over the centuries: the castle-keep of the twelfth century is a far cry from the multi-roomed palace of the fifteenth century. To further complicate the problem, it is necessary to make a definite distinction between the house types in the north and those in the south of the country—a distinction that lies not only in the cultural influences felt in these regions, but also in the very materials employed for construction.

Consequently we should begin with building materials. A "civilization of brick," the other a "civilization of granite," is the way the geographer Orlando Ribeiro characterized the two approximately equal areas into which Portugal can be divided.[1] In the south, although stone is present, it is rarer than in the north and of more varied kinds. Accordingly, people preferred to build houses of brick or mud and plaster and reserved limestone for nobler kinds of construction. In the north, stone, especially granite, abounds. Therefore, most homes were, and are, constructed of stone, particularly granite. Hence, this is one general characteristic of the medieval house in the north, if we are looking for one: stone as the basic material utilized, whether for seigniorial residences, or for commoners' huts.

Years before, this same writer had designated these two "civilizations" by geographical terms—the "Mediterranean" and the "Atlantic," which were joined together in the political entity called Portugal.[2]

On the historical plane, we would be tempted by interesting approximations. It is the area of "brick" and the "Mediterranean" in which the culture of Rome is firmly established and develops and in which that of Islam is superimposed later on. In the area of "granite" both Romans and Moslems penetrated only with great difficulty and the latter only superficially. It is also here that the most typical archaisms persist, that Germanization is most deeply rooted, and that the Christian Reconquest gives birth to the "barbaric" County of Portugal.

Throughout the medieval period, and even later, the south is characterized by flourishing urban centers, in sharp contrast to the dispersal of the northern population. The principal cities and their closest concentration are located in the southern zone of the country; even as late at 1527, the south contains twenty-five cities with more than two thousand inhabitants, as against only eight such centers in the central and northern provinces.3 Consequently, it is impossible that the techniques of civic construction and the improvement in housing would not have particularly developed there.

The Roman tradition had imposed a type of seigniorial house common throughout the Mediterranean hinterland and extended, moreover, to other, more distant regions. In the organization of the villa, or large property, the fulcrum of rural exploitation was situated in the so-called *villa urbana,* or country house, "a single-story building formed by four joined sections enclosing a garden, along every side of which ran a veranda or cloister." Each one of these sections was divided into rooms, many of which could be reached only by the veranda. Outside of one or two reserved for receptions or parties, these rooms were small because there was little space available. As for building material, stone was required for the solidity of the foundations. The rest could be made of mud and plaster, less expensive and faster to build with. Only the very rich gave themselves the luxury of constructing a mansion totally of stone. Mosaics, marble, bas-reliefs, and paintings decorated the walls and disguised the poor quality of the building construction.

In this country house lived the *dominus* (lord) with the members of his household. Nearby, a new nucleus of buildings came to form the *villa rustica* and the *fructuaria,* where the kitchens, servant quarters, barnyards, granary, etc., could be found. Three or four structures were arranged around a patio, the *cohors* (court).

Scattered throughout the whole estate were the *casae* (cottages), homes of the peasants who cultivated several parcels of land. Their homes usually had a single room, the kitchen, where their whole life concentrated around the hearth. There they ate and lived together; there women and children slept, while the men made do in the hayloft located over the stables. Of course, this house might contain a greater number of rooms, consonant with the wealth of the peasant; nevertheless, the principle of the common room, the kitchen, was always maintained.4

The Roman city house was quite different from any of these. In the city, the lack of space led to multi-storied structures. Thus, there appeared not only in Rome but in almost all the cities of the Empire "residential blocks" which came to be more than six floors high. In these constructions, although the principle of the inside patio was not usually abandoned, it is obvious that its practical utility changed, being used now as a simple courtyard for light and ventilation. On the front of the building, which opened onto the street, windows were added and verandas appeared. At other times, columned galleries with one or two levels were built. Inside stairways made of stone or of wood gave access to the various floors.[5]

The typical Moslem house followed identical building principles, as they were dictated primarily by the climatic conditions of the Mediterranean world. In the country, the dwelling was low—a single floor with four blocks arranged around a patio, or two-storied in the case of richer homes. In cities, buildings again rose in several levels, but continued to be centered upon the inner courtyard, for the windows opened onto it and the private galleries of one or two floors ran around it.[6]

The greater intimacy of Moslem family life and the circumspection imposed upon women obliged certain special practices, unknown in the Roman home, and were translated into the forms of construction. Thus, for example, the entrance hall and access to the inner patio were cut with bends in order to forestall indiscreet glances of passers-by in the street. Each window was delicately barred with metal or wood. Great use was made of the mushrabiya, a Moorish balcony totally enclosed by a wooden grating, from which women could look out without being seen. The mushrabiyas permitted feminine curiosity free expression, exactly as do modern venetian blinds; they also contributed to refreshing the apartments in regions that are much more subject to the summer heat than to winter cold.

One of the principal differences between the Roman and the Moslem house was in the roofs: tile roofs of one or two slopes in the case of the Roman house, a roof terrace or flat housetop for the Moslem. The predominance of the tile roof of one slope over the roof terrace on houses in the Algarve and Alentejo is explained also by the colonization of Berber elements, originating from a region where that type of roof was preferred.[7]

The medieval Portuguese house reflected all of these tendencies, but it was also adapted to the particular conditions of each period. The battles of the Christian Reconquest and the general instability of the first centuries often obliged the wealthy man to remove from his mansion to the nearest fortified redoubt or to convert his very home into a fortress. Cities were enclosed with walls, restricting the area allotted for buildings, compelling the house to be multi-storied and the street to be narrowed. The density of rural population was reduced, and whenever possible, the dispersion of the population gave way to a concentration which guaranteed greater security and better conditions for defense.

In spite of everything, the house of the south remained rooted to the traditional principles of Roman and Moslem construction. The dwellings, at least of the greater number of the inhabitants—whether they were artisans in the city, or tenant farmers and small landowners in the countryside—were low structures, generally reduced to one or two levels. In Lisbon in the twelfth and thirteenth centuries, the great majority of houses had a single *sobrado*, or wooden floor, at times accompanied by a *sótão* (ground floor) and a *cova* (bunker) which extended the space for residence or for storage of foodstuffs. Thus, in 1261, Ausenda Joanes sold a house on the public square in the parish of St. Estevão with a wooden floor and six small bunkers inside and three others in front of the door.[8] Stone and lime were utilized, along with mud and plaster and adobe, as construction materials. In 1191, the Crusaders wanted to burn Silves, which they had reconquered. But "the houses were built in such a manner that even when one was burning, the building next to it would not catch fire, because they were covered with bricks, the walls were earthen, stuccoed with cement, and there were few walls of wood."[9]

Beginning in the middle or end of the thirteenth century, foreign wood was imported.[10] It is customary to believe it destined for naval construction, but there is no proof that its use for civilian purposes was minimal. Actually, documentation is sufficient to direct our attention to the frequency of houses made of wood. A document from the end of the thirteenth century tells us of "houses . . . with their balconies overhanging the street as is customary in the land of Lisbon."[11] In April of 1369, a good part of Lisbon burned, the fire destroying all the houses on Blacksmith's Street (Rua da Ferraria) and a large part of New Street (Rua Nova), the principal thoroughfare in the city. In 1373, the Castilians set fire to it, "and burned all of New Street, and the parish of Madanela [Madalena], and of St. Gião, and the whole Jewish quarter, the best part of the city."[12] Much later, wood had to be imported from the recently discovered islands, as the chronicler Zurara attests.

The streets, whether in Lisbon or in other cities, were narrow. In the middle of the twelfth century, Lisbon's "buildings are crowded together so tightly that except for those of the merchants, streets with widths greater than eight feet are difficult to find," declares a witness.[13]

The government finally had to take measures to counter the narrowness of the streets. "The streets should be sufficiently spacious so that people can walk and ride down them without impediment," Afonso IV decreed in 1329, in a period when the number of multi-leveled houses was accelerating.[14]

With the passage of time, high buildings became more common, perhaps because of the influence of processes used in Northern Europe. In the mid-fifteenth century, Zurara, exalting the work of Henry the Navigator, speaks of the "great heights of the houses, which reach the sky, which were built and are built with the wood from those lands [the Azores and Madeira]." [15] Nevertheless, the buildings, even in Lisbon, were never very high. Even in the middle of the sixteenth century, the existence of buildings on the New Street of the Merchants (Rua Nova dos Mercadores), "all with three and four wooden floors" (that is, three or four stories high), was considered worthy of note.[16] In the same period, the average number of families (or hearths) per house did not exceed 1.6 in Lisbon—that is, one or two families resided in each building.[17] And it must be remembered that Lisbon has always been by far the largest center of population in the country.

The low house of one level, or a maximum of two, consequently constituted the rule in Portugal during the Middle Ages. Whenever possible, it had an adjoining patio, sometimes called a *curral* (corral), besides the garden, vegetable garden, or orchard, features which are still common today (Fig. 57).

Let us differentiate between these buildings by social hierarchies. Naturally, then, we will begin with the king's residence.

There is little information available about the royal palaces during the early years of the Monarchy. Guimarães and Coimbra were the preferred residences of the rulers until the middle of the thirteenth century. Little or nothing concrete is known about the palace of Guimarães. The present castle dates from much later, possibly from the time of Dinis (1279–1325) or João I (1385–1433). Inside, the living quarters occupy a small space, with half a dozen rooms filling two floors. It is difficult to recognize in such a small house the residence of a Count Henri, certainly used to more space and comfort in Burgundian lands. There remains the more probable hypothesis that the palace may have been located outside of the castle walls. For the Coimbra palace no information has survived. In all likelihood, it was located on top of the hill dominating the modern "Baixa," where later on we will find the palace of Alcáçova, on the site today occupied by the university.

Until the sixteenth century, the monarchs traveled a great deal. A study of the royal itineraries reveals their passage through cities, towns, and villages throughout the country, from the Algarve to Minho, with

Fig. 57.   Fifteenth-century gardens.

more or less leisurely stays in each one. Obviously palaces did not
exist in all these places, nor were there a great many wealthy bourgeois
houses where the kings might rest. As a rule, therefore, the kings lodged
in the monasteries, abundantly disseminated throughout Portugal and
having an abundance of well-arranged and comfortable cells. When, in
his wanderings, the ruler did not encounter a religious house to
use as a shelter, then he had to resort to the most important private
dwelling or take shelter within the walls of the castle, in the rooms of
the commander of the castle. In rare cities there were *estaus,* or collective lodgings, the ancestors of modern hotels.

From the end of the thirteenth century on, royal investments in the construction of residences became more liberal. The endemic warfare with the Saracen had ended. The times had changed, security was more generalized, the interest in the residence and in inside comfort more conspicuous. The customs and decoration of refined courts from the other side of the Pyrenees, particularly that of the king of France, were imitated, and came to replace the Moslem example as models of good taste and of elegance. Before the end of the fourteenth century, some large Portuguese royal residences had been constructed or remodeled: the palaces of Lisbon, Leiria, Santarém, and Coimbra, as well as the summer estate that was to be the origin of the palace of Sintra. In the following century, the palace of Évora was built.

Erected on the site of the residence of the Moslem fortress commander, perhaps using its foundation, the royal palace of Lisbon—the palace of Alcáçova as it passed into history—was inhabited by almost all of the Portuguese monarchs until the end of the 1500's. As a result of the enlargements, improvements, and adjustments of many periods, it did not display on the outside anything of particular architectural interest. It consisted, rather, of a mass of buildings of various dimensions, arranged irregularly at the capricious whim of the different monarchs and because of the practical necessities of available land. "It has no particular architectural form, for it had been built little by little in different periods," says the secretary to Cardinal Alexandrino, who visited Portugal in the sixteenth century.[18] But it was large and comfortable. The area which even today can be ascribed to it—inside the walls of the castle of St. George, before reaching the castle proper —would exceed perhaps two acres (8,000 square meters). The palace of the Marquis of Cascais, which was built on the foundations of the old royal palace of Lisbon and approximated the dimensions of the old palace, contained more than 285 feet (87 meters) of façade, with an average depth of nearly 131 feet (40 meters).[19]

The description of the interior of the palace made by Cardinal Alexandrino's secretary confirms a certain internal grandeur and complexity in its arrangement of rooms. The large reception hall, perhaps already built by the beginning of the sixteenth century, measured approximately 118 x 44 feet (35 x 13.4 meters) and was divided by columns like a church, with a central nave and an unknown number of side aisles. A dozen rooms filled the principal wing of the palace, in which were situated the royal chambers, reception and dining halls, and the lodgings reserved for guests. A round vestibule that was reached by going up a wide stairway gave access to the building. Outside, the few iconographic documents which we possess (from a much later period,

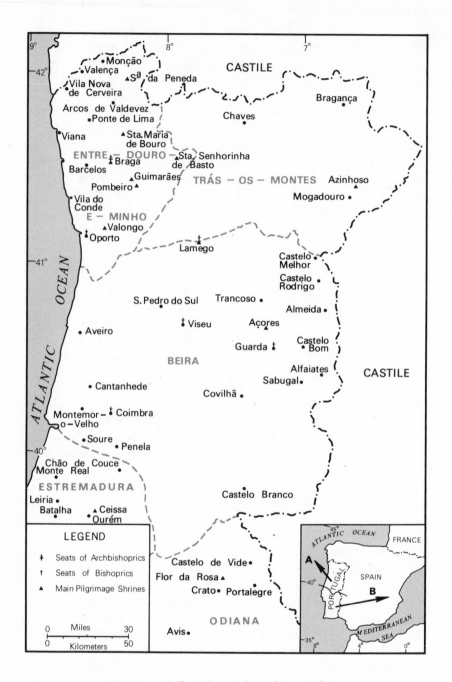

Map 2a. Medieval Portugal, northern provinces.

9° 8° 7°

• Penela

Monte
• Real   Chão de Couce   Castelo
                                      • Branco
   •Leiria   BEIRA
Batalha   •Ceissa
Nazaré•   Ourém •Tomar
Alcobáça•   Porto
             de Mós   Abrantes   Castelo   CASTILE
             Torres   de Vide
             Novas
   •Óbidos   Flor
 •Serra d'El-Rei   da Rosa▲
Atouguia   Crato• Portalegre
ESTREMADURA
        Santarém•
Torres   Ouguela•
Vedras   ▲N. Sᵃ das Virtudes
   •Alenquer•   •Avis   Campo•
Arruda• •Vila Nova da Rainha   Maior
    Tojal
Sintra Unhos•   Estremoz•   Elvas•
   •Frielas•   Vila Viçosa•
Odivelas•   Olivença•
Belas• •Sacavém   Arraiolos
Belém▲ ‡Lisbon   •   Montemor—
Almada   o—Novo•
      •Palmela   Espinheiro▲‡Évora Terena▲
Setúbal•
                                          Monsarás▲
Cabo •Sesimbra   Mourão•
Espichel   Alcáçovas•
                              Portel•
                     Alvito•
                                          Moura• Noudal•
              ODIANA
                     Beja•
                           Serpa•
              (ALÉM—TEJO)

                                          Mértola•   CASTILE
              •Odemira

                              Alcoutim

              ALGARVE   Castro•
          Silves‡   Marim
    Lagos•   Loulé• Tavira•
S. Vicente▲   Faro
do Cabo

ATLANTIC OCEAN

—39°

—38°

—37°

Map by the University of Wisconsin Cartographic Laboratory

Map 2b.   Medieval Portugal, southern provinces.

however) reveal a group of three or four buildings in juxtaposition with each other, two to three stories in height, crowned by some pointed towers in the Gothic style. The secretary of the cardinal attests that the construction was of stonework and that a labyrinth of inside stairways and ladders, added to galleries and balconies, complicated the internal structure.[20]

Another royal palace in Lisbon was that of St. Martinho. It was located in front of the church of that name, in the place occupied today by the prison of Limoeiro. It dates perhaps from the Moslem period and was the royal residence until the reign of Dinis. Later Fernando even lived there with Leonor Teles. Afterwards it was used as the Mint, but it again housed members of the royal family at the beginning of the fifteenth century: Duarte lived in it while a prince (before 1433), and it is possible that it was the residence of the crown prince for some time. By the reign of João III (1521–57), it was already being used as a prison. The plan of Bráunio, dating from the end of the sixteenth century, shows it to be of greater magnificence and architectural style than the very palace of Alcáçova.[21]

The palace of Leiria, where tradition conjures up Dinis (1279–1325), was in reality built much later, toward the end of the fourteenth century. The palace of Dinis was located somewhere else, presumably outside of the castle walls, near the church of St. Peter. Built on the orders either of Fernando or João I, the palace of Leiria must have been one of the most beautiful ones of the Portuguese Middle Ages. Not only was it favored by a magnificent location on top of the mountain, dominating the village, but it was also graced by the uniform disposition of its rooms, in studied agreement with a harmonious and coherent plan. Certainly, from the architectural point of view, it was one of the most splendid examples of Gothic style.

The main building, between the two towers, was a rectangle of 108 x 68 feet (33 x 21 meters), divided into three floors. One ascended an outside stairway of stone (the material used for the whole building) that led to the majestic floor on the upper story. There one proceeded from a vestibule to the great hall, which measured about 52 x 26 feet (16 x 8 meters) and was located over the open gallery. On each side, in the tower sections, were three rooms perhaps intended to be quarters of the king and the royal family. The room arrangement on the lower level was identical. The ground floor was not meant for residence, but only for the granaries, wine cellars, etc. A fourth floor, corresponding only to the upper parts of the towers, held another six rooms in which to live. In all, therefore, the palace of Leiria consisted of eighteen rooms and two halls. Some of these compartments were provided with chimneys and fireplaces. The lighting of the great hall could not have been of the best, since it received only the indirect light from the outer gallery.[22]

The vegetation of Sintra was as lush in the Middle Ages as it is today. Kings and great lords were attracted either by the possibilities for a quiet country estate, or by the inexhaustible resources the area offered as a hunting reserve. Naturally, therefore, the construction of homes which might be used as a lodging for royal visitors followed. By the fourteenth century or even before, there existed in Sintra a residence where Queen Saint Isabel (first half of the fourteenth century) lived. A little later, Beatriz, wife of Afonso IV, also spent summers there. But the great building transforming the original residence into a true palace, where all the later kings enjoyed more or less leisurely stays, dates from the end of the century with the advent of the first ruler of the Avis line.

The palace at Sintra reflected Mudéjar architecture, which had attained its apogee in civic construction in Castile in the fourteenth century and had influenced Portuguese construction by the mid-fifteenth century. The style, especially used in seigniorial and royal palaces, required an increasing use of Morisco artisans. Although the Gothic structural model was never forgotten, Moorish workmanship impressed the strong stamp of Mudéjar art on buildings, particularly in decoration (ceilings, ornamental tile wall coverings, and tile paving).[23]

In the first half of the fifteenth century, the palace of Sintra was composed of a ground and second floor (with a tower), divided into twenty-six rooms in all (Fig. 58). There were also two terraces, kitchens, and a chapel. The total surface occupied was a little less than 0.2 acres (1,000 square meters). A terrace some 40 x 14.7 feet (12 x 4.5 meters), probably roofed, gave entrance to the palace through a great hall, over 78 feet (24 meters) in length. There were two large chambers attached to it—the "chamber of the magpies" and the "chamber of gold"—two smaller rooms (in one of which João I was accustomed to sleep), a clothes closet, a small chapel, and a privy. The kitchens were placed in a structure apart with a roof terrace. The second floor was divided into more, but smaller, rooms. There were two large rooms, corresponding to the large hall below, which measured, respectively, 66.3 x 27.5 feet (20.3 x 8.4 meters) and 54.1 x 34.4 feet (16.5 x 10.5 meters). Four roomy quarters were adjoined to four chambers intended for the affairs of state —the chamber of dispatches, the "chamber where Vicente Donis writes," "the little room of the scribes," and "the little room for the secretary." There were two chapels as well, a larger room where it was usual to

Fig. 58. The royal palace of Sintra, in Estremadura. Early 16th century.

say mass, a wardrobe closet, and four privies, one of which was only a "little closet in which to urinate."[24]

In the first half of the fifteenth century, the palace of Évora was begun, on the initiative of King Duarte. His son Afonso V continued building it.[25] João II accelerated construction for the celebrations of the marriage of Crown Prince Afonso in 1490, Manuel carried it on, and João III may have concluded it. What remains of the building to-day, even after the work of restoration—two floors, divided equally, with two enormous halls on each and a central vestibule—hardly permits an appraisal of the comparative grandeur of the main structure, obviously intended for receptions, parties, banquets, and other formal occasions.[26]

Other, smaller royal palaces existed, traces of some of which still remain today, on the Serra d'El Rei (fourteenth century), on Monte Real (thirteenth and fourteenth centuries), in Chão de Couce (fourteenth century), in Frielas (fourteenth century), in Vila Nova da Rainha (fourteenth century), in Coimbra (fourteenth century), in Belas (fifteenth century), and elsewhere.[27]

Among the Portuguese, the castle rarely performed the functions of a permanent seigniorial residence, as was the case on the other side of the Pyrenees. Constructed as a bulwark for defense, as a rule it enclosed a small area, strictly necessary for military maneuvers and equipment. The dwellings built within the walls were meant for the commander of the fortress (the *alcaide*) and the personnel attached to him. Of course, this residence could be placed at the disposal of the king or of a great lord whenever other lodgings were scarce. But this dwelling place was merely temporary. For normal residences, kings and nobles ordered other buildings erected, purely civilian in nature, although often located near castles. If there was an *alcáçova*, or fortified terrain, adjoining the castle itself, residences were commonly built inside the fortified area: this was the case in Lisbon, Santarém, Leiria, and elsewhere. (In this case, however, the castle took the name *castelejo*, or "little castle," while the term *castelo* was applied to the whole of both the castelejo and alcáçova.) Few of these dwellings remain today, and these few have more often than not become ruins of scant significance. There was a royal residence ("some palaces with wooden floors") in the castle of Penela, where Prince Pedro (1392–1449) lived. In the castle of Beja, João II stayed overnight at various times in a small palace that still exists today: it has two floors, with a dozen rooms inside. Elvas also had a palace within its fortress. That of Óbidos dates from the fourteenth century.[28] And there were others.

At the entrance of the castle of Sesimbra was the residence of the commander, one of the few which managed to survive through recon-

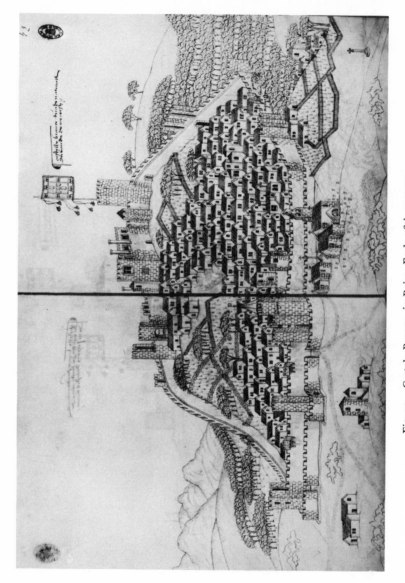

Fig. 59. Castelo Branco, in Beira. Early 16th century.

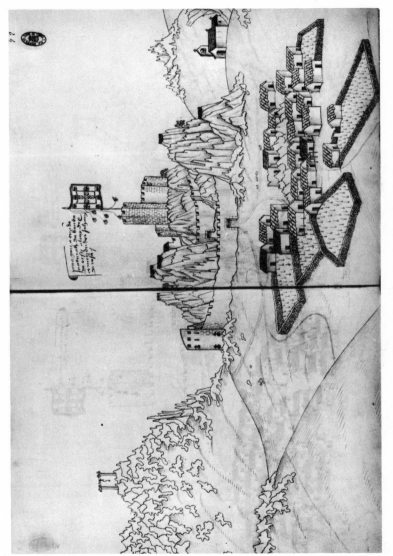

Fig. 6o.   Castle and village of Penha Garcia, in Beira. Early 16th century.

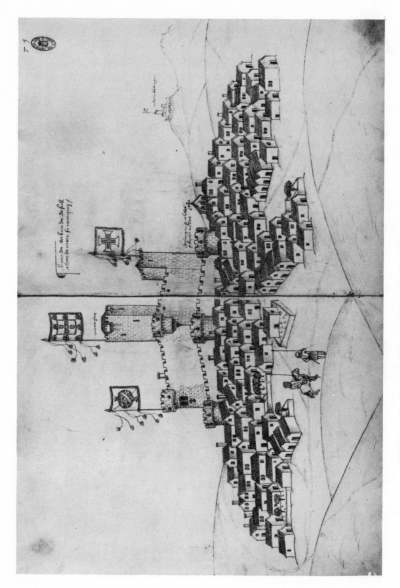

Fig. 61. Castle and village of Almeida, in Beira. Early 16th century.

Fig. 62. Castelo de Vide, in Alentejo. The lord's house is on the left; notice also the arch at the top of the main street. Early 16th century.

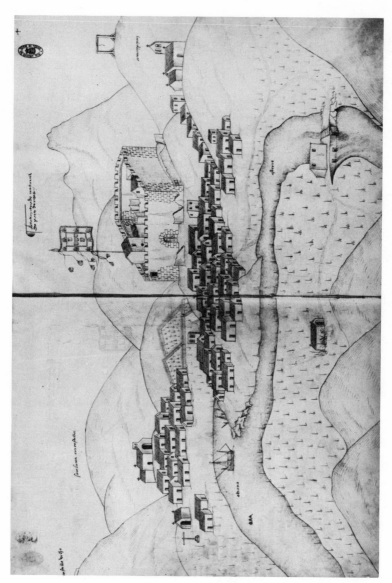

Fig. 63. Castle and village of Alcoutim, in the Algarve. Notice the water mill. Early 16th century.

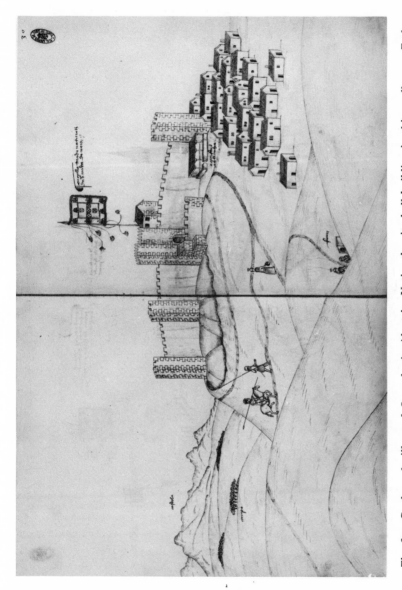

Fig. 64. Castle and village of Ouguela, in Alentejo. Notice the city hall building in this small town. Early 16th century.

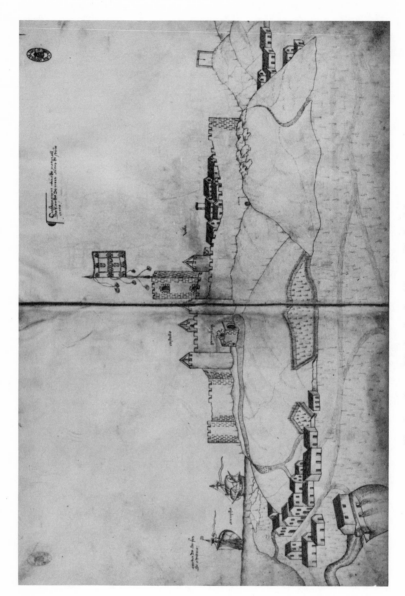

Fig. 65. Castro Marim, in the Algarve. Early 16th century.

struction. It was made up of the usual ground and second floors. Only the second floor, however, was used as a dwelling, as the five ground divisions of the first floor were used for storing firewood, for the wine cellar, and for housing haystacks, stables, and the cistern. The floor above, reached by ascending a brick stairway, contained four rooms besides the kitchen: a large hall used for receptions and for dining and three rooms, with chestnut wood paneling on the walls and ceiling, for sleeping and clothes closets. All these rooms had wooden floors and possessed windows opening onto the outside. In an annex, two rooms, each with alcoves, were used by the servants of the household. The large hall and the kitchen faced the south.[29]

The *Book on Fortresses* by Duarte Darmas, which dates from the first decade of the sixteenth century, allows us to evaluate the frequency and size of residences intended for the commanders in the Portuguese castles. Many such residences were no more than a single hall, where the governor ate, lived, and slept, and which certainly had the characteristics of the "house" of the Roman peasant. Others, much better arranged, had two, three, or four "rooms with wooden floors." Only occasionally were larger dwellings found: the castles of Mourão, Sabugal, Vilar Maior (near Sabugal), and Mogadouro each had five rooms; Mértola, Serpa, Noudal, Terena, and Olivença had six; Elvas, eight; and Moura, the best of all, displayed the luxury of nineteen rooms with wooden floors! (Fig. 66.) For recreation and also expediency, some castles included yards, vegetable gardens, and orchards. Moura, superior in everything, even flaunted an orange grove. What they all had on their grounds were single-room buildings in abundance —simple old constructions with floors of beaten earth, sometimes with a covering of straw, where household utensils were kept and food was deposited for safekeeping. The servants had to sleep there as well. In the castle of Mogadouro, there was a corral "in which were penned all kinds of rabbits."[30]

As a matter of fact, a good many of the dwellings, especially those of the common people, were covered with thatch (Fig. 67). In the mountains of Montemuro in the mid-sixteenth century, "there is no house with roofing tiles, but all of thatch, and all had dirt floors." In the cities, roofing tile was used, sometimes coated with whitewash. Broomstraw was also used as a covering.[31]

As we have mentioned before, the great lords had homes scattered throughout the countryside, in the center of their lands, or located in the cities. All, or almost all, of these homes have disappeared over the centuries. Generally small, confined to a single floor, or two at the most, completed by a tower, they suffered successive transformations

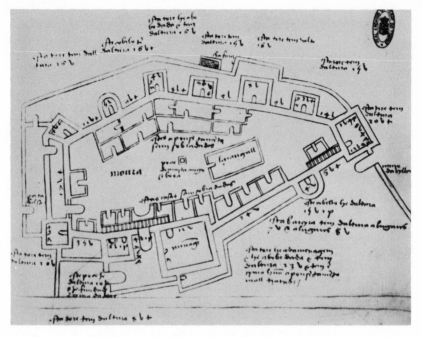

Fig. 66.   Plan of the castle of Moura. Early 16th century.

which disfigured them completely, or they were demolished when the
large manor house in the Renaissance style became fashionable, and a
necessity, beginning with the sixteenth century.

The increase in the construction of seigniorial palaces is noted
especially in the fourteenth and fifteenth centuries. In Barcelos, the
counts with the oldest title of nobility in Portugal possessed a palace
from an indeterminable date. Constable Nuno Álvares—who bestowed
it, with the title, upon Prince Afonso, the royal bastard, in 1401—
resided in it. Afonso, a great constructor of palaces, began the construction of a monumental work, only completed in the following century
(Fig. 68). In Ourém, the residential palace of the same Constable was
not judged worthy by his grandson, who constructed a new and more
elegant dwelling improperly called a castle.

Other seigniorial palaces covered the kingdom: in Arraiolos there
was one on the fortified grounds of the castle that had been completed
by 1315; in it the Count of Arraiolos resided until he fell heir to the
dukedom of Bragança. In Olivença, also in the enclosed sanctuary of the
castle, the counts of this name lived from the fifteenth century on.
Toward the end of the 1400's, the first Baron of Alvito laid the founda-

Fig. 67. Peasants' houses. Early 16th century.

tions for a palace. The village of Alcáçovas also harbored a majestic
palace: the primitive construction dating from the time of Dinis was
remodeled in the fifteenth century; in it, in 1447, Afonso V received
the embassy of Garcia Sanchez de Toledo. The palace of Viseu, in the
1300's, belonged to the kings of Portugal, and there Duarte was born.
The first duke, Henrique, lived in it for a long time. The Marquis of
Montemor owned a home inside the walls of the castle. In Canta-
nhede was raised the manor house of its counts, the future Marquis of
Marialva. And the lord of Penela, Prince Pedro, had a palace built in
which he often stayed. Nuno Álvares, the largest landowner at the end
of the fourteenth century, had residences distributed throughout the

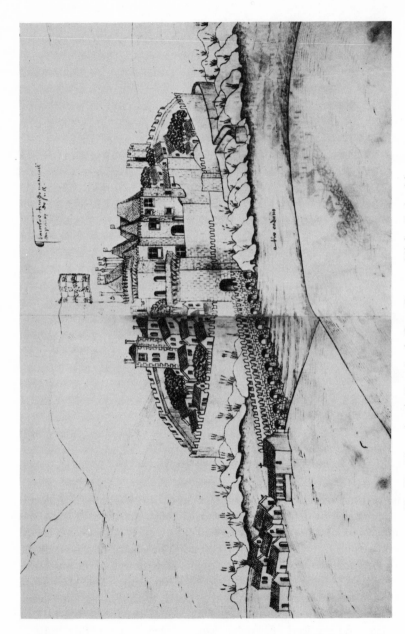

Fig. 68.   The palace in Barcelos, in Entre-Douro-e Minho. Early 16th century.

many lands in his possession as well as several palaces in Lisbon, according to his biographer. In Porto de Mós, the original palace was remodeled by the Marquis of Valença in the middle of the fifteenth century. No district of the kingdom possessed as many manor houses as did Minho in the fifteenth century.[32]

Nevertheless, the greatest constructor of seigniorial dwellings in fifteenth-century Portugal was unquestionably the first Duke of Bragança, Afonso. From the beginning to the end of his long life, he received various titles and resided successively in several cities. He left each one beautified with a palace, of increasing grandeur.

He began, as we saw, in Barcelos, where by preference, he lived between 1401 and 1420. Then he built the palace in Chaves, which was already habitable at the time of the death of Countess Beatriz, his first wife. In Vila Viçosa he ordered a palace raised in the fortified area of the castle. His crowning glory, however, was undoubtedly the palace of Guimarães, built between 1420 and 1438. Afonso had traveled in England, Italy, and Palestine; and it is possible that the civilian architecture he observed outside Portugal (principally in Italy) may have affected the style of his palaces. Actually, the Guimarães palace is in many respects an anticipation of the Renaissance palaces of the sixteenth century. It consists of four large blocks in the form of a rectangle, with three floors, around a central, quadrangular patio, with a gallery and flanked by towers. There were more than forty rooms, not including the chapel and the cellars. The whole arrangement of the building, and many of its features, mirrors a feeling of comfort and convenience that indicates the beginning of a new age in civil construction: there are an inordinate number of chimneys which lead to hearths used for heat; rainwater is piped, thanks to a perfect network of drains inserted in the walls, and there are drains in the privies; there about stairs for servants, verandas, and so forth.[33]

In the *Loyal Counselor,* Duarte describes briefly the basic compartmentation of a nobleman's manor. It should include a hall, "in which everyone from his manor who is not a fugitive enters, and also the strangers who want to come in." Next comes a more modest "chamber in which to wait," or antechamber, "in which the tenants and some other notables of the realm usually are." Then there should be the "chamber for sleeping," then an inner room called the *trescâmara,* "where they are accustomed to dress," and finally the chapel.[34]

The palaces whose room divisions are known to us follow this ideal scheme. In the palace of Sintra, we find a distinction made between halls, chambers, and clothes closets, in addition to the chapel, kitchens, and privies, obviously excluded from Duarte's theoretical plan. In the description of the palace of Lisbon, there is also mention of halls, chambers, antechambers, and chapels. Evidently, the diversification of rooms and their purposes was in direct proportion to the wealth and power of the noble in question. The separation of the sleeping chamber and dressing room, or clothes closet—thought indispensable in this period—arouses much interest. The antechamber, or *câmara de paramento* (from the verb *parar*, "to stop, stay"), is nothing more or less than the modern living room. In the fifteenth century (as in the previous centuries), a dining room still was not thought necessary. People ate in any spot—whether in the hall, or in the antechamber, or even in the bedchamber itself—on tables set up for this purpose and dismantled immediately afterwards. Further on, we will see the importance of this practice in the furniture of the house as a whole.

Of the "middle" residence—or rather, the dwelling of the burgher, of the smaller rural proprietor, of the knight-villein (cavaleiro-vilão)— we know little. In all likelihood, it would approximate more the style of the Roman house, with a single room centered on the hearth, than the intricate form of the majestic manor or the royal palace. Even the residence of the infanção, a member of the lower nobility in the first centuries of the monarchy, could be included in this simpler type of house. Is this not what an interesting song of derision, which Pero da Ponte wrote in the thirteenth century, reveals?

> Whoever might wish to take a nap
> I will advise him the best way:
> As soon as he has dined, he should think of going
> To the kitchen of the infanção.
> And he will find such a cold kitchen,
> That a like cannot be found among the king's men.
>
> I will tell you still more:
> I, who slept there once,
> Had not had such a good nap
> Since the day I was born,
> For God never wanted a fly
> To sleep in such a place,
> For it is the coldest thing I have ever seen.[35]

But, just as in the noble home or even in the peasant dwelling, so in the style of the "middle-class" house, many transformations were recorded as time went on. In the fifteenth century, the lesser noble, the knight-villein, and the burgher began to demand more comforts and a much more intricate type of residence than before. There still exist in Portuguese villages a considerable number of Gothic houses, all of them from the fifteenth or sixteenth centuries, which in spite of their barren appearance, a manifestation of not inferior crudeness of workmanship, already reflect distinct progress in the concept of living. In the south, particularly, the Gothic house seems to have experienced an internal improvement accentuated by Moorish or Oriental influences. As wood was rare, construction was done preferably in mud and plaster, stone, and brick. Roofs are vaulted, with tiles to fill the empty spaces of the stone arches. Part of the tile roof is flattened for a terrace. The outsides of these houses have very little decoration—just a coating of whitewash to cover everything. Inside, the rooms are small, the floor plans confused, the differences in levels and steps frequent. Flooring is made of bricks, or of tiles in the form of mosaics. (In Évora at the end of the fourteenth century, tiles to "tile chambers with" were baked a palm in length and two fingers in breadth.) More decorative tiles are employed in the wainscoting or on the stairs. Some ceilings were of carved wood (called *alfarge*); these have vanished without a trace.[36]

In spite of all these changes, the residences of the common people were still considerably removed from the minimum of comfort and ease known elsewhere. The amazement of Zurara, in his *Chronicle on the Capture of Ceuta (Crónica da Tomada de Ceuta)*, although attributed to peasant villeins, shows the astonishment that the very nobles felt, faced with the luxurious dwelling places of the Moors: "Here there were such houses among those people, for in this realm there was no hovel, and there were found as lodgings large houses tiled with bricks glazed with delirious colors; and the ceilings overlaid with olive wood, with beautiful roof terraces surrounded with very white, polished marble; and soft, yielding beds, and bed linen of imaginative, fancy needlework, as you see the labors of the Moors generally are . . . we, paltry ones, who in our native Portugal walk through the fields gathering our harvests, fatigued with the length of time, and late at night we have no other repose but poor dwellings which, in comparison with these, resemble pigsties."[37]

Medieval furniture never occupied much space in the interior of the houses.[38] If the pieces preserved today from that era are few, and documentary references are also scanty, it is because there really were few pieces of furniture.

The most important piece of domestic furniture was the bed. In the twelfth and thirteenth centuries, whoever possessed an inhabited country estate, a yoke of oxen, forty sheep, a donkey, and *two beds* moved from the social class of peasant to that of knight.[39] The charters decreed that a bed was always to be the last object to be used to answer for debts. Many wills include the bedstead as a gift to friends, servants, or pious institutions.

By "bed" or "bedstead" the medieval man did not always merely understand, or mean, the piece of furniture alone, but also the bed linen which covered it. And the set of textile articles which made up the bed clothing of that age was far from negligible. On the contrary —and again increasing in amount in proportion to the wealth of its owner—bed linen was appraised as the equal of, or even worth more than, many objects of jewelry or costly gems. Good textiles were expensive in themselves, and priceless embroidery, often of gold or silver thread, converted a pillow or a counterpane into an extremely rich furnishing.

The number and variety of beds increased as time passed. Even so, the "Apocalypse of Lorvão," which is from the twelfth century, already shows an extremely interesting bed (in which Jezebel is committing adultery) typical of the Roman style, without a canopy, of gracefully molded wood, and with decorative fillets on each pillar at the head and foot of the bed (Fig. 69). In wealthy homes, the bed might even be laminated in gold.[40] Later on, with the appearance of the Gothic style, the style in beds was modified. The famous canopy appears, with curtains to envelop and isolate each bed, and the wooden surfaces came to be abundantly decorated (see Fig. 70). In addition to bedsteads themselves, chests in which the bed linen (this seems to be the meaning of *almafreixe*) was kept during the day were used as bed frames; simple, broad, wooden benches, which could be moved easily, were also utilized.

Over the heavy wooden beams of the bed was placed a mattress of straw or hay, which the medieval Portuguese documents refer to as

Fig. 69. Twelfth-century bed from the "Apocalypse of Lorvão."

Fig. 70. Canopied bed. 13th century.

culcitro, culcitra, or even *almadraque;* on top of this mattress, another
one of wool or cotton would be placed; finally, on top of this was yet a
third, of feathers. Clearly the luxury of a bed with three mattresses
occurred only in rich homes; the poorer had two, or only one of straw.
Over the mattresses was sometimes placed a cloth pad, the base for
the linen on top: thus in the inventory of her trousseau (mid-fifteenth
century), Princess Beatriz, wife of Fernando, future Duke of Viseu,
registers "a cloth pad for the mattresses." In this same period, cases of
good cloth—for example, a fine cotton—were sometimes slipped over
the mattresses. The use of sheets made of fine cloth still was not common; they were known and used on the beds of the wealthy, but even
here they were considered objects of the greatest luxury. The inventory of Beatriz' trousseau mentions only "two sheets of French cloth."

Over the sheets, or directly over the finer mattresses, were laid the
bedcovers, of cotton, wool, or furs, consonant with the owner's means.
These included the *alfâmbar,* corresponding to the modern blanket of
fluffy wool, and the *almucela,* much lighter than the alfâmbar and
sometimes made of expensive fabrics, such as silk or purple cloth.
These two terms, of Arabic derivation, were gradually replaced from
the fourteenth century on by the terms *cobertores, cobertais,* or *cobertas*
(blankets); by the fifteenth century, the phrase *cobertores de papa*
(woolen bedcovers) had replaced the term *alfâmbar.* Covers of rabbit
fur, lined with cloth, were common. Beatriz carried with her three
scarlet covers, two others of fine cloth, and four of white frieze. As a
synonym of *cobertor,* there also appears the term *manta,* perhaps referring to a more decorative type of cover to be placed on top. The inventory of the Chapel of St. Clemente mentions mantas from Flanders,
two *viadas* (striped covers), and three covers with designs of dogs or
lions. The infirmary attached to the chapel owned two blue mantas
from Aragon.[41]

Finally, a *colcha* (counterpane), more or less luxurious and embroidered, was placed on top. Plain bedspreads of a single color, orna-

mented counterpanes ordered from abroad ("a French *barrada* spread"), bedspreads of purple cloth or of wool—all appear in the medieval texts, designated at times by the terms *sobrecamas* or *cobrecamas*. At the betrothal of Beatriz, daughter of Fernando, to the Count of Cambridge, Edward (grandson of Edward III), in 1381, there was "a cobricama of black carpet with two large figures of the King and the Queen in the middle, all in large and small seed pearls, according to the requirements of the place where it was used; the embroidery around the border was all of embellishments in the form of arks made of seed pearls, and inside identical figures of pearls, embroideries of the genealogies of all the nobles in Portugal, with their arms around them; and this ornamentation for the bed was afterwards given to King Juan of Castile when he married this same Princess Beatriz... and it was praised in Castile as a very sumptuous work, whose equal could not be found there."[42] The Duchess of Viseu, in the middle of the fifteenth century, owned cobrecamas of sable.

The *pulvinar,* or Roman pillow—generally stuffed with feathers and mentioned in Portuguese documents, since they were written in Latin —seems to correspond to the vernacular *chumaço,* or *chimaço* (stuffed pillow), also Latinized as *plumazo* (feather pillow). Such pillows of feathers or wool were used, either of a single color or patterned— checkered (*acedrenchado*), for example. The terms *chumaço* and *plumazo* disappear around the beginning of the fifteenth century in favor of *almofada* (pillow). Beatriz had twenty-seven large feather pillows of French cloth, besides as many others of lesser size in her trousseau. *Almadraque* might also have denoted a type of large, quite expensive cushion, as it was filled with feathers. Certain almadraques, more modest, contained wool instead of feathers. The *alifafe,* the *cabeçal,* the *travesseiro,* and the *faceiró* were all closely related types of smaller pillows which today are difficult to define with complete accuracy. A 1349 will mentions "cabeçais of such a size they and their wives fit on them." Pillowcases (called *fronhas* or *panos*) for the faceirós begin to be mentioned in the fourteenth century.[43]

At the end of the thirteenth century, the prices of some of these pieces of bed linen were included in the "Inventory and Accounts" of the household of Dinis. These prices, shown in Table 1, allow an appraisal of the scarcity of each item. By way of comparison, one ell (approximately 0.76 yards) of scarlet cloth—the most expensive fabric in that period—cost 5 libras; one arrátel (340 grams) of pepper, 17½ soldos; one dozen citron fruits, 5 soldos; and one pair of high boots, 1½ libras.

The Gothic bed, especially of the more well-to-do people, included canopy and curtains (Fig. 70). In her wedding trousseau, Beatriz

TABLE 1
Prices of Items of Bed Linen, Late Thirteenth Century

Item	Libras	Soldos	Dinheiros
Alfâmbar	8	7	3½
Almadraque	6	14	9½
Feather chumaço	2	16	8
Almucela	2	5	0
Woolen chumaço	0	17	8

Source: "Inventários e Contas da Casa de D. Dinis (1278–1282)," in *Arquivo Histórico Português,* X (Lisbon, 1916), 41–59.

brings bed curtains of various materials and decorations: of crimson, mulberry, and blue brocade; of embroidered gray damask; of gold and silver leather; of cloth of arras; and so on. These curtains were hung on cords or iron chains adjusted afterwards on the canopy, which was of bright-colored, fine, transparent cloth.[44] In an elegant chamber, it was customary to put up curtains on the bed to match the counterpanes. Consequently, Beatriz carried with her three complete sets, which were rotated at her pleasure.

After the bed, the most important piece of domestic furniture was the *arca,* or chest (Fig. 71). It was used for everything, even as a bed, as previously mentioned. In the chest were kept the household linen, the various items of clothing, books, dishes, and objects of adornment. During the Roman period, chests were very plain, with little or no decoration, though they were sometimes provided with appliqués of iron. They were always of wood, with quite resistant, heavy locks to preclude attempts at breaking into them and stealing their contents. From the fourteenth and fifteenth centuries on, they were made lighter and adorned in the Gothic style. The front and sides received a large amount of ornamentation; the lid curved upward in the middle; the strength and the crudity of shapes gave way to an elegance and exquisite mannerism quite appropriate to the age. In the 1400's the Italian influence created chests inspired by coffins and sepulchers, with Renaissance decoration and carved feet, still lighter and even more elegant than the Gothic ones.

Queen Beatriz, wife of Afonso IV (mid-fourteenth century), bequeathed several chests in her will. Another Beatriz, one hundred years later, possessed four large chests from Flanders and another dozen lined with leather, "for carrying things."

A small cousin of the chest was the *cofre* (box). It was used principally to hold jewels and other tiny objects, but also found frequent use as a reliquary. Every mansion of the nobility contained dozens of small coffers of all sizes and shapes, with the most imaginative and varied ornamentation, made of wood or metal, and recipient of the most

Fig. 71.   Chest, 13th century.

splendid appliqués. A duchess of Viseu, for example, owned coffers of amber, inlaid boxes from Germany, large, plated ones sent from Flanders, small chests lined with leather from Aragon, etc., making a total of seventeen.[45]

In the Middle Ages, the cabinet was very unusual, and there are no references in Portuguese documents to the use of furniture of this type in private homes. The cabinet was used at that time primarily in the churches, to store religious objects and vestments. Only in the fifteenth century did it begin to compete with the chest in lay residences. On the artistic plane, the cabinet reflected both the Roman and the Gothic influence.

Chairs were few. Usually people sat on chests or on the beds, and frequently on the ground. In this case, the Islamic custom was the determinant in Portugal. Men and women, but especially the latter, preferred to sit on the floor on carpets and cushions.

The formal chair, or *cathedra,* was a quite heavy and expensive piece of furniture reserved for the head of the family. From the thirteenth century to the fifteenth, it customarily had a canopy. The Romanesque cathedra was simpler, resembling a modern armchair. One of these chairs, made of gracefully worked wood and with a cushion on the seat, can be seen in the "Apocalypse of Lorvão" (Fig. 72). Other chairs called *faudesteuils* in France were lighter and collapsible, of a shape reminiscent of the Roman and Byzantine thrones. They corresponded to the royal seat, possessing a low back that was not quite high enough for a person to lean back upon and often lacking arms as well (Fig. 73). In the "Old Testament by Lorvão" ("Testamento Velho de Lorvão"), which dates from the thirteenth century, one of the illustrations shows just such a chair, with a red cushion on the seat, functioning as the royal throne. They disappeared from Europe about the end of the fourteenth century, only to be reintroduced by the Italian Renaissance at the end of the following century. Joint stools were even used during the Middle Ages, although Portuguese documents seem unaware of them.

Fig. 72. Chairs. 12th century.

Fig. 73. Throne-shaped chair, 13th century.

What we find in most abundance are benches, or *escanos,* with or without backs, longer or shorter, but never just a single seat. Their manufacture was as a rule very simple: a straight plank placed over two trestles on either end. When there was no back, the bench was set against the wall. Benches were covered on more formal occasions with velvety cloth or with other richly woven fabrics, which were called *bancais;* cushions were also frequently employed. The use of small benches as footstools was common.[46]

Starting with the fifteenth century, buffets and sideboards began to be used on any of several floors where tableware was displayed in the wealthy homes. Small casks, sometimes made of expensive, ornamented wood, were placed on supports in the halls or chambers, somewhat in the manner of the modern cellarets in nightclubs. The Duchess of Viseu even owned a gilded hogshead for wine.[47]

Fig. 74. Chair. 15th century.

One of the typical pieces of furniture of the Middle Ages was the *estante* (lectern), on which the voluminous codices of that age were rested, as it was impossible to hold them in one's hands or even on one's knees. Such desks could be made of wood or of iron.[48]

The table was a piece of furniture less highly esteemed than in the following centuries and was not always considered an indispensable article. Since it was frequently carried from room to room, its basic characteristics were lightness and a relative strength, traits not demanded of the bed or the chest. Often, it consisted only of a board mounted over trestles.[49] By the fifteenth century, however, a few hand-carved tables make their appearance, being used as decorative furniture. Beatriz took with her "an inlaid table from Germany," and other references indicate the growing importation of tables from Flanders and Germany.[50]

And with this, the inventory of furniture is concluded. Of course, in the bedrooms there were also mirrors on the walls, basins, and other objects for the toilette. Small portable washbasins called *aceteres* were used for bathing: a document of 1359 records "two lavatories, which are called *aceteres,* and a dozen basins, and four bowls." An inventory for the same period mentions another washbasin made of Morisco brass. In the trousseau of Duchess Beatriz there was a gold and white lavatory weighing 16 marks (8 pounds, or 3.68 kilograms).[51]

Toward the end of the fourteenth century, the first mechanical clocks were introduced into Portugal. Of recent invention, these were such large and complicated pieces of furniture that only kings and great lords could afford the luxury of owning one. The Duke of Lancaster offered one of these *horológios* to João I.[52]

The kitchen, besides the fireplace, contained roasting spits to cook the meat and other indispensable implements suspended from the rack and pinion: pots, cauldrons, large pans, water jugs, earthenware jugs, roasters, spits, porringers, shallow earthen bowls, frying pans, grills, mortars, etc., of clay or tin, consonant with the wealth of the residence. Pottery utensils were designated by the generic name *olas* in Portugal; their manufacture comprised one of the most important facets of national industry. In an inventory made in 1362, the kitchen that served the monastery of Avis is described in the following manner: "There was found in the house of Maria Vieira, in which the cooking was done, these articles: a large cauldron; likewise, two old copper pans and two copper bowls; also two iron spoons, one of which was perforated; likewise, an iron soup ladle; also three iron spits, two large ones and one small one; also small grills with six supports and four feet; also two small *catores* [?]; also seven whole cleavers and two broken ones; also a small wooden trough; also some large iron kettles and other, smaller ones; also a basket of needlegrass and a mortar and a pestle."[53]

The symbols of comfort and of elegance in medieval residences were the coverings for the walls and the wooden floors. During the period, Portuguese artisans produced famed leather which even came to be exported abroad. The cold walls of stone, mud and plaster, or tile were covered, totally or partially, with it, as were the wooden floors and wooden benches. From the workshops of the tanners came rectangles approximately 0.04 to 0.08 inches thick (1 to 2 millimeters) in average sizes of 26 x 16.8 inches (66 x 45 centimeters), which were intended to be used as phylacteries on altars, as valances, canopies, and even as cushions on the bed. These leather articles, at that time called *godemecis,* were preferably made from cowhide, calfskin, sheepskin, and goatskin. Tanned and polished, they were made in smooth textures or delicately tooled, either monochromatic (golden, for example) or, after the fifteenth century, bicolored (carmine and silver, dark red and silver). The best tooling came from Cordova and other cities in Moslem Spain. Aside from embellishing the room, leather helped insulate the corner where the bed was placed, whether from the heat or from the cold, or even from the multitude of insects. Other types of leather, evidently less sumptuous, were placed under the bed like a large carpet. In southern Portugal, leather was used to cool houses during the summertime and prevent the entrance of swarms of insects. For this reason it was removed when winter arrived. In the north, the uses of

Fig. 75.   Interior. 15th century.

leather were often limited to valances, the coverings of the canopy, or the headboards of beds.[54]

Completely covering the walls with textiles was much less common, yet such is also to be found in the wealthier homes. The fiancée of Prince Fernando, brother of Afonso V, included in her trousseau "some draperies for the walls of the chamber, of blue satin with edgings of crimson velvet," others of gray damask, and still others of serge in four pieces.[55] The fact that in one case reference was specifically made to four pieces leads to the supposition that some draperies existed for only two walls, or even a single one.

Whether to warm the rooms in wintertime, or to decorate them on the occasion of parties or receptions, or even for the compartmentation of a large hall whenever necessary, the Arras tapestries or drapes were put up temporarily and later taken down. Garcia de Resende tells us in the *Cancioneiro Geral:*

> I have bare rooms,
> (You can come whenever you wish)
> With some drapery hung up.[56]

Perhaps only in the royal palaces or in those of the great lords were tapestries permanently kept on the walls.

In her trousseau, Beatriz included no fewer than a dozen Arras curtains.[57] In the palace of Guimarães, the Count of Barcelos kept a priceless collection of tapestries on which were shown the long, complicated histories of Hannibal, Hercules, Theseus, Julius Caesar, Alexander, Troy, and others.[58] The royal palace of Alcáçova in Lisbon contained extremely sumptuous panels of cloth to hang up. In fact, the majestic Portuguese manors were always more richly decorated on the inside than on the outside. João I, for example, referring to a hall decorated for a party, remarked: "Whoever could doubt that he will not lose his weariness in seeing the hall so very well outfitted in such rich cloth?"[59]

The flagstone, tile, or wood floors were covered with skins, carpets, and woven mats of rushes, all of which were frequently employed on the peninsula because of the Moslem influence. Moreover, the use of straw mats was not confined to the poorer homes: the residence of Dinis, when he was yet a prince, had forty-two plain mats and ten Moorish ones. The mat was better suited than the carpet to the floors of beaten clay in the homes of the common people. Here, straw was also used to reduce, if only a little, mud on wet days in winter or dust on the sunny days of summer.[60]

Although less common, because more expensive, the carpet was found in relative profusion in medieval Portuguese homes. Documents from the twelfth to the fifteenth centuries are full of references to carpets. Duchess Beatriz had at least twelve.[61] In the description of the wedding of Duarte in 1428, the ornamental role of tapestries and other panels and of carpets is quite well emphasized:

> A good part of the cloister of St. Clara, through which the Princess had to pass, was adorned and paved with carpets, and at the door of the church — that is, inside in the choir of the nuns — was a rich cloth of crimson brocade which covered the place where the blessings were to be,

and the bolt of cloth crossed the whole church just as up a street; it went up a stair to the choir where Queen Isabel lies, and all this road was thus decorated and covered with carpets and the choir was totally ornamented with Arras cloth, inside the Church as well as outside and completely covered with carpets from the altar.[62]

Daylight was admitted into the house through doors, large windows, and vents. In the southern part of Portugal, outside openings were reduced to the bare minimum, at times limited to the entrance alone; in such cases, illumination was gained by means of the internal patio, onto which the various rooms opened. Only in the sixteenth century did the Portuguese start to use glass panes in windows with relative frequency. Colored glass panes were employed only in churches; in homes, the harsh brightness of sunlight was reduced by covering the windows with paper, oiled cloth, or sheets of fine parchment.

Protection against the sun and against the cold was achieved either by means of movable persiennes which opened outwards, by inside wooden shutters still used today in many parts of Portugal, or even by curtains and drapes of woven fabrics, lighter or heavier, more or less opaque, consonant with the owner's wealth. Drapes also hid the doors in the homes of the well-to-do.[63]

At night, light was obtained from the fire in the hearth or from oil lamps, wax or tallow candles, and resin torches. Wax was much more expensive than tallow, and so candles of that material were used principally in churches and monasteries. Nevertheless, Fernão Lopes testifies that Pedro I ordered five thousand large candles and torches made with six hundred arrobas of wax for the festivities which he ordered when he made João Afonso Telo a count and conferred knighthood on him.[64] Each candle or torch thus contained 0.12 of an arroba of wax, or nearly 2.9 pounds (1.32 kilograms). According to the charter of tolls for Lisbon in 1377, wax candles entering the harbor of the Tagus were exempt from customs duties. Wax candles and torches were sold with colored bottoms, generally green. Hanging oil lamps had slender wicks in proportion to those in wax or tallow candles.[65] The documents are filled with references to silver or iron *castiçais* (candlestick holders), to *tocheiras* (holders for torches), and to *candeias* (oil lamps). In the chapel of St. Clemente, near Oporto, there was a large iron *candeeiro* (lamp) that burned oil.[66]

Houses were generally heated only by the kitchen hearth. In certain seigniorial residences, however, fireplaces had been built in the chambers and halls. In one of these, concealed by a portiere, a noble had to answer the call of nature out of obvious distress—to the considerable scandal and derision of the court of Afonso V.[67] Of course, braziers were also used for heating.

There were, just as there are today, several systems for the ownership of homes: possession free and clear, possession by renting, and possession by long-term lease, or emphyteusis. In the case of rental, the lease was established according to a contract between the landlord and the tenant for one or more years. Generally, the payment of rents was made yearly, in money or in kind, though the time of the annual payment varied according to when the contract was made. The usual periods of payment were St. Michael's Day (September 29), Easter Sunday, Christmas Day, St. John's Day (June 24), and St. Martinho's Day (November 11). Rents could also be paid in two or three installments—Christmas and Easter, St. John's and Easter, etc.—and frequently were. The tenant had to pay the whole rent if he left the house before the contract had expired; in the same way, the landlord, if he ousted his tenant ahead of time in order to let the dwelling to another, lost his rent in its entirety. If the renter, however, bought a house to live in, he did not have to satisfy the rent on the one he had left for the period remaining to the end of the contract. In Lisbon, thirty days before the end of the term of lease, the landlord had to inquire of the tenant if he wished to continue to rent it or to notify him that he must vacate it at the conclusion of the lease.

The emphyteusis, or long-term lease—much more common—presupposed the lifelong possession of the house by the renter, with or without the right to transfer it to his children, by means of the payment of an annual rent, at the times and under the circumstances referred to above for the lease.[68]

Just as today, permits for the construction or repair of houses were necessary. In Oporto, in the middle of the fourteenth century, the erection of battlements on stone houses without license of the bishop was forbidden.[69]

4 : HYGIENE AND HEALTH

SOME nineteenth- and twentieth-century historians have pictured the Middle Ages as a paradise for filth. "Nul bain pendant mille ans," asserted Michelet; and people believed it. Even today the medieval period is popularly thought of in this way.

Nevertheless, this judgment is untrue. Without going to the opposite extreme of ascribing to the people of the Middle Ages habits of cleanliness that represent an achievement of the modern age, let us determine exactly what the hygienic practices were at that time. Certainly, they were no worse, nor any better, than those of many other periods.[1]

Moreover, those practices varied from the North Sea to the Mediterranean, from the Atlantic coast to the Russian borders. Conditions were different, so naturally customs were different. The European Far North, much colder, favored hygiene less; furthermore, the North was the home of more or less barbaric cultures in which little attention was given to hygienic refinements. On the other hand, in the South the whole Greco-Roman tradition of worship of the body and civilized development had established the prolonged bath as a habit over the centuries. The warm climate also favored pleasure in water during the greater part of the year. After the Roman Empire had disappeared, Islam continued and even improved the practices of cleanliness, both for the individual and the group.

Habits of neatness are not always allied with tradition and geography if they are not accompanied by certain indispensable conditions, however. Cleanliness is much more of an adjunct of wealth, for example, than is normally thought. Below a certain level of material well-being, only rarely can cleanliness be found. In the same way, for a city or a culture to benefit from hygienic practices, it must have at least a minimum of economic resources and of technical-scientific knowledge, both within the framework of a social structure and within an adequate political-administrative organization. Yet, once the Empire was destroyed, the concept of public works practically disappeared in the Roman world north of the Mediterranean. Kings and feudal lords

were not concerned about the repair or construction of roads, aqueducts, and public facilities. Now, for water to be abundant in daily
life, dams and aqueducts must first be built. For a street to be paved
and thus avoid mud and the accumulation of filth, stone (or clay)—
often existing only in distant deposits and consequently needing an
adequate transportation system—is a basic requirement. In every case,
a source of money or of other means of payment, as well as of labor—
neither always abundantly available in the Middle Ages—is the underlying problem.

Regulations on hygiene were therefore a purely local subject. Each
municipal council, for better or worse, made its own arrangements
concerning the water supply and its utilization, the pavement of
streets, and general cleanliness. Everything depended on the greater
or lesser administrative capacity of the officials, as well as on the greater
or lesser economic prosperity of the land. Furthermore, factors of
geography—the abundance or scarcity of water, a prolonged drought, or
a hard winter—had a decisive influence. Individuals, in their day-to-day
existence, acted in accordance with all these conditions as well as in
conformity with persistent, age-old habits and customs. Is the individual of whom we are speaking from Évora, in the heart of the Roman,
and later the Moslem, march? Is he the "new" Christian of the thirteenth century, the son or grandson of Moslems, frequent visitors at
the public baths, as their religion demanded? Is he from Braga, in the
very center of the old Suevian kingdom, in the remote north, so little
exposed to the Moslem cultural influence? Or is he the "old" Christian
of the twelfth century, son or grandson of crude Asturians or of
"Frankish" immigrants little accustomed to luxurious refinements?
Of course, hygienic habits will vary from the southern Soleimão to the
northern Gumersindo, from southern Silves to northern Bragança; and
they will also vary from one period to another. Although, as the centuries pass, the noble on his manor in Minho gradually becomes accustomed to practices of cleanliness which his barbarian ancestors were
ignorant of, at the same time, the Morisco peasant in a vegetable garden
in Lisbon gradually forgets the hygienic customs of his civilized grandfathers.

Documentation is niggardly in details relating to the individual, but
here and there some information on his habits of cleanliness exists.
He paid a great deal of attention to the neatness of his wardrobe.
From the north to the south in Portugal, public washerwomen could
be seen doing the washing of household linen and clothing. In the
middle of the sixteenth century, there were in Lisbon alone 3,500
launderesses, each of whom could serve some five to six families, not

counting the priests, courtesans, and foreigners they also served. Numerous slave women, a real novelty in Portuguese daily life before the end of the fifteenth century, were also recorded during the same period.[2] The soap industry had a certain significance in medieval Portugal, as is indicated by the fact that its profits were granted as a reward to important persons. Among these was Prince Henry the Navigator (and after his death, Prince Fernando, his nephew, and his successors), who received the monopoly of all the soap factories in the kingdom. Black soap and white soap were made from olive oil and ashes. Apparently, the industry became generalized throughout the whole country and often assumed the characteristics of a domestic industry.[3]

Filthiness in clothing was considered to be an atonement, and as a result, it is possible that such a state might have been more frequent during the Middle Ages than in the periods of less intensive religious fervor. Princess Saint Joana (mid-fifteenth century) wore the same chemise for months on end, suffering terribly from the multitudes of lice which were bred in it.[4] Although cases such as this were perhaps not unusual, they always aroused admiration, and this deed is praised by her biographer as evidence of her capacity for sacrifice. As a rule, however, clothing was changed relatively often, at least among the well-to-do classes. Beatriz, the wife of Prince Fernando (brother of Afonso V) had nearly two dozen chemises in her trousseau.[5]

The habit of combing one's hair (and beard), curling it, perfuming it, and otherwise devoting a great deal of attention to it is well documented by the references to combs and by the proliferation of barbers throughout the Middle Ages. (It is true that the duties of a barber were much broader at that time than they are today. He was used as a bloodletter and even as a doctor.) Poems of the period mention washing hair, as for instance that very beautiful song of the cancioneiro:

> Mother, I went to wash my hair
> At the fountain, and since,
> I have regretted it.[6]

The practice of washing the hands during the day has also been proven; we have already seen how it was customary to "bring water for the hands" before and after every meal.[7] Wills, inventories, and other lists mention towels and napkins. Beatriz, in the mid-fifteenth century, owned so many that their number is not even indicated on the list of her trousseau: there were "napkins for wiping the mouth" and "towels for wiping the hands," besides a wash basin, "water basins for the hands" ("two with pipes and two without pipes"), and even a basin in which to wash her hair.[8] The Moslem habit of daily ablutions must have had some influence on the practices of the Portuguese to the south of the Tagus or even the Mondego.

The public baths, so common among the Romans and the Arabs, were generally condemned by the Christian ideology as too favorable to licentiousness or to the degeneration of social customs and habits. Many baths were therefore destroyed or closed after the peaceful triumph of Christianity or after the Reconquest of the Moorish territory. It was impossible, however, to eradicate completely an ancestral custom, and public baths thus continued to exist throughout Portugal during the Middle Ages. Baths remained open in the large populated centers like Lisbon and Oporto, and in smaller towns such as Setúbal, Loulé, Faro, Tavira, Castro Marim, Alfaiates, Castelo Bom, Castelo Melhor, and Castelo Rodrigo. It is true that we know very little about their practical operation, and some scholars tend to include them among simple medicinal hot springs. In Alfaiates, Castelo Bom, Castelo Melhor, and Castelo Rodrigo, the baths were open every day from sunrise to sunset, reserved on Sundays, Tuesdays, and Thursdays for women, and for men on the other days. Fines were established for transgressors. There was even a bathkeeper at the disposal of the public. It was customary for the nobles, infanções, or knights and the respectable ladies to bring along a companion, either a squire or a maid, for whom nothing was paid. Nevertheless, the impression remains that attendance at the baths was limited to people of wealth.[9]

Portuguese literature abounds in references to baths, complete or partial, in rivers, where people washed or soaked their feet, face, and hair:

> If today my love
> Should find out, he would go with me,
> For I am going to bathe in the river.[10]

Although here they would not have to fear the prohibitions of the magistrates on promiscuity in the bath, it is not very likely that men and women refreshed themselves or bathed completely nude. As "bathing suits," the maidens' long chemises or the men's undergarments worked perfectly. References here and there lead one to think that bathing in the ocean was not entirely scorned in the Middle Ages.[11]

Within the houses there were washstands[12] and certainly bathtubs as well, without speaking of the frequent basins which have already been cited.

A cleanliness compatible with the resources of the period prevailed inside the houses. With floors of beaten earth, it would be more difficult to maintain impeccable neatness, yet the frequent removal of the straw that was strewn about the floors certainly helped. With floors of brick, tile, stone, or wood, the methods of cleaning would not differ essentially from modern ways. It is interesting to observe that at the end of the thirteenth century one of the famed Portuguese exports to Flanders consisted of needlegrass brooms called *balaises*. In southern Portugal, the internal and external walls were whitewashed. It was customary to perfume the interiors by burning certain herbs or other aromatic essences; even in this — and probably in the practice of whitewashing as well — Portugal owed a great debt to the Moslems.

The homes of nobles contained privies, of which it is impossible today to discover details. There is no information available as to what extent privies existed in the homes of burghers as well. During the reign of Duarte (1433–38), the palace of Sintra had four of these *privadas* with the dimensions of 4 x 3 ells (9 x 6.88 feet), 3½ x 3 ells (8 x 6.88 feet), 3½ x 2 ells (8 x 4.59 feet), and 3 x 2 ells (6.88 x 4.59 feet). None of them was much larger than the simple urinal also in the palace (a "little closet in which to urinate"), which did not exceed 3½ x 1½ ells (8 x 3.44 feet).[13] In the palace of the dukes of Bragança in Guimarães, rainwater, channeled into pipes, drained through the privies.[14] In his will, dating from the middle of the fourteenth century, Bartolomeu Joanes, a well-known and wealthy merchant, requires that the hospital he founded should contain a privy.[15]

The Roman practice of constructing kitchens away from the main body of the house was still sometimes observed in Portugal during the Middle Ages. The large manor houses generally had a courtyard that separated the kitchen from the rest of the rooms to avoid odors, dirt, and insects. In the will just cited, Bartolomeu Joanes directed "that there be a kitchen set off to one side in which they can cook well, so that nauseous smells will not spread through the house." On the other hand, in the great majority of homes the kitchen was, as we have seen, the very center of family life.

In cities and villages, the responsibility for an adequate water supply fell to the councilmen, who arranged for the construction of fountains and the canalization of the waters for them. Such cities as Lisbon, Santarém, Évora, Oporto, and Coimbra contained a large number of fountains, and constructions were even undertaken to obtain a greater volume of water. The care of these fountains was incumbent on the magistrates of each council.[16] Some cities also installed pipes at an early date to drain off rainwater, and thus avoid floods.[17]

The cleanliness of the streets—above all, in times of plague, as we shall see—aroused even more concern from the councils (and from the king himself). The *Afonsine Ordinances* declare that the market officers (*almotacés*) "each time will have the city cleaned of manure and evil odors, every person being responsible for that section of the street in front of his door; and in each parish they will have the dunghill removed and the manure thrown out in the places provided for it every month." They should also police each city or village so that "a dunghill may not be created in it nor dung or any other garbage thrown around the wall, and so that the sewage mains of the city or village and the water aqueducts are not stopped up." Much less "will they consent to beasts or dogs or other dirty and stinking things being cast into the city or village streets; and those who do so are to be made to remove them." [18] Thus it was decreed officially. One may rightfully suppose that practice was something else entirely. The fact that city ordinances on the same subject were reissued by the councils from time to time is an obvious acknowledgment of the continuation of such abuses.[19]

The practice of throwing slops out the window (called *água vai*) forestalled, or at least hampered, any effective attempt at cleanliness. In 1484, João II ordered that measures be taken against the "overturning of chamberpots," whose contents were flung out where they should not be. Apparently there were "reserved places" for pouring them out—on the beaches, for example—but many people paid no attention to such ordinances and persisted in emptying this filth on the streets. Consequently, the dungheaps and the garbage mounds, incubators of plague in the opinion of the period, were plentiful. It was desirable that all this filth be removed, João ruled, and that "all of the streets and alleys should be very clean." Two years later, he went to the point of ordering the construction of a complete system of sewers for Lisbon, "in which they may deposit their body wastes."[20] The actual construction of such a system, however, was still to take a long time.

Outside the towns, human waste was used to manure the fields, as it still is today. Thus, filth did not pile up in front of each door but was scattered around rather easily, the only privies being the fields, the herb gardens, and the orchards themselves.

Cobblestone or tile paving in the streets, a prerequisite for the cleanliness of the cities, dates at least from the reign of Dinis (1279–1325) in Portugal, when the New Street of the Merchants received stone paving. Later on, paving continued, but at a much slower rate, both in Lisbon and in other cities. At the end of the fifteenth century, the city council of the capital continued to pass statutes in this vein. In Évora during the same period, a similar measure was ordered for some streets. Each inhabitant of the city was to undertake, as his duty, the paving of the part of the street that was in front of his house, contributing the necessary stone and gravel as well. Efforts of this sort took time because they required the cooperation of all the inhabitants, which was not always easy to obtain.[21]

We have already seen that deficiencies in the medieval diet made certain diseases much more frequent than they are today. Resistance to infections was also quite reduced, with the result that epidemics spread easily.

There were several of these epidemics in Portugal during the twelfth, thirteenth, and fourteenth centuries: in 1190–91, in 1202, in 1223, in 1333, for example. The words "plague" or "pestilence" almost always designate them. Nevertheless, it has been proven that the true plague, the bubonic, was introduced into Europe only in the middle of the fourteenth century. The other epidemics, often in the trail of famines or war, exhibit different medical characteristics: they probably were dysentery, influenza, and so on. From the mid-1300's on, the frequency of these epidemics increased, for several reasons that need not concern us here. In Portugal, plagues or other contagious diseases of the epidemic type raged in 1348, 1356, 1384, 1415, 1423, 1432, 1435, 1437–38, 1448, 1458, 1464, 1477, and 1480–97.[22] The true bubonic plagues struck in 1348—this year saw the greatest of all, known as the Black Death— and again in 1384 and 1415.[23] This means that every Portuguese in the fourteenth and fifteenth centuries experienced two or more epidemics during his lifetime and of course had relatives and friends taken by them. There were plagues, as that of 1480–97, that lasted for years on end, with alternating phases of recrudescence and mildness. It is therefore understandable that doctors, pharmacists, quacks, sorcerers, and even philosophers and politicians had all mobilized their efforts in an attempt to discover effective preventive measures and remedies against the plague.

The causes of the epidemics were, from the scientific point of view, unknown. In the *Loyal Counselor*, Duarte mentions the influence of the stars and pollution of the water besides, obviously, the will of God.[24] The *Profitable Rule Against the Plague (Regimento proveitoso contra ha pestenença)* adds tainted air to this list. Accordingly, the removal of human or animal corpses from public places, the cleaning of cesspools, sewers, dunghills, and other bodies of filth, the purification of the air by fire, and the burning of aromatic or medicinal herbs were recommended.[25] During the plague in Évora in 1490, João II ordered the complete evacuation of the city for several days, while cattle were allowed to graze freely within it and absorb the bad smells; then the houses were fumigated, and walls and even streets whitewashed. Pesthouses were also set up, and the avoidance of contagion was attempted as much as possible. During the plague in Coimbra in 1477–79, the people of Oporto established a hygienic cordon around their city to forbid entrance to everyone who came from Coimbra. When cases of plague were observed in a street of Oporto in 1486, it was resolved to wall off this street and isolate the respective inhabitants. Other times, at the beginning of an epidemic, all the sick were carried to the special pesthouses outside the walls of the city. When a plague abroad was learned of, officials forbade entrance at the frontiers or required passengers and ships to submit to a quarantine. Such regulations were quite rigorous, especially toward the end of the fifteenth century, and seem to have been quite efficient.[26]

None of these measures succeeded in checking the plague when it raged intensely, and each person was compelled to take the preventive steps which he thought expedient for his own safety. Above all, of course, advises the *Profitable Rule,* "the man owes it to himself to put his evil practices to one side and to embrace good ones; that is, a man must first confess his sins humbly, because holy penitence and confession are a great remedy as they are more valuable and efficacious than all medicines." The second most salutary measure was flight from the infected locale. All the doctors, echoed by the father confessors, advised it. "But because many could not change their residence without suffering a great loss," famous precautions against the plague were developed. These were, in addition to precautions of a general nature, abstention from sexual pleasures; moderation in eating and drinking; "avoiding the daily bath"; avoidance of gatherings and contacts with other people; use and even overuse of water with vinegar to wash hands, faces, and the insides of houses; and staying at home as much as possible.[27]

Among the remedies, a special virtue was attributed to badger powders. In a famous letter written in the 1430's, Dr. Diogo Afonso Mangancha instructed King Duarte on the method of compounding them. One began by inebriating a badger on a wine filtered through camphor and blended with a compound of gold, seed pearls, and coral. The animal then was decapitated, all of his blood drained, and his heart and liver removed. The mixture of the blood with the powders should be effected under a "slow sun" or in the "heat of a fire." The composition of the powder was as follows:

2 ounces of very fine cinnamon
1 ounce of *geuaana* (?)
½ ounce of verbena
¼ ounce of ginger or saffron
⅛ ounce of fine clove
1/16 ounce of myrrh
1/32 ounce of aloes
1/64 ounce of fine "unicorn horn"*

Two ounces of paste resulting from pulverizing the heart, liver, and even the skin and teeth of the badger completed the mixture. This compound, dissolved in wine or in water seasoned with vinegar, was given to the patient. It was essential that the powders not be old— that is, that they should not have been made up more than a year before. If this were to happen, the results might be negative. This befell Dr. Diogo Afonso's own wife, for she died in his arms after having swallowed powders already dried and older than six years.

Once the remedy—"the best possible thing against the pestilence"— had been taken, the patient had to lie down, cover up warmly, and perspire for some six hours, without sleeping, eating, or drinking; afterwards, he should wash, put on a clean shirt, and again lie down, on the side of the bed that was untouched by sweat. He could then eat and drink, but only bread soaked in cold water and water. If the pain of the swellings persisted, it was permissible to bleed him in the aching leg or arm.

Many other remedies were known and prescribed against the plague. One of them was based on the blood of a bull mixed with roots of various trees and bushes. It was recommended, in any case, that people drink strong potions of vinegar and liquids diluted with vinegar, avoid sweets, and eat chicken, roasted kid, and dried fish.[28]

Ailments of the eyes, very common because of the deficiency of vitamin A in medieval diet, are mentioned frequently in contemporary medical treatises and collections of prescriptions. Two great Portuguese doctors, Pedro Hispano (the future Pope John XXI) in the thirteenth century and Velasco de Taranta in the fifteenth century, studied inflammation of the eye and prescribed medications to cure it. Aches and inflammations were combatted by the application of a countless number of preparations from animal, vegetable, and mineral ingredients, in which the gall bladder and the liver played outstanding roles. An eyewash of bladder of swallow, bladder of partridge, fennel seed, rue herb, and white wine was believed extremely effective. Egg whites

* See p. 30.

Fig. 76. Sick man. 15th century.

and yolks, dog milk and human milk, rosemary, lung of ram, goat, or hare, ashes of human manure, urine mixed with honey—all these were ingredients for the cure of ailing eyes. In his treatise on medicine, the *Philonium*, Velasco de Taranta also recommends recourse to bleedings and purgatives, the use of linen compresses soaked in various cooked emollients, and abstention from wine and meats. To relieve the pain of inflammation of the iris and of conjunctivitis, Velasco advised that the patient be isolated in a darkened room and protected from wind and dust, with frequent washings of the inflamed eyes.[29]

These remedies, as well as similar remedies for ailments other than those of the eye, have a certain scientific base. But besides these, how many superstitions existed! As a cure-all, the same Pedro Hispano advises wearing a little bag with the eyes of a magpie, a crab, or a wolf around one's neck![30] In some prescriptions mentioned later in this chapter, doctors resort to sorcery, portents, and other acts of witchcraft.

A rather complete compilation of prescriptions has survived from the thirteenth century, part of which was written by a famous medic of the period, the Dominican Friar Gil. For "mist over the eyes," "tearful eyes," "swelling of the eye," "bloodshot eyes," or "a sore in the eye," numerous remedies were prescribed. Let us look at some.

For bloodshot and tearful eyes
Take dry rue and grind it into a powder, mix it with honey, and put it in the eyes; and you will be healed. For this take the juice of the rue and mix it with seeds of white lily and put it on the eye.

To remove a sore from the eye

Take the juice of rue and the gall from a buck-goat and apply it to the eye.

To remove mist over the eye

Take equal amounts of the juice of rue, the juice of wormwood, the juice of fennel buds, the juice of vervain, the juice of blackberry buds, and the milk of a woman who has had a man child and mix all this with honey and wash the eyes with it.[31]

In the fifteenth century, much more complicated remedies were prescribed. One of them—that known as "water for the eyes"—required the passage of water through an intricate filter with egg whites, alum, rock candy, "milk of a woman delivered of a son," rosewater, and other ingredients.[32]

There were doctors who specialized in eye ailments in Portugal, just as in the rest of Europe. In 1434, for example, King Duarte enacted a charter of privileges for a certain Master Nacim, a Jew, "because we know for a certainty that he is a master in the art of the eyes and he is qualified and fit for that office by some cures which we have seen performed at his hands in our royal presence." By the terms of this charter, Nacim had the power to grant or deny the license of practicing medicine to all the future ophthalmologists in the country. We can find similar cases throughout the fifteenth century.[33]

Medieval practitioners even reached the point of performing operations on the eyes. One of the most common was the extraction of cataracts. The patient was first prepared through diets, purges, clysters, and bleedings, a complete absence of coughing also being necessary. Then, on a clear day, at the third hour (9 A.M.), the moon being in quadrature, outside of the sign of the Ram, when the conjunction and the opposition were at 15°, the precarious surgery could be undertaken. The patient was seated, and an assistant of the doctor held his head steady. Meanwhile, the surgeon climbed up a step and began to cover the healthy eye of the patient with cotton and bandages. Making the sign of the cross, the surgeon carefully inserted a silver or gold needle into the white of the eye, dexterously moving it in the direction of the internal angle. Avoiding injuring the veins, he pushed the cataract and pulled it downward until the whole thing was placed over the aperture in the iris. The operation concluded, the eye was washed with egg yolk and oil of roses. The patient was then left in the dark for several days, always with his healthy eye bandaged. Another frequent operation was that of the excision of lachrymal fistulas by a surgeon's lancet or razor, which was followed by the cauterization of the wound.[34]

Skin diseases constituted another common scourge in the Middle Ages, in part the consequence of wearing woolen clothing directly over the skin. Among these diseases, the most notorious and wretched, although far from being the most widespread, was leprosy. The Crusades may have helped its diffusion in Europe. Portugal, precisely on account of having the least contact with crusades, never experienced leprosy as fully as did the countries beyond the Pyrenees. The number of leper houses never exceeded some sixty-odd, which corresponds to a proportion of one for every 15,000 inhabitants; this is a low percentage if we compare it with that of France or of England.

Leprosy was believed to be incurable, and the idea that doctors might attend infected persons in the leper houses was not yet anticipated. In spite of this, some collections of prescriptions indicate remedies to use against this terrible disease. "To impede leprosy," says a thirteenth-century prescription, "cook the ashes of mallows in water and wash your eyes with it." The *Poor Man's Treasury (Thesaurum Pauperum)* recommended the application of the wine in which had been cooked a serpent from an arid and barren mountain, or of burlap soaked in the oil in which a viper had been cooked.

Lepers were never regarded with a great deal of aversion in Portugal. They were not generally obliged to wear marks of special identification nor to employ rattles or small bells when they strolled about. The *Registers of Noble Families* contain several examples of the marriages of such lepers and of their acceptance into society. In the fifteenth century, when the practices of hygiene had evolved and health was perhaps valued more highly, some official measures were taken to segregate lepers. Doctors were to take care to "send those contaminated people away, as it is a contagious disease that spreads from one person to another."[35]

Many other skin diseases are recorded in this period. Boils, mange, and ringworm are mentioned even in the *Cancioneiro Geral* by Garcia de Resende.[36]

It was especially to treat skin diseases that the use of mineral waters became generalized. The application of water from hot springs was obviously a very old practice, but it seems to have progressed during the Middle Ages. There is evidence dating from the twelfth century of the treatment of skin diseases in Portugal by the use of such water. Lepers went to bathe in the hot springs of Lafões, near St. Pedro do Sul, for example. But other illnesses as well—rheumatisms, swellings, infections, etc.—received some relief in the mineral-water springs that burst to the surface in many areas of the country. Swimming pools and baths were constructed for medicinal purposes, as is amply documented, and were frequently used.[37]

Against toothaches, the products recommended are numerous, aside, of course, from prayers.[38] From roots with medicinal uses (turnip roots, mallow root), various juices (onion juice, cucumber juice poured into the ear), or products even stranger (pig dung, dog's milk, the warm liver of a ferret, snake's flesh cooked after being pounded a great deal) to those that were purely superstitious (celery root worn around one's neck, a grain of salt wrapped in a spider's web, a centipede pierced with a needle and then touched to the painful tooth as many times as the number of wounds inflicted on the insect), the processes of treating teeth appear in practically every compilation of prescriptions. Velasco de Taranta wisely points out that the habit of picking one's teeth with metal objects is one of the causes of toothache. He describes tooth decay and recommends that the carious teeth be filled with camphor after they have been cleaned with wax. If, in children, the milk teeth were slow in appearing, mothers had only to massage the children's gums, anoint them with butter, and fortify their bodies with broth of meat and marrow.[39]

Stomach disorders were cured with roasted liver of goat dipped in strong vinegar and eaten along with biscuits; or with eggs poached in vinegar; or even with roast pigeons stuffed with beeswax, accompanied by red wine or rainwater in which a red-hot poker had been plunged. But the disorder still persists? Then, "if the diarrhea lasts so long that it becomes a continuous straining, he should avoid all fruits excepting quinces or medlars or sorb apples; he can eat as much as he likes of the latter fruit, however always with something else, and drink the distilled juice of quinces." Anointing the sides of the body and the back with a powder of goat dung mixed with egg whites was also advised. If diarrhea should occur, one had to eat toasted partridge feet ground into wine, or eggs roasted with sumac. Rubbing the abdomen with egg whites or with well-sifted goat dung and tying a bandage on top of it was equally efficacious. So was submitting the derrière to the vapors of vinegar cooked with figwort leaves.[40]

Rheumatic or arthritic illnesses were cured with a plaster resembling a quite modern prescription:

Mix Galician linseed with as much water as needed to make a paste, and put it in a dyed cloth, and as soon as it is at a temperature that the patient can stand, place it where the pain is; do this five or six times altogether; do this for three or four days. And when this is done each year for nine days or longer, if the weather is cold, wear a covering of doubled linen or of wool over the place that hurts.[41]

Fevers were treated with inhaled drops of the juice of spring herb, "as much as may be contained in a nutshell." In addition, certain prayers were considered particularly effective.[42] For the gout, alder buds distilled in hot water were prescribed.[43] The infections that created swellings and abscesses were fought with an endless number of remedies—leek leaves fried in pork fat, for example—which made the swollen gland burst.[44] The wounds of war, caused by sword or lance, were so common that the people of the Middle Ages knew how to cure them with relative efficiency. The open sore was generally cauterized after being cleaned.[45] The concerns of a medicine still crude though highly developed in practice went to the point of prescribing remedies for the times when the "nipples of the breast collapse" or "for the nipples of women when giving birth" (a warm plaster of earthworm fried in butter was supposed to work very well).[46]

Superstition closely accompanied the practice of medicine. For the man who had a rupture, the advice was to "write this phrase from the Gospel—*In principio erat verbum et verbum erat*—in a silver vessel and wash it and give this water to the patient to drink for three consecutive mornings." For lumbago, "take a piece of paper, and write these names on it and tie it on the arm: *in nomine patriz et fili et sprituy sancti amen* (cross) *sana me domine sanabor salvum me fac et salvus ero quonyam laus uia tu es* (cross) *zera* (cross) *zera. phi* (cross) *zeebeel* (cross) *zelguch* (cross) *et antany* (cross, cross, cross) and three Solomon's seals." [47]

Measures to revive persons who had fainted or drowned were known and practiced. The arms and legs were bound vigorously for this.[48]

Bleeding and purging were considered useful in most treatments, but also as preventives of diseases. A collection of prescriptions from the thirteenth century recommends bleeding five times a year: in March and in April, to avoid the "fire in the eyes"; in May, to combat fever; in September; and in October, against unwholesome humors and abscesses. The constitutions of the monastery of Pombeiro advise the monks to be bled every two months. Those of the monastery of Tojal (Viseu) are counseled to do so twice a year. Similar measures were advised in other monasteries.[49] Still, there were those who protested against these excesses in the name of prevention. Duarte, for example, realized that if a person was quite healthy, he should avoid purges, bleedings, and self-induced vomiting. On the other hand, he recommended the frequent consumption of what were known as "collective pills" (made of saffron, myrrh, and *acefar* [?] kneaded with fennel juice, citron juice, rose water, or white wine), a kind of cure-all against every disease.[50]

During the course of the Middle Ages, the number of bloodletters multiplied, most of them devoid of any knowledge of medicine. Barbers often performed the bleedings. Nevertheless, bleeding was not so easy as might be thought at first sight. One had to know not only the veins but also which ones were best according to the seasons of the year. In March the "vein of the head" in the right arm was selected, the recommendation being that only some three fingers of blood be drawn. In April, May, and October, the *arcal* vein in the right arm was preferred. But in September, the vein in the left arm over the *arcal* was bled. Besides this, the leech had simultaneously to be a little of the astrologer, since bloodletting produced good results only when the heavenly bodies (especially the moon) were in the appropriate positions. He had also to know how to differentiate between favorable and unfavorable days. The Roman tradition, joined to the Moslem, had led to the classification of the days of the year as propitious (the old fortunate days) or adverse (the ominous days). But the latter, in their turn, could be still further subdivided into canicular, unfortunate, and ill-omened days. Canicular days, or dog days, were considered "distempered," that is, there was no heavenly equilibrium nor any equilibrium in the temperature. There were nearly one hundred dog days each year. The thirty-one unfortunate, or mortal, days were favorable to bad accidents and were found in every month, especially in January.* The twenty-four ill-omened days of the year corresponded to bad spots in the blood. In all, therefore, 155 days out of the year were considered adverse.[51]

In diagnoses, enormous importance was attached to the analysis of the urine. There are theories on its color and density in almost all of the medieval medical treatises. The general appearance of the patient was also considered. Certain external signs on the patient were considered deadly: thus, "if the sick man has a pain in his face and if it should be swollen, and if the left hand should be stretched over the chest and if he should touch his nostrils frequently, this is a bad sign that he will have died before the end of another two weeks." In the same way, "if the sick man should have a headache and have lost his good sense, scrutinize both knees and if they are so swollen and hard that there is no feeling, country people say it is a fatal sign that he will die nine days later."[52]

To attendance at childbirth were connected the many superstitions that accompany the birth of children at all times. Here, as for all ailments, recourse to religious protection was regarded as indispensable; as advocate of women in labor there was Nossa Senhora do Ó, depicted as pregnant in many images which exist in Portugal. Abortion

---

* The unfortunate days were January 1, 2, 4, 7, 11, 15, and 20; February 16 and 18; March 15 and 25; April 8 and 15; May 7, 15, and 17; June 16 and 18; July 7; August 18 and 20; September 8, 16, and 21; October 10 and 16; November 15 and 16; and December 6, 7, and 11.

was known and practiced, justified when the mother's life was in danger, although certain religious precepts prohibited it. How to instigate premature birth was also known. At the time of the birth of Prince Fernando (1402), son of João I, the doctors declared the life of the pregnant queen to be in danger and resolved, with the assent of the king, to give the queen a cooked medicine of herbs to induce labor. She refused, as it almost certainly would result in the death of the infant. Then João I "threw the potion which he held in his hand to give her on the ground," and both commended themselves to divine protection.[53]

Everything that has been said thus far demonstrates the importance of medicine in daily life and the frequent appeal to doctors, surgeons, apothecaries, quacks, and sorcerers. The king and the great lords always had in their service a doctor and, in certain cases, a druggist to fill prescriptions. Among physicians, or authentic doctors, there were even distinguished specialists of this or that illness. We have already mentioned the ophthalmologists. There were others: "master of correcting arms and legs for those who are crippled"; surgeons; "masters who know how to cure goiters for men and women." The simple surgeon was ranked below the physician in the medical hierarchy. Bloodletters were even less esteemed.[54]

Documents testify to the existence of pharmacies (boticas), distributed throughout the country but especially concentrated in the cities. One of the most famous was that of the monastery of Alcobaça, which dates from the fifteenth century. The abuses in the exercise of pharmacy, which many practiced without knowing anything about it, led to a regulation of pharmacies and pharmacists in the fifteenth and sixteenth centuries. Candidates for the profession had to be examined before receiving their certificates as druggists. Apothecary shops were required to have five books: the *Pandectae medicinae* by Matthaeus Sylvaticus, an Arab compilation dating from the fourteenth century; Mesua's *De simplicibus,* an Arab text from the eleventh century; the *Antidotarium* by Nicolau Myrepso, a thirteenth-century work dealing with the composition and effect of medicines; the *Liber servitoris,* another Arab treatise; and the Fifth Book of the Canon of Avicenna. Every druggist was also obligated to own three measures for ounces— one for medicated syrups, another for waters, and the third for oils— besides the appropriate weights (wheat grain, drachma, ounce, and pound) and, naturally, the simple and compounded medicines. The pharmacies and their supplies were subjected to supervision by the doctors.[55]

Toward the end of the fifteenth century, all the remedies then in use were tabulated by the head doctor to the king, Master Rodrigo, with the consent of the councilmen. The list gives us a rather complete idea of the stores of each medieval pharmacy. They sold waters (for example, of fennel, purslane, mint, quince, or maidenhair), conserves (of roses, pumpkin, oranges), drinks to stimulate milk bearing in women who were nursing (of rose juice), medicinal plasters, flowers and herbs, drugs, spices, marmelades, honey, oils (rose-colored, camomile, linseed, sweet almond), pills, powders, medicinal syrups, treacles (a medicine composed of various powders and commonly used as an antidote against poison), and ointments, besides innumerable Latin medicines, now difficult to identify. Nearly 170 different products are registered, with prices which range from a real (for ordinary waters) to sixty and eighty reais (for rhubarb and *spiquanarde,* the latter, one of the Latin medicines that cannot be identified). Even spongecake was sold![56]

The domestic compounding of remedies also flourished in medieval Portugal. Everyone had his own remedies, and the relative ease in obtaining most of the ingredients—in the milk or blood of animals, or in the flowers, herbs, and roots of the countryside—led everyone to consider himself a pharmacist. Doctors took advantage of this and competed against the druggists in the manufacture and sale of the more complicated remedies.

Medicine and pharmacology were based on the triple Latin, Arabic, and Hebrew influence, although the Christian Middle Ages had experienced some improvement, and in certain cases, gone beyond these three traditions. Galen, Hippocrates, Isaac, and Avicenna were cited and invoked constantly; and medicine was always prescribed in Latin. Doctors and surgeons were permitted to possess "books about the arts written in Hebrew."[57]

Patients were usually treated at home. The modern concept of hospitals cannot be said to have existed in the Middle Ages, except, perhaps, for the infirmaries in the monasteries. The "hospitals" mentioned in the documents usually were no more than places of seclusion or asylums (for the poor, sick, or insane), permanent or temporary, with very little medical attendance or none at all. As the principal types of medieval hospitals, we find leper houses, asylums, shelters, children's hospitals, hospitals with hot springs, pesthouses, and hospitals for regeneration of women. Asylums, hospitals for children, and hospitals for women were really hospices, with the primary duty of serving as inns for travelers. The hospitals with hot springs, which were actually hotels, lodged the sick for treatments in medicinal waters. Finally the

leper houses and the pesthouses provided shelter for the sick afflicted
with contagious diseases that required isolation, either temporarily or
permanently. With the passing of time, many of these "asylums" came
to specialize in the acceptance of patients for whom hospital treatment
was provided. By the fifteenth century, one can speak of true hospitals;
all, however, were very small (the maximum was twenty-five beds), and
there were very few of them. Only after the great reform in relief,
undertaken during the reigns of João II and Manuel I with the creation of the hospital of All Saints and the founding of the *misericórdias*
(charitable institutions), did the history of the Portuguese hospital
truly begin. But this would carry our story into the modern period.[58]

5 : AFFECTION

HISTORY can record how people dress, where they live, sometimes even what they eat. It is more difficult to tell how they love. Only infrequently, and with great effort, can the intensity and the form of affection be glimpsed, in a fortuitous raising of the curtain of modesty or through an unintentional barrier of silence (for the ways and customs of love seem so natural to those concerned as to be unworthy of description).

Someone once wrote that history is limited to persons who are more than twenty years old. So it is, in truth. The whole world of childhood and adolescence escapes the interest of the researcher and indeed the possibility of being captured by him. We would like to know how affection between parents and small children was expressed; how the children were cared for, educated; how they played, and with what; what the problems that troubled them in puberty were, and how they overcame them. Of course, many of the attitudes and practices of the Middle Ages still persist, little changed, among what are called the lower classes. Consequently, it would be of especial interest to study the behavior of the upper classes—the royal family, the nobility, the greater bourgeoisie. One medieval Portuguese king—Afonso V—ascended the throne when he was little more than six years old, in 1438. Yet the chronicler tells us very little about the method of his education, about the toys with which he amused himself, about the companions with whom he laughed, about the friends for whom he had a high regard. It is true that the shorter human lifespan obliged the adolescent to become a man and to act as such at quite an early age. Between fourteen and sixteen years of age, sovereigns received charge of the government, and their minority was taken from them.[1] At eighteen, they generally reached the status of adulthood. Youths only fourteen or fifteen years old performed feats of war. Twelve-year-old girls became wives. To what degree situations such as these were considered normal or exceptional is something that needs to be studied. To what extent premature aging hastened the transformation of the child into an adult is a topic which even today has not been carefully investigated.

In the *Loyal Counselor,* in a famous chapter ("On the relationship which we had with the King, my lord and father, may his soul be with God"), Duarte discourses on the love between fathers and sons, and about the relationship between the two.[2] The basis of his theory is said to be his experiences in the midst of the Avis family. Even allowing for the natural exaggeration resulting from the desire to offer perfect standards of morals and conduct, sufficient material is left to enable us to draw a few conclusions. The facts related apparently refer to the period after the death of Queen Philippa (1415). The princes were no longer adolescents: Duarte was twenty-four years old, Pedro twenty-three, and Henrique (the future Henry the Navigator) twenty-one. It is true that the younger ones, João and Fernando, were only fifteen and thirteen years old; however, this chapter does not appear to allude to them. And there is complete silence about Isabel, the future duchess of Burgundy, at this time eighteen years old.

Although they are grown men, the behavior which the princes affect towards their father would be more appropriate to boys not yet in their teens. Absolute respect and veneration, carried even to the point of refusing the manifestation of their own individuality, was the rule. "In the affairs which we dealt with or talked about with him, we did not wish to advance our own projects, but we would affirm our whole desire and pleasure in offering to accept his decision without any hindrance." Even in their revelries and on hunting trips, diffidence and the yielding of their own pleasure to the greater pleasure of their father was exalted: "In riding and hunting, when we were with the aforesaid lord, we would make small account of the mirth which we used to have in it in order to always increase his, regretting a small annoyance caused him more than the loss of all the venison or the frustration of the whole hunt." They never became bored with their father's conversation nor argued with him: "If we had some talk in which our judgment and opinion might disagree with his, even though later we found our plan to be correct and better, we would never refer to it; rather, if he again told us his idea was better, we would humbly accept his pronouncement." They always praised him and obeyed him, telling the truth about everything. They strove to act in accordance with his wishes and never to betray annoyance "because he had acted contrary to our pleasure and will." This feudal submissiveness, quite characteristic of the period and closely related to the ideals of devotion between persons, had its complement in the just, fair, and courteous lord: "By the aforesaid lord, our king, since we reached the age of remembrance, never in anger were we struck, nor did we receive a harsh word, nor did we feel that sometimes we were not loved or in his good graces, but we received many benefices and great honor from him until the end of his very honorable days."

Such an atmosphere of harmony and of friendship extended to the relationships among the brothers. There was no envy, no "inordinate covetousness," no avarice, no desire, no haughtiness. In sports, discussions, and ideas, one never rebelled against the others.

Objective reality of a model family? Hazy memories? Or rather an hypocrisy necessary for the improvement of the behavior of the king's subjects, to "provide a good example" which the times needed so greatly? Duarte himself was aware of how extraordinary the facts which he narrated were and of how little credit they might receive. "It seems to me," he says, "that this should have been disclosed to a few select persons, because if those people who do not entertain such ideas and habits see it, they will prefer to criticize and to contradict me, than to seize profitable instruction on how to act toward their lord or friends from it." And the later fate of the princes of Avis was not very harmonious with the wholesome principles taught them by João I. There were quarrels among the brothers—Pedro and João against Afonso, Count of Barcelos; later Pedro against Henry the Navigator, who furnishes the king with soldiers to kill the "rebel." There was half-hearted fraternal love in the episode of the imprisonment of Fernando by the Moslems at Tangier (1437) and the abandonment to which he was voted. There was practical incitement to the revolt of Duarte's young son Afonso V against his mother—and the consequent exile of Leonor. And so the story goes.

Actually, the precepts of the eloquent king appeared as a norm of conduct that was not very convincing and even less to be copied, but rather to cause astonishment in this turbulent period which marked the end of the Middle Ages.

If we leaf through the pages of the *Books of Genealogy* (*Livros de Linhagens*) and the chronicles themselves, we discover that fratricides and parricides did occur: there is even the case of the noble who had his mother sewn in the skin of a bear and threw her to mastiffs because she meddled in his affairs with his mistress. But such incidents are almost always the exceptions, recorded as extraordinary phenomena and for this very reason worthy of mention. It is not believable that in the midst of the upper classes, habit could be transformed into the most absolute violation of the prevailing written and oral law. In a society so markedly patriarchal as that of the Middle Ages, obedience

toward and veneration for parents were conspicuously the rule governing relationships, whether theoretical or practical.

Children did not usually leave their parents' home until they married. "The children are in the power of the parents until they enter into
matrimony," says a twelfth-century charter. "Everything belongs to
their parents and they may not keep anything for themselves against
their parents's wishes."[3] Emancipation did not exist. On the contrary,
if a son behaved in an unworthy manner, or if he rebelled against
paternal power, his father could evict him from the house and cease
to consider him as a son, completely disinheriting him. This total integration of the son into his family was dispelled only by the death of one
of his parents. At this time, the heir received his inheritance and became independent, losing the condition of "family-son." Beginning
with the thirteenth century, however, certain changes occurred in favor
of a greater filial liberty, namely in the possibility of children having
their own possessions at their disposal.[4]

Adoption of children or of adults by couples or individuals who
had none was quite common. Once the confirmation of the king was
received, the adopted children entered into the bosom of the family
with all the rights and duties that belonged to genuine sons and
daughters.[5]

Incidents of incest seem to have been more frequent then than in
modern times. The *Books of Genealogy* mention several love affairs
between brother and sister, followed by abduction and carnal knowledge. The extent of this practice would merit a detailed and dis-
passionate study, all the more if the Middle Ages corresponded, as
one English historian would have it, to a period in which incestuous
unions were tolerated and viewed with light aversion by society.[6]

The whole gamut of tender premarital feelings is depicted in the
poetry of the cancioneiros. Whether uttered by enamored nobles or
by villeins, the expressions used had much in common and must not
have changed greatly between the thirteenth and fifteenth centuries.[7]

> Mother, a knight passed by here
> And left me enamored of him.

To go to the first meeting, the maiden seeks her sister's company:

> Sister, come see my love with me.

Afterwards, the meetings alone increase. Among the villeins, the
freedom that the maiden enjoys is greater than that among the upper
classes. But even so, in certain cases, the wretched girl complains:

> I am watched as no other woman
> Has ever been, my love, or ever shall be.

Actually, there are acquiescent mothers who assist and guide the love affairs, sometimes with disastrous results:

> Mother, you who told me
> To lie to my lover,
> What advice will you give me
> Now that he has gone away?

The passion is overwhelming—

> Never have I seen such a love of a lady
>   like unto my love

—and it frequently leads, especially outside of the aristocracy, to pre-marital relations:

> Arise, my love, you who sleep on cold mornings;
> All the birds of the world sang of love:
> I am so very happy.

or

> When I used to sleep with my lover,
> The night did not seem to last any time at all.

Then there is the marvelous period of happiness, merrymaking, and the urge to tell everyone the great joy of being in love:

> Mother, I went on a pilgrimage
> To Faro with my love,
> And I have returned deeply in love with him.
> So much did he tell me:
> He swore that he would die
> For me, he loves me so well!

Everything smiles around her:

> I see a lovely day, for I see you here.

Life would be impossible without the presence of her beloved:

> I cannot, my friend,
> Live
> With yearning for you . . .
> And therefore dwell,
> My love, where you can
> Speak to me and see me.

Afterwards, the bitternes of love comes. There is jealousy:

> He who delays so long in coming,
> If he desires another love,
> And not my own, I would want
> To die today, this very day.

resentment:

> I went, Mother, to St. Mamede, where I thought
> My love might come, and he was not there;
> And I left as sad as I was beautiful.

anger:

> He is the head of a depraved dog,
> For there is no fidelity in him:
> He is talking to another woman.

The sweethearts are later reconciled:

> Eyes of a traitor,
> Come back now, for I have already forgiven you.

But the situation has changed considerably. He wants to leave; she begs him to forget about her:

> You wish to go away, my love,
> From here, to make me sorrowful,
> And since you want to leave
> This place . . .
> Leave my heart completely
> And then go.

She suspects that it was her friend who stole him from her and swears vengeance:

> She who stole my love from me . . .
> You will see a woman running
> After me crying and I will not want to give him
> to her.

And finally, the break and the discord common in love:

> And if I were to have another lover, he would
> lie to me . . .
>
> I was all accompanied by lies . . .
>
> I, pretty thing that I am, as long as I may live,
> Never again will I believe in love.

Of the simple, everyday practices inherent to courting, we know little or nothing that may be dated, or is precise, or is limited to the medieval period. In compensation, the traditional habits of the Portuguese people may be retraced to the Middle Ages, to still older periods, habits, and superstitions connected to love. Playwright Gil Vicente had already mentioned picking a marigold apart as a method of fortune-telling in the early sixteenth century.[8] The superstition of a young woman's rubbing stones to obtain a bridegroom goes back to prehistory.[9] All kinds of enchantments, sorcery, religious invocations, linked to the most ingenuous practices of divination, interpretation of dreams, etc., can be detected in the medieval period because they have lasted down to modern times.

Aristocratic love assumed more complicated forms. It was not expressed in such a free and objective manner. In the declarations of love, in the vows expressed, in the complaints, and in the despair, it always attempted to hide itself beneath an exquisite formalism or courteous conventionalism. Between the expression of love and of gallantry there was little difference. Love was conceived in the Provençal manner, as a "service." The knight "served" his lady during the time that might be necessary to earn his reward. This service consisted in dedicating his thoughts, poetry, and deeds to her; in being in her presence on certain occasions; in not leaving without her permission; and so on. The servant was to his lady as the feudal vassal was to the suzerain; in fact, in thirteenth-century Portuguese, the lady was called *senhor,* the same word as "lord":

> *E que queria eu melhor*
> *De ser seu vassalo*
> *E ela minha senhor?*

> And what better could I wish
> Than to be her vassal
> And she my liege?[10]

We should not let the platonic idealism of this love, manifested in endless songs and repeated from the twelfth century to the fifteenth, make us forget the other side of the coin. The ardent desire for something more than chaste contemplation or "service" repaid with suffering is clearly evident in many texts and is emphasized by the facts. Carnal unions before marriage were not unusual. Even in the books accepted as exemplars of deportment, in the genre of the *Romance of Amadis (Romance de Amadis)* or of the *Quest for the Holy Grail (Demanda do Santo Gral),* extramarital love affairs are exhibited without pretense. In the *Romance of Amadis,* for example, Oriana is possessed by her lover on a green meadow.[11] The frequency of adultery

Fig. 77. Entertaining a lady. 15th century.

Fig. 78. Two lovers hunting. 15th century.

required the drafting of more severe laws and provoked harsh condemnation by the moralists.

Love, in the conventional or the highly refined platonic forms, was the almost obligatory theme of the medieval lyric of the aristocratic type. At the end of the fifteenth century, what model of love to follow, and how it should be reflected in human conduct, was debated heatedly in Portugal. The famous polemics of the *cuidar* ("to care for") and the *suspirar* ("to sigh for") may be used as an example. Two nobles, Jorge da Silveira and Nuno Pereira, in love with the same lady, argue and come to lead factions over preference for cuidar (fretting or silent melancholy) or for suspirar (manifestation of one's suffering through moans and sighs). Jorge da Silveira, an adherent of suspirar, argues that

Not that I go about sighing
For the one who gives me such grief,
And goes on treating me in this way;
For the pain she inflicts has already
Destroyed me completely.
To suffer is the first cause,
But after having suffered
My sighs go on unabated
Until they have stilled my very last breath.

To which Nuno Pereira answers:

To have the ability to sigh,
My lord brother-in-law, is an indication
That by such manifestation one can get things off his chest.
But there is no room in me for such sighing,
For my suffering prevents it.
Because it is so intense,
She for whom I am in such a state
Must be going about asking:
Has Nuno Pereira died yet?

And the controversy proceeds in tens of stanzas, with the help of numerous partisans of one or the other sentiment.[12]

Beyond all this hyprocritical conventionality, contradicted in practice by the violence of passions, there was a sincere cult of certain ideal forms cherished as the supreme objective of love and defended by poets and philosophers. This theory was possibly as meaningful for the thirteenth century as for the fifteenth, but the first Portuguese exposition of ideal love appears in Duarte's *Loyal Counselor*. Here, he theorizes on love as a universal concept that comprises four states of affection: well-wishing, desire of doing good, love, and friendship. By well-wishing, he means a vague feeling of fraternity, "the universal name by which we can say rightly that we like everyone we do not dislike." Desire of doing good, "which is more special," is felt for intimate acquaintances; only a very few "have such regard for everyone." Love corresponds to what we ordinarily call love today: "Principally, [the lover] desires above all else to be loved, to possess, and to attain for always a very intimate affection with whomever he loves in this way. And like a blind man or a galley slave, he often does not take care of his health, nor fear injury." There should be moderation, however: "Love in any case we may regard as questionable if it grows so great that it blinds or subjugates." Whenever passion troubles reason, one should reject love, "because if we were to renounce being guided by right reason and good understanding, what would we be worth?" Although Duarte acknowledges the virtue of love as a means of purification, especially among the young, to counteract the current depravity of the aristocratic environment, he still disapproves of it as hindering an authentic Christian life: "It is true that love makes young people behave better and defends them from some practices customarily found in the houses of the lords; but because of the danger which often grows out of love, it much behooves those who want to live virtuously to avoid this bondage."

Finally, there is friendship, which the monarch considers to be the truly superior and exemplary emotional state. Friendship partakes of the other three phases, but it differs from all of them, exhibiting their advantages but avoiding their inconveniences. "The friend has the advantage of the first two [well-wishing and desire of doing good] in that he loves his friend especially well, and thus he wishes to do things for him as he would want them done for himself. [Friendship] differs from love in that friends love guided principally by the understanding, and it differs from the others [well-wishing and desire of doing good] by involvement of the heart. The desire of being loved differs from friendship in yet another respect, because friends always think that they are so, for in any other way they would not have such regard for each other, that they can say each is another 'I.' " Far from being passionate, friends "do not desire an affection so constrictive and continuously close as lovers, nor so intense, because when the friend must take his leave, even though he may feel nostalgia for his friend, he bears it confidently and well." It is friendship which is felt for one's parents, brothers, and sisters.[13]

Marriage was considered the base of emotional life during the Middle Ages. In a civilization labeled Christian, it is not surprising that the ideal of matrimony should be presented as the ultimate end of all earthly love. Were not the very nuns married to Jesus Christ? Had not Christ himself married the Church? In a patriarchal but monogamous society, with its foundations in the family, only through marriage could sexual longings be realized perfectly within a Christian context.

Various methods of marriage were practiced in medieval Portugal. Among these was the Roman custom of marriage: a simple agreement between the two parties, solemnized or not by religious ritual. To Christianity, matrimony as a sacrament was considered indissolvable. Hence the rejection of divorce, which was popular in Roman society. Hence also the growing preoccupation of the Church to impress a religious stamp on the basic contract.

"I take this woman; I take this man."* These simple words, known as *palavras de presente*,† declared under oath between a man and a woman legally able to form a union, were enough to perform the marriage. The presence of witnesses was not necessary. It was enough for the young spouses, now living together, to announce to whoever might wish to know that they had pledged love and devotion to each other.

This very simple marriage ceremony was especially suitable for the humble, unable to pay for the attendance of a priest to bless their union, too poor to require a notary to draw up a contract in proper form for division of property, too poor even to celebrate the event with wedding feasts or dances. But it also suited clandestine lovers whose families were opposed to their marriage, and even seducers, who thus acquired consent for the carnal liaison. Afterwards, if one of the partners behaved badly, it was easy to deny that a marriage had really taken place without witnesses to verify the promises exchanged. The birth of children produced, so many times, perjurers, men indifferent or monetarily unable to manage a family.[14]

The Portuguese of that age called these clandestine marriages, though valid in their practical effects, *casamentos a furto* ("dissimulated marriages") and *casamentos de pública fama* ("marriages of public rumor"), according to whether they took place in secret or were recognized by well-known cohabitation. Even the palavras de presente were considered unnecessary for the validity of the union if a man and a woman lived together for seven years uninterruptedly, acting like spouses, regarding themselves as such, and were thus acknowledged by the neighborhood.[15] "Every marriage," says a thirteenth-century law, "may be performed with those words which the Holy Church requires, provided that the contracting parties are ones who may marry without committing a sin. And every marriage which can be proven, whether it be secret [*a furto*], or whether in a public manner [*conhoçudamente*], will be valid, if those married in this way are of legal age, as is customary."[16]

From this necessity of proof would come, in modern times, the uniformity in the marriage ceremony performed through the intervention of the Church. The period from the twelfth century to the fifteenth century, however, was still far from such conformity. The frequency of clandestine marriages worried the Church, which did not cease to denounce this practice and to fulminate with the most powerful excommunications against the betrothed who disdained to appear in the temple. Fernando I and Leonor Teles married secretly: "And it is

---

* "Ego te recipio in meam; et ego te in meum."

† "Words of the present," as opposed to "words of the future," or betrothal.

certified," says chronicler Fernão Lopes, "that before the King slept with her, first he took her as his wife, her sister and a few others being present, all of whom kept this thing secret."[17] This, in spite of the law which Fernando's father promulgated in 1352 stating that "all the marriages which were performed in the parish should be in the presence of the parish priest and the scribe." Although sent in the style of a circular letter to all the prelates of the kingdom, it had not been long before the law had been generally forgotten.[18] In the middle of the fifteenth century, the practice was still common, according to an official report by the archbishop of Lisbon on his visit to several parishes within his diocese:

> We find that some lay persons of the aforesaid city and archbishopric [Lisbon], not considering carefully how the holy sacraments of the Church should be given and administered to the faithful Christians by the priests who are her ministers and governors, to whom through God and by the aforesaid Church is contained the ministration, are moved with rash audacity to marry in private places within their homes, in such a way going contrary to the holy canons and decisions of the Holy Church, from which it often follows that wicked husbands and such woman repudiate their aforesaid marriages to the great detriment of their souls and consciences.[19]

Even clerics in the lesser orders married in this way, making use of "the secretiveness to deny the marriage and protect themselves under canon law."[20] The excommunication that resulted from such a marriage could be lifted only after "the couple and those who had received them, before being absolved, had spent three Sundays at the door of the church, outside it, while the masses at tierce were said, barefoot during the whole mass with brambles around their necks, thick and uncovered, in such a way that they may be in plain view of everyone, and the witnesses each will appear one Sunday in similar fashion."[21]

Preceding the marriage, what was known as the betrothal took place, at least among the nobility. This corresponded to the modern engagement period. A marriage, whether based on affection or convenience, was officially approved. The sum to constitute the dowry or the earnest money was agreed upon. The date of the marriage was set. If the social class of the betrothed couple justified it, a formal legal document of the event was drawn up. And everything received the blessings of the Church.[22]

The normal, solemn wedding ceremony was that known as *casamento de benção* ("the blessed marriage"). It was held in the church, or at its door, with the participation of a priest, who received the couple and blessed the union. The banns, or announcements, although

decreed by Innocent III in the Fourth Lateran Council, became widespread only little by little. Even in the middle of the fifteenth century,
many marriages neglected them, later encountering hindrances that obstructed the union. Consequently, publication of marriage banns for the
three Sundays previous to the formal act was again made obligatory.[23]

The bride who was married in the church wore a veil over her head,
a very old ritual contemporary with early Christianity. The exchange
of rings after the blessings was the Spanish variation of the symbol
of the earnest money, or dowry, with which the husband presented
his wife in German law. But the ring—of gold with gems for wealthy
couples, more modest both in metal and ornamentation for poor
couples—also signified the promise of marriage at the betrothal and
the love of the spouses in the wedding.[24]

The earnest money, or dowry, paid by the husband to his wife
signified the purchase of her body. This Germanic practice, contrary
to the Roman custom of the endowment of the woman by her father,
was in effect in Portugal during almost the entire Middle Ages, particularly since it was reinforced by an identical Moslem rite. When
the dowry justified it, a formal letter of grant was drawn up, the
carta de arras ("letter of settlement").[25] Kings were accustomed to give
magnificent dowries to their wives. Fernando settled Vila Viçosa,
Abrantes, Almada, Sintra, Torres Vedras, Alenquer, Atouguia, Óbidos,
Aveiro, the royal estates of Sacavém, Frielas, and Unhos, and the land
of Merles in Riba Douro on Leonor Teles.[26] João I, besides bestowing
on Philippa certain lands, gave her "the revenue of the customs and
tolls and of the Timber House, from all of which she could have had
20,000 gold dobras quite readily if she had wished to spend them all."[27]
Even among the less well-to-do, the earnest money could be considerable. The Usages of Riba-Coa* in the thirteenth century specified
that a dowry should consist of twelve maravedis (twelve pounds of
dinheiros), two fangas (3.14 bushels) of wheat, one pig, a yearling, five
rams, and fifty large gourds, each with the capacity of one cântaro
(5.8 gallons), filled with wine.[28]

The usual juridical rule was that of equal participation in the
administration of property. The woman disposed of her own belong-
ings, however: these included the trousseau, consisting of clothing,
household utensils, furniture, etc., which she brought to the home; the
wedding presents given the bride by her parents, relatives, bridegroom,
and guests; and her inheritances, received by the woman and subsequently transferred, freely, to her own heirs.[29]

---

* Riba-Coa was the medieval name given to the area between the rivers Coa
and Águeda in northeast Beira, close to the Spanish border.

There were many variations in the rites of marriage, changing from region to region in the country. Some corresponded to Moslem practices; others, to German, Roman, or Hispano-Roman customs; others were even connected to remote prehistorical and protohistorical tradition.

Usually, the bride was given to the groom by her parents. In Minho, however, a scene of violence was customarily feigned: the relatives dragged the young woman out of the house and carried her in a festive procession to her new home. In front of it walked a boy carrying a distaff filled with linen and the spindle.[30] Gradually, the Church succeeded in establishing that the surrender of the bride should be made through its mediation, after the prayers and the blessings.[31]

Other, more curious rituals could accompany the wedding. In weddings by proxy, the stand-in of the bridegroom pretended to sleep with the bride. João Rodrigues de Sá, the proxy of João I, did this, getting into bed with Philippa of Lancaster.[32]

A missal from the Middle Ages casts some light on the customary practice in weddings. This missal originates from the other side of the Pyrenees and represents the French tradition more than the Iberian, but it may have been followed in Portugal, since the trans-Pyrenean influence was quite marked in matters of the Church. The bride and groom were advised to arrive at the church by nine o'clock (the tierce, or the third hour). The priest then asked if there was any bond of kinship existing between the two receiving the sacrament, and if they were in love. Next, he blessed the ring and read the contract of the marriage settlement which had been brought by the groomsmen. Then he gave the ring to the bride, who received it wearing gloves if she had never been married before or without gloves if she was a widow. Picking it up again, he slipped it on the thumb, the forefinger, and the middle finger of the bride, while he recited invocations to the Trinity. Then came the time for the groom to pronounce the formula "With this ring I thee wed, with this gold I thee honor, with this dowry I thee endow." The priest blessed the coins, symbol of the marriage settlement, thus beginning the marriage mass. In the midst of the service, between the Our Father and the breaking of the bread, the bridal couple approached the altar; the parents of the bride gave her to the priest who handed her over to the groom; both lay down full-length on the floor, with his right hand on her shoulder; finally, altar boys covered them with a sheet. The ceremony ended with the nuptial blessing.[33]

When nobles and other powerful men were to wed, it was customary for the groom, with a friend, to go from house to house collecting gifts.

This practice led to violent scenes, because the youth, taking advantage of his social position, frequently demanded more than was owed by his vassals. At other times, disdaining to make the trip personally, the groom sent his castle commander, steward, lesser nobles, and goodmen on his land to collect the presents. Obviously, there followed all too frequently scenes of genuine extortion and rapine. These practices were based on the traditional law that the people contribute to the marriage of their lords.[34]

Fabulous sums were sometimes spent on these weddings. The sixteenth-century *Manueline Ordinances*, referring to medieval practices, attempted to moderate such expenditures. Because especially in Beira, in Entre-Douro-e-Minho, in Trás-os-Montes, and in Riba-Coa "ostentatious weddings and baptisms are habitual and accustomed to be held, in which men spend, if not squander, much of their estates; and besides this, the assembling of so many people at such weddings and baptisms results in deaths of men and in other evil deeds," such feasts were declared prohibited, and invitations to have dinner and supper with the bridal couple were forbidden to persons who were not close relatives, under pain of a whipping or banishment if disregarded. And, continued the *Ordinances*, "the relatives of the fourth degree will give nothing to the aforesaid wedding."[35]

When the bride had been married before and widowed, costly celebrations were usually not held. For the marriage of Constable Nuno Álvares with Leonor de Alvim (second half of the fourteenth century), "there was no feast nor should there have been, because she was a widow." The wedding took place with total simplicity, in the house in Vila Nova da Rainha (Estremadura) where King Fernando was staying.[36]

Marriages of kings and nobility were held with great pomp. In Oporto, when João I was married (1387),

the whole city was occupied in joyful attention to this feast. And everything being ready on that day, on Wednesday the King left his lodgings and went to the Palace of the Bishop where the Princess was. And on Thursday the people of the city all went jointly in merry bands of players and dancers on all the streets and squares, which had many decorations and delights. The principal streets through which this celebration had to pass were all strewn with fragrant greens and herbs. And the King, richly dressed in cloth of gold, came out of the palace riding a white horse; and the Queen on another, very majestically adorned. On their heads they wore golden crowns richly ornamented in small pearls of great price. Neither was riding a little in front of the other, but both were side by side. The grooms led the horses of the most honorable persons who were there, and everyone on foot was very well adorned. And the Archbishop

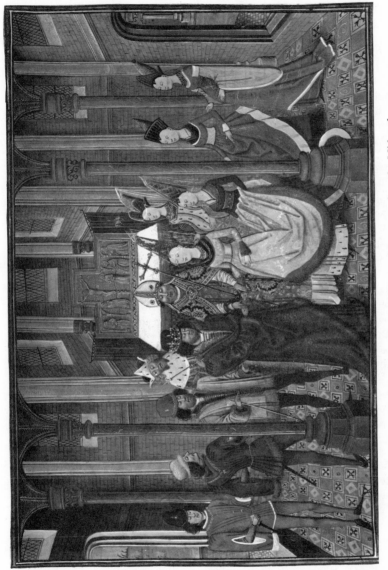

Fig. 79.   Royal marriage of João I and Philippa of Lancaster in 1387. Mid-15th century.

led the horse of the Queen by the reins. In front of them went pipes and
trumpets and other instruments which could not be heard; ladies, daughters of nobility, and those of the city sang, walking behind them, as is
customary at weddings. There were so many people that they could not
be governed nor ordered, for the space was so small from the palace to
the church. And thus they arrived at the door of the Cathedral, which was
very near, where Rodrigo, bishop of the city, was already festively dressed
in his pontifical robes and waiting with the clergy. He took them by the
hands and pronounced those words which the Holy Church orders to be
said in such a sacrament. Then he said mass and delivered the sermon:
and this service ending, the King and the Queen returned to the palace
that they had left, with similar festivity, where they were to eat. The
tables were already beautifully decorated, and with everything that be-
hooved them, not only where the newlyweds were to sit, but also the
places arranged for the bishops and other illustrious persons of the nobility and bourgeoisie of the city, and ladies and maidens of the palace
and city. And the master of ceremonies of the wedding feast was Nuno
Álvares Pereira, Constable of Portugal; great nobles and knights were
bearers of the towel and food and other services, for there was an abundance of dainty dishes prepared in fantastic ways. While the dinner
lasted, tumblers who knew their profession well, such as the leaps called
mensas and the royal leap and other graceful things, performed before
them; when these finished, everyone rose and began to dance, and all
the ladies sang with great delight. Meanwhile the King withdrew to his
chamber; and after the supper, at the evening party, the Archbishop and
other prelates, with many torches blazing, consecrated the bed with those
blessings which the Church directed for such an act. And leaving the
King with his wife, the others went to their own chambers.37

Another magnificent marriage was that of Prince Duarte, in 1428,
performed in Coimbra. It is narrated in a letter written by Henry
the Navigator to his father:

And Tuesday evening it was decided that their marriage should take
place on Wednesday. And the manner in which it was performed, with
the blessing which you bestowed on the Prince my Lord, on this first
evening, the decoration was in this manner: a large part of the cloister
of Santa Clara, through which her ladyship the Princess had to pass, was
adorned and carpeted with rugs, and at the door of the Church, which is
within the nuns' choir, was a rich length of scarlet brocade which covered
the place where the blessings were to be given; and the bolts of cloths
crossed the whole church just as through a street; it went up a stairway to
the choir where Queen Isabel lies, and this whole way was adorned and
covered like this completely with carpets, and the choir was completely
decorated with arras tapestries, both the part inside the church as well as
the part outside and completely covered with carpets all the way from

the altar, and a length of velvety blue satin laid on top of the carpets ran
through beneath the nuptial bed, and went up to the wall and was ten
lengths wide; and the front and the canopy of the altar were of very
sumptuous scarlet brocade, and the covering of the bed and the dorsal
which was above was also of quite splendid scarlet brocade. The cushion
on which they had to kneel was wholly of gold cloth without other needlework, and the altar was quite beautifully adorned of silver just like yours
as well as the other one here, and the bishop performed the service with
your miter and crosier, so that thanks be to Heaven, everything was well
arranged. And the Princess was in the chapter, and the Prince my Lord
came from his lodgings on a horse, handsomely dressed, wearing a very
richly embellished houppelande and an emerald as a brooch, and my
brothers Prince Pedro and Prince Fernando walked on one side of him
and I and my brother the Count walked on the other, on foot, and in
like manner, many other nobles. And we proceeded in this way to the
doors; and there the Prince dismounted and went on foot to the choir,
and Prince Fernando and the Count were there with him, while Prince
Pedro and I went for the Princess. And we brought her to where the
vows were made; and my Lord the Prince came, and the chanter of Évora
made a small bow and received them and performed the service. The
Princess was splendidly dressed. Torches were carried by Fernando,
Sancho, Duarte, Fernando de Castro, and the other illustrious young
lords who were there. And then the mass was prayed by the deacon and
subdeacon and everything done as pontifically as if it had been sung; and
two hundred dobras were the offering. And by the end of the service,
the Princess was so tired because of her houppelande, which was very
heavy, and from the oppressive heat generated by all those good men
who were there, and the torches which were so intense, that when we
began to leave she fainted. And we dashed some water on her face and
she awoke. And all the men left there, but the women stayed. The best
man was the Count and the bridesmaid, the Countess. And Lady Guiomar
carried the trains of the gowns. The Prince returned in the manner in
which he came, and when night came, we went for the Princess in the
monastery because she had eaten there, for it to appear that she had
married from the house of Queen Isabel [late thirteenth, early fourteenth
centuries] and thus was of Aragon; and everyone understood from the
saintliness of the aforesaid Queen Isabel that this was done very well and
honorably for her house. And the Princess rode and my brother Pedro
and I held the reins at the neck of the horse, and we both were on foot,
as were Prince Fernando and the Count and all the other nobles all the
way to her house. And she rode on a dove-gray horse with the golden
ornaments that the Prince sent her which Your Grace saw; and there
were some sixty torches which squires carried; and in her train came, also
on foot, the Countess and Isabel de Ataide and other ladies and maidens.
And after she was left in the chamber, we danced and sang a little while
in the palace, and the Prince came there and had his footstool and the

cloth for the footstool. And the hall was completely decorated. And he
was served wine and fruit by all of us: Prince Pedro brought the cloth,
and I the sweets, and Prince Fernando the fruit, and the Count the wine;
and after he drank, we said goodnight to him and withdrew to our own
rooms. And as the final touch to the writing of this letter, I understand
that for some little while now her grace the Princess has been your daughter completely.[38]

There were no wedding costumes as we know them today. The bride
and groom wore the most splendid clothing they owned, or had
clothing expressly made, but it was not essentially different from the
formal dress used at balls or at other solemn ceremonies.

In marriage, as in the conventions of love, the inconsistencies between
ideal and actuality were profound. Between husband and wife, the
emotional ideal should be perfectly attained, partaking of all four
states of affection put forth in the *Loyal Counselor*. "If it is not so,
they cannot reach its perfect state," Duarte declares dogmatically,
but he immediately adds: "Some entering such an estate [marriage],
will understand how they may love perfectly in all four ways of
loving, which I believe that few are predisposed to reach for want
of moral excellence, wisdom, or good intentions, which there must
be in each of the partners." Sadly disbelieving in the ability of most
people to achieve fully the ideal of marriage, the monarch clearly
comprehended the moral transformations of his century. It is true that
he hastened to amend this skepticism so that no one might suppose
that discord or indifference prevailed in the royal family or in the
court: "Those who have reached such [an emotionally perfect mar-
riage] will recognize well how truthfully I have written of this science,
thanks to Our Lord well practiced among us." And, further on, with
the same moralizing preoccupation with defense of appearances: "At
present I do not know nor have I heard of the wife of a knight nor
of another man of good report in my whole kingdom who has a
reputation contrary to her honor in defense of faithfulness. And there
are more than a hundred ladies whom the King and the Queen, their
graces my Father and Mother, may their souls be in Heaven, and we
have married in our palaces, and it pleased Our Lord that as far as
I know never did one fall into such an error since she was married."[39]
All this defense of aristocratic morality was no more than a conventional drapery to hide the quite different reality of this period, as the
documents clearly reveal.

In a society in which most marriages were arranged by agreement
between the parents of the betrothed, or between the groom and the

parents of the bride, it is understandable that the problem of the existence of love between husband and wife became an important theme of discussion. One of the most discriminating monarchs that Portugal ever had, João I, came to perpetrate the unprecedented outrage of marrying ladies and gentlemen of his household without even apprising them of the fact until the evening before! Certain of "the high discretion and agreement" of the women whom he thus forced into marriage, he did not so much as disclose the name of their future husbands, to whom they were introduced only on the occasion of the ceremony: "The King has sent us to inform you that you should be ready to marry tomorrow." The men did not receive greater consideration from him: "On the next day the King himself led the bridegrooms to the chamber of the Queen and there told each one that woman whom he should receive in marriage, to whose command there was no contradiction," even though, adds the chronicler maliciously, "only one lady managed to marry the one she liked." Later on, the complaints of the newlyweds became so loud that the King of Good Memory swore never again to become involved in matchmaking.[40]

Marriages were arranged as early as the birth of the children. Betrothals took place at a very tender age. The formal marriage was common among adolescents only fourteen, fifteen, or sixteen years old, especially among the privileged classes. What could marital love signify for a "matron" fourteen years old bound to a forty-year-old adult? Or even to two fifteen-year-old adolescents?

The interference of third persons extended to the very system of sexual relations. Between husband and wife, the Church prohibited them as sin during menstruation, after pregnancy was verified, after the birth of the child until the mother was purified, as well as at certain periods of the year: during Advent, in Lent, on Sundays, and on holy days. The offender was compelled to confess his sins and received pardon only through the sacrament of penitence.[41]

From the twelfth century on, one of the themes discussed in the literature of the cycle of the Round Table was "that true love does not exist in marriage."[42] Kings and queens, nobles and clerics, ladies and maidens comment on it. The ideal love of the troubadour lyric had nothing to do with matrimonial ties. Daily experience confirms this thesis. Possibly there was never another period in history more prolific in adultery, illegitimacy, and extramarital love than the Middle Ages. Adultery, especially common among the nobility, constituted a serious problem in a society which pretended to condemn it without pardon, in the light of the rigid ethics of Christianity.[43] Numerous and severe

laws on immoral love, constantly renewed, betray the obvious fact
of the frequency of the sin.

Annulment of marriage took the place of the lack of legalized
divorce. The Church forbade marriages between relatives up to the
eighth degree of kinship. This restriction was later reduced (1215) to
only the fourth degree. Marriages between cousins were permitted
only through dispensation, difficult to attain, or at least onerous,
especially in the closest degrees. But in such a small society, so closed
as the Portuguese aristocracy of that time appears to have been, it is
easy to understand the relative frequency of illegal marriages between
relatives. Subsequently, as Herculano says so well, "when boredom
came to settle upon the conjugal bed of the noble, or a new love
troubled his heart, it was almost always to a kinship, genuine or
feigned, which he resorted in order to break the ties that had become
odious to him. The inevitable consequences of these facts are easy
to anticipate. Dissensions among the most eminent families, atrocious
revenge, private wars, rupture of domestic ties, and severance of filial
piety must emerge from this."44

Adultery could result from violent love between a man and a married woman, caught up in what was known as "spiritual conversations."
Saint Thomas Aquinas, in the thirteenth century, calls attention to
the danger that such meetings constituted. In the fifteenth century
Duarte was to comment on the same theme in the *Loyal Counselor*.

Theological and pious topics were very much in vogue at that time
as the theme of lofty conversation. In the long leisure hours of high
society, lords and ladies amused themselves by debating on the divine
nature, the appearance of the angels, or the theory of the virtues.
Before long, they discovered spiritual affinities. It is understandable
that the customary rudeness of masculine contacts should have found
complement and relief in gentle conversation with women. Nevertheless, the moralists scathingly denounced it:

> When [men] are acquainted and carry on conversation and have some
> familiarity with any woman, which is or seems to be spiritual, as they
> want the motive of such a friendship to appear good, nevertheless, the
> great familiarity and friendship with such persons is nothing if not a
> gentle peril, a delightful and poorly disguised injury, painted in the
> colors of goodness, to which intimacy, the more it grows, in like amount
> the principal basis and the first reason on which and for which the afore-
> said affection began decreases, and thus more and more the purity of
> each is hurt, and temptations corrupt both to seek an opportunity for
> their corporeal union.

Fig. 80. "Spiritual conversation." 15th century.

And it all was consummated in the most lascivious love, in adultery, and in the necessity of deceiving others and of changing confessors frequently.[45]

The end of the fourteenth century and the whole of the fifteenth— periods of profound incongruities in the social and moral scheme— also witnessed an increase in the number of illegitimate children. Of course, only the privileged classes enjoyed the ability of obtaining a letter of legitimacy for their natural children from the king, but concubinage and moral intemperance were also more frequent among these classes. A statistical study of the concessions of letters of legitimacy reveals an obvious increase in illegitimate childbirth beginning with the last quarter of the fourteenth century. The epoch of João I, so often mentioned as an example of morality by authors who take literally the pompous declarations of the chroniclers and of Duarte, nicknamed the Eloquent King, on the contrary displays an unbridled state of violation of the moral code by the nobility and the clergy. Between 1398 and 1408 alone there were granted 575 letters of legitimacy, an average of almost sixty per year! All in all, the reign of the

Master of Avis, João I, shows some two thousand legitimacies, and that of his son another three hundred.[46]

The acts of violence committed by nobles on virgins and widows are well known and mentioned often as a feudal characteristic of the Middle Ages (although, as a matter of fact, much in an exaggerated vein has been written on the subject). The custom of the times allowed the lords to lodge in the homes of commoners when they traveled. It may be imagined how such billeting could result in criminal assaults on the wives and daughters of the lower classes. In the very convents of nuns the turbulence of the nobility was not moderated, creating all kinds of spiritual denunciations and legal prohibitions.[47] Afonso IV (1325–57), living in a period in which occurrences of this order began to worry the rulers, established by law that nobles who violated the honor of women must marry them or recompense them if they were already married.[48] In the sessions of the Cortes, the grievances of the people against violations of the moral code by the nobility never fail to be raised.

The moral condition of the clergy was no worse than that of the laity, though some would declare it so. But because his actions generated more numerous and stringent civil and ecclesiastical laws and because he was under the rule of celibacy and continence, the priest acquired a special notoriety. Since priests were protected by canon law, only in well-defined cases did the Church agree to the interference of civil authorities in the sins of the clergy. This would happen, for example, when a priest had been seized in a flagrant sin with some woman he was confessing during the performance of his spiritual duty.[49]

It was common for priests to live with their mistresses, temporarily or permanently. They had offspring by them, raising the children "at home" in a perfect domestic setting. At the Cortes of 1401, the people complained about the fact that many clerics were living with mistresses, flaunting their concubines in public and dressing them much better than the legitimate wives of the laymen. Many women, in fact, preferred a union such as this to a normal marriage, as a means of satisfying their desires for luxury and wealth. The scandal was so great that many laymen refused to receive the sacraments from the hands of priests considered public paramours.[50]

High dignitaries of the Church fathered offspring from the north to the south of the country, taking advantage of their position or of the property that they had received to enter a petition to the king for letters of legitimacy for their many children. From 1389 to 1438, two archbishops, five bishops, eleven archdeacons, nine deans, four chanters, seventy-two canons, and nearly six hundred priests—without counting clergymen of minor orders, those who gave rations to the poor, and others—received such letters.[51]

Among the ranks of the regular clergy the violation of continence was no less. Abbots, friars, and monks lived with mistresses, *teúdas e manteúdas* ("possessed and maintained"), or pursued love affairs here and there, producing and legitimizing infants. In the same period mentioned above, no fewer than four hundred abbots and priors of monasteries obtained documents of legitimacy for their children from João I and Duarte. Many of them were fathers several times: there was, for example, Lourenço Roiz, abbot of St. Salvador do Souto in Rebordães, father of five children born of two different mothers (two and three children respectively), or Martim Vasques de Rebelo, abbot of St. Paio of Caria, with eight offspring, also by two mothers, both servants in his household (three and five children respectively). João Dores, abbot of Santas, was more constant a lover: his five children were all born of the same mother.[52]

Nor were the sisters and nuns, beginning with the abbesses, ashamed to petition for letters of legitimacy for the products of their love affairs. The infractions of chastity by the professed in the religious-military orders are well-known. The famous Fr. Álvaro Gonçalves, prior of the Hospitalers, legitimized seven sons, one of whom was Constable Nuno Álvares. Thirteen masters and priors from all the orders (Christ, Avis, Hospital), besides twenty-four commendators, entered petitions for legitimations from João I and Duarte. The friars of Santiago could marry, but that did not cause them to refrain from sowing children outside of matrimony.[53] Many troubadours, who courted women and extolled the charms of love in songs, were clerics.[54]

Against adultery committed by clergy or laymen, the penalties imposed were nevertheless quite severe. The Church censured with excommunication sacrilegious persons who might fornicate inside the very churches or go to bed with nuns. Mistresses of clerics or of married men were numbered among the excommunicated along with their respective paramours. Twelfth-century civil law ordered mistresses of clerics thrown into prison. Only much later, after a century had passed, did it forbid the existence of mistresses at the royal court and prohibit the legacies and gifts settled by married men on their mistresses. He who deflowered a virgin or slept with a widow was obliged to marry her. Bigamy was punished with death. Anyone who committed adultery with a married woman with her consent was to be punished with exile and his goods confiscated as the property of the Crown if he was a noble; if he was not, he was to be condemned

to death. In the borough charters, the punishment given for violent
rape was a severe fine. The woman so ravished had to run immediately
to the public square and scream in front of everyone "See what John
Doe did to me!" so that justice might be done her. Procuresses and
pimps would be flogged the first time, with proclamation made of it,
and expelled from the land, losing their goods to the king; if they
repeated the offense, they received the death penalty.[55]

Affronted husbands were entitled to complete official protection.
A law by Afonso IV confirms the custom "that every married woman
who commits adultery against her husband, if her husband kills her
for this, although he had not actually caught her in the adultery, the
husband will not die for this crime, nor should there be any penalty
of justice imposed." That is why in the mid-fourteenth century Prince
João, son of Inês de Castro, can murder his wife Maria Teles with
impunity. The adulterer could also be slain by the outraged husband,
without the consequence of judicial prosecution. If the adulterer
should be a knight or a noble with a manor, however, the penalty of
death could not be inflicted, "out of reverence of his person and status
of chivalry or nobility." Nevertheless, if the husband, a dishonored
peasant, had the impudence to kill the adulterer, he would "only"
suffer a public whipping and exile for one year.

From the notorious paramour were exacted high fines, which reached
2 to 4 percent of the paramour's possessions. Upon the second offense,
the fine was reckoned as double, on the third as quadruple, with the
woman flogged, and on the fourth, the offender was imprisoned until
an order of the king released him.[56]

As the expedient substitute for concubinage, prostitution enjoyed high
favor, obtaining the tolerance and complaisance of the whole society.
Meretrizes (harlots), *soldadeiras* (hired servants), *mancebas* (concubines), *mulheres de segre* (women of the world), "women who 'do' for
men"—all were more or less the same as today's prostitutes. There
were, however, certain differences between these groups of women,
both in way of life as well as in social category. A soldadeira accompanied the jesters, roving about to the royal palaces, the manor houses
of the nobility, or the palaces of the high dignitaries of the church.
Traveling by foot or on horseback and serving as companion, assistant,
or maid, the soldadeira danced and sang to the sound of the jester's
instrument. In the social hierarchy, she would have been equated with
him or placed just a little lower. She came to interest the troubadours
as a theme for love songs.[57] There are numerous songs of scorn that
refer to her, however, and in time, the soldadeira lost what little credit
she still enjoyed and approximated the common harlot. As early as

1261, a law forbade her to remain more than three days in the royal palaces.

The clear distinction between harlots, soldadeiras, and mistresses does not appear much before the fourteenth century. Until that time, generalized concubinage and the situation of dancing, tumbling, and being willing to love for wages (a soldo) diluted the ranks of prostitutes. The concern in regulating prostitution, segregating it from the "decent" life, and branding and demeaning it was the inevitable consequence of the moral slackening at the close of the Middle Ages, with the inherent necessity of moralizing ex cathedra. And so the laws of Afonso IV were issued, ordering the zoning of prostitutes in special districts of each city or village. They were to reside there and were not to leave. And their luxury was also checked: "Let no woman of the world throughout our kingdom make in one year more than one pair of clothes [i.e., one dress] of Arras material or other material of comparable value; nor may she wear gold nor silver on her girdles nor ornaments on her veils nor on her chemises." And still more: prostitutes were obliged, as were the Jews, to wear signs on their clothing that labeled them clearly. Yet it is questionable whether these arrangements were implemented continuously. Pedro I (1357–67), who was more tolerant, lifted the harsh measures taken by his father against the luxuries of the "women who 'do' for men." The very location of the brothels was far from being strictly zoned. The zoning was repeated in the fifteenth-century Ordinances, but by the end of the fifteenth century, the people again complained that harlots lived among honest women in violation of the law.[58]

Actually, tolerance was great and the prerogative of husbands to sleep with prostitutes came to obtain the express recognition of the king. In the Cortes of Évora in 1436, the representatives of the city asserted: "It sometimes happens that honorable men come to this city and lodge at the inns and desire to sleep with single concubines, and send to the brothel for them to come speak to them at the inn because they are not the sort of men to go to the brothel"; the representatives went on to request: "Let it please your grace, that even if the aforesaid single harlot sleeps with him in the said inn, that he not be punished nor yet the innkeeper, seeing that he consented to it." And the virtuous king Duarte, author of the treatise on morals known as the Loyal Counselor, promptly conceded the petition—"we answer that you ask well"—as long as the girls did not transform the inn into a brothel, returning to their dwellings the following morning.[59]

The existence of pimps is attested by extensive documentation. There were ruffians (or tafuis, "dandies"), who kept mistresses in prostitution, "placing them in the inns to publicly sleep with the travelers, taking for themselves everything the girls so earned in the aforesaid sin; and so much so that if they become bored there or do not earn enough to be content, they take the girls to the villages and cities of which they hear greater fame, for there they earn more and there they put them in the public brothels." Some of these pimps were even squires. A law of Afonso V punished them with exile. For villeins, the penalty inflicted allowed flogging and exile.[60]

In the *Royal Compilation of Law (Fuero Real)* by Alfonso X, the Wise (thirteenth century), which was the law in Portugal for a long time, one clause established: "Because once in awhile a man lusts after men to sin with him unnaturally, we decree that anyone whoever he may be who commits such a sin, that as soon as it may be known, both will be castrated in public. And then, on the third day, let them be hung by their legs until they die."[61] The fifteenth-century *Afonsine Ordinances (Ordenações Afonsinas)*, besides condemning homosexuality, moralized on the subject:

> Above every other sin, the sin of sodomy surely appears to be the most obscene, repugnant and immoral, and there cannot be found another so abhorrent before God and the world as this one; because not only through it is committed an affront to the Creator of nature, Who is God, but also it can be said that all created nature, heavenly as well as human, is greatly outraged. And as the natural philosophers said, even if men only mention it without any other act, so great is its aversion that the air cannot tolerate it, but it is naturally corrupted and loses its natural purity. And it can even be read that because of this sin God launched the flood upon the earth, when He ordered Noah to construct an ark in which he and his family might escape by whom He reestablished the world again; and because of this sin He destroyed the cities of Sodom and Gomorra, which were the most outstanding which were in the world at that time; and for this sin, the Order of the Templars was obliterated throughout Christendom in one day. And because according to the quality of the sin, thus one should be gravely punished: therefore we decree and we institute as the general law that every man who should commit such a sin, in whatsoever manner it may be, should be burned and reduced to ashes by the flame, so that never may there be a monument to his body and sepulcher.[62]

All this theoretical loathing was a stage curtain scarcely disguising the reality of the scene. Homosexuality frequently appears in the Middle Ages, and does not arouse, in practical life, a horror of the evil person. It even inspires poetic themes and gives rise to several songs of derision and slander *(cantigas de escárnio e mal-dizer)* accepted by the contemporary cancioneiros.[63] In one of them, Pero da Ponte attests to the frequency of this practice among the nobles of the court. In its turn the *Cancioneiro Geral* by Garcia de Resende explains some aspects of both masculine and feminine homosexuality, along with masturbation.[64] And the greatest Portuguese chronicler, Fernão Lopes, does not hesitate to cast suspicion upon Pedro I, who loved his squire Afonso Madeira "more than should be spoken of here" and ordered him castrated out of obvious jealousy.[65]

6 : WORK

IN the introduction to Title LXIII of Volume I in the *Afonsine Ordinances,* the three estates of society are defined: "Defenders are one of the three estates which God ordained to maintain the world, quite in the same way that those who pray for the people are called orators, and those who till the soil to raise what men need in order to live and sustain themselves, are called maintainers; thus those who are to defend these two groups are called defenders."

The preceding chapters have dealt especially with aspects of daily life pertinent to the "defenders" (nobility) or to "those who pray" (clergy). In this chapter the "maintainers" (commoners) will receive almost undivided attention. For in theory, only the common people had the duty and indeed the right to work. When, toward the end of the Middle Ages, many nobles, clerics, and even kings were devoting themselves to the lucrative practice of commerce, there was an endless stream of protests from the third estate against this intrusion into their legitimate domain. Just as it was generally forbidden for a villein to enter an order of chivalry—a characteristic of and synonym for nobility —so also the laws pertaining to the nobility expressly forbade the knight to attempt to earn money, removing him from the order "if he publicly engaged in commerce."[1]

Thus only the commoner had to cope with the problem of selecting a profession or of developing its practice. Now the text of the *Ordinances,* reflecting the traditional classification, speaks only of those who "till the soil." It is obvious, however, that the phrase is written with an allegorical meaning. The foods of the soil are the bases of life. Therefore, the plowman or farmer, as the "maintainer" par excellence of mankind, becomes the symbol of the laborer. Nevertheless, the allegory was clothed in a double meaning. In the Middle Ages, agricultural activity monopolized the attention of the majority of the population. Consequently, the farmer had to be considered the outstanding worker, for he was most prominent in the production of goods for consumption.

There was no "class" of plowers or farmers, nor did this term "class" mean in the Middle Ages what it means today. Among those who lived from agriculture, there were many categories. Without speaking of the slaves, whose number was insignificant in the period from the twelfth century to the fifteenth, we may cite the serfs (not the same as the slaves because they were bound to the land they worked and because they could not be separated from it at the lord's whim), tenant farmers, freeholders or inheritors, and a vast group of personal bound laborers such as domestic serfs, house servants, menservants, and others, all included in the generic term *malados*.[2]

In the early days of the Monarchy there were very few villeins— that is, persons who were not nobles and not clergy—who held full ownership of the land which they farmed. That number grew, especially after the mid-fourteenth century, when many burghers of the city began to invest capital in land and to become small or modest rural landowners. Nevertheless, the percentage of rural property fully owned by those who actually worked it remained very small.

Thus the majority of the people cultivated land which did not belong to them, paying a fixed annual rent (either established by a contract of emphyteusis or a contract for a limited number of years) to their lord, whether he was the king, a noble, or the Church. Even those who held an allod, or full ownership, had to pay a tax to the king, although it was lower than that on other lands.

These assessments were generally very high. On the lands leased on a contract of emphyteusis (*a prazo* or *a foro*), the farmer had to pay a base installment payment (the rent) which varied between one-third and one-tenth of his total production. Besides this rent, he was still liable to many other payments varying from land to land: *direitura* (a kind of invariable tax), *eirádega* (a tax on cereals, wine, and other products), *jantar* (a tax originally destined to feed the lord), *jugada* (a tax levied on cultivated fields), labor services, and the usual tithe to the Church. The tithe was deducted before any of the other taxes, as the tenth part of all the fruits produced. The rent and other taxes were based on the remaining nine-tenths. By the contract of sharecropping (*parceria*), the "partner," or sharecropper (*parceiro*)— that is, the direct exploiter of the land—retained only one-fourth to one-half of his produce, not counting the smaller taxes that always existed. On the royal lands, subject to the direct administration of the king's deputies, the farmer had to pay a share of costs, which was estimated at between one-sixth to one-third, though apparently usually falling closer to the latter. Added to this percentage was an infinity of other taxes—*direituras, eirádegas, jantares,* etc.—ordinarily set at a fixed rate.

Without intending to mention all the forms of ownership and taxation on them, it seems that, in general, a small allodial proprietor would never pay less than one-tenth or one-ninth of his total production; and that in the case of inhabitants of royal lands and other kinds of farmers, the total assessment could amount to more than seven-tenths of total production. All this, in short, meant that the situation was distinctly unfavorable for the Portuguese farmer.[3]

Rents and other taxes were paid throughout the year on the day established in the contract. On Easter, on St. John the Baptist's day, on St. Mary's day in August, on St. Michael's in September, and at Christmas, the farmer went to the house of the comptroller's representative—the steward—and gave him the two capons, the dozen eggs, the alqueire (about 33 pounds) of wheat, and the almude (about 33.6 quarts) of wine or of olive oil that the contract for the grant of land or, more simply, tradition had assigned him. When it was a case of rent proportional to production, the farmer generally received a visit from the steward or from the tithe collector of the parish church, who came to his plot of land to ascertain the amount payable. Obviously, the tithe or the rent received often fell short of the amount due, but, there always existed the "control" of neighbors and of the steward, both of whom knew quite well how much had been collected in the grain harvests and the fruit crop and the number of casks of olive oil or of wine.

Payments in money were not rare and increased as the centuries passed. A dinheiro (denier) or a half-maravedi settled the debt paid to the steward. Later on, paying emphyteutic rents and especially lease rents (as the contract of leasing was becoming more generalized) totally in money replaced payment in kind. Sometimes the peasant was given the alternative of paying either in kind or in money, whichever was most convenient for him. If the farmer had gone to the market or the nearest fair and received a few dinheiros for the sale of goats or for measures of millet there, he would probably prefer to pay his rent in cash. But generally he paid in produce.

Labor service, or corvée (Port. *jeira*), was the most onerous form of tribute. Serfs, tenant farmers, small landowning peasants, and even, in certain cases, knight-villeins (cavaleiros-vilãos) were required to spend as many as three days of the week in work away from their own

Fig. 81. Harvesting grain, picking grapes, and making wine. 12th century.

land giving such labor service to their lord or to the king. Some had
to repair fortresses or construct palaces (the services known as
anúduva); others, to haul thatching or sheaves of besom and straw to
cover the roof or the ground floor of the seigniorial mansion; still
others, to furnish labor to the kiln for roofing tile and to the oven for
baking bread; and others, to supply domestic labor in the palace. Less
frequently, assignments properly agrarian—such as sowing, plowing or
harvesting—were required. Until the Reconquest ended, every knight-
villein and part of the foot peasantry were obligated to military service
once a year for military expeditions into Moorish territory. During
this time, work in the fields was left to the women, the aged, and the
incapacitated. Gradually, and moving from north to south, this practice became obsolete. Foray, scutage, and militia were owed now only
if war threatened the country. A tax, similar to the modern "military
tax," was substituted for them otherwise.[4]

   In the day-to-day grind of his work, the farmer probably experienced problems that were not much different from the ones farmers
cope with today. He worried about the good and bad agricultural

years. He fertilized the soil; he plowed it as many times as might be necessary; he sowed; and he reaped using the instruments and techniques which tradition had handed down to him and which have lasted into the twentieth century. He might be concerned about the future of his sons if more than one male survived him, since the land he cultivated was indivisible. The second and third sons had to seek a livelihood somewhere else; they generally found it not too far from their father's land, acquiring some unoccupied estate or more inhospitable stretch of land which they had to clear laboriously for farmland. For a long time, however, the high mortality rate balanced the no less high birthrate, so that problems of "placement" seldom had to be dealt with.

The emphyteuta, or the direct tenant paying a fixed annual rent, along with the small allodial proprietor, constituted the upper class of the population in the country. Many of them were sufficiently well-to-do to possess a horse and weapons of war, which integrated them into the economic-military class of the knight-villein. They frequently lived in small towns and villages, organized in municipalities, which they administered as notables or "goodmen." Under their orders, as under the orders of the king's stewards and of the nobles on the lands which they directly exploited, lived a much more numerous group of serfs and salaried employees who performed the rough and tiring work.

All during the twelfth and thirteenth centuries, the serf of the glebe was winning his freedom and becoming either a sedentary tenant farmer or a day laborer. The latter class especially increases in the fourteenth century, when a genuine floating work force comes into existence in the countryside, offering its labor to whoever needs it or pays the best.

In 1253, these wage earners were formed into a hierarchy of *abegão* (foreman), *mancebo de lavoura* (servant farmer), *azemel* (carter), *cachopo de lavoura* (young boy who helps to farm), *mancebo de vacas* (cowherd), *conhecedor de ovelhas* (shepherd), *conhecedor de porcos* (pig herd), *mancebo de ovelhas ou de porcos* (boy who helps with the sheep and pigs), *cachopo de gado* (boy who helps with the cattle), and *mancebo* (a general handyman).[5] The abegão, who was the person in charge of the overall care of the livestock rather than a true overseer or tenant farmer, received five gold morabitinos, two quarteiros (about 8.5 bushels) of grain—half of which was wheat and half barley—twelve côvados (9.18 yards) of coarse woolen cloth, six varas (7.2 yards) of coarse linen, and two pairs of shoes as his year's wages. This type of salary, in money, cereals, and articles of clothing, persisted with variations, throughout the Middle Ages as a result of the limited monetary

Sowing   Harvesting

Threshing   Cutting grass

Making wine   Feeding hogs

Fig. 82. Farm laborers. 15th century.

circulation and the scant penetration of commerce. The mancebo de lavoura received three libras (which means that he would receive 720 dinheiros of an alloy of silver and copper, since the libra, like the soldo, corresponded to money never actually minted), twenty measures of cereals (half wheat and half barley), and cloth and shoes in the same proportions as the abegão received. The azemel, a sort of carrier, besides being given the same wage in cloth and shoes, received five gold maravedis. The other workers were paid proportionately. The lowest laborer, the mancebo, received thirty soldos (360 dinheiros), a tunic, two shirts, a toque, and two pairs of shoes.

More than a century later, this whole system of salaries had changed. Foremen, hoers, pruners, people who tied grapevines to stakes or poles, men and women who worked in the vineyards, weeders, harvesters of grainfields, and reapers of wheat had their salaries listed every day (the original meaning of *jornal*—a day's pay) and limited to money. Beyond this, they were entitled, at best, to dinner from the landowner. During part of the reign of João I (1385–1433), they again received their wages in measures of wheat or millet, because the devaluation of money prohibited a reliable price scheduling. These modifications reflected the changes in society. In 1253, most foremen, farmers, and farmhands still lived on the land of their lords, even though they worked as salaried employees. They were the genuine servants (*mancipia*) of the countryside. In 1379, the situation had altered, and the day laborer, whose salary is put on a price list, greatly resembled the modern rural proletariat.

All in all, the salary of the rural laborer rose considerably between 1253 and 1379. This phenomenon worried the upper classes and the bourgeoisie and led to a number of laws and municipal ordinances that established maximum salaries and sought to tie the laborers to the lands on which they lived. It can generally be said that there never were salaries unencumbered by laws in Portugal during the Middle Ages. From time to time, either the councilors or the king would remember the coercive principle and revive the old price lists, modifying them as necessary. Nevertheless, the scarcity of laborers overlay all these measures and compelled successive increases in their salaries, mainly in the second half of the fourteenth century and in the beginning of the fifteenth century.

Laborers were also far from having the right to choose their own work. Those who did not have land of their own were obliged to work for a wage on the lands of someone else. Furthermore, the children of those hired for wages could not escape the paternal situation and seek other employment in the cities. The law constained them to hire out for wages as well. Measures of this nature—such as the *sesmarias* law, a law governing land grants and actual soil tilling—sought to avoid a lack of labor and to combat the agricultural crises that had arisen as a result of an inadequate labor force. But laws and ordinances were powerless to forestall the move of a large part of the rural population from the countryside to the city. Servants fled from their masters or preferred to hire out for wages on a weekly basis instead of by the year, as tradition directed, in order to have a greater freedom of movement. Vagabonds and beggars covered the country. In the council of Lisbon and its territory, the right to choose one's own work was completely recognized by the close of the fourteenth century.[6] Later, it is true, restrictions would return.

We generally confine the term "artisan" (*mesteiral*) to the workers in mechanical trades of craftsmanship or industry. But the expression as used in the Middle Ages included, besides these, some lesser tradesmen such as carters, retailers, and butchers; certain rural laborers, such as the millers; and even fishermen.[7]

It is extremely difficult to enumerate all the manual professions which existed in Portugal from the twelfth to the fifteenth century. The "Organization of the Processions of Évora," which dates from the close of the 1400's, provides the following generic chart, although a bare outline, of these jobs and of the hierarchy into they were fit:

> *First*
>   goldsmiths, silversmiths
>   tinsmiths
> *Second*
>   clothshearers
>   candlemakers
> *Third*
>   carpenters and sawyers
>   masons in brick, stone, and mud and plaster; streetpavers;
>   pavers; limemakers; diggers
> *Fourth*
>   potters
>   tilemakers and brickmakers
> *Fifth*
>   cordmakers
>   breechmakers
> *Sixth*
>   saddlers
>   target makers
>   silk spinners

Seventh
  weavers, wool combers, carders
Eighth
  "men of arms":
    barbers
    blacksmiths, farriers
    armorers, cutlers
    harness makers, scabbard makers
    spearmakers
    tinkers
Ninth
  crossbowmen
  gunsmiths
Tenth
  tailors
Eleventh
  cobblers
  curriers and tanners
  men who make leather bottles and wineskins
Twelfth
  draymen
  innkeepers
Thirteenth
  carters
Fourteenth
  fruit dealers, women street vendors, grocers
Fifteenth
  women bakers
Sixteenth
  fishwives
Seventeenth
  kitchen gardeners and orchard tenders
Eighteenth
  butchers and retailers[8]

Some important artisans are missing from this list: the coopers, the ropemakers (perhaps included in the fifth category), the caulkers (there were none in Évora), the coppersmiths (in the eighth category), and the furriers, for instance. Some were subdivided into highly specialized categories. Within the craft of the cobblers were over a dozen subgroups specializing in the manufacture of high-laced boots, shoes properly so called, buskins, open-toed wooden clogs, boots, and so on. Of course, such specialization was to be found only in the large centers of population, such as Lisbon or Oporto.

There were never a great number of craftsmen, if compared with the number of farm laborers. In the mid-fifteenth century in a city like

Fig. 83.   Fishing. 15th century.

Fig. 84. Coopers mending tuns.
15th century.

Lisbon, where maritime commerce and overseas voyages already held
an outstanding place in the economy, there must have been no more
than fifty caulkers. Lisbon had not even a dozen blacksmiths in the first
half of the thirteenth century; there were a few more cobblers—some
three dozen by the end of the century. In 1308, there were slightly more
than fifteen coopers in the capital. These numbers rose to 150, 100,
400, and 180 respectively by the middle of the sixteenth century.
Guimarães, ancient burg and distinguished "industrial" city, reckoned
less than fifty tradesmen, all told, in the third quarter of the fourteenth
century. In Oporto there were some twenty shoemakers in 1401 and
as many coopers in 1486. Two smaller towns show a similar phenomenon: in Alenquer (Estremadura), the craftsmen totaled 12 percent of
the population as against 54 percent made up by farm laborers (end
of the fifteenth century); in Arruda dos Vinhos (Estremadura), only
9 percent of the population were artisans while 80 percent were farm
workers (1369).[9]
    In the cities and in important towns, the crafts were zoned or
grouped by professions on the same streets. Even today the names of

streets have persisted as an excellent illustration of this arrangement. There is the Street of the Cobblers, the Street of the Leather Makers, the Street of the Goldsmiths, and the Street of the Silversmiths, in Lisbon; the Street of the Smithy, the Street of the Cobblers, and the Street of the Shops in Oporto; the Street of the Bakers, the Street of Earthenware, the Street of the Matmakers, and the Street of the Cooperages in Coimbra; the Street of the Tanners and the Street of Leathers in Guimarães. The zoning of professions began to be observed in the twelfth century; it developed especially in the fourteenth century and began to be officially ordered after 1351. But it was never achieved in its entirety.[10] In the middle of the sixteenth century, the public official João Brandão appealed to the king apropos of the New Street of the Merchants in Lisbon:

> Your Highness should order that fourteen types of professions, which further on I will name, may not all be on that street; for just as on the other streets it was thought well to group the craftsmen, from whose profession the street takes its name, this street should appear having everything according to its name. And since the others were entitled to be quite methodically arranged, this ought not to be less deserving than the others, and especially as there is as much space in the city and streets as there is.[11]

The zoning of the crafts had begun by being the rule of the artisans themselves before becoming an obligatory principle decreed by the councils. By gathering on the same street, the craftsmen in each profession felt better protected against possible violences and abuses; and they mutually watched over each other in the quality and quantity of the products, the prices for which they were sold, and the methods used in attracting customers. Zoning also made the customers' search easier. Later, the process came to facilitate supervision by the aldermen and the collection of excise taxes, besides, as a royal letter of 1385 justifies, working toward the "good organization and greater beauty and stateliness of the city [Lisbon]." [12]

Thus, on the principal streets of Lisbon and Oporto, different masters plied the same trade in shops lined side by side, displaying at their doors the same products and quarreling with each other over the clientele. The shop, either owned by the master craftsmen or rented, was simultaneously a factory, and customers could often oversee for themselves the quality of the work and the final touch given the article, whether it was a pair of shoes or a barrel for wine. In time of war, shops might even become weapon depots. Toward the end of the fourteenth century, the municipality of Évora ordered that "henceforth all the shoemakers, doublet makers, tailors, goldsmiths, armorers, swordmakers, cutlass makers, and oil lamp makers, and in like manner all the other artisans, may each have his shield and lance where he works, and the merchants have lances in their shops, and so soon as they may hear any calling or shouts and noise, they will immediately run out with their arms at the first hint of trouble and help to capture the criminals." [13]

Each shop constituted a small artisan unit. Factories in the modern style where hundreds or thousands of laborers work under the orders of a boss did not exist. If the population multiplied and a single shop was no longer sufficient for the increase in consumption, the remedy was in the opening of a new shop and not in the expansion of the first one. In this series of artisan cells, the house and the tools belonged to the master, generally rented to him by the king or by a great lord (later on we will find affluent proprietary burgesses; they are the ancestors of the great industrialists of the modern age). Under the orders of the master worked the laborers (*obreiros*) or journeymen (*sergentes*), numbering two or three, rarely more than half a dozen. Lastly, apprentices (*aprendizes*) or young boys helped and ran errands. The master or the apprentices probably attended to the customers. Even in the mid-sixteenth century, the average number of occupants of each Lisbon shop in any of the various professions was three or four persons.[14]

For an example, let us look into a workshop of a blacksmith in Évora in the last quarter of the fourteenth century. A master needed one workday to forge a quintal (a hundredweight) of iron into eleven or twelve iron plows, or eight hoes, or sixteen dozen horseshoes with their respective nails. Two men—the journeymen—hammered the iron, while a fourth—the bellows treader, certainly still an apprentice— "played" the bellows. A youth called the *ganha-dinheiros* (coin earner) brought in the iron, firewood, and coal for the forge; the water to cool the metal; and finally stacked up the horseshoes or the nails. The smithy therefore occupied five persons. (See Table 4.) It is interesting to note, by the way, that almost all the blacksmiths in the city were Jews and Moslems.[15]

The supervision and regulation of the trades developed gradually after the twelfth century. In Portugal, corporations did not exist before the end of the fifteenth century, and the regulation of the crafts took place only in the two centuries following. Nevertheless, it is possible to find certain traces of organization. Besides the already mentioned street zonings—the basis of the whole future structure—the workshops formed brotherhoods of a religious nature after the first quarter of the thirteenth century. For a long time it was not obligatory for the artisan to join the brotherhood of his trade, although it may be supposed that most did so. The brotherhood afforded practical advantages, such as protection in case of illness, many times a special hospital (an asylum or an inn, it is understood), besides manifesting the religious and charitable sentiments of the time.[16] Probably only the master were allowed to join. Later, adherence became practically compulsory, and the initial spirit of the brotherhood was gradually lost.

In the last quarter of the fifteenth century, a brotherhood of seamen existed in Oporto. In a meeting of the Council,

> by the aforesaid masters it was told the aforementioned magistrates and officials and good men that they knew how they, the brotherhood of St. Peter, did each year on the day of Corpus Christi the best that they could for the honor of the said feast. And that in the aforesaid city lived some sailors who did not wish to contribute to the aforementioned brotherhood, as they were obligated to do and as was customary. That they requested that, inasmuch as the said sailors enjoyed the privileges that were rendered to all, that they [the Council] constrain them to pay [their dues] to the aforementioned brotherhood. And if they did not wish to pay, that henceforth they might not enjoy those said privileges, and might lose their privileges.

The council decided that all the mariners listed as members on the roll kept by the steward of the brotherhood were obliged to pay the dues and participate in the procession.[17]

These arrangements bring us to a discussion of privileges, another cause of the future corporative organization. The object of each master artisan was to enjoy the privileges that exempted him from various grievances of an economic and military nature. Among them were the duty of providing lodging to nobles (*aposentadoria*), of yielding horses whenever necessary, of paying extraordinary taxes (*pedidos*), of being detached to accompany levies of prisoners or to transport money over long distances, of being recruited as a crossbowman for the army, and of being obliged to accept guardianships or trusteeships against his will. Some master craftsmen, directly connected to the court or to influential persons, received such charters of privilege as personal grants. But collective privileges could be achieved only by the assemblage of the men of a particular trade into a relatively homogeneous group. There were still other privileges that varied from profession to profession, such as exemption from payment of the transfer tax on materials or on imports and exports. In the last third of the fourteenth century, King Fernando granted exemption from price-fixing (*almota-çaria*) of their wages to the caulkers and shipwrights of the royal dockyards (the royal magazines at the quay) of Lisbon. In the mid-fifteenth century, a charter exempted from payment of the transfer tax all the contract work undertaken by the carpenters of the River Bank of Lisbon for manufacture of ships. A royal charter of privilege to three hundred carpenters of the same Bank dates from the close of the century. In 1455, up to forty caulkers in Lisbon were exempted from paying extraordinary taxes, a privilege later extended to Viana, Faro, and Vila do Conde.[18]

Of course, there were rules governing whether an artisan could title himself a caulker or a carpenter and become a member of the group included in the royal privilege. There was always a representative of the king who "examined" the candidates and decided whether they had the qualifications to be accepted in the trade. This examination in Portugal corresponded to the famous test of a masterpiece that elevated the journeyman to a master in other countries.

The regulation of this examination became detailed in time. Toward the end of the fourteenth century, there was already in the royal ship-yards a master of carpentry among whose responsibilities was that of examining the naval carpenters and giving them the certificate of confirmation. Only afterwards did they petition the monarch for a

Fig. 85. Shipbuilding in Caminha, at the mouth of the Minho. Early 16th century.

charter of appointment as a carpenter of the royal magazines.[19] At the end of the fifteenth century, this "curriculum" was obligatory for all master artisans who wanted to work for the State.

At least from the fifteenth century on, the most important trades in terms of numbers of craftsmen had elected or appointed representives, generally two of them. They were known as controllers (*vedores*). In 1379 in Évora we find controllers of the tailors of multi-hued textiles, controllers over the tailors in linen cloth, controllers of the shoe-makers, and an attorney (*procurador*) of the Moorish shoemakers, all of them apparently elected. In Oporto by the beginning and in the middle of the fifteenth century, however, there were already controllers appointed by the municipal council: thus the controller of the coopers, the controller of the ropemakers, and the controller and marker of the tinsmiths. The functions of the controllers were varied. They gave advice on the scheduling of prices proposed by the councils or by the king; they guaranteed good order within their trade; they represented the trade before the authorities. In 1412, the council of Oporto decided that supervision should be established over the cobblers, tailors, weavers, and blacksmiths to control the prices of their respective products. For this purpose, a person from each trade was summoned, "from those who you understand are of the best qualities," to discuss the agreement to be established with the council. This was the begin-ning of the compulsory inspectorship that João II officially decreed in 1487: each trade was to have two controllers, "so that they might meditate on the grievances and differences which might occur, espe-cially in the application of the taxes." [20]

From a union of the various elements mentioned above came the regulations (*regimentos*) of the mechanical professions. The first known dates from 1489 and refers to the cobblers—whether makers of boots, shoes, thick-soled ladies' shoes, or clogs—and tanners in Lisbon, who already owned the hospital of St. Vicente, where it was customary for them to assemble. This regulation established that

(1) no master could employ a journeyman or apprentice except at the usual salary paid weekly;
(2) no master could cut sheepskin, black or dyed, except for the manu-facture of house slippers, and provided he gave its work to "boys up to ten years old";
(3) no master could permit work to be executed without his knowledge and verification;
(4) no one could buy leather except tanned and in bundles;
(5) no master engage apprentices for money, but only by time: a boy

ten to twelve years old or less, for a period of four years; a boy
more than twelve years old, for a period of three years;

.   .   .   .

(7) no journeyman or apprentice could set up his own shoe shop without apprising the controllers and judges ordered by the trade to
examine samples of his work.[21]

Sometimes abuses in the verification of the competency of the
"mechanic artisans" (a name generally given to all the craftsmen) were
recorded. Before the precise regulations of the sixteenth century, the
aldermen of the councils interfered in the examination, disregarding
the representatives of the trades appointed as examiners. Évora complains to João II of such occurrences in the Cortes of 1481: "Your
people are wronged by the chief alderman, because having, as they
have, a charter from your father, may he be in holy glory, by which
he orders that the mechanic artisans be examined by the examiners
whom the city prescribes, as they have ordered, . . . he, the chief alderman, wants the said craftsmen to be examined by himself and by the
officials whom he orders, who do not know anything about it." [22]

Outside interference was even more to be dreaded in the fixing of
prices. Usually, each council established municipal ordinances to prevent the rise of prices. From time to time, they modernized them
because prices had to rise, or the clamor of the persons whose interests
were affected would have become intolerable. Sometimes the king
intervened in the price-scheduling, fixing general prices for the kingdom or part of it.

Nevertheless, before the second half of the fourteenth century, the
principle of freedom in prices was frequently observed. It must be
noted that the price schedulings, proposed and decided by the goodmen, or notables, of the municipalities or by the functionaries of the
court, were generally applied to the products of craftsmanship. Cereals,
wine, olive oil, and other agricultural produce, whose commerce en-
riched the goodmen, seem to have almost always been excluded from
the lists.

Not just the "industrial" articles were taxed. This control also fell
over the salaries. The percentages of "profit" that each master was to
receive for his manufactured article were rigorously regulated; the
salaries of the journeymen and the apprentices as well as of the rural
day laborers were fixed.

Some of these regulations are of great interest because they allow us
to know, in detail, such things as the formation of the costs of production for various articles and the percentages granted to the remunera-

tion of labor costs. Around 1480, in the prices of some types of shoes, the materials absorbed between 68 and 78 percent, the remaining 22 to 32 percent being allotted for the remuneration of the labor. In horseshoes and other iron objects, 78 percent of the cost went to materials (including taxes), and 22 percent, to labor. For doublets, on the other hand, the materials required took 90 percent of the cost. And in products of the saddlers (reins, bridles for horses, harnesses, whips, sword scabbards, sword belts), 79 to 91 percent of the price went for material.[23] Labor costs included capital and work. The master was remunerated like any journeyman, receiving additionally what was called *ganho e cabedal* (profit and capital), in consideration for the workshop and the equipment that he owned. This surplus was fixed, varying therefore in its proportion relative to the work required: it could be one-half, one-fourth, one-sixth, one-eighteenth, and so on. On rare occasions, there was a small profit to round out excessively complicated sums. The artisans who worked for the court—for example, those who made footwear and clothing—received the greatest profits.[24]

The numbers which we have for the end of the fourteenth century confirm a division of the costs in a similar proportion.

In "industry," the situation could be quite different. The manufacture of roofing tile, for example, required a small expenditure for material but an enormous one for the number of workers needed, whose activity was necessary for several days. Women came in to help their husbands and to earn part of their salaries. For example, in 1380 in order to make a batch of 10,000 tiles, six men and eleven women had to work ten days making the tile and another two and a half days molding and baking it; the resulting expenditures are shown in Table 2. The bill itemizing the total cost of tile manufacturing might be presented as shown in Table 3. On the other hand, the bill for the manufacture of iron articles (eight-pound plows) might be presented as shown in Table 4.

The techniques employed by Portuguese artisans did not vary greatly during the Middle Ages. Some practices even persisted without major alterations until the twentieth century. There is ample documentation on the processes used in the manufacture of clothing, footwear, leather belts and straps, articles of iron and steel, pottery, and many other objects.

Artisans and rural laborers generally worked from sunrise to sunset. They were supposed to rest on Sunday, but there are many examples of violations of the Sunday rest. The Jews always tried to keep the

TABLE 2
Cost of Labor in Tilemaking, 1380
(per 10,000 tiles)

Type of work	Man-hours required		Salaries[a]	
	Men	Women	Men[b]	Women[c]
Tilemaking	30	30	10.10.10	4.10.0
Baking	6	30	2. 2. 0	4.10.0
Total	36	60	12.12. 0	9. 0.0
Total, all salaries[d]			22.7.0	

[a] In Portuguese libras, soldos, and dinheiros (1£ = 20s. = 240d.).
[b] At the rate of 7s. per day for master craftsmen.
[c] At the rate of 3s. per day.
[d] Includes 15s. for unknown items.
Source: *Documentos Historicos da Cidade de Evora*, ed. Gabriel Pereira (Evora, 1885–91), pt. 1, pp. 141–42.

TABLE 3
Cost of Manufacturing Tile, 1380
(per 10,000 tiles)

Item	Cost	Percentage of total cost
	£. s. d.	
Labor and other costs	*37. 9. 3*	*83.2%*
Labor[a]	22. 7. 0	
Other costs[b]	15. 2. 3	
Materials and breakage	*7. 10. 9*	*16.8*
Firewood[c]	3. 7. 6	
Breakage (1,000)[d]	2. 19. 3	
Tools	0. 14. 0	
Use of oven	0. 10. 0	
Total	*45. 0. 0*	*100.0*
Cost per thousand	4. 10. 0[e]	
Cost per tile	0. 0. 1.08	

[a] See Table 2.
[b] The rough reckoning estimation, the sales tax (*sisa*), and other unspecified items.
[c] Fifteen loads at 4½s. per load.
[d] Based on the estimate that approximately one-tenth of each batch of tiles would be lost through breakage.
[e] Raised to £5 in 1382.
Source: *Doc. Hist. Evora*, pt. 1, pp. 141–42.

TABLE 4
Cost of Forging a Hundredweight of Iron, 1380
(for iron plows)

Item	Cost			Percentage of total cost
	£.	s.	d.	
Labor[a]	2.	12.	0	23.2%
Materials and				
other expenses	8.	9.	10	76.8
Iron[b]	7.	0.	0	
Coal (8 sacks)	1.	4.	0	
Sales tax	0.	3.	6	
Firewood (3 loads)	0.	1.	0	
Transportation[c]	0.	1.	0	
"Avoirdupois"[d]	0.	0.	4	
Total	11.	1.	10	100.0
Cost per iron plow	0.	18.	6	

[a] Distributed as follows:

Salary for two hammerers	1. 4. 0
Salary for the master craftsman with tools and house	1. 0. 0
Salary for one bellows blower	0. 8. 0

[b] One hundredweight (a quintal) yielded twelve plows.
[c] Paid to the "coin earner"; see above, p. 193.
[d] A tax levied according to weight.
Source: *Doc. Hist. Evora,* pt. 1, pp. 147–48.

Sabbath, often obliging Christian subordinates to work on Sundays. In the beginning of the fifteenth century, it was decreed in Oporto that artisans might not work from sunset on Saturday until sunrise on Monday. Fishermen were forbidden to go out on the sea before Monday morning, but in 1406, those of Lisbon were permitted to move their departure up to Sunday at the Ave Marias. And in 1456, the Pope acquiesced, even to allowing them to fish for sardines on Sundays and holy days, except on the principal feasts of Jesus Christ and Our Lady. The sale of meat, wine, and bread was prohibited on Sundays until after the people had been to mass.[25]

The holy days were equally respected, sometimes even more rigorously, even though they were very numerous. In the fourteenth and fifteenth centuries, the principal feasts observed throughout the country (besides the local cults) were the following:

Circumcision	January 1
Epiphany	January 6
St. Vincent	January 22

St. Brás	February 3
Holy Thursday	variable
Good Friday	variable
Holy Saturday	variable
Annunciation	March 25
St. Catherine	April 1
St. Antão	April 4
St. George	April 23
Finding of the Holy Cross	May 3
Ascension Thursday	variable
Corpus Christi	variable
St. Anthony	June 13
St. John	June 24
St. Peter and St. Paul	June 29
St. Mary Magdalene	July 22
Santiago (St. James)	July 25
St. Mary of August	August 15
St. Laurence	September 5
All Saints Day	November 1
Christmas	December 25

Some of the holidays were purely judicial and were not observed by the farmer or the artisan. Such was also the case with the three days before and the two days after Pentecost, the week following Christmas, Easter week and Low Sunday week, all the feasts of Christ and Our Lady, from the middle of July to August 15 and from the last week of September until the end of the third week of October.[26]

Commercial life, at least for those in subordinate positions, was as regulated as that of the mechanic artisans. But it is necessary to remember, as we have observed before, that the greater part of the smaller merchants (sellers of meat, vendors of fruit, etc.) were included within the class of artisans.

The regulation of the markets continually absorbed the city councils and gave rise to a great number of city ordinances. The various commodities were also zoned: around 1380, the council of Évora decided there should be three streets for the sale of meat at retail; on one, goats and kids should be sold, on another, ewes and lambs, and on the third, rams. After the slaughtering in the city corral (at least thirty head per day were required for consumption in Évora), the meat went to the butcher's shop, where it was cut up. From there it went to the market. In the meat market on Saturdays, Sundays, and Thursdays, there were open butchers' chopping blocks, two for beef and two for mutton.

A curious detail: it was ordered that the heads of the animals should not be separated from their bodies until all the meat had been sold. And the butchers and retailers were required to refrain from bloating the meat displayed for sale.[27] Vegetables, fruits, and potherbs were not to be sold in the public square, but rather in stands assigned for that purpose in the location designated. The residents of each city or town had first priority over itinerant peddlers in the assignment of these vending stands.

The lack of a standard of weights and measures led to amazing variations from council to council and to the constant necessity for comparison. In Évora at the end of the fourteenth century, the council decreed a monthly comparison of the measures of cereals, salt, wine, olive oil, and honey; of the varas (1 vara = 3.6 feet) of textiles; and of the weights of metals, meats, soap, etc. For these latter items, the goldsmith—surveyor of weights and measures for the council—was the person entrusted with determining the standards of the arroba (approximately 33 pounds), the half-arroba, the quarter-arroba, and the arratel (one pound).[28]

Bread had to be sold by weight and not by measure.[29] The bakers charged with making and selling it were generally women, just as were most of the vendors of fruit, potherbs, and vegetables. None of these were included, obviously, in the classification of artisans.

Also excluded from it were numerous men and women street vendors who went from door to door offering their products: laundresses; manual laborers and wage earners, who became quite important at times, such as those of Lisbon and Oporto who did the work of stowers; street cleaners and unloaders of garbage; women helpers in various

Fig. 86.   Peddler. Early 16th century.

trades; ragpickers; and so many others that in numbers they exceeded those of the master artisans and and the burghers and corresponded, in the cities and villages, to the mass of tenant farmers, serfs, and day laborers of the rural environment. There were also retailers and street vendors who brought commodities by the gross to then sell them retail, for themselves or for someone else.

About them we know very little even yet; just as paradoxically, we know little about the true bourgeoisie, the elite of the working world, the urban equivalents, in Lisbon and Oporto, of the provincial knight-villeins. The greatest merchants were those in textiles. They were the most affluent, the most respected, and the most numerous within their class. The merchants in dyed cloth (imported from abroad) were distinguished from the merchants in linen, the merchants in silk, the merchants in wool, and the *marceiros* (traders of thread, ribbons, and other items related to cloth). There were also merchants who exported and imported cereals, fruits, weapons, and military supplies, and manufactured a variety of articles. Frequently, they engaged in several of these activities at the same time.

Their role in the hierarchical society of that period is seen quite well by their place in the procession of Corpus Christi: they walked immediately before the scribes, and apothecaries, and the notaries. Practicing their business without hindrances, exempt from the regulations of the artisans, enjoying privileges that they could buy with the fortune they had saved, the merchants elude documentation, which is preoccupied with the bylaws and statutes of labor and municipal ordinances. On the other hand, not reaching the degree of merit that might make them worthy of mention, they generally escape the attention of the chroniclers. These are the reasons why their activity becomes so difficult to analyze.

Apothecaries, physicians, scribes, notaries, teachers, and judges constituted another class, the intelligentsia of the late Middle Ages, in which were placed the public functionaries of the period as well: judges of the court of appeals, magistrates, judges of civil and criminal courts, attorneys, royal scribes, bailiffs, town criers, accountants, controllers, stewards, bailiffs, and jailers; besides all the officialdom of the councils (judges, councilmen, aldermen, attorneys, castle commanders); and, finally, the important offices of the administration and the army, belonging as a rule to members of the nobility—castle governors, commanders, captains, hunters, chamberlains, controllers of the treasury, and so on.[30] Their total number was not more than a few hundred before the end of the fifteenth century. The personnel of the court—

youths of the chamber; chapel boys; boys of stirrup and hunt; yeomen of the wardrobe; crossbowmen of the council; men of the arsenal; youths of the treasury and accounts; butlers; those in charge of the linen of the royal household, of storage of venison, of storehouses for furniture, kitchens, and others; the chief cooks; the cooks' helpers; etc.—did not number many more than a hundred either.[31]

The majority of learned people were clerics, many with minor orders only, but belonging by right and in fact to the ecclesiastical world. Yet, particularly from the thirteenth century onwards, the number of noncleric bureaucrats and royal counselors grew rapidly. In the fifteenth century this situation was greatly modified, laymen sharing more and more in the tasks of administration.

Civil servants and the personnel of the royal household were paid monthly or yearly. Their salary was in money, besides, many times, cloth and grain. A youth of the chamber earned no more than a blacksmith's helper, but he also received free housing, bed, and board. The chief cook earned approximately as much as the master saddler, but surpassed him in actual wages because of the extra gratuities.

In work schedules, the public official had a great advantage over the craftsman. The number of hours varied with the duty, but it could be as few as four, as was the case with the personnel of the Exchequer (Casa dos Contos), who were obligated to be present only between six and ten o'clock in the morning during the summer, and eight to eleven o'clock in wintertime. Just the same, absences and abuses were recorded. When old age arrived, the official received complete retirement and continued to enjoy the privileges inherent to the office.[32]

From the figures given in Table 5, the reader can ascertain the similarities and differences of some prices and salaries in the thirteenth, fourteenth, and fifteenth centuries.

TABLE 5
Prices and Salaries in Portugal in the Late Middle Ages[a]

	1253		1379–81		1480	
	Soldos	Grams of silver	Soldos	Grams of silver	White reais	Grams of silver
Prices						
Alqueire of wheat	2	2	40	20.8	15	1.8
Alqueire of barley	1	1	25	13	8	0.9
Mantle[b]	3	3	9	4.6	20	2.4
Tunic or doublet[b]	1.5	1.5	7	3.6	40	4.8

TABLE 5—*Continued*

	1253		1379–81		1480	
	Soldos	Grams of silver	Soldos	Grams of silver	White reais	Grams of silver
Prices						
Pair of boots	—	—	30	15.6	80	9.6
Pair of shoes	4	4	14	7.2	30	3.6
Quintal of iron	—	—	240	124.8	600	72
Horseshoes (4)	2.5	2.5	5	2.6	19	2.2
Horse harness (complete set)	240	230	—	—	100	12
Sack of coal	—	—	3	1.5	16	1.8
Vara of linen	3	3	—	—	17	2
Côvado of good foreign cloth	20	20	—	—	300	36
Mark of silver	240[c]	230	440	230	1,896	230
Mark of gold	1,760[d]	0	4,400	0	20,952	0
Approximate salaries per work day						
Master blacksmith	—	—	20	10.4	40	4.8
Master saddler	—	—	—	—	40	4.8
Master tailor	—	—	—	—	25	3
Journeyman blacksmith	—	—	12	6.3	25	3
Master carpenter	—	—	10	5.2	—	—
Journeyman carpenter	—	—	4	2	—	—
Master mason	5	5	10	5.2	—	—
Hoer or foreman	0.5	0.5	4	2	—	—
Chief palace chef[e]	—	—	—	—	33	4
Court barber[f]	—	—	—	—	21.6	2.6
Youth of the king's chamber[g]	—	—	—	—	15.5	1.8

[a] See Table 2 for an explanation of the soldo. White reais (*reais brancos*) were equivalent to soldos in the late fifteenth century; the currency system was as follows: 1 gold cruzado = 20 leais = 400 reais brancos = 4000 reais pretos.

The medieval measures used are as follows: alqueire = approx. 33 lb.; quintal = hundredweight; vara = 3.6 ft.; côvado = 27.5 in.; mark = 230 grams.

[b] Work only.

[c] 12 libras.

[d] 88 libras.

[e] Monthly salary in 1480 of 1,000 reais brancos.

[f] Monthly salary in 1480 of 650 reais brancos.

[g] Monthly salary in 1480 of 466 reais brancos.

Sources: The data for 1253 was taken from the 1253 law of price regulations, published in João Pedro Ribeiro, *Dissertações Chronologicas e Criticas sobre a Historia e Jurisprudencia Ecclesiastica e Civil de Portugal*, 2nd ed., III, pt. 2 (Lisbon, 1857), 66–67; that for 1379–81 was drawn primarily from *Doc. Hist. Evora*, pts. 1–3; and that for 1480, from *Livro Vermelho de D. Affonso V*, Ineditos de Historia Portugueza, III (Lisbon, 1793), pp. 507–12.

7 : FAITH

THE role that religion played in the life of medieval man was of much more significance than it is in the life of modern man. His whole day-to-day existence, from birth to the tomb, unfolded under its influence. This was not because he had a more intense faith or a more profound belief in God. It was because he felt less revulsion at the thought of subordination to supernatural beings. As a consequence of scientific ignorance, most of the events which governed human existence were attributed to hidden forces, and the world, from its beginning until its end, was explained in terms of Christianity. It also had to fill the life of each man, from presiding at his birth, through his growth, until his death. Religion imposed itself because it was more necessary.

On the eighth day after his birth, the child was baptized. Both nobles and peasants followed this custom. The baptism was performed in the church by a priest, except in case of an emergency. There were generally three godparents *(compadres)*—two men and a woman if the child were a boy, two women and a man if it were a girl. For royal baptisms, this number might be increased: thus, for Prince João, future João II, who was carried with great pomp to the Cathedral of Lisbon to be baptized (mid-fifteenth century), Henry the Navigator and the Prior of Crato, Vasco de Ataíde, acted as godfathers; and Princesss Catarina, the Marquise of Vila Viçosa, and Beatriz de Vilhena, wife of Diogo Soares, were godmothers. (It is true that another version assigns to the Prince only the three godparents prescribed by the rules of the Church: these were the Duke of Bragança, the Prior of Crato, and Beatriz de Vilhena.) Finally, the priest who performed the baptism and the husbands and wives of the godfathers and godmothers were considered godparents of the child as well. In all, therefore, the minimum number of three could easily be raised to seven.[1]

The baptism involved a complete ritual that did not change very much as the centuries passed. It was celebrated by parties and banquets, in accordance with the social position of the family. At the baptism of Prince João,

Prince Fernando, brother of the King, carried the Prince in his arms up to the Cathedral, covered with a canopy of cloth of gold which was carried by Pedro de Meneses, Count of Vila Real, and Vasco de Ataíde, the Prior of Crato, who walked in front, and Fernando, Count of Arraiolos (whom the King made the Marquis of Vila Viçosa a few days later), and Fernando, his oldest son (who afterwards became Count of Arraiolos), who walked behind. Fernando de Meneses carried the saltcellar, and the pitcher and basin as the offering were brought by Leonel de Lima (whom King Afonso later made Viscount of Vila Nova da Cerveira with the title of "Dom" for himself and his son João de Lima).[2]

The sacrament of confirmation, along with baptism, penance, communion, and extreme unction, was included in the list of obligatory sacraments for each devout person. The imposition of the holy oils could be received at a very tender age, however. Thus it is that King Duarte in 1435 decides "to order the holy oil sprinkled on his children with great solemnity and magnificence, and great feasts having been commanded and large expenditures paid for this purpose, with the Princes and the principal people of the kingdom gathering on the designated day." This, in spite of the fact that his eldest daughter, Princess Filipa, was but five years old, the future King Afonso V was only three, and Prince Fernando was just two.[3]

Even before reaching the age of reason the child submitted to a new religious ritual, for which a blessing and special prayers were prescribed: the first haircut.[4]

Christian instruction followed. The Church recommended the teaching of the catechism to small children. Monks and friars were especially in charge of this task. A great number of Christians, however, grew up with only a scant knowledge of the most elementary precepts of their faith. Consequently, it was impressed upon the priests that during the mass on Sundays and on holy days, they should recite slowly and distinctly the Our Father, the Hail Mary, and the Creed, and that during Advent and Lent, they should do the same for the Ten Commandments, the works of mercy, the mortal sins, the sacraments, and the theological and cardinal virtues.[5] Even so, religious training was so neglected in different parts of the realm that in the mid-sixteenth century the action of the Bishop of Lamego within his diocese was singled out for praise:

> For there is no boy or girl, either in the villages or in the city, even including those who wander with the livestock up in the mountain, who do not know the Our Father and Hail Mary and the Creed and Salve Regina and the commandments, and assist at mass; so that the children teach their fathers and mothers, and this is done in the bishopric of Your Lordship, by the teachers and primers which Your Lordship ordered

placed in every church of your bishopric, so that every day at dusk they make all the boys and girls of the parish come, and they teach them. The which is a very holy work, for there is no one who does not rejoice to see the instruction and the knowledge of the children, especially in the villages and mountains, where they did not even know the Our Father until Your Lordship ordered them to be taught.[6]

The Fourth Lateran Council (1215) had made it obligatory for all the faithful to receive the Communion of the Body of Christ on Easter every year under pain of excommunication and of privation of ecclesiastical burial. Christians who had reached the age of reason were moreover invited to "confess in private and in sincerity all their sins to their own priest at least once every year." [7] These obligations were expressed in several Portuguese ecclesiastical texts in the Middle Ages: the faithful should be confessed sometime between Epiphany Sunday and the beginning of Lent, and take communion on Easter Sunday. Nevertheless, more frequent use of the two sacraments was recommended. In 1385, the city council of Lisbon asked their archbishop to force the people of his diocese to confess themselves three times a year, at least: at the beginning of Advent, the beginning of Lent, and two weeks before Pentecost. A fourteenth-century penitential believed it an obligation to take communion on Christmas Day, Holy Thursday, Easter Sunday, Pentecost, and the feast of Corpus Christi. By no means was attendance at the eucharistic table as frequent as it is today. A devout person like Constable Nuno Álvares, for example, received communion only four times a year: at Christmas, at Easter, at Pentecost, and on the feast of the Assumption of Our Lady.[8]

There was practically no variation in the form of these two sacraments. Confession was heard in secret, generally by one's personal confessor in the respective parish. Communion was administered in the form of the Host in churches, just as it is today.

The penances received in that period did vary greatly from those of today, both in type and in quantity. Penitentials surviving from the Middle Ages give us an idea of the frequency of the sins committed and the vehemence of the punishments. These were so harsh sometimes "that some penitents preferred to enter monasteries; for the religious life, considered a second baptism, relieved them of some of the obligations inflicted." The most violent penalties included fifteen years of penitence, with a prohibition from receiving the sacraments, along with fastings and continual mortifications. This was imposed on incestuous sodomites (sin of homosexuality with one's brother), those who practiced copulation with animals, incestuous heterosexuals, the

burners of churches, and assassins of priests unless there were extenu-
ating circumstances. Ecclesiastical sodomites incurred punishments that
ranged from seven to fourteen years in accordance with the position
of the cleric. Willful homicide earned between seven and ten years;
if the victim was the murderer's wife, he could never again drink wine
or cider, take a bath, ride a horse, or participate in group amusements.
Violation of the fourth commandment—honoring one's parents—and
theft of religious ornaments were punished with seven years. Thefts of
other natures drew penances lasting from one to two years. If, however,
the cause of the theft had been hunger, the penalty was only two days'
fasting. Other, lighter sins were judged indulgently: "If someone
bathes in a bath with women and sees them nude, and even if it is
his own wife, he must fast for two days on bread and water." Sexual
relations during the periods proscribed by the Church required between twenty and forty days' fasting. In the general definition of the
sins, there were "sins of the ears," that is, listening to trivial songs
being sung, not hearing the hours of God with total devotion, and
so on. He sinned through taste who "became repulsive in eating or in
drinking, as Saint Bernard says, opening his mouth very widely or
smacking his lips, like an animal, or spilling the foods or the wine on
himself or on the table, or repulsively sticking his whole hand or all
his fingers into the bowl, or returning the chewed bread to it, or smear-
ing the rim of his glass with grease, or vilely dirtying the cloth." Thus,
one quite civilizing function of the Church in the fourteenth century
was the inclusion of unrefined behavior in the series of offenses
requiring penance and correction. One could also sin through smell
by "taking carnal pleasure in smelling spices or potions or flowers or
herbs or foods or other things with a good scent, not out of praise to
God, but for immoderate sensual pleasure," and by placing "such
corporeal scents on the reliquaries or on the vestments or on the other
ecclesiastical things for any worldly intention."

Almost all the penances could, however, be discharged by prayers or
by alms. Forty psalms prayed on one's knees, or seventy prayed on foot,
accompanied by the charity of giving a poor person food to eat,
equalled one day spent fasting on bread and water. Five dinheiros
performed the same redemptive service. Even the vows of pilgrimage
(except to Jerusalem) could be redeemed by alms, through the approval
of the bishop.9

This possibility had a double consequence. On the one hand, it
facilitated absolution for wealthy sinners, who constantly distributed
considerable sums of money to the poor and to the coffers of the

churches. On the other hand, it constrained the great mass of devout commoners to prayer, obliging them to haunt the churches and ask pardon from God. In the former case, it was a means of enriching the clergy and promoting assistance to the poor. In the second, it accustomed people to attendance at churches, to the practice of devotions, and to the rejection of deep-rooted pagan habits.

Medieval man was much more subject to the danger of imminent death than is modern man. Hence the custom, sanctioned by diocesan rules, of confession to lay persons (even to women) in moments of danger when no priest was present (without the sacramental character, it only manifested contrition). In a skirmish with the Moors during the first half of the fifteenth century, the Portuguese were in grave danger, in spite of the bravery of their captain, Duarte de Meneses. "But although the strength of the captain might be so great, . . . there was none, however brave he might be, to whom it did not appear that he was closer to death than life; so withdrawing two by two, some confessed and others commended their souls and possessions to those who might escape alive." [10]

Attendance at mass and other ceremonies of the Church,* fasts and abstinences, and pilgrimages reflected the religiosity of the medieval Portuguese more than receiving the sacraments.

Hearing mass was one of the most common practices in the Middle Ages. The churches, especially those in cities, were filled every morning by a multitude derived from the several classes, which, if not devout, at least was disciplined in the performance of a social duty. There were an abundance of church feasts, and the private veneration of the saints was widespread. Masses in honor of particular saints were well attended. Kings and mighty lords heard mass daily. This practice, however, varied with the times. In the middle of the fourteenth century, for example, attendance at masses, at least by the nobility, was neglected. Constable Nuno Álvares, who was later beatified, heard two masses each weekday and three on Saturdays and Sundays, "which was a good example in Portugal, especially to those in the Palace, for before he did so, few attended them." In the early fourteenth century, Queen Saint Isabel also heard mass officiated and sung daily. From the Regiment of the Royal Chapel ordered by King Duarte (1433–38), we must conclude that the monarch heard mass every day. One of

* These included rituals and blessings for the first harvest, the new fruits, a newly completed building or well, and so on. Similar ceremonies, of course, are still observed today.

the obligations of the boys in the chapel consisted in asking the ruler, every night, where and at what hour he wished to hear mass on the following day.

The length of masses varied greatly. At the minimum, it took half an hour for a mass to be said; however, high masses, which could not take less than an hour, were very frequent. Clearly, the sermon was in addition to this. The time that nobles and commoners spent in church during the year compels admiration. It is not surprising that a queen such as Philippa of Lancaster in the last years of her life (early fifteenth century) should spend the greater part of the day in the chapel or in church: "For as soon as it was morning, she immediately went to the church, where she stayed until noon, and as soon as she had eaten and taken a little rest, she subsequently returned to her prayers," the chronicler tells us. He continues later: "The greater part of her pre-occupation was in praying, and every day she prayed the canonical hours according to the practice at Salisbury, and the hours of Our Lady, and the prayers of the dead, and the seven psalms along with many other devotions, and she often prayed the entire Psalter, and certain vigils at other hours." Saint Isabel and even Nuno Álvares proceeded in almost the same manner. King Duarte, whose professional duties could not spare him, permitted himself hours and hours of public devotion throughout the year just the same. On Christmas night, Palm Sunday, and Holy Saturday, he spent five consecutive hours in holy offices, with masses, a sermon, offertories, processions, litanies, and canonical hours. On Purification, Ash Wednesday, Holy Thursday, Good Friday, Pentecost Sunday, and the anniversary of the death of Queen Philippa, the religious ceremonies filled from three to three and a half hours. Any of the other services, which might be in addition to the simple spoken mass, occupied from one to two hours. And this was not a particularly rare thing during the year.[11]

To these must be added private devotions carried on at home. The habit of praying the canonical hours was observed, and no lord or lady could dispense with his own Book of Hours. Each palace, mansion, and humble residence contained its shrine, where the images of the saints, votive lights, and prie-dieus were arranged for prayer. During Lent, the pious paroxysm attained its height. Relatives gathered to observe Lent together. Fasts on bread and water and total abstinences were then exaggerated. One example among many was the custom of Prince Pedro (1392–1449), who slept fully clothed on a bed of straw during this period. Nuno Álvares was accustomed to fast three times a week. The Church ordered abstinence from meat every

Friday on which some feast did not fall and recommended fasts on the vigils of the principal saints.[12]

Through pilgrimages, medieval man achieved a double purpose: he satisfied, on the one hand, his devotions as a Christian, fulfilling his promises and redeeming sins; he broadened, on the other, the narrow horizons in which he normally lived, searching for adventure on the trip, observing new lands, and meeting other peoples.

All through Portugal were scattered churches, chapels, and hermitages, shrines of miracle-working images which were the objects of zealous devotion. The king, the powerful lord, the wealthy merchant, and the humble peasant sought relief for their sorrows there, gave thanks for victories or prosperous business or good harvests there, did penance for the sins of flesh and spirit there. On the pilgrimage, nobles mingled with plebeians and with clerics; men found themselves with women and children. A man might travel comfortably, on horseback or in a litter, with an escort of soldiers or servants; or humbly, on foot, often barefoot, without attending to lineages or social distinctions.

There were shrines in the countryside as well as in the city. It was fashionable to visit this or that statue, famous for its miracles; but with rare exceptions of shrines whose popularity persevered, the places sought out in the fifteenth century were not the same as those of the twelfth century. And there were also shrines of a uniquely local stamp, besides "provincial," "national," and even "international" ones.

In the twelfth and thirteenth centuries, the sites visited on pilgrimages were located almost exclusively in Entre-Douro-e-Minho and in Beira. The South was still infidel or had just been reconquered. The

Fig. 87. Shrine at Sabugal. Early 16th century.

fame of its miracle-working saints, if it had them, had not been divulged for the time being. In Minho and in Douro, people went to the shrines of St. Geraldo of Braga, St. Maria of Bouro, Our Lady of Peneda, St. Maria of Pombeiro, Our Lady of Oliveira, St. Salvador of Valongo, St. Eleutério, St. Mamede, St. Maria of Lago, St. Servando, St. Clemenço of the Sea, and many others. King Sancho I (1185–1211) went to the shrine of St. Senhorinha of Basto to give thanks for the cure of one of his sons.

Farther south the important centers of pilgrimage in Estremadura begin to appear in the fourteenth century: Our Lady of Nazaré, Our Lady of Virtues (the "Fatima of the fifteenth century"), Our Lady of Cabo (whose famous processions of the candles date from the Middle Ages), and in Lisbon, St. Maria of Escada, St. Maria of Luz, and St. Maria of Belém. The Constable moves to St. Maria of Ceissa (Ourém) after the battle of Aljubarrota (1385), while João I prefers to go farther north, to Guimarães. In Trás-os-Montes, the Azinhoso shrine and, a little more to the south, the shrine of St. Domingos of Queimada, near Lamego, are visited. João II and the whole royal family go there in 1483 "to request with rich offerings, which they presented Him, that in answer to their prayers and merits, God might grant him children." St. Maria of Leiras, Our Lady of Mileu, and St. Maria of Açores were famous shrines in Beira. In Alentejo pilgrimages were made to Flor da Rosa, St. Maria of Espinheiro, Terena, and Monsarás. In the Algarve there was the famous St. Vicente of Cabo, an extremely ancient shrine sought out by the Mozarabs during the period of Moslem captivity and center of pilgrimages from Christian Portugal. It was still fashionable in the early fourteenth century, when Prince Afonso, the future Afonso IV, visited it; afterwards, devotion to it seems to have faded.

In the overseas territories, St. Maria of Africa in Ceuta, which the Portuguese conquered in 1415, acquired fame quickly. It became an obligatory place of pilgrimage for the mariners who made a port of call there. Rescued from the sea in 1463, King Afonso V and all the high dignitaries who accompanied him made their way to the temple "in shirts and barefoot" as a sign of their gratitude.[13]

The more daring, more devout, or wealthier Portuguese also undertook pilgrimages to the great international shrines: Santiago de Compostela, Our Lady of Guadalupe, Rome, and Palestine—to mention only the most famous. Pilgrims from northern Portugal journeyed frequently to Santiago; Queen Saint Isabel went on such a pilgrimage. Our Lady of Guadalupe, in Castile, was very fashionable toward the end of the Middle Ages as a Spanish religious center, although it did not have the truly international character of the Galician shrine.

Afonso V "went on a pilgrimage to St. Maria of Guadalupe" in 1474, taking advantage of its location to meet with the sovereigns of Castile. The Saintly Constable also planned a pilgrimage to Our Lady of Guadalupe.[14]

Fewer Portuguese went to Rome, and fewer still reached the Holy Land.[15] Even so, there were many pilgrims, principally priests, who ventured to such faraway lands. Of the nobility, Prince Afonso, illegitimate son of João I, who visited Palestine, and Prince Pedro, his half brother, who passed through Rome, can be cited.

Inns were staggered along the principal routes of pilgrimages. There came to be some two hundred of them scattered throughout medieval Portugal. As a rule they were very small, but they offered to the exhausted traveler, in exchange for alms, the comforts he might desire: a bed or a simple bundle of straw, a good fire, water, and a frugal meal.

The pilgrim to Santiago wore a distinctive dress decorated with the famous scallop, emblem of the Compostelan saint. The pilgrim also wore a hat with a broad brim and leaned on a staff, as did almost all travelers on foot.

Once his destination was reached, the devout person visited and venerated the relics displayed: bones and scraps of flesh from a saint; the saint's clothing or hair from his beard; jewelry that a saint had touched; and so on. This earned indulgences, one of the strongest motives for pilgrimages: so many days of absolution from penance if

Fig. 88. Pilgrims. 13th century.

one entered such and such a church on a certain day, confessed, and received communion. One had, however, to be on guard against the false preachers of indulgences, those wanderers dressed in religious habits who sought to fill their pockets at the expense of the credulous piety of the faithful. The pilgrim spent a few days at the shrine, sleeping in the church next to the relics or by the saint's tomb; observed wonders or felt that a miracle had been wrought on himself; presented, if his promise had been such, votive offerings of wax for the cure of persons or animals; purchased images, keepsakes, or relics for a good price; and undertook the trip home, tired in body but clean in spirit and content with the many things he had seen and the many things which he had to tell.

Certain pilgrimages were prepared and documented just like a modern sight-seeing trip. Long journeys required special itineraries, true guidebooks in which all the details of interest were compiled—the obligatory ports of call, the shrines that should be visited along the way, etc.—and the distances estimated. There has survived from the end of the fifteenth century a Portuguese "Book of the Pilgrimages of the Entire Holy Land." There also exist books of miracles, or registers, in the form of a list of the miracles produced by the various saints of devotion. In Portugal, especially in the fourteenth and fifteenth centuries, books of miracles by Saint Anthony, Queen Saint Isabel, the Martyrs of Morocco, Our Lady of Oliveira, Bom Jesus, and even by the Saintly Constable Nuno Álvares were known.[16]

Devotion to particular saints also varied during the Middle Ages. Besides the saints of an "international" character, common to all Christianity, others of a local stamp, native to the Iberian Peninsula or intimately connected with it, were venerated. This was the case with Saint Martinho of Dume; Saint Frutuoso of Montélios; Saint Isidore of Seville; Saint Justa and Saint Rufina; Saint Veríssimo, Saint Máximo, and Saint Júlia; and Saint Irene. This was also true of Saint Vicente and Saint James the Greater. In the twelfth, thirteenth, and fourteenth centuries, new saints were introduced through the trans-Pyrenean influence or by more recent canonizations: that was what happened with a Saint George or a Saint Martin, a Saint Anthony, a Saint Francis, a Saint Dominic, or a Saint Isabel. Some of the "old" saints remained. Others were relegated to the category of local patron saints. Still others were purely and simply forgotten. The fate of a saint also depended very much on the devotion of the members of the royal family or of the high church dignitaries and the nobility. Saint Vicente, patron saint of Lisbon, became very fashionable in the fourteenth and fifteenth centuries, after a period of less significance, thanks to the devotion of João I, his children, and Afonso V. Saint Catherine was the favorite saint of the latter ruler. Toward the end of the fourteenth century, Saint George was elevated to national patron saint, to the detriment of Saint James (Santiago), as a result of English or Italian influence. The importance acquired by some religious orders involved the cult of their respective patron saints: for instance, Saint Francis of Assisi, Saint Dominic de Guzmán, and Saint Eloi from the thirteenth century, besides Saint Anthony and Saint John the Evangelist. Saint Laurence was also very popular in the fifteenth century.[17]

It is especially after the thirteenth century that a modification in general religiosity is observed throughout Western Europe. Though dogma is maintained in its essence (was it maintained in its concept?), religious practices undergo a profound alteration. The whole movement involved a reaction against the coldness and the formality of the ritual. The period demands a greater involvement of sensibility and emotion in religion. It also demands a greater participation of the faithful in God, a more emotional and more direct union of man with Christ. The mendicant orders preach love and humility as the essence of Christianity. They champion a sanctification of daily life by an intimate contact with nature, the living work of the Creator. Charitable practices develop; the interest of the rich in the poor increases; sanctuaries, hospitals, leper colonies, and inns are founded everywhere. The faithful gather in brotherhoods of charity. New devotions appear, such as the cults of the Passion of Christ, of the Most Holy Sacrament, and of Our Lady. The problems of the Immaculate Conception and the Assumption of the Virgin divide the Christian intelligentsia. The feast of the Holy Ghost also constitutes a novelty in this final epoch of the Middle Ages.[18]

The devotion to Our Lady was doubtless quite ancient; the Incarnation on March 25 was especially commemorated. But there is an enormous growth in Marian devotion after the thirteenth century, especially in the fourteenth and fifteenth centuries. It must also be connected to the exaltation of the woman, patent in the literature of the period, and to the influence of religious orders such as the Cluniac, Cistercian, Franciscan, and Dominican. At the end of the fifteenth century, more than a thousand consecrations to Mary can be seen in Portuguese churches, chapels, and hermitages. In these are included all the cathedral sees and a large number of the monasteries. But the provinces in the central and southern parts of the country, re-Christianized in the thirteenth and fourteenth centuries, are the ones that display the greater number of such dedications. We have already seen how many Marian shrines were the objectives of pilgrimages. Most of these centers became famous only after the fourteenth century.

The Nativity and Assumption, which the Franciscan friars (and some Dominicans as well) accepted and preached to the people, were celebrated. The Purification, the Annunciation, and the Maternity (Senhora do Ó) were also observed. In the fourteenth century, the feasts of Our Lady of Neves and of the Immaculate Conception were introduced, or became popular; in the fifteenth century, that of the Visitation appears. Even though dating from the beginning of the thirteenth century, the devotion of the Immaculate Conception spread only slowly. In 1320, the bishop of Coimbra, the Frenchman Raymond Évrard, ordered "that in our cathedral church of Coimbra a feast should be held every year, on the eighth of December, on which day the Virgin, the glorious Holy Mary, was conceived, just as is done in other lands." And in fact, the devotion had been known for a long time in France.[19] The cult of the Seven Sorrows of the Virgin and of the Holy Rosary also began in the 1400's. The first known candle to Our Lady of Cabo was lit in 1431. The popularization of the Salve Regina can be observed during the fourteenth century; at the battle of Aljubarrota (1385), the whole army recited it.

In 1264, a bull of Pope Urban IV had established the solemnity of Corpus Christi. Toward the end of the reign of Afonso III (1248–79), this feast had been introduced into Portugal, rapidly becoming popular.[20] In the fourteenth and fifteenth centuries the celebration of the Most Holy Sacrament was among the most solemn in the Portuguese Church, especially because of the magnificent procession to which it gave occasion. During the whole eight days of Corpus Christi, the Most Holy Sacrament was displayed in the churches, with the accompaniment of lights, perfumes, and canticles.[21]

A "Regiment" of the most important processions of the Kingdom, dating from the beginning of the reign of João II (1481–95), allows us to evaluate the magnificence of the procession of Corpus Christi. In this procession, representatives from all social classes and all the professions took part. In front walked the butchers, dragging a bull by ropes. Other butchers and retail meat merchants on horseback, carrying the standard of their profession, surrounded them. The gardeners and orchardists followed, conveying a cart on which had been built a "solid machine of boards and painted burlap, which represented a garden plot with its hotbeds, flower beds, scoop wheel, canebrakes, and vegetables." Their standards and insignias were decorated with floral designs in allusion to their work. After them came successive groups of fishwives, bakers, women street vendors, and fruit vendors, all in their gayest clothing, dancing to the sound of fifes. Following them came the carters and innkeepers, guarded by the Three Magi, whose litter "in its contrivance" they carried. Cobblers and others of similar occupations (curriers, tanners, and leather bottle makers) flanked three masked persons who represented a "very well dressed" emperor and two kings. Alongside the cobblers, the row of the tailors wound "around the serpent temptress of our mother Eve." The soldiers' turn came next: two lines of the fifty crossbowmen that every city and village was required to maintain, ready for action, festively adorned. Afterwards, on one side came the gunsmiths of the king, and on the other, the crossbowmen of the royal council and the crossbowmen of the cavalry. Then, in two wings, came those known as "men of arms"—barbers, blacksmiths, armorers, cutlers, farriers, saddlers, scabbard makers, spearmakers, and tinkers. They displayed unsheathed swords in their hands and carried a litter with Saint George killing the dragon, watched by a page and a maiden. The weavers, wool combers, and carders were under the protection of Saint Bartholomew, whose litter they bore on their shoulders. They pulled a figure of the devil bound by a rope. Saddlers, manufacturers of daggers, and silk weavers came in a parallel row, carrying the image of Saint Sebastian, their patron saint. After them, on one side, came the cordmakers and breechmakers with the image of Saint Michael the Archangel expelling the devils; on the other, potters, tilers, and brickmakers brought the image of Saint Claire and her two companions. The litter of Saint Catherine was carried by carpenters, masons, streetpavers, bricklayers' assistants, excavators, "and others who repair houses," divided equally into two rows. The shearers and candlestick makers, with enormous, flaming torches mounted on tin holders, formed the following group.

Next in the procession came the parade of the most noble and the wealthiest trades: goldsmiths and tinsmiths, also with blazing torches, carrying the litter of Saint John. A grave pause introduced the flag of the city and the royal banner, proudly carried by the standard-bearer and by the aldermen on horseback. A farce by some youths came next, in which they portrayed a group of the apostles, evangelists, and little angels. The way was now opened for the passage of the rich bourgeois merchants of linen cloth and of silk, solemnly holding their torches and leading two horses by their reins. Then came the affluent merchants in woolen materials (dyed cloth), also with flaming candles. The scholars and authorities followed: these were the scribes, military scribe, apothecaries, notaries for reports, judicial notaries, attorneys, the king's investigators, clerks for orphans and for the aldermen, royal scribes, judges, and councilmen. "As a contrast to these unusual, diverse scenes . . . the monastic communities followed: . . . black friars,

gray friars, white friars, brown friars, friars in every sad color; Augustinians, Benedictines, Cistercians, Dominicans, Franciscans, Beghards.
Then there came an endless number of knights in the orders of Christ,
of the Hospital, of Avis, of Santiago, preceded by their respective
masters and commendators and followed by the lay friars and servants
at arms. Then, the magistrates of the court, the official of the crown,
and the monarch himself formed a group surrounding the triumphant
Host carried in the hands of the bishop." All the nobility lent, with the
luxury and brilliance of their clothing, an unsurmountable note of
splendor to the procession of Corpus Christi, which concluded in this
fashion.

This arrangement was common to three other processions: one purely
religious, that took place on the day of the miracle of wax; two commemorative of civil events, on March 2 for the victory of the battle of
Toro in 1475 (which both the Portuguese and the Castilians of that
period considered a victory) and on August 14 for the triumph at the
battle of Aljubarrota.[22]

Besides these, there were obviously many other processions, varying
in time and locale. Each region, town, or village celebrated its patron
saint, just as they all do today. Before the regulation of João II, even
the processions observed nationwide differed from district to district.
In Coimbra, for example, the procession of Corpus Christi would
come out of the church and cloister of Santa Cruz, circle around the
churchyard and reenter. Only ecclesiastics took part in it.[23] To oppose
pagan vestiges and to celebrate the victory achieved at Aljubarrota
(1385), the city council of Lisbon decided to promote solemn processions on the following dates: January 1, directed to the cathedral and
in honor of the Circumcision; May 1, directed to the hermitage of
Our Lady of Escada and in praise of the Virgin Mary; the day of the
Holy Cross, at the church of the same name and in celebration of the
True Cross; the day of Saint Vicente, with a pilgrimage by the representatives of the various trades to his tomb in the cathedral; the day
of Saint George, with a pious procession to the church of his invoca-
tion; the day of the Martyrs, with a solemn procession to the church
of the Saints; the eve of the birth of the Virgin, with a procession to
the Church of the Martyrs; the eve of the Purification of the Virgin,
with Our Lady of Escada as its destiny; the vigil of the Annunciation,
with a pilgrimage to Our Lady of Paraíso; August 12 and 13, with the
barefoot penitents heading in a procession to the monasteries of
Trindade and St. Francis, respectively; and August 14, with the

solemnity of the procession of Corpus Christi and its destination at the church of St. Maria of Graça. It was specified that on the days of the last three feasts, "the Salve Regina [should be] sung with the litany in the cathedral and in the other churches. . . . And all the parishes should attend church, or at least one person from each household."[24]

One of the most celebrated processions at the end of the Middle Ages was the procession of the naked. Symbol of an age of mysticism and an expression of devotion, these processions were found in various European countries, including Portugal, from the second half of the fourteenth century on. The persons taking part in them appeared with little clothing, perhaps only in a shirt or with a bare torso, always barefoot, defying the inclemencies of the weather and often all scourging one another. At the time of the plague in 1423, a certain Vicente Martins o Grangeeiro made a promise to visit the sepulcher of the Martyrs of Morocco in Coimbra every year, accompanied by his sons, all of them unclothed from the waist up. Neighbors and acquaintances began to accompany him, and soon the procession became famous and drew innumerable participants. It was held in midwinter, on the sixteenth of January. The penitents met in the monastery of St. Francisco da Ponte, where they confessed, received communion, and heard a high mass. Then, dressed only in breeches or in a cloth to their knees, they formed an awe-inspiring and impressive procession which made its way to the monastery of Santa Cruz, in which are found the bones of the martyrs. The procession was repeated every year until the seventeenth century, but by that time it caused so many indecencies, mockeries, and so much laughter that it was prohibited in 1641. Authorized again some years later, it was discontinued definitively only toward the end of the eighteenth century.[25]

Although already long in existence, the devotion to relics and medals increased in the period under consideration. It was common for kings, nobles, clergy, and commoners to wear relics (sometimes genuine gems in gold, silver, and precious stones), blessed medals, cilices, and other symbols of Christian veneration. Certain relics were so highly esteemed that they were passed from father to son by inheritance. It is common to find mention of relics left to heirs in the royal wills. On the point of death, Philippa of Lancaster gave a piece of the Holy Rood to each of her three oldest sons and to her husband. Henry the Navigator later said "that as well as he could remember, after the aforementioned Holy Rood had been given to him, that he had always worn it, except for a single day when he had absentmindedly removed it in taking off a shirt."[26]

Although it was not until the Council of Trent in the mid-sixteenth century that Church ritual became standardized, the liturgy in the medieval Church did not vary greatly. It is true that from region to region, according to the dioceses or the religious orders, there were certain differences in the devotion. In the prayers recited by the priest at the beginning of the mass, in those which preceded the reading of the Gospel, in those which came before the offertory, in those which led to communion, in the last prayers, and in still others, small variations could be noted. Generally, sermon, admonitions, banns, etc., took place after the offertory. Each diocese, even each church, disposed of considerable freedom in fixing the calendar of its liturgical feasts. Outside of the sacrifice of the mass,[27] the liturgy of the Middle Ages included certain rites of a dramatic character, usually in its final part. At Lent and Easter, there was a whole theatrical spectacular concerning the Passion of Christ. On Ash Wednesday the penitents were symbolically expelled from the church: the bishop took the first penitent by the hand and led him to the door, and holding hands, all the others went with him. The ceremony symbolized the expulsion of Adam and Eve from Paradise. On Palm Sunday the solemn enthronement of Jesus Christ was held. On Holy Thursday (or even on Palm Sunday) there was the ceremony of the reconciliation of the penitents with the whole diocese, assembled in the main cathedral. The ritual of the sepulture was held on Good Friday. And so on. At Christmas the reading of the genealogy of Jesus was performed. The Regiment of the Royal Chapel, instituted by King Duarte, points out the most important feasts of the Church and describes the required ceremony.[28]

The influence of foreign religious practices seems never to have been very great in Portugal. Very early, the Roman ritual had imposed itself, replacing the Mozarab. Certain queens or particular high dignitaries coming from beyond the Pyrenees introduced styles that sometimes lasted for a long time. For instance, Philippa of Lancaster made the liturgical customs of Salisbury fashionable, and they continued to be followed by her sons in their private devotions.[29]

The ceremonies were very often accompanied by song and solemnized by the burning of incense and other perfumes. The Regiment of the Royal Chapel gave special attention to liturgical singing. First of all, it commends instruction in this art from childhood: children seven or eight years old should be trained and raised to sing and officiate in the chapel, and they should be taught to sing correctly. Voices are then considered: "The voices of the chaplains should be known, who is to sing as alto, and who as contralto, and who as tenor." Precautions should be taken so that the voices harmonize and blend with each other. They should not sing falsetto or off-key: "Let them not choose songs higher than they can easily reach." And the song should be happy or sad consonant with the seasons.

One of the characteristics of medieval religious song was its comprehensibility to the faithful. In Church, the Christian was expected to accompany the priests, or at least to listen to them, understanding what he heard. Consequently, "what they sing should be something that all those who have to sing it know quite well."[30]

In addition to the colors still worn today in ecclesiastical vestments, yellow and blue were seen. For the religious services, the priests wore a flowing alb, a chasuble, an amice, and a stole. White and falling to the feet, the alb was unchanged in form from the thirteenth century to the fifteenth. The chasuble of the twelfth century looked more like a mantle; in the thirteenth or fourteenth century, a new type of chasuble appeared, slashed on both sides and with a different cut on the sides and in front. Deacons and priests wore dalmatics, whose shape, during the Middle Ages, changed only in the type of sleeves: very short in the twelfth century, long in the following century, again shortening in the fourteenth century. The dalmatic of the fourteenth century was slit on the sides. Footwear conformed with the fashion of the period, with points more or less accentuated. Miter, crosier, cross, cape, etc., were not very different from the modern ones.[31]

Except for the offices, there was no completely standardized ecclesiastical outfit. The priests wore clothing resembling that of the lay people, in spite of constant attempts at regulation by the Church. In 1311, the Synod of Bergamo had ordered the use of the lay skullcap to prevent other, more complicated head coverings. From the thirteenth century on, bishops and canons used the rochet—a white gown— as normal dress. The diocesan council of Braga in 1333 forbade the use of multihued clothes to parish priests, prescribing for them clothing in shades of black, brown, and white only. The style of wearing clothes open in front was prohibited, the council deciding the priests should always wear round, closed cassocks, neither very short nor very long, with black palliums lined in the same color and simple leather belts, without any decoration.[32] In the beginning of the fifteenth century, the archbishop of Lisbon decreed that the clothes of the clergy

> should be proper to their estate and that they should not be of green cloth, nor red, nor two halves of different colors, nor striped, nor fringed, nor any shorter than mid-calf, nor so long that they drag on the ground,

nor slashed on the sides, nor in back (except for those who owned an animal on which they rode, and when this is the case, they can have slits in the back of the garment measuring two handspans, even though they are not riding); nor may they wear mutton-shaped sleeves, nor collars so high that they rise above the neck, . . . nor wear doublets bound at the collar with ribbons or leather strings, nor wear sleeves wider than one and a half spans, nor open mantles, except when they ride (though they can wear those which they already own until the second synod); nor may they wear buttoned short capes, nor shoes with points longer than three spans . . . nor green shoes, nor red, nor flowered.[33]

In the middle of the fifteenth century, both regular and secular priests wore high caps, identical to those which the fashion of the period prescribed for lay persons (see, for example, Fig. 2).

The principal symbol of the clergy ought to have been the tonsure and cut of their hair. Many, however, were negligent in maintaining it properly. As a result, the Constitutions of the Archbishopric of Lisbon ordered that "all the clergy in holy and beneficed orders have their hair cut short and shave their tonsure and beard every two weeks."[34]

Priests were not supposed to carry weapons, but many defied the laws, arousing the protests of the people over this. In the Cortes of Evora in 1481–82, complaints were raised against the bearing of arms and the style of long hair worn by priests.[35]

The clothes of monks, sisters, friars, and nuns were not essentially different from the twentieth-century garments worn by such people.

Fig. 89. Benedictine and Cistercian monks. 15th century.

A medieval church was not intended to be the place of worship only. Given the lack of other public buildings, it was also used as a meeting place and even as the premises for amusements. In the church, neighbors often gathered in a council to discuss the most diverse subjects. In the church, dances were held, troubadours and jesters were heard, short religious dramas and mystery plays were presented. In the church, people ate, drank, and slept whenever necessary. During mass itself, it was not uncommon—especially in the villages—for the parishioners to question the priest about thefts or losses they had suffered.[36]

For all these reasons the man of the Middle Ages did not respect the church as does the modern Christian. He spoke out loud, laughed, argued, and worked inside its walls. The priests themselves did not hesitate to give a bad example. A visitation of 1473 reported that the canonical hours were often badly sung, because the beneficiaries talked a great deal in the choir, even abusing and striking each other. Criticism of and punishments for cases of this nature can be found throughout the Middle Ages. The penitentials threaten with punishments both corporeal and spiritual all those who might talk in church while praying or listening to the canonical hours.

Not all the churches were provided with seats for the faithful. Even in the beginning of the fifteenth century, the archbishop of Lisbon ordered that benches be placed in every church of the diocese, which indicates that many had none.[37]

If respect for the house of God was not great, the consideration of the people for the ministers of the faith was even less—not because the priests were more licentious, corrupt, or ignorant than the nobles or the bourgeoisie, but precisely because they were not distinguishable from them. In their habits, in their ambitions, even in their dress, the bishops and priests were like the rest of the people. In another chapter we have already seen how the frequency of concubinage among ecclesiastics aroused successive protests from the peoples assembled in the Cortes, and how some even refused to receive the sacraments from the priests who kept mistresses. On the other hand, the examples afforded by the rulers did nothing to enhance respect for the clergy. In their battle to centralize royal power, practically all the medieval Portuguese kings fought and humiliated the Church, including many individual clerics, bishops, and friars. Since the king was the natural protector for the great mass of the population, the people followed his lead in their attitude toward the clergy.

Naturally, there was considerable difference between monks and friars in the opinion of the people. The Benedictine monk, hidden in his monastery, receiving his rents, and cultivating music, literature, and the arts in the leisure of his wealth, would perhaps be respected, sometimes hated, but rarely loved. On the other hand, the Franciscan friar, in contact with the people, begging at the doors or in the public square, preaching from the height of the pulpit or on a simple pillar in the open air, had to deserve more veneration and esteem. It is true that as time went on, the friar changed his style of life. Pampered and protected by great and small, he grew wealthy and became "bourgeois." As essentially urban orders, the mendicants and preachers benefited materially from the economic spurt of the cities and forgot their original goals. The friar in caricature, who passed into history and legend as being enamored of a good table, dissolute, and potbellied, was essentially the Franciscan or the Dominican. In fact, the moral decadence of the regular clergy had begun to worry both ecclesiastics and lay people by the end of the Middle Ages.[38]

The organization of laymen into brotherhoods, a means of participating more intensely in ecclesiastical activity and an intermediate phase between Christian life in the world and religious life in a community, denotes a trend at the end of the Middle Ages. In principle, the brotherhood joined Catholics from all social origins in devotion to the same saint or participation in the same act of religious fervor. The brotherhood almost always applied itself to well-determined purposes. It made use, in the greater number of cases, of factors of economic or professional fellowship, which became the basis of the future corporations.

The first Portuguese brotherhoods are documented in the early thirteenth century: there was one for blacksmiths in 1229 and another for merchants in the same century. Still others, under the protection of the Holy Ghost and of Saint Francis, are numbered among the pioneer groups. Cobblers and butchers had their own inns in the same period, which leads us to presume that they gathered in brotherhoods also. And the movement continued without interruption during the entire late Middle Ages. Each trade or group of related professions had its brotherhood, invoked its saints, and displayed its special banner. Each brotherhood was more or less well-to-do, according to the degree of wealth of its members. It disposed of houses, vineyards, and grainfields. It received rents. It supported hospitals and lent assistance to disabled or elderly colleagues.[39]

Other brotherhoods emerged for very different reasons—for example, that of the Servants of the Bom Senhor Jesus Cristo, founded in 1432 in Lisbon to implore divine mercy during the plague. The Dominican Friar André Dias was its creator and established its seat in the monastery of St. Dominic.[40]

In the middle or at the end of the thirteenth century, there was created in Évora—and, there is a strong possibility, in many other cities of Portugal as well—a brotherhood of charity, formed by the good men who had made the pilgrimage to Jerusalem. Although supposedly a charitable organization, this brotherhood bore more resemblance to a modern alumni association than to anything else. The brothers held a meeting once a month and attended a ceremonial banquet on one Sunday in January every year. It is true that here they shared their feast with the poor. Among themselves they were to preserve harmony and submit all their differences to the arbitration of their peers. They lent each other material and moral aid in case of sickness or death. Each paid six dinheiros "for his soul" and a half a maravedi of jewelry as initiation fee. They elected a majordomo and a crier for their financial and administrative business.[41]

In spite of being profoundly Christian, the Middle Ages did not signal the end of paganism in daily religion. All kinds of practices linked to the ancient gods persisted obstinately in the habits of the people, especially among the lower classes. Although hidden behind the façade of Christianity, which lent names of saints and Catholic feasts to the forces of nature and the pagan devotions, worship of nature was quite actively preserved throughout the Middle Ages, drawing denunciations and threats from the Church and from the more enlightened laymen. To this cult were connected all kinds of superstitions, which are carried on in part even today. Thus there arose, especially outside of the cities, a complex fusion of beliefs and practices, in theory baptized with Christianity but in practice quite remote from it. The Penitential of Martim Perez establishes a long list of superstitions that must be considered sinful by the confessors and consequently punished. Typically pagan believers were those who believed in the stars and such signs. Then came a long series of superstitions. Many believed that women shrank, went out at night, and flew, going to suck blood from animals — a typical conception of a witch and vampire. They believed in fairies and the effectiveness of the crowing of a cock to drive devils away. They also believed in the Evil eye, in evil spells, witchcraft, omens, and fortune tellers, which gave rise to very lucrative "professions" because of the demand for this sort of thing. Some prepared love potions, "indecent and obscene things," which were given to husbands, lovers, and sweethearts to drink. Others recited incantations and cast evil spells of a magical sort to kill someone from a distance or, more simply, to dry up the milk of livestock. There were individuals particularly trained in calling up demons and other evil spirits. Others, both men and women, prayed for plagues that would inflict injury on their victims.

The Our Father, the Creed, the Psalms, the very Gospel were used for cabalistic interpretations. The Constitutions of the Archbishopric of Lisbon protest, in the beginning of the fifteenth century, that the sacred Host and the chrism are used to prepare amulets.[42]

It must be emphasized that the age truly believed in the power of magic and in almost all these superstitious practices. The power of such forces was naïvely attributed to demonic influences. So, in the name of religion, it was necessary to prohibit superstitions and condemn their practitioners. The famous royal charter of 1385, whose objective was to purge idolatry in order to please God during the grave predicament through which the country was passing, refers in its preamble to the "grave sins which in this city of Lisbon have been practiced since very ancient times, and extraordinarily idolatrous sins and wicked customs of the gentiles, which had been maintained for a long time," and consequently determines:

> no person may use nor effect fetishes, nor bonds, nor summoning up of devils, nor incantations, nor casting spells, nor making cabalistic figures, nor evil spells, nor interpreting dreams, nor working enchantments, nor may he cast lots nor read fortunes, nor produce divinations in whatever guise that may be forbidden . . . nor may one lay his hand on another, nor measure the waist, nor cast an evil eye or any similar glance, nor pour water through a sieve, nor give any remedy whatsoever for the health of any man or animal that is not advised by the art of medicine. . . .
>
> They also establish that from now on in this city and its territories, Januaries and Mays cannot be sung, nor songs to any other month of the year, nor may they pour whitewash on their doors in the name of Janus, nor may they steal water, nor cast fortunes, nor disturb water, nor perform any other work secretly, as was done before.[43]

It is hard to speak of atheism in medieval times. The period from the thirteenth century to the fifteenth did not lack incidents of heresy and blasphemy, however. The State tolerated religions like Judaism and Islam, although it favored the conversion of Jews and Moors. But it placed under the authority of the law those Christians who abjured their faith.

The end of the Middle Ages brought with it an increase in doubt and in deviation from orthodoxy, as it similarly brought a growth in religious fervor and mysticism. "For some time here," say the *Afonsine Ordinances,* "through their sins some people fell and are falling into the very grave error of heresy, saying and believing and affirming things which are against Our Lord God and the Holy Mother Church." But lack of faith was ancient. A law from the time of Dinis (1279–1325) had ordered that those who did not believe in God or in the Virgin, or who blasphemed, were to have their tongues torn out and then they were to be burned. By the time of Afonso V, apparently it had become impossible to apply the law in all its severity, perhaps because blasphemy and doubt had become so widespread. Many times, in the bitterness of life or in the din of a brawl, God or the Virgin was denied, "furiously." Such "free expressions of one's emotions" — for they were nothing else — earned the lightest punishment: a fine of one thousand reais for nobles and knights, whipping at the pillory for peasants with a needle pierced through their tongues. To deny the saints involved only five hundred reais as a fine, or penitence for five Fridays in the form of a procession around the church, with a bramble around one's neck. But if a person denied them "with the intention and the idea of abjuring his faith," he then fell under the jurisdiction of heresy and was punished as a heretic, with death.[44] A law by Fernando I (1367–83) testifies to the concern of the authorities (as much civil as ecclesiastical) for the disdain with which many excommunicants calmly awaited the lifting of their excommunications. It seeks to constrain them to request absolution and to do penance for their sins, under penalty of various fines. Such was the levity of spirit with which, at the end of the Middle Ages, people contemplated a spiritual penalty apparently so much to be feared by well-educated Catholics.[45]

8 : CULTURE

THE education of a youngster depended, as a rule, on his situation in society, on his material resources, and on the geographic location in which he spent his childhood and adolescence. Providing primary education or compulsory education was not considered the duty of the Crown, or indeed, of anyone. The only exception recorded is religious instruction. And this was often the only means whereby a minimum number of persons could achieve a minimum amount of education. Children were expected to learn the mysteries of the Faith, the most important prayers, and the form of assisting at the services. Each bishop had the obligation of fostering catechistic instruction in his diocese. We have already seen how the actual execution of this duty resulted in a certain cultural outburst on the primary level in the bishopric of Lamego.[1] Other such cases may have occurred during the Middle Ages. Most of the time, however, the goodwill of the prelates or of the priests was not enough. Rather, they lacked the ways and means of translating their educational duty into practice. The regular clergy was thinly scattered over the country. Each monastery that was not one of friars was a potential school, but a school often poorly situated, far from the important centers of population, and consequently of little cultural impact. Franciscans and Dominicans could walk from territory to territory and bring instruction with them — when they themselves were educated. But there were few of them; and the tasks of preaching, of hearing confessions, and of fighting against heresy, paganism, superstition, or religious indifference absorbed them. Besides, their settling down arrived quickly. Secular clerics were always scarce and badly equipped, even for the specific religious functions. Many priests, as well as many friars, did not know how to read or write. What instruction could they provide in this case?

Joined to this were the difficulties of communication and transportation; the price and the scarcity of books and writing materials; the inability of peasant or artisan fathers to comprehend the importance of educating their sons; the low living standards of most of the population. Consequently, it is not difficult to understand the reasons for the widespread illiteracy.

Yet illiteracy, in the modern sense, did not necessarily imply a lack of culture in the Middle Ages. Neither for the masses nor for the elite could literacy be judged on the basis of reading and writing skills. The primary means for transmitting both theoretical and practical knowledge was oral. Popular traditions, romances, proverbs, and sermons played as important a role in medieval education as do books today. Church frescoes and sculptures, the liturgy, and religious drama could also be instructive.

In the cathedrals of the peninsular west, the existence of schools is attested from the eleventh century. They were used exclusively for the education of the clerics, but many children who were supported by ecclesiastics or destined by their parents for the religious life also took part in them. Coimbra, Braga, Lisbon, Oporto, and probably other diocesan churches accordingly had their schools or simply a schoolteacher, as the Lateran Council (1215) had recommended.[2]

In addition to these episcopal schools, there were others in the monasteries. Documents indicate the existence of those at Alcobaça and Santa Cruz by the twelfth century. Many others, of which evidence has not survived, were distributed among the various monasteries of Portugal.

What was taught in these schools? In the first place, to read and write Latin: this was the course known as grammar. For this purpose there were some compilations, known throughout Christendom, which were written by the Latin authors of the Later Empire (fourth century). But only the culturally developed monasteries and cathedrals, like the one at Alcobaça, possessed such implements of instruction. In most schools education was carried out either through copies of extracts from these books, or only as an exercise of the memory of the schoolmaster. For practicing reading, the various books of the church existing everywhere — the missals, antiphonaries, Bibles, etc. — were employed. Gothic script was learned exclusively, and alas for the student who took liberties in writing and imparted his own personality to the letter! The standards were exhibited to be copied, not to be corrupted by new scribes! Besides learning to trace the several letters of the alphabet (only twenty-three: the I was still not differentiated from the J, nor the U from the V; W was unknown) and to recognize their numerical values (what are known as Roman numerals with rules a little different from those used today), and besides learning to read words by the juxtaposition of letters, it was also required of the scholar to memorize the numerous abbreviations which were then normally utilized in writing. Even today, it is rare for the Portuguese to write out such words as *Dom* and *São* instead of using the abbreviations *D.* and *S.* The scribes of the Middle Ages never thought of writing *Jesus* or *Christ* completely; the usual forms, originating from the Greek, were *Ihu* and *Xpo.* In addition to these, many others sprang up: *Dns* instead of *Dominus*, *nr* for *noster*, $\underset{m}{i}$ instead of *mihi*, and so on. This habit, against which the grammarians will protest in the sixteenth century, came principally from the scarcity of parchment and the resulting necessity of writing a great deal in comparatively little space.

And so they learned to read and write in Latin. But in Portugal from the twelfth to the fifteenth centuries, no one spoke Latin any longer except to foreign ambassadors. Consequently, there was a need for dictionaries in both Latin and Portuguese. Explanatory dictionaries in Latin were used internationally. In Portugal there has survived a small glossary of verbs from the mid-fourteenth century giving the Latin form and its Portuguese translation. Certain translations clearly reveal concepts which differ from modern ones: thus, the verb *dogmatizo, dogmatizas, dogmatizare* (literally, "to dogmatize"), further defined as *instruo, doceo,* is translated as "to teach." And *dicto, dictas, dictare,* translated as "to dictate," is the synonym of *litteras conpono* ("I compose letters").[3]

Even though Portuguese had been the official language since the reign of Dinis (1279–1325), private schools and schoolmasters never taught it until the end of the Middle Ages. Somewhat as in the case of the modern dialects, Portuguese was heard in the cradle, then spoken naturally, and was written (by those who knew how to write) without having been learned. Hence the fact that the written language considerably approximated the spoken language. But since all of those, or almost all, who could read and write Portuguese had begun by learning Latin, it is evident that they would seek to Latinize as many words, rules of syntax, and idiomatic expressions as they could. The first texts in Portuguese, dating from the beginning of the thirteenth century, are almost literal translations from the Latin original, which can be detected in practically every phrase. Only with the passage of time was the vernacular perfected and rendered independent of Latin. The increase of translations into Portuguese in the 1300's and 1400's contributed considerably toward this development. Prince Pedro, by the first half of the fifteenth century, had already commended some rules for good translation.

After grammar, some schools taught dialectics. This was the study of certain rules of logic believed essential for the rational arrangement of phrases, written as well as spoken. The syllogism was studied specifically, based mostly on Porphyry, commentator on Aristotle. Dialectics was considered very advanced material, however, and only those who intended to continue their studies risked it. Moreover, few schools in Portugal had teachers in this branch of knowledge.

Once he knew how to read and write, the student was qualified to attend the university. Today we consider the university to be a center for higher courses of study, separated from primary schooling by a long intermediate step, secondary education. Not so in the Middle Ages. The university functioned much more like a high school, sometimes even as an extension of grade school, than as a union of colleges in the modern manner.

People of all ages attended the university. As a rule, it was in the adult years that the desire to learn, or the financial capacity of acquiring education, came to the person. The university student generally did not have the time nor the ability to work. There did not exist, as there does today, freedom to work nor placement services. Consequently, in the years spent in Lisbon or in Coimbra, the scholar had to live on his income, or the poorer ones, by begging alms, which was not a rare occurrence. Nevertheless, there is no lack of cases of young boys barely in adolescence enrolling in the university after having profitably attended grammar schools. There was a large percentage of clerics, or of candidates to the clergy. Even sons of the nobility attended the university, perhaps without any intention of finishing a course and earning a degree, but at any rate acquiring a certain amount of knowledge without equal in the culture of the court salon. In the *Chronicle of King Fernando,* Fernão Lopes relates that, about 1378, Prince João rode swiftly to Coimbra (where the university functioned between 1354 and 1377), accompanied by some of his vassals, with the firm intention of murdering Maria Teles: "And crossing the bridge, arriving at the wall, the Prince called one of his men and said, 'You know this city and its entrances and exists better than anyone else here because you have already been here studying.' " [4]

Although officially created toward the end of the thirteenth century, the *studium generale* (the name then used for the university) was no more than a simple public school, little more advanced than the previous episcopal and monastic schools until the 1400's. Even during the fifteenth century, the university had little importance; the degrees which it conferred obtained little validity, even in the interior of the country; and not even remotely could it be compared with the universities at Oxford, Paris, Salamanca, or Bologna. As a matter of fact, the great mass of Portuguese students seriously wanting to learn continued to seek out these schools and many others like them, whenever financial conditions and their adventurous spirit allowed them. We even find them going to Cologne, where they study Theology and the Arts.5

Although it may be customary to divide the medieval university into faculties and there may be a tendency to equate them with the modern idea, the truth is that in Portugal each so-called faculty represented only a chair. There were, on the lowest level, the chairs of Grammar and Dialectic (Logic), constituting the faculty of Arts. The course, which progressed a little beyond the knowledge acquired before university enrollment, lasted three years and conferred the bachelor's degree, after a public examination.

One could also study for a bachelor's degree in the chairs of Medicine (the sources do not clearly indicate whether this curriculum was studied simultaneously with or after the arts). Medicine embraced two branches—Physics and Philosophy, the latter being subdivided into Natural Philosophy and Moral Philosophy—but excluded practical medicine. Studies were based principally on Aristotle's treatises on the nature of people and things, on birth and corruption, on the shape of the world, on morality, and so on. Of the physicians, Galen and Hippocrates were glossed.

The illustrious faculties were those of Law: Civil Law (Laws) and Canon Law (Edict and Decretals). In the chair of Civil Law, Roman law was studied; in that of Edict, the basis of canon law; in that of Decretals, the decretals of Pope Gregory IX and Boniface VIII. It was the only modernized faculty of truly practical interest. Not only were canonical decisions of daily application studied, but the new papal canons were also added to the curriculum—as, for example, the *Clementinas,* rescripts compiled by Clement V and published by John XXII in the first half of the fourteenth century. Theology was not studied at the Portuguese university until the mid-fifteenth century. There were, nevertheless, courses of theology in several monastic schools, especially those of the Dominicans and Franciscans.

Beyond the bachelor's, the university, through the archbishop of Lisbon or one of his vicars, conferred the degrees of licentiate and of doctor. To be granted the degree of licentiate, the student had to follow a course of study for seven to nine years, undergo examinations, and pay expensive gratuities. The title of doctor required, in addition to this, public examinations and pompous ceremonies, which were very costly for the candidate. Consequently, only wealthy individuals or those subsidized (in the case of the clergy) could hope to rise to the summit of the university hierarchy and become a *lente* (university professor).

During the Middle Ages, there were never more than two dozen professors in the Portuguese studium generale. In the beginning of the fourteenth century, that number was only five; by the beginning of the fifteenth, it had only risen to fifteen teachers. There were classes in the morning and afternoon. The most important were those in the morning, also called "ordinaries." They began at six o'clock in the morning (the "prime" hour, "prime" chairs, "prime" teachers), which was regarded as the most propitious hour for learning! In the afternoon were the "extraordinary" classes, on secondary subjects and entrusted to less important professors. The school year lasted till August 25, but it was subject to many interruptions by the holidays and feasts of the Church. Each chair was required to have "two public and solemn acts" every year, rather like the modern examinations, in which the students' capacity for debating was put to the test.

On the margin of "official" education, there existed in Lisbon and Coimbra private teachers, with or without a bachelor's degree, who for their own profit performed the function of "expounders" (tutors).

We do not know, not even approximately, how many students there were in the medieval Portuguese university. Naturally few, about a hundred, if we are to judge by the size of the teaching staff. Even so, they created problems for the authorities and people, especially with respect to public order, food, and lodging. The university, a corporation of scholars, had its privileges, just as any other corporation or brotherhood. One of them, perhaps the most important and the one that led to the most friction between town and gown, respected the administration of its own justice — what was known as the "academic law."

Hitherto we have spoken of the "official" education administered in schools. But a large number, possibly the majority, of the educated population had received their knowledge in another form and also transmitted it in a different way.

The cultural level of the nobility increased with the passage of time. Nevertheless, the illiteracy of the kings and great nobles has been much exaggerated. It is not creditable that Count Henri (late eleventh century), coming from Burgundy—a region relatively developed in the economic sphere for the eleventh century—was illiterate. Nor is it probable that his widow, surrounded by French cleries belonging to the cultural elite of the time—remember the monks of Cluny—would have completely neglected the education of his son Afonso Henriques (b. 1109). Afonso's son, Sancho I, is known to have been a poet. It is to be doubted that, interested as he was in letters, the monarch would have denied the rudiments of grammar to his children—Afonso II (b. 1185), for example. By the time of his son, Sancho II, the cultural troubadour atmosphere, though only incipient, was already a reality in Portugal. Even so, would the ruler ignore primary education?

To know how to read and write doubtless represented an advanced stage of education for the period. But even if he were erudite, what forms of educational broadening could a king or a noble receive in his court or in his provincial manor?

From time to time wandering minstrels or invited troubadours would visit the palace. Both groups told stories and legends, declaimed poetry, played instruments, and danced. Beyond mere entertainment, such activities compensated for the lack of books.

The cultural atmosphere began to improve after the mid-thirteenth century, at least at the court. Afonso III and his vassals, returning from France in 1245, introduce new and refined habits from the other side of the Pyrenees. Afonso not only writes verse and enlivens parties with prose narratives, but at the same time initiates a fruitful movement in the acquisition, production, and copying of books. In the following century, the movement proceeds and even accelerates. Among the books that most interest the aristocracy are treatises on hunting and related sports. Several books on such subjects as veterinary science (treatment of horses), falconry, riding, and hunting are published.[6] The kings themselves make the arrangements in this regard, when they are not writing or are not styled the authors of books (as in the cases of the *Book on Hunting* by João I and the works by King Duarte). It is interesting to note that these treatises, frequently read or heard by the nobles, transmitted a great deal of empirical knowledge about zoology, veterinary science, medicine, and nature.

The vogue in chivalric romances also enters Portugal. In the fourteenth century, *Amadis de Gaula* is written. During the whole of this century, and the two following, books of chivalry are fashionable and beguiling, especially to young people. Constable Nuno Álvares, when an adolescent, "had great relish for them and used to listen to and read books of such stories a great deal: he would especially read the story of Galahad, in which is contained the substance of the Round Table."[7] This, and similar comments, reveals the increasing presence of books in the homes of the nobility.

The pleasure in books, whether in reading them or in hearing them read, becomes more and more accentuated. Monasteries lose their monopoly on libraries. In the Portuguese court, books had existed for a long time, but with King Duarte (1433–38) their number rises to eighty-three volumes. Afonso V (1438–81) expands this library, installs it in a special section of the palace, and furnishes it with two large tables for reading.[8] Other aristocrats, like the Dukes of Bragança, the first Marquis of Valença, and the princes of the royal house—many of them cultured and well-traveled—have their own libraries as well.

In the middle of the fifteenth century, Duarte advocates the spread of education among the aristocracy:

> The youth of good lineage who are raised in such a house in which it can be done should be taught right from the beginning to read, write, and speak Latin, continuing with good books in Latin and in the vernacular as good guidance for a virtuous life. . . . Also the books of moral philosophy, which are of many types to provide instruction in good habits and in the pursuit of the virtues, should be seen and taught, and everything pertinent to them, well practiced. And those books on instruction in war, with the approved chronicles, are very pertinent reading for the lords and knights and their children, from which are derived great and good examples and wisdom, which render valuable aid in times of necessity, with the grace of the Lord.[9]

There was another trend, it is true, to which Duarte expressly refers ("Here since some say such literature does not befit men of such estate . . ."), that reproached so much "scribble" in men meant for acts of courage and military virtues. Those people did not take into account the changing times, which also worried Duarte—the old habits, he notes, are being lost and replaced by conversation with women, interest in style, ball games, song, and dance.[10]

The types of books suggested by the monarch corresponded to the literature in vogue ever since the fourteenth century: works of a moralistic stamp or of religious exaltation; chronicles and romances; besides, obviously, didactic works. Interest in the classical authors which is beginning to appear, is generally confined to treatises of the same type. The translation of Aesop's *Fables* into Portuguese belongs to the fifteenth century.[11]

The spread of these and other books could not be extended to a vast public. A book was expensive and hard to come by. Except for religious works—such as Bibles, missals, antiphonies, and other books of the divine office, the necessity of disseminating which put into motion dozens or even hundreds of translators—literary works of any other kind underwent "publication" of one, two, or three exemplars. It was specifically ordered to copy book A or book B because the king or a great lord had expressed interest in owning it. More copies of books of chivalry were certainly produced, but never more than ten of any one book. Sometimes only the passages regarded as being of greatest interest were copied. This phenomenon was also extended to legislative codices, the separate laws, the chapters of the Cortes, and so on.

The book thus was like the painted panel, the tapestries illustrating long stories, the objects of jeweler's craft, the ermine mantle, and the relic: to possess one was a luxury, and only the richest were able proudly to exhibit a "library." The spread of education through reading, therefore, remained restricted to a part of the aristocracy, and to the clergy, owing to its institutions of a collective nature. All of this explains the importance and the favor given cultural transmission by the auditory method and by oral tradition.

The documents do not allow us to evaluate the cultural index of the peasant or the artisan. Comparisons of an ethnological nature with the rude inhabitants of some modern hamlets of Trás-os-Montes or Beira perhaps help us. They did not know how to read or write: they employed rudimentary processes for counting. Often, they did not even know the Christian prayers; in the absence of a church, they still practiced a pagan worship of adoration of the forces of nature. The difficulty of transportation and communication shackled them perpetually to the land where they were born and which they farmed. At best, they would go to the nearest fair or, at long intervals, they would take part in a pilgrimage in the vicinity. What education could one of these men have? He knew the name of the king and had heard stories told of his wealth and of his acts of justice. As he was much nearer than God, the king symbolized the rectification of the grievances received from the lord, the attentive listener of the complaints of the "little people," the infallible and merciful judge. The peasant was more familiar with the great lord or the petty noble, whose lands he tilled; he was completely cognizant of the noble's demands, his violences, his physical exactions. Then he knew the money, the difference between gold and silver alloys, the price of all commodities, and the value of the alqueire and the almude. He had heard tell of Lisbon and of its grandeur, but he did not believe that such a large village with so many people and so much wealth could really exist. Of foreign lands, he was well aware of the border position of Castile because he had already been to war and had seen and heard the enemy. He had a slightly vague idea about the Pope because he knew people who knew others who had actually beheld him by making a pilgrimage to Rome. For the rest, he confused the Emperor sometimes with Jesus Christ, other times with the Pope, and not a few times with an enchanted monarch reigning over fairies and angels. They

Fig. 90. Learning how to count ("The Dialogue of the Numbers"). 12th and 13th centuries.

Fig. 90 (cont.).   Learning how to count.

told him of other countries and of other kings, rich and powerful, but
he could not conceive that they might be greater than the king of
Portugal. Furthermore, that interested him very little. He had rather
to think about the quality of the seed, the perversity of the year, and
the diseases striking his sheep—when not afflicting his wife and children. He was capable of telling by the passage of January if the year
would be one of abundance or one of hunger. He knew perfectly how
to foresee rain, thunderstorms, and heat waves. He calculated the time
of day quite well from the height of the sun. He also knew how to
perform sorcery, how to lay a curse effectively, and how to recognize
when someone had put a hex on him. His wife healed all wounds with
prayers and incantations.[12]

The cloth merchant established in Lisbon or in Oporto would not be
as versed as the noble in moral philosophy or in romances of chivalry.
Nevertheless, he was in possession of a sum of knowledge which is
much more familiar to us today. Besides reading and writing the
various types of letters with rapidity, he knew how to count (sometimes not very well), adding, multiplying, and dividing numbers which
could be quite large and converting libras into soldos (1 libra = 20
soldos) and soldos into dinheiros (1 soldo = 12 dinheiros) rapidly. He
was informed on all the exchanges and knew the value of silver in
relation to gold. He was able to distinguish, without excessive labor,
between a florin and a noble or between a tournois and a maravedi.
The extent of his business gave him a broad knowledge of geography:
he was familiar with the whole coast from Lisbon to Bruges or London, and had precise ideas about Scandinavia and eastern Europe; the
East he knew from Lisbon to Venice through his own experience;
farther toward the east, he was even capable of discoursing on Constantinople and on the Moslem world. He corresponded with his
associates and representatives and with many foreign colleagues: he
wrote in Latin, but he was capable of reading letters in French,
Castilian, Aragonese, or the principal Italian dialects. He knew very
well who the princes reigning in the various states were, and he was
well informed about their foreign policy to the extent to which it
could affect his business. With the king of Portugal he was on intimate
terms. Had he not just lent him a considerable amount of money for
the expenses incurred by the war?

He did not have much time in which to read. He was fascinated
by legends of distant lands, however, and from time to time, by moral
apologies and the lives of saints. He envied the magnificent and care-
free life of the noble knight. He memorized the lineages of the prin-

cipal families and aspired to one day be made a knight or to receive
a coat of arms.

He was, finally, completely versed in his profession. He knew the
whole technique of the textile industry, of dyeing, and of ornamentation of cloth. He also knew the markets; he sensed—a little by instinct,
it is true—the law of supply and demand, the basis of wealth. He was
knowledgeable about the "industrial" development of the country.
He knew the principal fairs where textiles were traded, the commercial
lines which concerned them, the processes of packing and of transportation. That gave him a clear vision of the districts and regions into
which Portugal was divided, of the resources and the power of purchase in each province, of the agglomeration and the dispersion of
people. Instead of the purely localistic view which was that of the
peasant, the vision of the merchant became national. Hence the fact
of his being the most qualified—perhaps even the only one qualified—
to take a seat in the Cortes or on the bench as the attorney of the
council and to formulate grievances with complete knowledge of the
causes and the least risk of committing a blunder.[13]

The physicians and the apothecaries were also guardians of culture.
They were simultaneously heirs to a wide traditional theory of medicine and to a certain practical experience resulting from the treatment
of malaria and the preparation of remedies. Philosophers and theolo-
gians, astrologers and physicians, druggists and charlatans—the
"doctors"—represented a curious type of scholar and scientist typical of
the medieval period.[14]

9 : AMUSEMENTS

EVEN in modern times, the kinds of diversions, their intensity, and their frequency are strongly conditioned by the social level and the material possessions of the people involved. In the Middle Ages, this relationship was even more strict. The great majority of what we consider typically medieval amusements were those of the nobility, as in the case of the tourneys or of the parties where ballads were composed and sung. The common people also had forms of merry-making and ways of forgetting the daily drudgery, but theirs were fewer and less refined. Let us put the clergy to one side, even though this is only in theory: wordly pursuits which kept them from their responsibilities to God were prohibited. In practice, the high clergy joined in the amusements of the nobility, while the lower clergy participated in those of the people. Of course, there were forms of amusements typically ecclesiastical, as the religious mystery plays and church singing, in both of which, moreover, the faithful also took an active part.

It is true that the members of the nobility had a good deal of free time. To be more precise, they had only free time. As we have seen earlier, nobility and engagement in remunerative professions were mutually exclusive. The function of the noble was not to work, but to provide protection with his weapons. The noble society thus was constituted of a body of officers always alert to the collective defense (which was that of their own interests). This was performed with gallantry when it was necessary. They exceeded the limits of their function, however, many times attacking and searching for war only for the pleasure of combat. The entire activity of the nobility in time of peace consisted of the exercise of arms and the maintenance of the strength of their bodies. (Consequently, at least theoretically, King Duarte justifies and recommends certain diversions which are apparently primarily for leisure and pleasure.) Medieval sports arise with the objective of training for war.[1] In these terms, the participation of villeins would have been regarded as absurd, except in unusual cases.

Nevertheless, there were exceptions in the social division of amusements. Some could at least be observed by everyone: for example, the bullfights, the mummeries, and even the jousts and tournaments. Others, although watched by nobles and commoners, excluded the participation of both, such as the Jewish festivals and Morisco merrymaking. Finally, all the members of medieval society were included in others: that was the case with the pilgrimages, the processions, the acclamations, and certain banquets offered by the king in moments of great happiness.

Hunting was among the most beloved activities of the nobility and the clergy, and was practiced the most frequently. In its various forms it was the pastime of kings and lords, who esteemed it, preferred it to everything else, and even theorized on it in glowing treatises. Nobles spent weeks and months on end in the hunt. In 1411 or 1412, the sons of João I decided to cross the Tagus and hunt in Odiana, "passing thus two or three months in their amusements."[2] Afonso IV provoked his counselors' criticism in the beginning of his reign by dedicating more time to the hunt than to the business of ruling. Fernão Lopes praises Pedro I for knowing how to harmonize speedy dispatch of governmental matters with hunts far from the court. Prince João, son of Inês de Castro, appreciated the chase to the point of rising "two or three hours before dawn, starting by night in winters and calms, to ride and run over rocky terrain and shady hills and to jump streams and brooks, which led to great accidents, in which he fell and the horses upon him."[3] And even Fernando, whom some insist on seeing as delicate and not very robust, loved hunting so much that "he said he would not rest until he had populated a street in Santarém with a hundred falconers."[4] For hunting in the Middle Ages was fundamentally of two types: venery (*montaria*), or hunting by furious pursuit of animals, and falconry (*cetraria*), or hunting with domesticated birds of prey.

A good part of the kingdom was covered with woods and dense forest, which favored the proliferation of every kind of hunting. Moreover, throughout Portugal were scattered more or less vast areas set aside as hunting preserves. The great zone of hunting lay south of the Tagus, in the vast uninhabited moors, where even today population is scarce. In the vicinity of Santarém, hunting was carried on with

excellent results in the beginning of the fifteenth century: "Let us go
to these mountains where, in the past, I often have found many huge
boars," João I says to his sons.[5]

The common people often protested against the extension of the
game preserves, but without any great results. The hunting reserves
did decrease gradually after the end of the fifteenth century, but this
was due to the increase in population and the necessity of clearing
new parcels of land for cultivation.

Other protests against the excesses resulting from hunting activity
are found. In the beginning of the thirteenth century, Pope Innocent
III censures Sancho I for obligating the clergy to provide dogs and
birds for hunting. At the end of his reign, perhaps as a token of sub-
mission, the monarch decides to exempt the canons of Coimbra from
lodging hawkers and falconers with birds of the king. And one of
the first acts of Afonso II (1211–23) was to free the humble people
from the obligation of furnishing quivers (linen sacks) for the transportation of the royal falcons. In 1258 his son Afonso III, in a tide of
economy or of concessions to the people, limited the hunting personnel
of his household to one hunter and four falconers. But by 1261 the
team had already been expanded by three more hawkers.[6] A hundred
years later all these laws had fallen into oblivion, and King Fernando
could parade numerous specialized hunting personnel, including
Moors trained in the domestication of herons and in the recovering
of lost falcons.[7]

The objects of the hunt were large animals like the bear, the wild
boar, the wolf, the fallow deer, the hart, and the wild ass. Bears still
abounded in the mid-fourteenth century in Beira and Riba-Coa; there
are suggestions of their existence in the documentation of the previous
centuries. Both the meat and skin were utilized. In 1414, near Portel,
Princes Duarte and Henrique (Henry the Navigator) killed a huge
bear, which they sent to their father, the king. Twenty years afterwards, the bear was already beginning to grow scarce in the country,
the species becoming extinct by the end of the century.[8]

The classic hunt in medieval Portugal selected the wild boar as its
objective. The principal game in preserves for this purpose were located in northern Odiana and in Beira. Afonso V, in defense of the
"art," prohibited killing mountain boars with traps, snares, and
crossbows, as was the custom of the people in defense of their crops.[9]
The *Book on Hunting*, by João I, is a complete treatise on hunting
wild boars, using the spear and a pack of hounds.

Falconry had its appeal and perhaps was even preferred during part
of the Middle Ages (Fig. 91). Special gloves were put on to hold the

Fig. 91. Hunting with a falcon. 15th century.

falcons or hawks. By the price schedule of 1253, a hawking glove made of the hide of roebuck or fallow deer cost twenty dinheiros; the best glove for falcons cost fifteen dinheiros; if the gloves were of sheepskin, the prices fell to six to ten dinheiros. The chains and other equipment to fasten the birds were priced similarly. The same law forbade the theft of eggs of goshawks, hawks, and falcons under penalty of ten libras per egg and loss of all one's possessions. Hunts for live goshawks were limited to the two weeks before the feast of St. John the Baptist (June 24). Hawks and falcons could only be caught "one out of three," that is, the third one.[10]

In 1318, King Dinis ordered his doctor, Master Giraldo, to translate into Portuguese a treatise on the diseases, cure, and treatment of hunting birds. Later, Fernando (who purchased birds from abroad) ordered a similar project to be undertaken by Pero Menino.[11] These books described in great detail the hunting birds employed—falcons-gentle, blue falcons, gerfalcons, hobby falcons, goshawks, and others—their habits, their illnesses, ways of treating them, recommended food, and so on. The chapter on food, for example, suggested milk from donkeys, goats, or cows; butter; chicken; hens; doves; and other delicacies. There was a special prescription for bathing the birds:

> When you want to bathe them, it must be done in this fashion: in the winter, do it in the sunshine, or if there is none, near a fire; and in the summer, in the shade. If it is a delicate bird, take an ounce and a half of well-ground and sifted pepper and a third of an ounce of that pepper also sifted and completely blended; then lay your bird down and sprinkle that powder between his legs, wherever it seems necessary to you. Then take a towel as hot as your hands can stand and roll it up, and put that hot towel on him two or three times, for the space of fifteen minutes. Afterwards clean his eyes and nostrils with a little cold water; then unwrap the towel and go out into the sun with him with a knife or sharp stick, and remove the lice which come out.[12]

Not just the birds were entitled to such care and prescriptions: there exist, from the same age or a little later, detailed instructions on the treatment of horses and hunting dogs.

Falconry and hunting were even recorded in the cancioneiros, as can be seen from this famous song of derision (thirteenth century):

> Sir Gil needed badly
> A little blue falcon
> Who would not fly
> From Sir Gil
> Nor even rob any crumbs!
>
> A little hare-chasing greyhound
> That one hare in a thousand
> Would not steal
> From Sir Gil
> But wag his tail and bark!
>
> A rabbit hound from the banks of the Sil
> Which would not kill time, nor be so vile
> That it wet
> On Sir Gil,
> Whenever it found a hare!
>
> And boots made of wild boar's skin
> Up to his hips
> Which would not tear
> On Sir Gil
> When he would scare up a hare! [13]

But one could hunt without the aid of hounds or falcons. Simpler than the chase or hawking was hunting with the bow and arrow, which, even so, maintained its distinction as an "art." A beautiful love song (*cantiga de amigo*) tells of the pleasure in this kind of hunt:

> Let us go, my sister, let us go to sleep
> On the banks of the lake, where I saw
> My love stalking the birds
>
> .   .   .   .
>
> By the banks of the lake, where I saw
> My friend walking, his bow in hand
> To shoot birds, stalking the birds. [14]

The bourgeoisie and villeins also hunted, but with practical purposes in mind (Fig. 92). The frequency with which wild animals and birds are mentioned as being sold in the butcher shops and markets throughout the country is sufficient proof of the profit from hunting. Rabbits, partridges, and fallow and other deer were hunted, not only

Fig. 92.   Peasants hunting with dogs. 14th century.

in the legal ways, but also—and even especially—the illegal, which appalled the sportsman. Nevertheless, the economic importance that game must have had in daily life led to tolerance by the advocates of the art of hunting. This is the reason why, in 1425, Duarte authorizes the inhabitants of Évora and its territory to hunt partridges and hares in the region (officially a game preserve) and to make use of nets, snares, and other traps. Only hunting with lights was prohibited.[15]

The multiplication in the number of wolves even led to the discontinuation of the habitual protection of game. Nobles and commoners were urged and even compelled to hold a regular beating of the woods to flush game, which in the fifteenth century was to take place every Saturday. Much the same happened as a result of the predation of eagles.[16]

A related sport was the art of riding. To sit a horse properly, to train it, to perform all sorts of maneuvers from high up on the saddle constituted what might be called the obligation of the noble. That is why Duarte, before 1433, wrote the famous *Book of Instruction on the Art of Riding Well*. Actually, the *Book on Hunting* had already dealt at length with the art of horsemanship. The *Art of Riding Well* is a complete treatise which must have served as a breviary to many a young knight. In it, he could learn everything that was necessary for the perfect rider, from the way to handle a horse and make appropriate use of reins and stirrup to the practice of jumping on the horse without any help. Treatises on veterinary science, which taught the internal "mechanics" of the mounts, could be used to complement Duarte's instructions.

Besides racing and jumping, genuine games were performed on horseback, as will be seen further on. In one of these—the *páreo* (race), in which two knights raced side by side holding hands—Prince Afonso died, toward the end of the fifteenth century.

To describe the multiple forms of the saddle, harness, and stirrups that existed during the Middle Ages, disclosing the changing techniques of manufacture and influences on style, is a task which obviously exceeds the objectives of this chapter. In every schedule of prices from the twelfth century to the fifteenth century, and even down to the nineteenth, the list of harnesses is always quite long and indicates subtle differences in the basic material, the execution, and the decoration. As Duarte says, from the appropriate harness frequently derived excellence in riding. A detailed study on riding, which has not been attempted as yet, would find abundant sources and would be an important contribution to history.

Once on horseback, the medieval noble could devote himself to a series of sportive exercises, all of them more or less violent. Of these, the most flamboyant and best known were doubtless the jousts and the tournaments.

Although the Portuguese texts mention both terms, it is difficult to distinguish differing concepts behind them. In principle, the joust was single combat with sword or lance fought between only two persons, while the tourney assumed the form of a battle between several persons. But there are cases of collective jousts. In 1414, in the parties given by Henry the Navigator in Viseu, "there were very grand jousts, in which Prince Duarte and those gentlemen who had come with him jousted against the princes and most of those nobles and gentlemen who were with them."[17]

Jousts and tournaments were among the most popular diversions of the aristocracy. They were generally held in a cleared, flat area (*teia*) surrounded by barriers, with platforms and a dais where the audience, which included numerous ladies, was seated. But there were instances of jousts and tourneys in the middle of the public road. For the celebrations of the marriage by proxy of Princess Leonor, sister of Afonso V, to the Emperor of Germany (1450), the king himself "challenged the knights for the royal jousts which were held on the New Street"— that is, on the principal artery of Lisbon. A passage in the *Book on Hunting* leads to the supposition that such a practice was usual.[18]

An obligatory spectacle, so to speak, at all the festivities, the tournament of the fifteenth century took on aspects of a theatrical presentation or of a contest of elegance, with the knights dressed at times in an exotic manner and contending for an established prize. In the aforementioned celebrations of 1450 were

> proposed prizes and very sumptuous awards for whoever most gallantly came to the field, and in this fashion jousted best. To which Prince Fernando came with his knights-errant* with tresses of fine silk like barbarians, on top of good mounts, in clothing covered with the figures and the characters of well-known animals, and others, misshapen, and all very natural. And Prince Fernando, as the best jouster, then won the prize, which was a rich cup, which he immediately gave to Diogo de Melo. And in the same fashion there came another six knights-errant of Prince Henrique, rich and in good armor; and after them, many others, who on the first day and on the others which the King held, jousted, in which were outstanding and marvelous encounters.[19]

The tournament could be quite dangerous, however, and even deadly for the fighters. In more barbarous times, it frequently degenerated into a genuine battle or was provoked as a settlement of accounts. The famous encounter of Arcos de Valdevez in 1140 was no more than a tourney of this type between the Portuguese and the Leonese.

The joust had its rules, not only in regard to the position of the adversaries but also in such matters as the type of weapons to use and the manner of delivering the blows. Duarte, in the *Art of Riding Well*, hands down some. One example may be selected:

> And to deliver a hard, shashing blow, you should strike on the instant of impact of the horse with both the body and arm relaxed. This I found very proper in tournaments, for if I attempted to hit with the arm alone relaxed, I delivered too light a blow, and if on the exact moment of impact of the horses, both body and arm were loose, the blow was heavier, to my great advantage. And this is my advice for whoever in a tourney wishes to deliver famous blows: that you will rarely wound your opponent if you do not do it on the first combined impact; resting firmly on your legs, relax your body and arm with the sword held tightly in your hand, deliver your blow not completely placed crosswise nor from top to bottom, but in a diagonal line inwards. And for this reason, it is desirable not to make small circles in a great tourney. . . .
>
> . . . and be quite attentive to keep from falling without profit, as happens to many at such a time. And when the first clash has passed, strike always in the place assigned, and as you have given one blow, immediately go to another one without trying to turn until you have crossed

* Jousters of the same party or faction were designated by the term "knight-errant" (Port. *aventureiros,* or *ventureiros*).

Fig. 93.   Knight. 14th century.

the whole field, claiming the places of the principal viewers. And when you see that some of your companions are energetically surrounding others, striking vigorously among them, scattering them on the point of impact of the horses, immediately cross and fall upon others.[20]

A variation of the jousts were what were known as the *canas* (duels by reeds). Instead of lances, the contestants on horseback used pointed reeds to attack each other. This game had its own rules, obviously quite different from those which governed tourneys. Reed duels were held at the wedding of Leonor in 1450, at that of Prince Afonso in 1490, and at many other festivities.[21]

The terms *bafordo* and *tavolado* both denoted the same diversion. It consisted, according to Paulo Merêa, of a knight's hurling his short javelin—which was also called a bafordo—against a palisade of boards in an attempt to knock it down. Already popular in the twelfth and thirteenth centuries, the bafordo even merited a minstrel's song:

> You went, my love, today
> To win the bafordo at the wedding feast.
> You beat all the others, and it pleases me.

In the fifteenth century, the expressions "throwing the tavolado," "hurling the tavolado," or "playing the távolas" were preferred, but the essence of the old game had not changed.[22]

Certain sports could be played either on foot or on horseback, but the latter was more frequent. These included throwing the spear and a kind of javelin known as a *barra* (rod), or maneuvering the sword in the same way. Every noble considered himself an expert in these activities, which were known as *braceria*—that is, the quality of being very strong and agile. King Fernando "was quite strong-armed—indeed no man could be found who was more so; he hit very well with a sword and hurled a spear well on horseback." As much could be said about Prince João and most of the nobles of the period.[23]

João I applies the term *ligeirices* (agility, rapidity, lightness) to the various modes of racing and jumping, with or without horses. One of them, usual in the beginning of the fifteenth century, consisted of "placing one hand on the cantle and the other on the pommel of the saddle, and jumping on the horse." Other exercises were running, jumping, jumping over an obstacle after a short run (a kind of obstacle race), and jumping with the feet together.[24]

Duarte champions the virtues of hand-to-hand combat in sporting exercise. There were professors of this skill, who taught the blows of a good fighter. At the end of the fourteenth century and the beginning of the fifteenth, public fights were fashionable, and João I himself was devoted to this recreation. Duarte complains about its neglect by the nobles of his period.[25] One fought in normal clothing or in a special boxer's outfit, which the texts do not describe but which must have been limited to a few brief pieces of clothing.

Finally, in the field of violent sports the game of *péla* (handball) must be mentioned. Duarte does not praise it; on the contrary, he includes it in the list of games that entertained the youth of his period to the detriment of the practices of knighthood. But João I considered handball very useful for training in arms: "Today in this age, some, when they are amusing themselves and it is necessary to perform in arms, play ball, because this game makes the members of the body supple."[26] There is no description of this ball game, but it probably was one of throwing the ball, perhaps with the intent of knocking down some obstacle or simply of hitting a distant point.

The nobility did not entertain itself solely by riding, sword play, or other violent sports. Nor, many times, did the weather permit it. Inside the home on winter evenings or when it was raining and thundering outside, the king, the lord, the vassals, and their families needed to pass the time in some way. Besides, the social transformations from the eleventh to the fifteenth centuries were in the direction of a more and more marked preference for the "peaceful," less bellicose distractions in which women could participate and where the company of the two sexes was emphasized.

Duarte complained, as we have already seen, of this change of habits, which came to Portugal a little later than elsewhere. The youth of his time preferred conversing with ladies, playing ball, singing, and dancing to horseback riding. Furthermore, fashion in clothing worried him exceedingly. Nevertheless, writing a quarter of a century

earlier, João I, with much more tolerance and openmindedness, applauded dancing and playing musical instruments, just as he praised
the utility of the handball game.[27]

One of the table games known and held in high regard in the
Middle Ages was chess, the invention of which dated from antiquity.
João I exalts it as able training for battle: the object of the game, the
basic rules, and the indispensable planning approximated military
strategy. Accordingly, it was not inappropriate for a knight to play
chess; rather, it schooled him in the tactics of actual conflicts. When
she married Fernando, in the mid-fifteenth century, Princess Beatriz
brought a chessboard in her trousseau.[28]

Card games, of Chinese origin, were introduced into Europe toward
the end of the Middle Ages. There is at least a trace of their existence
in fifteenth-century Portugal, although neither João I nor Duarte
mentions them. They were, apparently, more popular among the
commoners than the nobility. They were found in the gambling houses
(tavolagens), those ancestors of the modern casinos or the cabarets,
where men drank, gambled for money, and encountered women of
low repute.

From time to time such taverns were prohibited. The first known
repressive law dates from the reign of Afonso IV (1325–57). Taking
into consideration that "many men, not regarding the good of God
nor the profit of the world where they are, they utter many and very
evil phrases, reviling God and His Mother and the Saints, because of
which vituperations many tempests come unto the lands, and we
noticing how men are induced by the game of dice to this sin and to
many others, specifically in the places where the taverns are accustomed
to be in the public squares; and that likewise great injuries and disasters develop among those who are in the habit of playing these
games and many others" and magnanimously disdaining "the many
revenues which we . . . up till now have received," the king forbade
the existence of taverns, whether public or private, under penalty of
a harsh fine.

This measure, it would seem, did not have the desired effect.
Fernando renewed the prohibition. João I forbade all gambling for
money (there were several such games). Pedro, while regent, included
these several laws in the ordinances of 1446. But the taverns always
reappeared, if they ever did really disappear at any time. In 1490,
when João II was in Évora, "it being certified that in Lisbon, in the
houses of one Diogo Pires, knight as he was called on foot, which were
next to the Square of Straw, dice and cards and other games were
played, by which they did a disservice to God Our Lord, His name and

that of His saints being cursed and blasphemed; as in everything he [João II] was a very Catholic prince, to prevent such a great evil, he ordered that, with notices of justice published in the same case, they should, as they were, be burned during the day, publicly."[29] Here is a member of the lesser nobility—a knight—the proprietor of a gambling house, where he would certainly receive other knights as well. The relative secrecy with which these taverns, prohibited by law, had to be operated certainly would have attracted the *jeunesse dorée* of the period, as it always attracts those of any age.

The game of dice was the most ancient, the most popular, and the most persecuted by the authorities. Nobles, commoners, and even harlots engaged in it. In the thirteenth century, the troubadour Pero Garcia Burgalês satirized Maria Balteira, a lady who liked to play:

> Maria Balteira, why do you play
> Dice, since you do not believe in them?
> Some news I will tell you that you may know:
> With all who meet you, you lose,
> For I tell you what I hear them say
> That you should not disbelieve,
> For you are already a grown woman, and yet you want to play.[30]

In 1304, nothing less than the penalty of death threatened whoever "throws or wishes to play any dishonest game, or in a game introduces crooked or loaded dice." In the fifteenth century, attitudes are found to be much softer, and the punishment is reduced to a public flogging, or to exile to the Islands and payment of a fine, or simply to banishment to Ceuta if the guilty party is a noble. The Constitutions of the Archbishopric of Lisbon, from the beginning of the fifteenth century, prohibit gambling with dice between December 24 and January 8, owing to the sanctity of the period.

In the time of João I, there were those—particularly rural landowners, merchants, and professional men—who might stake at dice everything they possessed or expected to own, even meat, fish, grain, vegetables, and drink. The law forbade such excessive stakes, allowing only "rounds of drinks" of wine ("save if it might be wine to drink immediately and pay for, costing no more than twenty soldos").

Other games of chance found favor with the public. Card games included *vaca* (a game resembling monte, in which the croupier extracted from the deck and placed on the table four cards for the players to bet on, one against the others, the winning partners being those who bet on the cards to appear first) and perhaps the game called *jaldete. Butir* and *porca* were games of throwing objects at a target, the latter resembling the modern ninepins. *Curre-curre*, not

introduced in Portugal until the late Middle Ages, corresponded in
some ways to the modern odd or even. A person held a certain number
of objects in his hand, saying, "curre-curre." The opponent answered,
"I am coming in," trying to guess how many objects there were. Other
games of chance were *torrelhas* and *dados fêmeas* ("female dice"),
possibly both variations on dice.[31]

The *Cancioneiro Geral* by Garcia de Resende mentions still other
games from the end of the fifteenth century, and even from the sixteenth: *aléo*, which was actually a stick with which to play ball;
badalassa, a kind of popular roulette; *conca* (quoits), a game of throwing objects at the base of lumps of earth; and so on. Similarly, the *pião*
(whirligig) and the games of *dinheiros secos* ("dry dinheiros") and
dinheiros molhados ("wet dinheiros") were played.[32]

Among themselves, or with the gallants who were visiting them, the
ladies also indulged in gambling. In the fifteenth century, games of
forfeit were introduced and quickly became popular as salon games.
Thus the ladies and maidens amused themselves, as an alternative
to the embroidering and sewing which tradition preserves as the
typical occupations of women in the Middle Ages.

Troubadours and minstrels played an outstanding role in the amusement of the nobility from the twelfth to the fourteen centuries. The
subject is too well known to require extensive discussion here, having
already been amply studied by historians and literary critics.[33] The
troubadour was generally a noble who composed the poem, and sometimes, the music for it, which minstrels played and sang. In the
Portuguese court, troubadours and minstrels increased after the mid-
thirteenth century, flourishing for nearly a hundred years and leaving
the tradition of their presence during the 1400's.

Today we designate as "minstrels" all these musicians, acrobats, folk
poets, or actors, because they were a little of everything, wandering
from land to land in the manner of itinerant circuses, stopping whenever there was an audience to applaud and reward them, naturally
preferring the residences of the mighty lords or the wealthy monasteries. But the terminology of the period drew a distinction among the
jograis, minstrels properly so called—those who played instruments;
remedadores—those who preferred to do imitations; *segréis*—those of
the highest category, who were presented in the courts; *caçurros*—the
most miserable and least esteemed, who addressed themselves exclusively to the mob, with crude and naïve "programs"; *soldadeiras*, whom
we have mentioned before—dancers, musicians, and semi-prostitutes;
and so on. Another kind of minstrel were the mimes, itinerant actors,

Fig. 94.   Troubadours. 13th century.

specialists in farce and other quasi-theatrical compositions, who fre-
quented the courts and presented the *arremedilhos*, ancestors of our
theatrical plays. In the fourteenth century, or perhaps even before, the
Goliards—vagabond clerics or wayward students who were half minstrels and half troubadours, themselves composing, reciting, singing,
and acting as clowns—appear in Portugal.[34]

In the king's court, and undoubtedly in the most important
seigniorial mansions, some minstrels were always established, becoming
sedentary in return for the promise of free residence and food and
assured employment. From them often came the fools, more famous
in legend and tradition than documented by history (Fig. 95). In 1258
the number of resident minstrels in the court of Afonso III was fixed
at three. The stay of soldadeiras for periods longer than three days
was forbidden.[35] Measures such as this must not have been effective,
and later laws completely omit reference to minstrels and soldadeiras.

The largest number of ballads sang of love, in all its various forms.
But there were many other types as well. Remote ancestors of the

Fig. 95. Buffoon, or fool.
13th century.

modern vaudevilles were the songs of derision and defamation (*cantigas de escárnio e mal-dizer*), which satirized events, customs, and persons in vigorous, caustic, sometimes obscene stanzas. One may presume that some were sung only in the presence of the king, the court, or the nobility of the provinces, for the "insignificant people" would not have understood them. For these people there was the buffoonery of the minstrels and the caçurros, capable of delighting their coarse senses and alleviating the sorrows of life.

Another genre of ballads had practical aims, aside from being purely amusing. This was the "informative" ballad, a rhymed and rhythmic way of transmiting news over great distances. In the *Cancioneiro Geral* of Garcia de Resende there are several of these ballads, dating from the end of the fifteenth century or the beginning of the sixteenth. But this type of ballad was much older, having developed in the early fifteenth century. In fact, in the *Chronicle on the Capture of Ceuta*, referring to the events of 1415, it is said that "a Jew, servant of Queen Philippa, who was named Black Juda and who was a great troubadour according to the ballads of that period, in a song which he sent to a squire of Prince Pedro, one Martim Afonso de Atouguia by name, [told] him the news of the court, relating everything that we said, and many other things, among which, in the final foot of the fourth ballad, he said . . . that the king would travel to the city of Ceuta."[36]

Although the sources are scanty, the impression remains that dance, song, and conversation were preferred to the ballad and the histrionic spectacular at the soirées at the end of the fourteenth century and in the fifteenth. Troubadours would always be applauded and appreciated; however, poetic composition itself is freed from the obligatory refrain and from musical rhythm to become a sequence of rhythmical words declaimed by their respective authors. On the other hand, dancing, definitely disdained by the noble two hundred years before, becomes an obligatory activity for the courtier of the fifteenth century.

There is very little information about the ballroom dances of the Portuguese court in the fourteenth and fifteenth centuries. Nonetheless, there is practically no text which does not mention them when speaking of public or private parties. João I praises dancing and playing a musical instrument, and speaks with delight of the rooms decorated for the balls of his time. Duarte testifies to the frequency of the dance as entertainment. At Duarte's marriage with Leonor, Henry the Navigator relates that at the party "we danced and sang a little while in the palace." The princess was very talented, and the bridegroom saw that in dancing and singing "and in any other thing which she could adopt of enjoyment, she seized it with goodwill; and she is quite gay and very wholesome, thanks be to God; and the singing of the Princess is praised a great deal and so is her playing of the virginal, and the dancing according to her personal style, and thus they say that she dances."37

The highly refined dances of the fifteenth century would have been only a few slow steps to the sound of soft stringed instruments, which the gentleman and the lady, or the knight with two ladies, performed face to face, holding one hand, with an abundance of bows and flourishes. Aside from these, there were more popular dances of the circle type, which were not absent from the palace parties. In these, there was singing, or at least some choruses were sung, with happier and faster music played with French horns, bass drums, and other wind and percussion instruments. Sometimes the dancers accompanied the rhythm by clapping their hands. Popular dance spectacles in the presence of sophisticated palace audiences were also common. Villeins were hired to sing and dance to their traditionally simple and unpretentious ditties in front of the king, the mighty lords, or illustrious guests.

The typical dances of the Jews and the Moors were very greatly prized. When Prince Afonso, son of João II, married, the king ordered "that from all the Moorish quarters in the Kingdom all the Moslem men and women who knew how to dance, play instruments, and sing must come to the celebrations. . . . It was ordered and obeyed that from the places closest [to Évora] beautiful girls who know well how to dance and sing should come to the aforesaid places, for they came with young jesters, dressed in their imaginative clothing." The German Rosmital, visiting the country in 1466, also tells us "of the manner in which the Saracen pagans perform their festivals."38

All the popular celebrations were based on music and dancing. The participants danced in a circle, sang, clapped their hands, and stamped their feet. The dance pervaded a good part of the love songs of the thirteenth and fourteenth centuries:

> Let us all three dance now, my friends,
> Under these flowering hazel trees.

There are dances for women alone and there are dances in which both sexes take part. (Were there also those just for men?) Some ballads speak of dances in the churchyards, which developed among the youth while their mothers prayed in the church.39 Singing and dancing enlivened the fairs and the pilgrimages and interrupted the rural labors. Men's choruses, singing a melody in unison or accompanying a solo, were to be heard throughout the provinces, rambling through the grainfields, threshing floors, and orchards, and lightening the drudgery of the crafts. In some places, the people utilized the very antiphonies of the church for lay ballads.[40]

All this musical folklore, which in good part has persisted down to our day, required musical instruments. The Middle Ages knew several and bequeathed us many.

The most frequent stringed instruments were the viola, the cittern, the lute, the harp, the psaltery, the rote, the symphony, the Moorish rebeck, and even the gigue, the bandore, and the virginal.

Resembling the modern violin, the viola could be played with a bow or plucked with a plume. It was perhaps the most fashionable instrument among the troubadours. The cittern (*citola*, also called *cedra* or *citolom*) corresponded to the present Portuguese guitar, and it already appears with this name in the fifteenth century. It is frequently mentioned in the troubadour lyric:

> Lopo began to tune his cittern
> So that he could play;
> And they gave orders to give him something
> So that he would stop.
> And then he immediately began to sing
> And they gave him another gift
> So that he would be quiet.

The harp, psaltery, and rote were only variations on the same instrument. The harp was played in a vertical position. On the other hand, the psaltery was played horizontally. The rote was a small harp. The virginal, more complex, was played by a keyboard. The princesses had already learned to play it in the first half of the fifteenth century.

Stringed instruments were not always preferred. King Pedro was charmed rather with the loud noise of the *longa* (a horn, a kind of shawm), the French horn, and the shawm, obligatory in any festivity. Other wind instruments mentioned are the *exabeba*(?), the *anafil* (a Morisco horn resembling a shawm), the *alboque*(?), the flute, the pipe, and the fife. The organ was also known in various sizes, now portable, now transported on the back of an animal. To play an organ required great skill and long apprenticeship: a song of derision cites Master Nicolau, who had learned to play the organ in Montpellier.

Finally, there were the percussion instruments—the drum (*tambor*, or *atambor*, with a variety of tabret), the tambourine, the *adufe* (timbrel), the kettledrum or barrel-shaped drum, and even castanets.[41]

Serious music was predominately religious, with a large variety of masses and of canticles for the various divine offices. Before the fif-

Fig. 96. Wind instruments. *Top,* twelfth
century; *bottom,* fifteenth century.

teenth century, there is no evidence of the use of polyphony, but in
·1415 a contrapuntal Te Deum was performed in celebration of the
victory of Ceuta. By the time of João I, the name of Guillaume de
Machaut (in Portuguese, Guilherme de Machado) was already known
in Portugal. The *Book on Hunting* prosaically compares his work to
the race of dogs after their quarry: "Here we can say quite well that
Guilherme de Machado did not create such a beautiful concord of
melody, no matter how fine it may be, as the dogs produce when they
are running well."[42]

The Regiment of the Royal Chapel by Duarte, which we have
referred to in another chapter, gives evidence of a certain develop-

ment of church music in Portugal at the end of the Middle Ages.

Toward the end of the Middle Ages, lay music took its first steps toward orchestral composition. From the time of João I, we know the names of several musicians, many of them laymen, who were attached to the court and produced instrumental pieces for it. Álvaro Afonso, possibly a priest, composes a service commemorating the capture of Arzila (1472), which is dedicated to the king. Musicians, singers, and minstrels, as well as musical instruments, are cited. Some

Fig. 97. Performance of religious music. 15th century.

nobles of high degree, as the Count of Ourém and the Count of Arraiolos, also had their private musicians. Tristão da Silva was the outstanding composer in the age of Afonso V, and the monarch himself, in the words of Rui de Pina, "was very fond of hearing music, and had a high regard for it from his own nature, which was unaffected by artifice."[43]

Throughout the year were staggered several dozen holy days and traditional holidays dedicated to provincial patron saints. They were the cause of processions, songs, and dances, more secular than religious, as we have had occasion to see. Certain commemorations, too, were more lay than religious: thus, for example, the festivities of the battle of Aljubarrota (1385) or the battle of Toro (1476). The battle of Salado (October 30, 1340) even had a commemorative hymn, which was sung in the special religious service. The hymn had quite secular lyrics, which extolled the military virtues of the Christians; it began with the following verses:

> Glory be to the Spaniards
> For this solemn victory
> Which the triune God
> Has conferred upon the Christians.
>
> .   .   .   .
>
> And He has saved, thanks to the Spaniards,
> All the Kings of Christendom;
> Therefore the Church to Christ
> Sings psalms for ever and ever.

These lyrics had been put to music already in existence—the hymn of the feast of All Saints. (This secular use of religious music was a common practice in the Middle Ages, even among troubadours and popular poets.)[44]

A description of the multiple celebrations of popular origin would be endless. They commemorated not only the happy events of Catholicism, but also those of paganism, masked with the character of Christian ceremony, and even purely pagan usages. That was the case of the Januaries and the Mays, which the authorities sought to suppress many times without effect.[45] The most important Christian feasts observed throughout the country were those of Christmas, Easter, St. John the Baptist, Corpus Christi, and All Saints Day. Jews and Moors similarly had their own celebrations. The usual entertainments at such festivities differed little from those of today. Then, as now, religious ceremonies (especially processions), markets or fairs, chiming bells, dances and songfests, and collective feasts, provided the typical color. Likewise, little difference is to be seen in the great urban celebrations commemorating the births, baptisms, or weddings of great lords. Nevertheless, some particular characteristics distinguish them. In the first place there were the bullfights.

Of Greco-Roman origin, the bullfights arose from the sacrifices of bulls in the amphitheaters and the arenas with the design of placating the fury of the diabolical gods. These fights were held in high esteem by the Moors and had already enjoyed several centuries as a tradition when the kingdom of Portugal appeared. The documents give evidence of their perseverance throughout the medieval period. Bullfights are mentioned by the twelfth century; by the fourteenth and fifteenth centuries, they were quite frequent at commemorative celebrations. At the marriage of Beatriz, daughter of Fernando, to the king of Castile (1383), "after dining they jousted and tourneyed and fought bulls." In 1428, Duarte wed; in Coimbra, where the wedding took place, "Lady Guiomar ordered that two bulls be run here for the Princess, and they ran them both at the same time, one in a corral [yard, patio] of the palaces and the other where the jousts were held in front of Santa Clara, and two of my men [Henry the Navigator's] awaited the one at the palace, because he was small, and they killed him very ably." It is not known if bulls to be killed were fought by men on foot or on horseback.

In 1450, during the celebrations of the marriage of Leonor to Frederick III of Germany, there was also a bullfight in Lisbon. As the German ambassador Nicolaus Lanckmann von Valkenstein narrates, "At midday the king commanded six brave bulls to run, and in the view of all the people came Moors of both sexes dancing and playing instruments. And they seized two live bulls, which they slaughtered and quartered and distributed in accordance with their custom." The description is too imprecise to allow us to draw conclusions from it about the kind of bullfights held in that period. It seems that the bullfight was performed in the Morisco style, with the capture and sacrifice of the victim (maintaining the Roman tradition) and the distribution of pieces of the animal's flesh by the "executioners."

In 1455, when Joana, sister of Afonso V, passed through Évora on her way to marry the King of Castile, bulls which were valued at between thirty-five thousand and thirty-six thousand reais brancos were run. Other documents of the municipality of Évora reveal that it was customary to fight bulls on the day of Corpus Christi and that in 1471, when Prince Afonso was born, "if it had not been raining so hard on Sunday last, we, old men and youths, would have had to contend with the bulls." This is obvious evidence of the participation of the commoners in bullfights, a little in the manner of the bullfights by amateurs or of the encounters with the bulls in Vila Franca.

The illustrations multiply: during the celebrations of the wedding of Prince Afonso in 1490, the city of Évora presented fifty bulls to be run, doubtless in a series of bullfights spread over the several days of the festivities.[46]

Less common but no less popular were the mummeries. A mummery was a masquerade involving exotic disguises which were slipped on to cause laughter or to impress the public. It was customary for the mummers to accompany their masquerades with histrionic gesticulation, in imitations symbolic of or inherent to a particular plot. Therefore, the mummeries and their antics can also be counted among the ancestors of theatrical performance, especially those of the comic theater. Much later relegated only to the carnival days, the mummeries and the masquerade balls were then an integral part of the amusements given during the year, when such amusements were out of the ordinary.

Henry the Navigator offered grand parties for his friends on the Christmas of 1414: in preparation, "the Prince sent to Lisbon and Oporto for bolts of silk and wool and embroiderers and tailors to make their liveries and mummeries, so that they would actually be worthy of his party." And his spectacle was a hit: "There were mummeries of such an extravagant fashion that the sight of them was a very great pleasure." Members of the nobility sometimes took part in the masquerade: "And in like manner, many other very excellent mummeries of nobles were held," we are told in regard to the celebrations of Prince Afonso's marriage. Other instances could be mentioned. Rui de Pina, in his narration of the wedding of Prince Afonso (1490), portrays with great realism the mummeries of that period:

> And on the following Tuesday, there was held in the hall of wood superb and very beautiful mummeries, in one of which the King, to instigate a joust in which he would be a defender, came as the first mummer, ornamented artfully as the Knight of the Swan, with a great deal of wealth, charm, and graciousness. He entered through the doors of the hall with a large fleet of great ships, set on bolts of cloth painted as stormy and natural waves of the ocean, with great thunder of ordnance being fired, and trumpets and horns, and minstrels playing instruments, with wild shouts and the turmoil of whistles by make-believe masters, pilots, and mariners who were dressed in brocades and silks, and the authentic, rich clothing of the Germans. The quarterdecks of the ships were of brocade, and the sails of white and purple taffeta, and the ship's rigging of gold and silk, stocked and completely full of flaming candles and oil lamps.

The flags, squared on the bottom, and the standards at the topsails were of the arms of the king and the princess. A large and beautiful swan with white and golden feathers came in front of the fleet on the water; and after him, in the prow of the first ship and piloting it, came his knight, who, fully armed, came out with his speech, in the name of the king, and gave the Princess a brief relating his intense desire to serve her in the celebrations of her marriage; wherein, by certain assertions of love, which he affirmed, he challenged and provoked with a joust of arms, with his eight champions, all those who might wish to fight for the contrary. And after that, with arms, trumpets, and officials selected for this, the brief, the challenge, the conditions of the jousts, and the prizes in them were announced in a loud voice; thus it would be for whoever most gallantly came to the field, as well as for whoever fought best. And after this the King sallied forth in his very luxurious masquerade dress and danced with the Princess, and in like manner the others with their ladies. And then there came other mummers of the Duke and of other nobles, who, with words and invention of great zeal and grace, accepted the same conditions, and by their briefs took upon themselves the challenge of the joust. And they danced that night, and there were many farces and festivities.

The function of the mummers here, as in other festivities, consisted in serving as heralds for the tourneys, announcing the number of contenders, the rules, and so on.[47]

The texts speak still further of *entremezes* (interludes), although the word seems to connote only the idea of amusement, without applying to a particular kind of spectacle: Thus, Rui de Pina speaks of a "hall of wood for banquets and Christmas Eve dinners, mummeries, bullfights, duels with reeds and jousts, and other interludes," and elsewhere, of "bullfights and reed duels and more mummeries and banquets and many interludes of great contrivance and great expense." [48]

When a great person was knighted or a title of high nobility was established, it was customary to hold celebrations, which could vary greatly in the kind of entertainments proposed. King Pedro I spent vast sums of money on large candles and torches for the festivities that accompanied the knighting of João Afonso Telo in the mid-fourteenth century. Planning to knight his oldest sons, King João I announced his intention to

order some regal celebrations to last the entire year, for which I will command to be invited all the nobles and knights who are of an age and disposition for such a deed that may be in all the kingdoms of Christendom, and I will order that in the said celebrations there be extraordinary jousts and great tourneys and very sumptuous banquets supplied with every kind of food which exists, both within my realm and outside of it.

And the dances and other amusements will be so many and of such nature that of them, as of all the other things, the people who see them shall say that greater or better than these they cannot hold.

Celebrations of his kind were relatively common, because knighthood was now being conferred upon townspeople, sons of "townsmen and merchants," who spent as much as they could on celebrations and amusements, since — as the nobles sniffed scornfully — "the essence of their honor lies in the fame of their expenditure." [49]

Money for splendid illuminations to penetrate the thick night of the times previous to gas and electricity was not spared. Torches, large and small candles, flambeaus, oil lamps, and fires were lighted in towers and belfries, placed at windows and on terraces, or were carried in long processions. Around 1455 or 1456, Afonso V knighted his brother, Prince Fernando, "with so much ceremony that almost the least luxurious aspect of this pomp was that one thousand torches, carried by four hundred gentlemen and six hundred squires of the most magnificent of the court, all dressed in a suit and livery, preceded this magnificent act." In the Évora of 1490 "very great luminaries" were ordered to distribute light "in the towers and the steeples of the churches in such a way that it lasts most of the night." Even at this early date, gunpowder was used a great deal to brighten the celebrations.[50]

All the festivities of consequence included more or less opulent, more or less satiating banquets, consonant with the money available and the distinction that was desirable to impart to the occasion. In 1490, Évora and several villages in Odiana jointly participated in lavish banquets honoring the princely wedding; the fare included 120 sheep, 1,200 chickens, 150 ducks, 100 kids, 60 suckling pigs, 12,000 reais worth of rabbits and partridges, seven arrobas of sweets, five arrobas of dates, 50 bowls of fried foods, and 30 bowls of honey cakes.[51] In Chapter 1 of this book we have seen descriptions of two of these banquets, typical of celebrations at the end of the Middle Ages. Between the serving of each dish, there were sometimes histrionic spectaculars, antics, dances, and music. On the other side of the Pyrenees, such "interludes" were known as entr'actes (entre-mets); as we have already seen, however, in Portugal the expression was utilized in a more generic sense.

From time to time, the kings took advantage of an event of special importance to present the people with dazzling spectacles of pageantry and assorted compositions. Such occasions also afforded a means of displaying wealth and impressing foreign visitors. Because of the heterogeneity of the diversions, such festivities could almost be compared to modern international fairs. They came to last longer than a week and included—in addition to the usual bullfights, reed duels, mummeries, tourneys, games, dances, and banquets—military parades, historical processions, exhibitions of folklore, and even short plays. Perhaps the most famous of such festivities were those ordered by Afonso V, from the thirteenth to the fifteenth of October 1450, on the occasion of the wedding of his sister Leonor to Frederick III of Germany. One modern scholar wishes to see—and he seems to be correct—theatrical performances in the entertainments alluded to in such festivities; and he compares favorably the farces described with the early sixteenth-century *Play of the Visitation* (*Auto da Visitação*) by Gil Vicente, the famous founder of the Portuguese theater.[52]

The festivities began on the thirteenth with a kind of historical procession. In front came kings at arms and heralds saluting the new empress in the name of all the queens of Christendom. They were followed by Ethiopians and Moors dragging a representation of a dragon and displaying their customs. Prince Fernando rode behind these at the head of his men at arms, all of whom were dressed in the same color. The procession continued with a parade of "savages," portraying the inhabitants of the Canaries. In the place of honor rode King Afonso V in front of his militia. The procession closed with a contingent of Germans, who came to greet their empress.

On October 14, a "theatrical" spectacular unfolded in the center of Lisbon, near the Cathedral. Actors in masks and costumes represented the Seven Electors of the Holy Roman Empire of Germany in the act of electing Frederick III; others depicted the Pope, the cardinals of the Roman curia, the emperor and empress, high dignitaries of the Portuguese Church, canons, and other clergy. After a symbolic blessing, youths dressed as angels approached, bearing the imperial crown and singing canticles of praise. Another setting symbolized paradise, with a high tower from whose windows angels emerged, "flying" and sprinkling roses on the imperial heads. Farther on, in another scene, could be seen the images of all the kings of Portugal down to Afonso V. There, addressing himself to the audience (almost twenty thousand persons, according to Valkenstein), a "doctor" delivered a laudatory harangue on the heroic achievements of the Portuguese monarchs against the infidels. In a sonorous and dramatic oration the story of the Prince Saint* was related; the audience shed copious tears. Then three girls representing the theological virtues appeared to exhort the

---

* Fernando, brother of Henry the Navigator, who died in Morocco a captive of the Moors.

empress to fulfill faithfully her duties as a wife and a Christian. In a final "apotheosis" a fountain appeared, spraying rose water over a delightful garden where various wild animals were seen. And to conclude the spectacular, thirteen prophets predicted all kinds of happiness for the empress.

On the fifteenth the bullfight was held in the area in front of the palace of Alcáçova. The magnificent military parade, in which the king and his army were preceded by heralds, dancers, and shawm players, took place on the sixteenth.

The festivities on the seventeenth began with a new procession in which Christians, Moors, barbarians, and Jews took part, dancing and playing. Then came the captain general of the sea, challenging the king of Portugal to combat. Several clamoring soldiers seated on the figure of a serpent, which had a horrible aspect and an arched, elevated neck, joined in challenging him to battle. Then the tourney was held, the king and his men fighting against Prince Fernando. The day closed with another procession, in which persons costumed as wild or mythological animals (elephants, unicorns, bulls, lions, capricorns, and bears) took part, alongside of and followed by the participants in the jousts.

On October 18, mummeries were held with a gigantic figure of a dragon parading and dancing in front of the royal palace. The antics continued on into the following day. On the twentieth, hunters with dogs and dead wild animals passed in review, followed by various men at arms. On the twenty-first, the mummeries recaptured the center of attention with another theatrical spectacular, in which the king of Troy and his sons participated. There were battles between pagans and Saracens, accompanied by tournaments and juggling acts on the twenty-second. The twenty-third was reserved for the folklore dances, in which Christians, Moors, Jews, and savage Ethiops and Canarians participated. On the following day, a great banquet with sumptuous decorations was given. After the feast there was music and dances, and "very soft voices, singing musical poems for two hours." Finally, the festivities concluded splendidly on the twenty-fifth with a great religious service in the Cathedral.[53]

10 : DEATH

WRITING in the first half of the fifteenth century on life expectancy and the theory of ages, King Duarte declared:

> The ages are divided in many ways, but one which the scholars propose, which seems good to me, calls the first period up to seven years old infancy, childhood till fourteen, adolescence until twenty-one, youth till fifty, old age until seventy, senility up to eighty, and from thence until the end of life decrepitude. And this agrees with the saying of King David, in the psalm which goes: "The days of our years are threescore years and ten; and if by reason of strength they be fourscore years, yet is their strength labour and sorrow."[1]

This text is truly revealing of the number of years which one could anticipate living during the Middle Ages. Old age was reached when a person had rounded half a century. Seventy years was considered the limit of life. More than this was regarded as exceptional and almost always "labour and sorrow." But that end was believed to be a goal that very few reached. Once past fifty, one attained the psychology of an old person. At fifty-three, Queen Philippa of Lancaster considered herself an "old woman" and consequently refused to flee the plague, which proceeded to harvest her.[2] Similar testimony appears here and there in chronicles and documents.

Autumn in the life of the medieval man began at about thirty-five years of age. In his own theory on age, Duarte writes that

> in the first, at seven, people change teeth; in the second, at fourteen, they are at an age in which they can marry; in the third, at twenty-one, they have finished growing; in the fourth, at twenty-eight, they attain their full strength and complete furnishing of body; in the fifth, at thirty-five, is attained perfect endeavor, advice, and natural understanding; and thenceforward, similarly every seven years, I perceive that they decline by other degrees naturally, although this cannot be seen so clearly, until completing the number of seventy years of age, at which time we must make an end of our days for the achievements of the present life.[3]

Observation of daily life would not yield different conclusions. Of the kings of Portugal only the two dynastic founders—Afonso Henriques and João I—exceeded seventy years in age. Only four reached "old age"—Sancho I, Afonso III, Dinis, and Afonso IV. The rest died in their "youth." The same was true of the queens and princesses. The average lifespan of more than sixty members of the Portuguese royal family from the twelfth century to the fifteenth was no more than forty-nine years, even disregarding the cases of infant mortality.

The increase in epidemics and a lowered resistance to infections after the mid-fourteenth century produced as a possible consequence a decrease in the number of years that the medieval man could rightfully expect to reach. He died more quickly, and he died in childhood, in adolescence, in the full strength of maturity. The Portuguese of the fifteenth century perceived this and commented on it. The scholars sought to deny it with specious arguments: "And this must draw us from that simple thought, for some think that men now live fewer years than they lived in the period of our grandfathers, while quite the contrary is shown, because many in this age live in a reasonable state of health." 4 Today, historical knowledge seems to support the first thesis.

Infant mortality was quite high, and the high birthrate was not enough to counterbalance it. The result was a stagnation (when not a decrease) in the number of inhabitants over a period of several centuries. Rare was the family that had not lost one or more children at a tender age, in childhood or in adolescence; this happened to all the Portuguese sovereigns with the exception of Afonso II. An investigation of the genealogical records from the twelfth century to the fourteenth shows that the average number of children per couple who survived was approximately two and that there were numerous homes where only a single child reached his majority.5 If such conclusions are arrived at in respect to the aristocracy, we may with much greater cause extend them to the common people, who were less protected by hygiene and diligence, and received less attention from the doctors.

If death is so near, if plagues and wars are common episodes repeated many times in the course of each generation, it is not surprising that the presence of death, the memory of death, the theme of death arises as a constant in daily life and in literature and art. More than ever the Church insists on the transitory nature of the pleasures of this world and upon the necessity for each Christian to meditate on his passage to eternal life. Hence, a soaring in religious fervor and in devout practices. Hence also, the constant renewal of prohibitions against everything that might swerve man from his Christian condition. This necessarily accompanies a passionate love for life and an unlimited desire to enjoy earthly pleasures while there is yet time. This subject has already been broached at various times in the preceding pages.

It is difficult to single out the most common reasons for the medieval mortality rate. There is little detailed information on the diseases of the period and their evolution. Beyond the plagues and other epidemics, which periodically visited the people and destroyed entire generations, a low resistance to illnesses of an infectious type is observed. When certain tumors or wounds appear, death rapidly arrives a few days later. Everything leads to the belief that there soon developed pronounced septicemias, impossible to detect or stop with the primitive procedures of medieval medicine. The "fevers" that victimized other persons would often be tuberculosis making easy progress. Sudden deaths caused by heart attacks appear to be rarer. Anemia, intestinal sores, and skin diseases also must have frequently caused death.

The handling of corpses varied according to social category. Kings and queens, members of the nobility, and high dignitaries of the Church underwent processes resembling embalming. The dead were treated with fragrant substances, perhaps inherited from the Moslem tradition, which were intended to hinder the decay of the flesh. There are frequent descriptions of finding the bodies of great lords undecayed when their tombs were opened after several centuries.

The clothing for the dead person also differed for a variety of reasons. Christian piety led to a great number of bodies being shrouded in religious habits. The desire to be interred wearing the habit of Saint Francis or Saint Benedict is commonly found in wills. When this was not the case, the dead person was clothed in his most luxurious garments (or simply in a shroud), adorned with jewels, and combed and perfumed. Over the body were placed sheets and bedspreads. If it was buried in the earth, a wooden coffin of a rectangular or trapezoid shape with a flat cover was sufficient. If the body was interred in a tomb, then it needed an outer casket of lead. Lime was used to hasten decomposition.

Queen Saint Isabel, whose body had to be carried from Estremoz to Coimbra, after being shrouded in the habit of the Clares, was wrapped in a sheet of fine linen. Over the body was next placed a counterpane of heavier cloth, a cover of rough, very coarse linen stitched with a needle, and finally another bedspread of white, heavy cotton. The corpse was then laid in a rectangular wooden casket over

Fig. 98. Burial. 15th century.

which was fastened a cowhide, with the hair turned to the outside for
greater protection, the whole being covered with a purple cloth also
carefully affixed to the casket.[6]

The fate of the corpse again depended on the social class to which
the dead man had belonged. Within the churches were buried only the
churchmen, the mighty lords, and those who, by their last wills or by
a donation in life, had "bought" a sepulcher in a holy place; except for
the beneficiaries of the Church itself, the authorization of an ecclesiastical entity (usually the bishop) was always required. Collective tombs,
corresponding to modern vaults, already existed at that time. To an
inquiry on whether a separate payment was necessary for each dead
person buried in such vaults, an archbishop of Lisbon in the early
fifteenth century answered that "it is the practice, customary of old
in our aforesaid archbishopric, when such a sepulcher thus had been
selected within a church by any person and the aforesaid church
endowed, that in the said sepulcher can be interred those of his lineage
in the direct line of descendance without giving more to the said
church, save if by chance they corrupt new land by making another
grave; this custom seems good and reasonable to us, and we order that
it be preserved." [7]

On the gravestone or the tomb were inscribed the name, relationship, age, and merits of the deceased, often accompanied by pious
captions extracted from holy books. Kings and great lords normally
deserved their portrait carved on top of it. On other tombs, which were
level with the ground, the contours of the figures of the dead were

carved. All this depended, in the last analysis, on the financial situation of the heirs and on their interest in preserving the memory of the dead person.

The burial of one of the common people was much less complicated. He secured, at best, the churchyard or the cloister of the monastery for the locale of his eternal rest. More frequently, he was buried in the cemetery. Contrary to what is commonly believed, cemeteries were not a creation of the nineteenth century. Throughout the Middle Ages, they existed and performed their social function. Always blessed by religious ceremonies, they were generally situated next to the churches, as annexes of territory belonging to them, and designated *passais* (presbytery lands). Other cemeteries, however, were located farther away, although always in the neighborhood of chapels or hermitages. Occasionally, they were located on the premises of castles, which for some reason had become useless, and even on lands belonging to private individuals.[8]

In the cemeteries, the recourse to common graves was perhaps more common than it is today. Serfs and slaves, beggars and other less fortunate people, none of whom could give the Church an endowment, received a collective grave. The procedure for burying slaves assumed scandalous aspects. During the fifteenth century, especially with the influx of African Negroes, it became customary to throw the bodies of these wretches into veritable dunghills, situated at the outskirts of Lisbon, without even taking care to cover them appropriately with earth. In order to remedy this situation, Manuel ordered in 1515 that a deep pit should be dug, with a wall of stone and lime built around it, where the corpses of the slaves could be piled and that quicklime should be thrown on them from time to time to promote rapid decomposition.[9]

Neither was it uncommon—especially in dealing with persons dying without the comforts of religion—to bury bodies in the fields or at the edge of roads, indicating the grave with a mound of rocks. The habit of each passerby's placing a rock on the crude funeral monument dated from antiquity.[10]

If most burials were normally connected with religious ceremonies of greater or lesser ostentation, consonant with the dignity and wealth of the deceased, there were, on the other hand, also cases of civil funerals, *avant la lettre*. In a visitation made in 1473, the archbishop of Lisbon discovered that when the dead were poor and their offering to the church minute, ecclesiastical attendance ceased: "Sometimes . . . the beneficiaries . . . do not want to go to such a dead man, and so he does not find anyone to bury him." [11]

The ritual which accompanied a death and burial goes back to remote antiquity. The pagan custom of hiring professional mourners (pran-teadeiras) to attend the deceased and to accompany the corpse to the gravesite persevered during the Middle Ages in spite of all the pro-hibitions to the contrary by both the Church and the civil authorities. It is obvious that only at the funerals of the wealthy could such a usage be maintained. King Dinis and King Fernando were mourned in this way, as were many others. The relatives of the dead man, his friends, and other guests served as voluntary mourners. They wept and lamented with loud cries, chanting traditional songs which expressed their sorrow in the face of their inconsolable loss. They plucked their hair and beards, covered their heads with earth or ashes, and so on. Against all these pagan rituals, which signified, in the final analysis, the little importance attributed to eternal life, priests and laymen protested ineffectually. In 1385, when the nation was faced with danger, measures were taken to insure Christian "purification," to instill moral principles into the habits of the people, and to eradicate the persistent stains of paganism. One of them, which the city council of Lisbon decreed and João I saw fit to confirm, asserted "that the tearing and plucking of one's hair in despair over the dead is a practice which comes from the Gentiles, and is a kind of idolatry, and is against the commandments of God"; and it forbade, under pain of fifty libras as a fine and having the corpse maintained in the house for a week, that "no man nor woman will tear or pluck his hair or cry out over any dead person or for him, even though it be father, mother, son or daughter, brother or sister, or husband or wife, nor for any other loss or death, not hindering anyone who wants to bear his mourning and cry, if he so wishes." This decree was later adopted in other parts of the kingdom. In Évora, a municipal ordinance of 1386 prohibited "that from this day forward any person tear out or pluck his hair or lacerate his face, or give voice to cries or shouts or make other noise for his dead, such as in accordance with a bad habit is practiced, and cry, because it is not so done nor customary in other kingdoms and pro-vinces saving only in these . . . because the burial of people should be effected with prayers and alms and offerings to God and divine services." [12]

Although reissued in 1402, the prohibition did not have the desired effect, even in the official sectors. At the funeral of João I (1433), mourning and weeping were great, by both the near relatives and the vassals. At that of Prince Afonso (1491), "then heads of great judgment were plucked and beards of great authority torn away; there was no face of any woman which had not been clouted and covered with blood by her very own hands and cruel nails," and when the funeral procession passed and during the solemn funeral rites, "very sorrowful cries and exceedingly sad lamentations" were heard everywhere. After attending an interment in the village of Tomar in 1466, the German knight the Baron of Rosmital reported that those "who are paid to mourn for the deceased are dressed in black dress and produce some tears, just as do those who among us jump in exultation, or are slightly intoxicated from having drunk deeply." [13]

The funerals were marked not only by weeping and wailing but also by singing and dancing. People visited the sepulchers periodically, sang lugubrious refrains over them, and danced around them. There was a pilgrimage to the tomb of the Constable Nuno Álvares every year on his birthday, in which Christian piety and devotion to the "saint" were on a par with pagan rituals of song and dance. The ballads written on the death of Prince Afonso reflect the same practice. And even in the funeral processions of Manuel I, in the midst of the sixteenth century, it is verified that this custom still persisted. [14]

Death was also celebrated with banquets or with light repasts, in accordance with the wealth of the family; bread and wine or vegetables were traditionally offered to the guests as the base of this meal. The ceremony could take place in the house of the dead man or in the church: "There is also this custom," narrates Rosmital, "that when someone dies, wine, meat, bread, and other food is carried to the church, and the relatives of the dead man accompany the funeral, dressed in white clothing appropriate for interments, with hoods like those of monks." The *Manueline Ordinances* permitted banquets at funerals as long as they were held outside of the churches. The commemoration was repeated on the anniversaries of the death, often at the site of the grave. [15]

The practice in regard to the composition of the procession did not differ greatly from the present practice. In addition to the professional mourners, relatives, friends, and acquaintances dressed in mourning accompanied the deceased. The coffin was carried by hand or on the back of an animal. A kind of litter for a casket, with poles to be placed on men's shoulders, was used, especially for the longer distances; and even carts were used. The body of King Fernando was transported from Lisbon to Santarém "on some poles covered with black cloth and carried on the shoulders of friars to the monastery of São Francisco." But the body of Afonso V was "placed in a casket and put upon a pack animal, which with crosses, torches, and clergy was led by the Count of Monsanto, who was there, and by other nobles to the monastery of Batalha." [16]

The religious ceremonies for funerals did not differ essentially from modern ones. In the principal churches of the country, coffins were placed on wooden biers, covered with black cloth on which white crosses were imprinted. Around the biers, candles and torches were arranged.* The souls of the dead were commended to God with prayers, litanies, swinging censers, and masses. The number of people praying such petitions depended on the wealth of the deceased and on the arrangements in his last will. In almost all medieval wills, funds, often quite large, were designated for masses for the dead. Property was donated to the Church in order that, with its interest, masses might be prayed perpetually for the donor. When kings died, all the great vassals and nobles of his household were summoned to the religious services for his soul. In the autumn of 1383, Nuno Álvares received "a message from Queen Leonor that the king was dead and that she ordered him to come immediately to the king's trental." [17] Masses for the dead were customarily held every month and on the anniversary of the death, with a rite resembling the modern ones.

There were also *saimentos,* more or less long corteges around the churches in which clergy as well as the common people took part, with intercessory prayers for the deceased. They were generally held once a week "according to ancient practice." The priests held the cross and sprinkled the churchyards and cemeteries with holy water. [18]

To the cult of the dead were linked a large number of superstitions and beliefs of a pagan origin, as can easily be supposed. These included the belief in tormented souls, in ghosts, in the revenge of the dead, in spiritualism, and so on; the minute description of such beliefs would be enough to fill a volume in itself. [19] Many of these usages and rituals of incantations persist in modern Portugal, at least among the lower classes.

Mourning was worn frequently, now for the dead, now for national disasters, now for unfortunate events occurring beyond the national borders, though without the exaggerated length and the minutely

---

* This aspect of the rite was modified only on specific orders from the court. When Queen Isabel died in 1455, the city council of Évora had ordered a bier and a simulated funeral (a religious ceremony with a cortege, as if the body were present), and had bought four pieces of black cloth for the necessary draperies. When they received instructions to the contrary, the council decided to take advantage of the material for mourning suits, against the tradition of using white; for this, they did penance in the Cortes of Lisbon held in the following year. (João Baptista de Castro, *Mappa de Portugal Antigo e Moderno*, 3rd ed., I [Lisbon, 1870], 276–77; *Documentos Historicos da Cidade de Evora*, ed. Gabriel Pereira [Évora, 1885–91], pt. 2, p. 78.)

detailed regulation which will be found in the seventeenth and eighteenth centuries.

Mourning lay more in the renunciation of the pomp of the world than in the convention of wearing a certain color. Signs of mourning were, consequently, clothing of homespun, worsted, or sackcloth — all coarse and poor materials — in contrast with fine cloths, silks, or luxurious brocades. Mourning was also seen in the cut and disheveling of hair, in plucking out beards or in letting them grow wildly (contrary to whatever the current style was), in the neglect of hygiene or of care

Fig. 99. Religious service for the dead. 15th century.

of the body, and so on. The poor came to wear their suits wrong side out, in the absence of any other way to display their mourning. When Maximilian of Hapsburg (the future emperor) was imprisoned by the citizens of Bruges, his cousin King João II donned mourning, "and his palace, and those of the queen and of the prince were immediately stripped of their rich panels of cloth and tapestries, which had been put up for the feast, and then all music and festivities ceased in it, and thus it remained afterwards until they received news of his release." After the death of Prince Afonso, "the King cropped off all his hair . . . and the Princess cut the golden hair that she had," and they ate "seated on the ground and off of vessels of pottery, deprived in every respect of all magnificence." [20]

Because unbleached and undyed homespun and sackcloth were whitish or yellowish, just as is burlap, white became a badge of mourning during the Middle Ages. Each person had at home a kind of cloak of coarse woolen cloth, with a hood like a friar's (called a *vaso*), with which he enveloped himself completely during periods of mourning. Such dress was the equivalent of the modern black tie and armband. Consequently, the entire realm could be covered "with hood and wool" quickly when the ruler or a prince suddenly died. The people came in homespun clothing to keep vigil over the corpse. It is recorded that the nobles all donned "mantles of homespun for sorrow" at the death, four days after his birth, of the only male child of King Fernando.[21]

Only the king and queen could wear black as a sign of mourning. When Fernando died (1383), the Count of Ourém, perhaps following a foreign custom, appeared dressed in black when all the other nobles were in homespun. That was criticized and reprimanded to such a point that the count had to resign himself to covering his black clothing with the customary white cloak. Duarte, the act of his acclamation over, "donned mourning in black and the princes wore homespun." At the death of Afonso V (1481), the new king, still "dressed in homespun, closeted himself in his chamber three days." At the time he ordered the Duke of Bragança executed, however, he wore "garments of black wool and closed capes," the color he assumed in mourning the imprisonment of Maximilian and the death of his son, the crown prince.[22]

In certain truly exceptional cases, mourning might be shown by the wearing of dark tones in place of black. It was, so to speak, a form of second mourning. In the reinstatement of the memory of Prince Pedro and the transfer of his corpse to Batalha, a ceremony directed by Henry the Navigator, the latter wore dark blue homespun or black.

The women who accompanied the procession "wore some sign of sorrow which was not black veils but those dyed a dark red." [23]

Black had begun to vie with white as an indication of mourning toward the close of the Middle Ages. It was the color of the funeral banners, the mortuary draperies, the biers, and the coverings for the coffins. But only in the reign of Manuel I (1495–1521) was it adopted as the official color of mourning in clothing.[24]

Mourning for parents was removed at the end of a year, the longest period of obvious sorrow. For their son Afonso, João II and Queen Leonor wore it only six months.[25] There is no information on the normal duration of mourning for relatives other than parents. It is not probable, moreover, that social regulations were as restrictive in the Middle Ages as they came to be in the modern period. If, at the end of a year, the king could remove mourning for his father, certainly the greatest of all, it can safely be assumed that the periods of mourning for other relatives were much shorter. This excludes the mourning of widows (and perhaps widowers), evidently permanent. Widows frequently donned religious habits, though this did not necessarily mean they took regular vows. Wearing the rough worsted of the Benedictine nuns or the Clares, the lady in mourning announced only her intention to exchange her worldly dress for clothing of sorrow and renunciation. When a lord died, the servants of the household wore homespun for an entire year.[26]

Reference
Matter

GENEALOGICAL CHARTS

KINGS OF PORTUGAL : HOUSE OF BURGUNDY

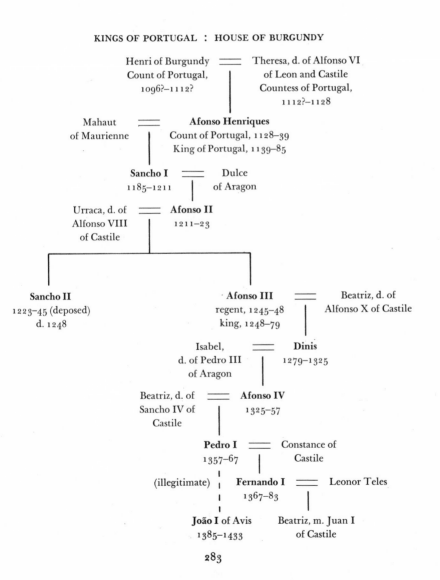

Henri of Burgundy ===== Theresa, d. of Alfonso VI
Count of Portugal,   of Leon and Castile
1096?–1112?   Countess of Portugal,
1112?–1128

Mahaut ===== **Afonso Henriques**
of Maurienne   Count of Portugal, 1128–39
King of Portugal, 1139–85

Sancho I ===== Dulce
1185–1211   of Aragon

Urraca, d. of ===== **Afonso II**
Alfonso VIII   1211–23
of Castile

Sancho II
1223–45 (deposed)
d. 1248

Afonso III ===== Beatriz, d. of
regent, 1245–48   Alfonso X of Castile
king, 1248–79

Isabel, ===== **Dinis**
d. of Pedro III   1279–1325
of Aragon

Beatriz, d. of ===== **Afonso IV**
Sancho IV of   1325–57
Castile

Pedro I ===== Constance of
1357–67   Castile

(illegitimate)   **Fernando I** ===== Leonor Teles
1367–83

João I of Avis   Beatriz, m. Juan I
1385–1433   of Castile

283

KINGS OF PORTUGAL : HOUSE OF AVIS

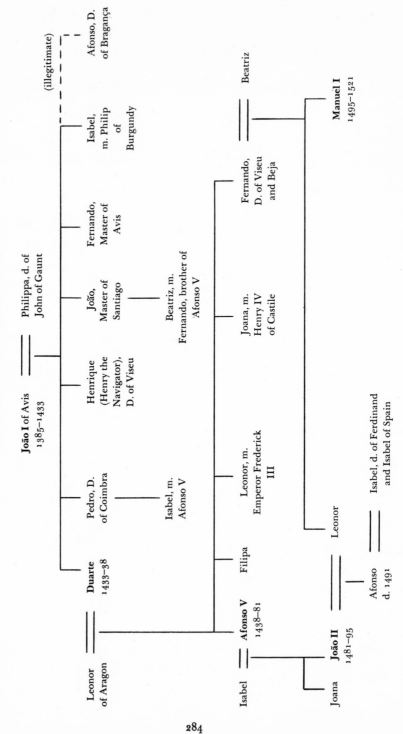

NOTES

ABBREVIATIONS AND SHORT TITLES

ANTT	Arquivo Nacional da Torre do Tombo, Lisbon.
BNL	Biblioteca Nacional of Lisbon.
Canc. Bibl. Nac.	*Cancioneiro da Biblioteca Nacional*, ed. Elza Paxeco Machado and José Pedro Machado, 8 vols. (Lisbon, 1949–64).
Canc. Ger.	*Cancioneiro Geral de Garcia de Resende*, ed. A. J. Gonçalves Guimarães, 5 vols. (Coimbra, 1910–15).
Doc. Hist. Evora	*Documentos Historicos da Cidade de Evora*, ed. Gabriel Pereira, pts. 1–3 (Évora, 1885–91).
Orden. Affonso	*Ordenaçoens do Senhor Rey D. Affonso V*, 5 vols. (Coimbra, 1792).
Provas	*Provas da História Genealógica da Casa Real Portuguesa*, ed. António Caetano de Sousa, 2nd ed., 12 vols. (Coimbra, 1946–54).

CHAPTER 1 : THE TABLE

1 See Henry Hamilton, *History of the Homeland* (London, 1946), p. 65, for the European case in general, and the use I made of this for Portugal in my licentiate degree dissertation presented to the Faculdade de Letras of Lisbon in 1956, "A Sociedade em Portugal nos séculos XII a XIV: Subsídios para a sua História," II (unpubl.), 358–59.

2 See the reasons on p. 337 in my dissertation; see also F. Funck-Brentano, *La Société au moyen age* (Paris, 1937), p. 22; Max von Boehn, *La Moda*, I (Barcelona, 1928), 299; Duarte, *Leal Conselheiro*, ed. Joseph M. Piel (Lisbon, 1942), chap. C, pp. 379–82.

3 See my article, "A Pragmática de 1340," offprint of *Revista da Faculdade de Letras* (Lisbon), 2nd ser., XXII, no. 2 (1956), 13–14, 21–23.

4 Oliveira Marques, "A Sociedade em Portugal," II, 338 ff.; idem, "A Pragmática de 1340."

5 *Canc. Ger.*, IV, 178–79, cited by Maximiano Lemos, "A medicina no Cancioneiro de Garcia de Resende," *Arquivos de História da Medicina Portuguesa*, n.s., XI–XII (1920–21), p. 175.

6 Teófilo Braga, *O Povo Portuguez nos seus costumes, crenças e tradições*, I (Lisbon, 1885), 115.

7 The text mentioned was edited by Maria José da Gama Lobo Salema in her study "Tratado de Cozinha, Século XVI (MS. I-E-33 da BN de Nápoles)" (unpubl. diss., Faculdade de Letras, Lisbon, 1956). All of the recipes quoted in this chapter are taken from her study.

8 Mário Martins, "O Penitencial de Martim Pérez, em Medievo-Português," *Lusitania Sacra*, II (1957), 92.

9 Oliveira Marques, "A Sociedade em Portugal," II, 341 ff.; also see *Orden. Affonso*, vol. I, title XI, pp. 78–79; Maximiano Lemos, "A medicina," p. 175.

10 ANTT, "Livro do Almoxarife Régio do Pescado," Fundo Antigo, bundle 156, no. 1.

11 João Pedro Ribeiro, *Dissertações Chronologicas e Criticas sobre a Historia e Jurisprudencia Ecclesiastica e Civil de Portugal*, 2nd ed., III, pt. 2 (Lisbon, 1857), 86–87; Oliveira Marques, "A Sociedade em Portugal," II, 341 ff.

12 For all this, see my study, *Introdução à História da Agricultura em Portugal: A questão cerealífera durante a Idade Média*, 2nd ed. (Lisbon, 1968); also see Maximiano Lemos, "A medicina," p. 176. On vegetables, see João Manuel Esteves Pereira, *A Industria Agraria: Apontamentos para a historia das industrias portuguezas, seculos XII a XIX* (Lisbon, 1895).

13 Fernão Lopes, *Chronica de El-Rei D. Pedro I* (Lisbon, 1895), chap. XXXI, p. 127.

14 Oliveira Marques, "A Sociedade em Portugal," II, 351–52; "Inventários e Contas da Casa de D. Dinis (1278–1282)," *Arquivo Histórico Português*, X (1916), 41–59.

15 *Leal Conselheiro*, chap. C, pp. 379–82.

16 Ibid.; Maria José Lobo Salema, "Tratado de Cozinha."

17 *Leal Conselheiro*, chap. C, pp. 379–82. See also Maximiano Lemos, "A medicina," p. 176.

18 *Chronica de El-Rei D. Pedro I*, chap. XIV, p. 57; *Crónica de D. João I* (Oporto, 1945–49), vol. II, chap. CI, p. 233.

19 Maria José Lobo Salema, "Tratado de Cozinha."

20 Oliveira Marques, *Agricultura em Portugal*, p. 196.

21 Ibid.; see also Oliveira Marques, "A Sociedade em Portugal," II, 352–56.

22 *Leal Conselheiro*, chap. C, pp. 379–82; João I, *Livro da Montaria*, ed. Francisco Maria Esteves Pereira (Coimbra, 1918), pt. 1, chap. VII, p. 41.

23 Joaquim de Santa Rosa de Viterbo, *Elucidario das Palavras, Termos, e Frases que em Portugal antiguamente se usarão* (Lisbon, 1798–99), I, 63.

24 *Provas*, vol. I, bk. III, pp. 377–78.

25 BNL, Códice Alcobacense, no. 208 ("Livro dos Usos da Ordem de Cister"), fols. 61–62v.

26 *Provas*, vol. I, bk. III, pp. 377–78; Oliveira Marques, "A Sociedade em Portugal," II, 368; BNL, Cod. Alcob., no. 208 ("Usos da Ordem de Cister"), fols. 61–62v.

27 See Oliveira Marques, "A Sociedade em Portugal," II, 361 ff.; Edmond Faral, *La Vie quotidienne au temps de Saint Louis* (Paris, 1952), pp. 163

ff.; von Boehn, *La Moda,* I, 301; BNL, Cod. Alcob., no. 208 ("Usos da Ordem de Cister"), fols. 61–62v.

28 *Doc. Hist. Evora,* pt. 1, p. 181.

29 BNL, Cod. Alcob., no. 208 ("Usos da Ordem de Cister"), fols. 61–62v.

30 Fernão Lopes, *Crónica de D. João I,* vol. II, chap. XCI, p. 217.

31 Oliveira Marques, "A Pragmática de 1340."

32 Quoted from the Biblioteca dos Classicos Portuguezes edition, vol. II (Lisbon, 1902), chap. CXXIV, pp. 88–90.

33 Ibid., chap. CXXV, pp. 90–92.

CHAPTER 2 : DRESS

1 Also see the illustrations in Albino Forjaz de Sampaio, ed., *História da Literatura Portuguesa Ilustrada,* I (Lisbon, 1929), 26 ff.

2 In *Portugaliae Monumenta Historica: Leges et Consuetudines,* I (Lisbon, 1856), 422.

3 Carmen Bernis Madrazo, *Indumentaria Medieval Española* (Madrid, 1956), p. 12.

4 See the pattern in Jacques Ruppert, *L'Antiquité et le moyen age,* vol. I of *Le Costume* (Paris, 1957), p. 33, figs. 64 and 65.

5 *PMH: Leges,* I, 422.

6 I am following the hypothesis of Elza Paxeco in "Guaruaya," *Revista de Portugal,* XIV (January 1949), 21–23. This article gives the principal bibliography on the subject.

7 *Cancioneiro da Ajuda,* ed. Marques Braga, I (Lisbon, 1945), 81, no. 38.

8 The designs are shown in ANTT, "Comentário ao Apocalipse de Lorvão" (c. 3, e. 3, p. 8, no. 160); for terms and documentation, see *PMH: Leges,* I, 743–44, and my "A Sociedade em Portugal nos séculos XII a XIV: Subsídios para a sua História," II (unpubl. diss., Faculdade de Letras, Lisbon, 1956), 370 ff.

9 "Inventários e Contas da Casa de D. Dinis (1278–1282)," *Arquivo Histórico Português,* X (1916), 41 ff.; see also my "A Sociedade em Portugal," II, 378 ff.

10 *Canc. Bibl. Nac.,* II, 370–71, no. 437.

11 Ibid., VI, 104–5, no. 1321.

12 See the illustrations in Forjaz de Sampaio, *História de Literatura Portuguesa Ilustrada,* I, 112 ff., among other publications.

13 The word *sobressaia* is used in a single case, in reference to the clothing of peons, as a synonym for *pelote* (A. H. de Oliveira Marques, "A Pragmática de 1340," offprint of *Revista da Faculdade de Letras* [Lisbon], 2nd ser., XXII [1956], 29). The first reference that I found to the surcoat dates from the 1265 "Livro dos Bens de D. João de Portel," in *Archivo Historico Portuguez,* IV (1906), 186, cited by Maria Otília Simões Martins, "Elementos para o estudo do vestuário nos séculos XIII–XIV e XV" (unpubl. diss., Faculdade de Letras, Lisbon, 1959), p. 72.

14 All these garments are discussed in my "A Sociedade em Portugal," II, 375 ff.
15 *Canc. Bibl. Nac.,* VI, 161–62, no. 1371.
16 Oliveira Marques, "A Sociedade em Portugal," pp. 375 ff.
17 These head coverings are illustrated in the following codices, all from ANTT: "Testamento Velho de Lorvão" (c. 3, e. 3, p. 6, no. 106), fols. 130v, 239v; "Livro da Sagrada Escritura de Lorvão" (c. 3, e. 3, p. 6, no. 105), fol. 27; and "Psaltério de Lorvão" (e. 3, p. 6, no. 95), fol. 107.

The 1253 law of price regulations was published by João Pedro Ribeiro, *Dissertações Chronologicas e Criticas sobre a Historia e Jurisprudencia Ecclesiastica e Civil de Portugal,* 2nd ed., III, pt. 2 (Lisbon, 1857), 59–72; by Alexandre Herculano in *PMH: Leges,* I, 191–96; by A. C. Teixeira de Aragão, *Descripção Geral e Historica das Moedas,* I (Lisbon, 1874), 334–40; and by A. G. Ramalho, *Legislação Agricola,* I (Lisbon, 1905), 88–94.
18 See especially the 1253 law of price regulations in the works cited in the previous note. See also my "A Sociedade em Portugal."
19 *Canc. Bibl. Nac.,* II, 380, no. 441.
20 See n. 18, above.
21 *Orden. Affonso,* vol. V, title XLIII, pp. 154–57.
22 See the 1253 law of price regulations; Oliveira Marques, "A Sociedade em Portugal"; and "Inventários e Contas da Casa de D. Dinis," pp. 41 ff.

The word *eixarafa,* or *enxarrafa,* which appears in the documents and which has been translated as "pouch" here, leads to problems, since it seems to denote, at one and the same time, a pocket and hood (see p. 52).
23 Ibid.
24 Oliveira Marques, "A Pragmática de 1340."
25 *Canc. Ger.,* I, 173.
26 Ibid., II, 350.
27 *Livro da Montaria,* ed. Francisco Maria Esteves Pereira (Coimbra, 1918), pt. 3, chap. II, p. 334.
28 Oliveira Marques, "A Pragmática de 1340," p. 29.
29 *Orden. Affonso,* vol. V, title XLIII, pp. 154-57.
30 *Provas,* vol. V, bk. II, pp. 241–42, 246.
31 *Canc. Ger.,* I, 300.
32 Ibid., IV, 161–66.
33 Ibid., I, 173.
34 *Crónica de D. João I* (Oporto, 1945–49), vol. I, chap. XIII, p. 33.
35 *Provas,* vol. V, bk. II, p. 280; *Canc. Ger.,* III, 335.
36 Ed. Joseph M. Piel (Lisbon, 1944), p. 35.
37 I, 300; IV, 405; and elsewhere.
38 Pt. III, chap. II, p. 332.
39 In, for example, *Provas,* vol. V, bk. II, pp. 270, 278.
40 Ibid., vol. V, bk. II, pp. 246, 257; vol. I, bk. III, pp. 385–87.
41 Ibid., vol. I, bk. III, pp. 385–87.
42 *Orden. Affonso,* vol. I, title XLIX, pp. 281 ff.

43 *Canc. Ger.,* I, 174.

44 *Livro da Ensinança,* p. 36.

45 *Crónica de D. João I,* vol. II, chap. CLXV, p. 361.

46 *Provas,* vol. V, bk. II, p. 259; vol. VI, bk. II, p. 9; vol. I, bk. III, p. 381.

47 Pt. 3, chap. II, p. 333.

48 P. 35.

49 *Livro da Montaria,* pt. 1, chap. III, p. 17.

50 *Canc. Ger.,* II, 174–75; IV, 189–90.

51 Fernão Lopes, *Crónica de D. João I,* vol. I, chap. XIII, p. 33; *Canc. Ger.,* I, 174, IV, 319.

52 See my "A Pragmática de 1340"; and Fernão Lopes, *Crónica de D. João I,* vol. I, chap. LIV, pp. 107–8.

53 *Doc. Hist. Evora,* pt. 1, p. 138. Only a tailor, already retired, knew how to make them in 1379.

54 *Provas,* vol. I, bk. III, p. 381.

55 Fernão Lopes, *Chronica do Senhor Rei D. Fernando,* Inéditos de História Portuguesa, 2nd ed. (Lisbon, 1925), chap. CLIII, pp. 456–57.

56 P. 34.

57 See the various references to terms designating footwear in my "A Sociedade em Portugal," II, 394–95; see also António Cruz, *Os Mesteres do Pôrto: Subsídios para a História das Antigas Corporações dos Ofícios Mecânicos,* I (Oporto, 1943), pp. lxxxiv–lxxxvii; and *Canc. Ger.,* I, 173. On cordovan, see *Dicionário de História de Portugal,* ed. Joel Serrão, s.v. "Cordovão." For an exhaustive analysis of Portuguese footgear at the end of the fourteenth century, see *Doc. Hist. Evora,* pt. 1, pp. 144–46, 176–78.

58 *Canc. Ger.,* I, 300.

59 Ibid., I, 184.

60 *Doc. Hist. Evora,* pt. 1, pp. 144–46, 176–78.

61 *Livro da Montaria,* pt. 3, chap. II, p. 334; *Crónica de D. João I,* vol. II, chap. CXXXVIII, p. 302.

62 *Canc. Ger.,* IV, 203.

63 Ibid., IV, 205.

64 Ibid., I, 183, IV, 362.

65 Cited by Joan Evans, *Dress in Mediaeval France* (Oxford, 1952), p. 62.

66 Carmen Bernis Madrazo, *Indumentaria,* p. 42.

67 See the great variety of terms which the ballads of the *Cancioneiro Geral* present, as, for example, I, 39, 174, 183, 299; II, 328; III, 278, 283, 335; IV, 177, 202 ff., 362.

68 The word *enxarrafa,* or *eixarafa,* seems also to have meant a movable pocket; see *Canc. Ger.,* IV, 324.

69 I, 174.

70 *Orden. Affonso,* vol. V, title XLIII, pp. 154–57. There are drawings of peasants in BNL, Códice Alcobacense, no. 376 ("Compendium Theologicae Veritatis"), fols. 3v and 81v; in ANTT, "Livro de Horas de D.

Duarte" (e. 3, p. 7, no. 140), fol. 120v; and elsewhere.

71 See the 1253 law of price regulations mentioned in n. 17 to this chapter.

72 Aarão de Lacerda, *História da Arte em Portugal* (Oporto, 1942–47), I, 426.

73 *Canc. Bibl. Nac.*, V, 294–95, no. 1139.

74 Some of these surcoats can be seen on recumbent statues.

75 There are drawings of crespinas in the "Testamento Velho de Lorvão" (ANTT, c. 3, e. 3, p. 6, no. 106), fols. 130v and 281, as well as in other sources.

76 *Provas*, vol. I, bk. III, pp. 289–96.

77 Ibid. On the general aspects of the cotte, see Michèle Beaulieu and Jeanne Baylé, *Le Costume en Bourgogne de Philippe le Hardi à la mort de Charles le Téméraire (1364–1477)* (Paris, 1956).

78 *Provas*, vol. V, bk. II, p. 241.

79 Ibid., vol. I, bk. III, pp. 289–96.

80 Ibid.

81 *Canc. Ger.*, IV, 179; A. de Sousa e Silva Costa Lobo, *Historia da Sociedade em Portugal no seculo XV* (Lisbon, 1903), pp. 433–40. The lady on the St. Vicente panels also wears a gargantilha.

82 *Provas*, vol. I, bk. III, pp. 289–96.

83 Ibid., p. 375.

84 Ibid., pp. 289–96.

85 Ibid.

86 Ibid.

87 *Cantigas de Santa Maria de Afonso X, o Sábio,* ed. Manuel Rodrigues Lapa (Lisbon, 1933), p. 46.

88 *Provas*, vol. I, bk. II, pp. 341–43.

89 *Orden. Affonso*, vol. V, title XLIII, pp. 154–57.

90 *Provas*, vol. I, bk. II, pp. 341 ff.

91 Beatriz owned a gold paternoster to wear around her neck (ibid., vol. I, bk. III, p. 290); the two ladies of the St. Vicente panels also hold paternosters. On adornments see also Costa Lobo, *Sociedade em Portugal,* pp. 433–40.

92 M. Braun-Ronsdorf, *Le Mouchoir,* in *Cahiers CIBA* (Basel), IV, no. 41 (May 1952); Fernão Lopes, *Chronica do Senhor Rei D. Fernando,* chap. CXXXIX, p. 428.

93 On the types of medieval fabrics, see my "A Sociedade em Portugal" and its bibliography. See also Beaulieu and Baylé, *Le Costume en Bourgogne,* pp. 23–24.

94 Oliveira Marques, "A Pragmática de 1340," p. 24.

95 See n. 93, above.

96 A list and description of the fragments of medieval textiles still extant in museums and private collections in Portugal can be found in Sebastião Pessanha, *Um Nucleo de Tecidos: Catalogo da Collecção do Auctor,* I–II (Lisbon, 1918–19); in the Museu Machado de Castro, Coimbra, *Catálogo-*

Guia: Secção de Tecidos, Bordados, Tapeçarias e Tapetes (Coimbra, 1943) ; and in the studies by Carlos Bastos, particularly *O Comércio e a Indústria Têxtil em Portugal* (Oporto, 1950), and *Subsídios para a História da Arte Ornamental dos Tecidos* (Oporto, 1954). For a comparison with Spanish fabrics, see Monasterio de las Huelgas, Burgos, *Guia turística* (Madrid, 1961).

97 José Leite de Vasconcelos, *A Barba em Portugal* (Lisbon, 1925), pp. 62–63 (on recumbent statues with beards from the twelfth century).

98 It is true that the recumbent statue of Odivelas represents the king with a beard, but it may have been carved later, in the midst of an "epoch of beards." Several recumbent statues of the fourteenth century, some of which are cited by J. Leite de Vasconcelos (ibid., pp. 64–65), display beards. Also see the illustrations in Aarão de Lacerda, *História da Arte em Portugal*, I, 429–60 passim, 605, 612; as well as the description of the recumbent statue of Fernão Sanches, the illegitimate son of Dinis, in the appendix to the Esteves Pereira edition of João I's *Livro da Montaria*, pp. 454–55.

99 "The ninth king was Fernando. . . . He was the first who began to shave his beard and to eat at a high table" (*Crónica de Cinco Reis de Portugal*, ed. A. Magalhães Basto [Oporto, 1945], pt. 2 [Capítulos Soltos], chap. 8, p. 249).

100 J. Leite de Vasconcelos, *A Barba*, pp. 62, 66–67.

101 "King Duarte is represented in the sacristy of St. Domingos on a small canvas one côvado high [less than a yard]. It is a full-body painting, despite the fact that the canvas is small, and is placed above the chests where the friars dress to say mass; it has no beard other than a moustache" (Artur da Mota Alves, *Os Painéis de S. Vicente num Códice da Biblioteca Nacional do Rio de Janeiro* [Lisbon, 1936]). There is no apparent reason to doubt the authenticity of this text, as Jaime Cortesão has shown in *Os Descobrimentos Portugueses*, I (Lisbon, n.d.), 426–27. An analysis which I applied to the writing, based on the photographs displayed by Mota Alves, also reveals a type of cursive writing used in the sixteenth century, with Gothic elements but already profoundly influenced by humanistic writing.

102 See Georg von Ehingen, *Itinerarium* (Augsburg: Raymond Fugger, 1600). The full-length portrait of the king in the *Itinerarium* is a sixteenth-century alteration, adapted for printing, of the original illumination. See the former in António Belard da Fonseca, *O Mistério dos Painéis*, I (Lisbon, 1957), 120–21, fig. 37.

103 The identification between João II and the portrait of a king of Portugal in the Kunsthistorisches Museum of Vienna, which Pedro Batalha Reis (*Um Retrato d'El-Rei Dom João II* [Lisbon, 1946]) proposes, is fanciful. The clothes and hat worn by the king in this portrait do not permit the portrait to be dated earlier than 1515. If in truth it does treat of a king of Portugal, then it has to be Manuel or João III (see Maria Fernanda

Gomes da Silva, "Sobre um Suposto Retrato de D. João II," offprint of *Palestra*, no. 21 [1965]). The testimony of Garcia de Resende also does not enable us to affirm that the Perfect Prince wore a beard: to say that the king "had a black and well-cared-for beard" is not the same as declaring he wore a long beard.

104 *Provas*, vol. I, bk. III, p. 375.

105 For all this, see Beaulieu and Baylé, *Le Costume en Bourgogne*, pp. 82–84.

CHAPTER 3 : THE HOUSE

1 In *Geografia e Civilização: Temas Portugueses* (Lisbon, 1961), pp. 17–78.

2 In *Portugal, o Mediterrâneo e o Atlântico: Estudo Geográfico*, Universitas, no. 5 (Coimbra, n.d.; 2nd ed., Lisbon, 1963).

3 See Orlando Ribeiro, s.v. "Cidade," in *Dicionário de História de Portugal,* I, 576.

4 Alberto Sampaio, "As Villas do Norte de Portugal," in *Estudos Históricos e Económicos,* I (Oporto, 1923), 82–83, 93.

5 Herbert Koch, *Arte Romano,* trans. Ernesto Martínez Ferrando, 3rd ed. (Barcelona, 1946), pp. 31 ff.

6 Aly Mazahéri, *La Vie quotidienne des Musulmans au moyen age: X^e au XIIIe siècle* (Paris, 1951), pp. 75 ff.

7 Ibid.; Orlando Ribeiro, *Geografia e Civilização*, pp. 92 ff.

8 Gérard Pradalié, "Lisbonne, de la Reconquête à la fin du XIIIe siècle" (unpubl. diss., Faculté des Lettres et des Sciences Humaines, Toulouse, 1961), pp. 49–51.

9 Alfredo Pimenta, *Anais e Crónicas,* vol. I of *Fontes Medievais da História de Portugal* (Lisbon, 1948), p. 170.

10 A. H. de Oliveira Marques, *Hansa e Portugal na Idade Média* (Lisbon, 1959), pp. 145–46.

11 Quoted in Pradalié, "Lisbonne," p. 121.

12 Fernão Lopes, *Chronica do Senhor Rei D. Fernando,* Inéditos de História Portuguesa, 2nd ed., IV (Lisbon, 1925), chap. XXXIX, p. 202, chap. LXXVII, p. 287.

13 Quoted in Pimenta, *Anais e Crónicas,* p. 121.

14 See also A. de Sousa e Silva Costa Lobo, *Historia da Sociedade em Portugal no seculo XV* (Lisbon, 1903), p. 124.

15 Gomes Eanes de Zurara, *Crónica dos Feitos da Guiné,* ed. Dias Dinis (Lisbon, 1949), chap. II, p. 13.

16 João Brandão, *Tratado da Majestade, Grandeza e Abastança da Cidade de Lisboa, na 2.ª Metade do Século XVI: Estatística de Lisboa de 1552* (Lisbon, 1923), p. 79.

17 A calculation made from the data of Cristóvão Rodrigues de Oliveira, *Summario em que brevemente se contem algumas cousas (assi ecclesiasticas como seculares) que ha na cidade de Lisboa,* ed. Augusto Vieira da Silva, 3rd ed. (Lisbon, 1938).

18 Alexandre Herculano, *Opúsculos,* 4th ed., VI (Lisbon, n.d.) , 81.

19 See the plan of the parish of Santa Cruz do Castelo, published by Augusto Vieira da Silva in *O Castelo de S. Jorge em Lisboa: Estudo histórico-descritivo,* 2nd ed. (Lisbon, 1937) , p. 17.

20 Herculano, *Opúsculos,* VI, 81 ff.; Vieira da Silva, *O Castelo de S. Jorge,* pp. 96 ff.

21 Augusto Vieira da Silva, *A Cêrca Moura de Lisboa: Estudo histórico-descritivo,* 2nd ed. (Lisbon, 1939) , pp. 168–70 and plate VII in the back of the volume.

22 Ernesto Korrodi, *Estudos de Reconstrucção sobre o Castello de Leiria* (Zurich, 1898) , fol. VI ff.

23 Raul Lino, *Quatro Palavras sobre os Paços Reais da Vila de Sintra* (Lisbon, 1948) , pp. 24–38 ff.

24 ANTT, "Livro de Conselhos de El-Rei D. Duarte," better known as the "Livro da Cartuxa de Évora" (MS. 1928) , fols. 177v–179v (*Doc. Hist. Evora,* pt. 3, p. 35) .

25 The Baron of Rosmital, who passed through the city in 1466, refers only to the episcopal palace and one other, belonging to Prince Fernando, brother of the king (see João Baptista de Castro, *Mappa de Portugal antigo e moderno,* 3rd ed., IV [Lisbon, 1870], p. 54) .

26 *Boletim da Direcção Geral dos Edifícios e Monumentos Nacionais,* no. 79 (March 1955) , *Palácio de D. Manuel, Évora,* pp. 6–9 and the respective plates; Túlio Espanca, *Évora: Guia Histórico-Artístico* (Évora, 1949) , pp. 87 ff.; idem, *Palácios Reais de Évora,* vol. III of *Cadernos de História e Arte Eborense* (Évora, 1946) .

27 Gustavo de Matos Sequeira, *Distrito de Leiria,* vol. V of *Inventário Artístico de Portugal* (Lisbon, 1955) , p. xviii; Vergílio Correia and A. Nogueira Gonçalves, *Distrito de Coimbra,* vol. IV of ibid. (Lisbon, 1952) , p. xxii; Fernão Lopes, *Chronica do Senhor Rei D. Fernando,* chap. CXXXV, p. 420; Rui de Pina, *Chronica do Senhor Rey D. Duarte,* Ineditos de Historia Portugueza, I (Lisbon, 1790) , chap. V, p. 85.

28 *Bol. da Dir. Ger. Edif. Monum. Nac.,* no. 91 (March 1958) , *Castelo de Penela,* p. 26; ibid., no. 77 (September 1954) , *Castelo de Beja,* figs. 4 and 14; ibid., no. 54 (December 1948) , *Castelo de Elvas;* ibid., nos. 68–69 (June–September 1952), *Castelo de Óbidos; Extremadura, Alentejo, Algarve,* ed. Raúl Proença, vol. II of *Guia de Portugal* (Lisbon, 1927) , p. 588.

29 Jorge Larcher, "O Castelo de Sesimbra: Sua história e um subsídio importante para a sua reconstrução," fasc. 4 of *Petrus Nonius,* II (Lisbon, 1940) , 269–70.

30 João de Almeida, ed., *Reprodução anotada do Livro das Fortalezas de Duarte Darmas* (Lisbon, 1943). On the dating of the *Livro das Fortalezas,* see Alfredo Pimenta, *Duarte Darmas e o seu Livro das Fortalezas,* Estudos Históricos, XXII (Lisbon, 1944) .

31 Rui Fernandes, "Descripção do terreno em roda da cidade de Lamego

duas leguas," in *Collecção de Ineditos de Historia Portugueza,* 2nd ed., V (Lisbon, 1926), 573; Fernão Lopes, *Chronica do Senhor Rei D. Fernando,* chap. XXXIX, p. 202; Teófilo Braga, *O Povo Portuguez nos seus costumes, crenças e tradições,* I (Lisbon, 1885), III.

32 Information collected from the *Guia de Portugal,* vols. II–III; *Bol. da Dir. Ger. Edif. Monum. Nac.,* several numbers; and *Inventário Artístico de Portugal,* vols. I–VI. See also *Chronica do Condestabre de Portugal Dom Nuno Alvarez Pereira,* ed. Mendes dos Remédios (Coimbra, 1911), p. 209; Adriano de Gusmão, "Solares Barrocos da Região de Basto: Ensaio de Pesquisa Artistica," offprint of *XVI Congrès international d'histoire de l'art,* II (Lisbon, 1954); Fialho de Almeida, *Estancias d'Arte e de Saudade* (Lisbon, 1921), pp. 260 ff. (on Castelo de Alvito).

33 Rogério de Azevedo, *O Paço dos Duques de Guimarães: Preâmbulo à Memória do Projecto de Restauro* (Oporto, 1942), pp. 38 ff., 43 ff., 60 ff., 72, 77, and 98; see also the criticism by Alfredo Pimenta, *A Propósito do Paço dos Duques em Guimarães,* Estudos Históricos, XIX (Guimarães, 1942); and *Bol. da Dir. Ger. Edif. Monum. Nac.,* no. 102 (December 1960), *Paço dos Duques de Bragança, Guimarães.*

34 Chap. LXXXI, p. 303, in the edition of Joseph M. Piel (Lisbon, 1942).

35 *Canc. Bibl. Nac.,* VI, 353, no. 1538.

36 Raul Lino, *L'évolution de l'architecture domestique au Portugal: Essai,* trans. Léon Bourdon (Lisbon, 1937), pp. 3–7; Orlando Ribeiro, *Geografia e Civilização,* pp. 96 ff.; Alfredo Guimarães, *Guimarães,* fasc. II of *Mobiliário Artístico Português: Elementos para a sua história* (Oporto, 1935), pp. xiii–xiv; and information found in *Guia de Portugal,* vols. II–III, the *Inventário Artístico de Portugal,* vols. I–VI, and other sources. See also *Doc. Hist. Evora,* pt. 1, p. 182.

37 Ed. Francisco Maria Esteves Pereira (Lisbon, 1915), chap. LXXXVIII, p. 236.

38 On medieval furniture, see Hermann Schmitz, *História del mueble: Estilos del mueble desde la antiguedad hasta mediados del siglo XIX,* trans. José Ontañón, 3rd ed. (Barcelona, 1952); and also the introduction by Guillaume Janneau in *Les Meubles,* I (Paris, 1945). The book by J. F. da Silva Nascimento, *Leitos e Camilhas Portugueses: Subsídios para o seu estudo* (Lisbon, 1950), has little of importance for the medieval period, although see pp. 23, 27–30.

39 A. H. de Oliveira Marques, s.v. "Cavaleiro-Vilão," in *Dicionário de História de Portugal,* I, 543.

40 *Canc. Bibl. Nac.,* VI, 89–90, no. 1306.

41 F. João da Póvoa et al., "Memórias sôltas e inventário do oratório de S. Clemente das Penhas e do mosteiro de N. S.ª da Conceição de Matozinhos dos séculos XIV e XV," ed. A. de Magalhães Basto, fasc. I of *Boletim Cultural da Câmara Municipal do Porto,* III (Oporto, 1940).

42 Fernão Lopes, *Chronica do Senhor Rei D. Fernando,* chap. CXXX, p. 410.

43 The sources on medieval bed clothing are numerous. The reader inter-

ested in the subject can consult my "A Sociedade em Portugal nos séculos XII a XIV: Subsídios para sua História," II (unpubl. diss., Faculdade de Letras, Lisbon, 1956), 416 ff. For the identification of terms of Arab origin, also see José Pedro Machado, *Influência Arábica no Vocabulário Português*, I (Lisbon, 1958). On the trousseau of Beatriz, see *Provas*, vol. I, bk. III, pp. 289–96.

44 *Provas*, vol. I, bk. III, pp. 289–96.

45 Ibid.

46 On chairs, refer to the works cited in the bibliography for furniture; to Guillaume Janneau, *Les Sièges*, I (Paris, 1949) ; and especially to Augusto Cardoso Pinto, *Cadeiras Portuguesas* (Lisbon, 1952), pp. 27–28, 37–38, 41. The drawings of the faudesteuil are in ANTT, "Testamento Velho de Lorvão" (c. 3, e. 3, p. 6, no. 106), fols. 85v, 305; see also the reproductions in A. Cardoso Pinto, *Cadeiras*, plates II, XI, and XII.

47 *Provas*, vol. I, bk. III, pp. 289–96.

48 Ibid.

49 This explains the ease with which Nuno Álvares, at the banquet celebrating the marriage between Beatriz and the King of Castile (1383), "lifted the table and with his foot kicked away its leg so that the table fell to the ground" (*Chronica do Condestabre*, chap. XIV, p. 38).

50 *Provas*, vol. I, bk. III, pp. 289–96.

51 Joaquim de Santa Rosa de Viterbo, *Elucidario* . . . (Lisbon, 1798–99), I, 48; Póvoa et al., "Memórias sôltas e inventário," p. 77; *Provas*, vol. I, bk. III, p. 295.

52 Alexandre Herculano, *O Monge de Cister, ou a Epocha de D. João I*, 20th ed., II (Lisbon, n.d.), 10.

53 Pedro de Azevedo, "Um inventario de seculo XIV," *O Archeologo Português*, VII (1902), 231.

54 Alfredo Guimarães, "Couros policromados de Córdova," in *Um Retrato de Nuno Gonçalves e outros Estudos*, Estudos do Museu Alberto Sampaio, II (Oporto, 1944), 48–51; see also idem, *Guimarães*, pp. xiv and 56, n. 1.

55 *Provas*, vol. I, bk. III, pp. 293–94.

56 *Canc. Ger.*, V, 324.

57 *Provas*, vol. I, bk. III, p. 293.

58 Guimarães, *Um Retrato*, p. 15, n. 1.

59 *Livro da Montaria*, ed. Francisco Maria Esteves Pereira (Coimbra, 1918), pt. 1, chap. II, p. 11.

60 See especially my "A Sociedade em Portugal," II, 416 ff.

61 *Provas*, vol. I, bk. III, p. 293.

62 Ibid., vol. VI, bk. II, p. 9.

63 See especially my "A Sociedade em Portugal," II, 430 ff.

64 *Chronica de El-Rei D. Pedro I* (Lisbon, 1895), chap. XIV, p. 57.

65 Maria Teresa Campos Rodrigues, "Aspectos da administração municipal de Lisboa no século XV," *Revista Municipal*, no. 103 (1964), p. 50.

66 Póvoa et al., "Memórias sôltas e inventário," p. 76.

67 *Canc. Ger.*, IV, 345–52.

68 *Orden. Affonso*, vol. IV, titles LXXIII–LXXV, pp. 258–64; Henrique da Gama Barros, *História da Administração Pública em Portugal nos séculos XII a XV*, 2nd ed. (Lisbon, 1949), vol. VII, bk. III, pp. 13–16; Oliveira Marques, "A Sociedade em Portugal," II, 414–16.

69 Oliveira Marques, "A Sociedade em Portugal," II, 432.

CHAPTER 4 : HYGIENE AND HEALTH

1 See the summary given by Manuel Gonçalves Cerejeira in his book *A Idade Média* (Coimbra, 1936), pp. 92 ff.

2 See, for example, the testimony of João I in his *Livro da Montaria*, ed. Francisco Maria Esteves Pereira (Coimbra, 1918), pt. 2, chap. I, p. 227. On the washerwomen, etc., see João Brandão, *Tratado da Majestade, Grandeza e Abastança da Cidade de Lisboa . . .* (Lisbon, 1923), p. 49.

3 On the soap factories and their owners, see Henrique da Gama Barros, *História da Administração Pública em Portugal nos Séculos XII a XV*, 2nd ed., IX (Lisbon, n.d.), 237–42.

4 Fernando da Silva Correia, "A causa da morte da Infanta Santa Joana: Uma história clínica do séc. XV," offprint of *A Medicina Contemporânea*, LX, nos. 24–28 (1942).

5 *Provas*, vol. I, bk. III, p. 292.

6 *Cancioneiro da Vaticana*, no. 291, cited by Cerejeira, *A Idade Média*, p. 98.

7 See Chapter 1, p. 29, of this book.

8 *Provas*, vol. I, bk. III, p. 295.

9 Maximiano Lemos, *Historia da Medicina em Portugal: Doutrinas e Instituições*, I (Lisbon, 1899), 54–60; Ricardo Jorge, *Origens & Desenvolvimento da População do Porto: Notas historicas e estatisticas* (Oporto, 1897), p. 26, n. 2; Luís Filipe Lindley Cintra, *A Linguagem dos Foros de Castelo Rodrigo* (Lisbon, 1959), bk. V, chaps. XXXIV–XXXV, p. 81.

10 *Cancioneiro da Vaticana*, no. 322, cited by Cerejeira, *A Idade Média*, p. 98.

11 Cerejeira, *A Idade Média*, p. 99.

12 See an example in *Provas*, vol. I, bk. III, p. 295.

13 ANTT, "Livro de Conselhos de El-Rei D. Duarte" (MS. 1928), fols. 177v–179v.

14 Rógerio de Azevedo, *O Paço dos Duques de Guimarães: Preâmbulo à memória do projecto de restauro* (Oporto, 1942), p. 62.

15 José Maria António Nogueira, *Esparsos: Arquelogia, Etnografia, Bibliografia e História* (Coimbra, 1934), p. 88.

16 Ibid.; *Orden. Affonso*, vol. I, title XXVI, p. 165; *Índice dos Elementos para a História do Municipio de Lisboa*, I (Lisbon, 1942), s.v. "Chafariz."

17 Eduardo Freire de Oliveira, ed., *Elementos para a Historia do Municipio de Lisboa* (Lisbon, 1882–85), I, 463n.

18 Vol. I, title XXVIII, p. 185.

19 For an example, see *Doc. Hist. Evora*, pt. 1, pp. 188–89.

20 Freire de Oliveira, *Elementos*, I, 347, 463n.

21 Ibid., I, 189–90, 380; *Doc. Hist. Evora*, pt. 3, p. 84.

22 Antonio da Cunha Vieira de Meireles, *Memorias de Epidemologia Portugueza* (Coimbra, 1866), pp. 33–35, 40, 201 ff., 214–18 ff.

23 Ibid., pp. 33–35, 40, 214 ff.; João de Meira, "A Peste de 1384, e as diversas *Historia da Medicina Portugueza*, n.s., II (1911), 179–92; idem, "Da Peste de 1415 e da palavra 'trama' significando 'bubão pestilencial,'" ibid., n.s., III (1912), 178–82.

24 Chap. LIV, pp. 233–34.

25 Facsimile edition (Oporto, 1962); *Orden. Affonso*, vol. I, title LI, par. 39.

26 Maximiano Lemos, *Medicina em Portugal*, I, 143 ff.; 148 ff.; Ricardo Jorge, *Origens & Desenvolvimento*, pp. 84–86.

27 *Regimento proueytoso*.

28 ANTT, "Conselhos de D. Duarte" (MS. 1928), fols. 99–102v, 254–255, 275–277.

29 Augusto da Silva Carvalho, "História da Oftalmologia Portuguesa até ao fim do século XVI" (Lisbon, 1939), offprint of the *Boletim da Sociedade Portuguesa de Oftalmologia*, II (1940), 6–7, 8–9, 12–13; Egas Moniz, "O Papa João XXI," offprint of *Biblos*, VI, nos. 1–2 (1930), 20.

30 Silva Carvalho, "Oftalmologia Portuguesa até ao fim do século XVI," p. 7.

31 Quoted in Maximiano Lemos, *Medicina em Portugal*, I, 24–25.

32 ANTT, "Conselhos de D. Duarte" (MS. 1928), fols. 256–257.

33 Francisco Marques de Sousa Viterbo, "Noticia sobre alguns medicos portuguezes ou que exerceram a clinica em Portugal" (pt. 3), *Jornal de Sociedade das Sciencias Medicas de Lisboa* (1895), p. 108; Augusto da Silva Carvalho, "História da Oftalmologia Portuguesa até ao fim do século XVII" (Lisbon, 1940), offprint of *Boletim da Sociedade Portuguesa de Oftalmologia*, II (1940), 1.

34 Silva Carvalho, "Oftalmologia Portuguesa até ao fim do século XVI," p. 8.

35 Augusto da Silva Carvalho, *História da lepra em Portugal* (Oporto, 1932), pp. 11–13, 159, 162; A. Rocha Brito, "História da Gafaria de Coimbra," *Arquivo de Dermatologia e Sifiligrafia*, year I, no. 1 (1931), 79; Maximiano Lemos, *Medicina em Portugal*, I, 50–52; João de Meira, "Os gafos do Nobiliário," *Arq. Hist. Med. Port.*, n.s., III (1912), 195–96.

36 Maximiano Lemos, "A medicina no *Cancioneiro de Garcia de Resende*," *Arq. Hist. Med. Port.*, n.s., XI (1920), 124–25.

37 Maximiano Lemos, *Medicina em Portugal*, I, 53–56.

38 BNL, Códice Alcobacense, no. 276, fol. 116.

39 Augusto da Silva Carvalho, "História da Estomatologia: Doentes, dentistas e odontólogos," *Revista Portuguesa de Estomatologia*, no. 1 (July 1934), pp. 10–15.

40 ANTT, "Conselhos de D. Duarte" (MS. 1928), fols. 264v, 265v–268v.

41 Ibid., fol. 265v.

42 Ibid., fols. 278v–279; BNL, Cód. Alcob., no. 276, fol. 116.

43 ANTT, "Conselhos de D. Duarte" (MS. 1928), fol. 282v.

44 Ibid., fols. 279–280v.

45 Doc. Hist. Evora, pt. 3, p. 81.

46 ANTT, "Conselhos de D. Duarte" (MS. 1928), fols. 268, 264–264v.

47 Maximiano Lemos, Medicina em Portugal, I, 22, n. 4.

48 João I, Livro da Montaria, pt. 2, chap. XX, p. 318.

49 Maximiano Lemos, Medicina em Portugal, I, 31–32; Doc. Hist. Evora, pt. 3, pp. 83–84.

50 Leal Conselheiro, chap. XX, p. 77.

51 Maximiano Lemos, Medicina em Portugal, I, 31; Doc. Hist. Evora, pt. 3, pp. 83–84.

52 Maximiano Lemos, Medicina em Portugal, I, 25n.

53 Augusto da Silva Carvalho, "Subsídios para a História das Parteiras Portuguezas," A Medicina Contemporânea, 3rd ser., 12 July 1931, p. 248; "Constituições do Arcebispado de Lisboa decretadas por D. João Esteves d'Azambuja (1402–1414)," Revista Archeologica e Historica, I (1887), 14; João Álvares, Chronica do Infante Santo D. Fernando (Coimbra, 1911), chap. I, pp. 6–7.

54 See the list of these doctors especially in Francisco Marques de Sousa Viterbo, "Medicos da Familia Real Portugueza" (pt. 1), Jorn. Soc. Scien. Med. Lisboa (1892), pp. 214–15; idem, "Noticia sobre alguns medicos portuguezes ou que exerceram a clinica em Portugal" (pt. 2), Jorn. Soc. Scien. Med. Lisboa (1894), p. 518; ibid. (pt. 3), Jorn. Soc. Scien. Med. Lisboa (1895), pp. 112–13, 163, 220 ff.; ibid. (pt. 5), Arq. Hist. Med. Port., n.s., V (1914), 28.

55 Pedro José da Silva, Principaes factos da Pharmacia Portugueza nos seculos passados (Lisbon, 1868), pp. 8–11, 12–14, 32; Doc. Hist. Evora, pt. 3, pp. 73–74.

56 Pedro J. da Silva, Pharmacia Portugueza, pp. 82–87; Doc. Hist. Evora, pt. 3, pp. 75–80.

57 Maximiano Lemos, Medicina em Portugal, I, 14, 17–18; Pedro José da Silva, Ensino da Pharmacia em Portugal e nas principaes nações da Europa (Lisbon, 1866), pp. 25–26.

58 On the history of hospitals, hospices, etc., see principally the following works: Fernando da Silva Correia, "Hospitais pré-quinhentistas portugueses: A lição da história," offprint of Imprensa Médica, IX nos. 23–24 (1943); idem, "Os Velhos Hospitais da Lisboa Antiga," offprint of Revista Municipal, II, no. 10 (1942); and especially, idem, Origem e Formação das Misericórdias Portuguesas: Estudos sôbre a História da Assistência (Lisbon, 1944); José Júlio Gonçalves Coelho, "Notre-Dame de Roc Amadour en Portugal (son culte—hôpitaux et hôtelleries): Memoire historique," offprint of Bulletin de la Société scientifique, historique et archéologique de la Corrèze (Brive, 1912); Maximiano Lemos, Medicina em Portugal, I, 42 ff.

CHAPTER 5 : AFFECTION

1 Rui de Pina, *Chronica do Senhor Rey Dom Affonso V,* Ineditos de Historia Portugueza (Lisbon, 1790), vol. I, chap. LXXXVI, p. 352; Henrique da Gama Barros, *Historia da Administração Pública em Portugal nos séculos XII a XV,* 2nd ed., III (Lisbon, 1946), 313–14.

2 Ed. Joseph M. Piel (Lisbon, 1942), chap. XCVIII, pp. 359–72.

3 "Fuero" of Cuenca, which also reflects the Portuguese case. See also Manuel Paulo Merêa, "Notas sobre o poder paternal no direito hispânico ocidental: Em torno do § CCVI do Foro de Cuenca," in *Estudos de Direito Hispânico Medieval,* II (Coimbra, 1953), 83.

4 Ibid., pp. 89–91, 97, and 108.

5 Guilherme Braga da Cruz, "Algumas considerações sobre a 'Perfiliatio,'" offprint of *Boletim da Faculdade de Direito* (Coimbra), XIV (1938), 5 ff.; Manuel Paulo Merêa, "Da minha gaveta (Silva Histórico-Jurídica), II: Sinopse histórica da adopção (perfilhamento)," *Boletim da Faculdade de Direito* (Coimbra), XXXII (1956), 182–94; idem, "Nótulas Histórico-Jurídicas, II: Sobre a adopção no século XII," *Boletim da Faculdade de Direito* (Coimbra), XXXI (1955), 372–76; idem, "Perfilhação," *Revista Portuguesa de Filologia,* VII (1956), 119. See also the complementary documentary collection added by Humberto Carlos Baquero Moreno, "Subsídios para o estudo da sociedade medieval portuguesa: Moralidade e costumes" (unpubl. diss., Faculdade de Letras, Lisbon, 1961), pp. 122–36.

6 G. Rattray Taylor, *Sex in History,* 2nd ed. (London, 1959). See especially p. 83; the medieval period would have been predominately "patrist."

7 I have used, on the following pages of text, some of the examples selected by José Joaquim Nunes, *Cantigas de Amigo dos Trovadores Galego-Portugueses,* I (Coimbra, 1928), 8–10, 15, and 28–29.

8 In *Auto dos Almocreves,* cited by Luís Chaves, *O Amor Português* (Lisbon, 1922), p. 48.

9 Luís Chaves, "Sobrevivências neolíticas de Portugal: Vestígios líticos, em concordância ou paralelismo, e na toponímia," *Arquivo de Universidade de Lisboa,* IV (1917), 58 ff.

10 Quoted in António José Saraiva, *História da Cultura em Portugal,* I (Lisbon, 1950), 290–91.

11 Ibid., I, 324, 331–32. See note 43, below.

12 *Canc. Ger.,* I, 5–129.

13 Duarte, *Leal Conselheiro,* chap. XLIV, pp. 176–78.

14 Alexandre Herculano, *Estudos sobre o Casamento Civil,* 5th ed. (Lisbon, n.d.), pp. 36 ff.

15 Ibid., pp. 49–50.

16 Ibid., p. 43. See also the *Fuero Real de Afonso X, o Sabio: Versão portuguesa do século XIII,* ed. Alfredo Pimenta (Lisbon, 1946), bk. III, pp. 81–84.

17 *Chronica do Senhor Rei D. Fernando,* Inéditos de História Portuguesa, 2nd ed., IV (Lisbon, 1925), chap. LVII, p. 247.

18 Cited by Herculano, *Casamento Civil,* p. 54.

19 "Visitação à Egreja de S. João do Mocharro d'Obidos por D. Jorge da Costa, em 14 de Fevereiro de 1467," *Revista Archeologica e Historica,* I (1887), 125; see also in the same periodical "Constituições do Archbispado de Lisboa decretadas por D. João Esteves d'Azambuja (1402–1414)," I, 108; and "Visitação do Arcebispado de Lisboa (século XV)," II (1888), 14.

20 Herculano, *Casamento Civil,* p. 53.

21 "Visitação à Egreja . . . 1467," p. 125.

22 On the betrothal of Beatriz, daughter of Fernando I, to the Count of Cambridge, see Fernão Lopes, *Chronica do Senhor Rei D. Fernando,* chap. CXXX, p. 410. On the ritual of betrothals, see Pierre David, "Le Missal de Mateus: Notes historiques et liturgiques," offprint of *Biblos,* XX (1944), 339.

23 Herculano, *Casamento Civil,* p. 59, n. 1; "Visitação à Egreja . . . 1467," p. 125; "Constituições do Arcebispado de Lisboa," p. 108; "Visitação do Arcebispado de Lisboa," p. 14.

24 Herculano, *Casamento Civil,* p. 37; Luís Chaves, *O Amor Português,* p. 58; M. Paulo Merêa, "Um problema filológico-jurídico: A palavra 'arras,'" in *Novos Estudos de História do Direito* (Barcelos, 1937), pp. 148–49.

25 M. Paulo Merêa, *Evolução dos regimes matrimoniais: Contribuições para a História do Direito Português,* II (Coimbra, 1913), 4; idem, "Mulher recabdada," in *Novos Estudos de História do Direito,* p. 82; idem, "Um problema filológico-jurídico," pp. 148–49; Frederico Francisco de La Figanière, *Memorias das Rainhas de Portugal: D. Theresa—Santa Isabel* (Lisbon, 1859), p. xv. Although dowries were given by the fathers of brides as early as the thirteenth century, the custom became widespread only much later.

26 Fernão Lopes, *Chronica do Senhor Rei D. Fernando,* chap. LXII, p. 255.

27 Fernão Lopes, *Crónica de D. João I* (Oporto, 1945–49), vol. II, chap. XCVI, p. 225.

28 M. Paulo Merêa, *Evolução dos regimes matrimoniais,* II, 58.

29 Ibid., II, 4–8.

30 João Baptista de Castro, *Mappa de Portugal antigo e moderno,* 3rd ed., I (Lisbon, 1870), 134.

31 M. Paulo Merêa, "Sobre o casamento de juras," in *Novos Estudos de História do Direito,* p. 136.

32 Cited by Teófilo Braga, *O Povo Portuguez nos seus costumes, crenças e tradições,* I (Lisbon, 1885), 243.

33 David, "Le Missal de Mateus," pp. 339–40.

34 Baptista de Castro, *Mappa de Portugal,* I, 135.

35 Book V, title XLV, pp. 156–58 (Coimbra, 1797).

36 *Chronica do Condestabre de Portugal Dom Nuno Alvarez Pereira,* ed. Mendes dos Remédios (Coimbra, 1911), chap. V, p. 11.

37 Fernão Lopes, *Crónica de D. João I,* vol. II, chap. XCV, pp. 223–24.

38 *Provas,* vol. VI, bk. II, pp. 9–10.

39 Duarte, *Leal Conselheiro,* chap. XLV, pp. 178–81. The reality of the situation was quite different, if we may believe Fernão Lopes. See what I say on p. 173.

40 Fernão Lopes, *Crónica de D. João I,* vol. II, chap. CXXXVIII, pp. 300–303.

41 Mário Martins, "O Penitencial de Martim Pérez, em Medievo-Português," *Lusitania Sacra,* II (1957), 97.

42 Teófilo Braga, *Tristão o Enamorado* (Oporto, 1914), p. 13.

43 In the *Amadis de Gaula,* carnal union outside of marriage between Elisena and King Perion is perfectly admitted as the normal product of love. The "sin" is repeated over a period of ten days in the chamber of the king of Gaula. The romance is of the greatest interest for the study of the practices of love in the fourteenth century and the tolerance given extramarital love affairs (see *Amadis de Gaula,* Tesoro de Autores Ilustres, LXIII–LXVI [Barcelona, 1847–48]).

44 Alexandre Herculano, "Memoria sobre a origem provavel dos Livros de Linhagens," in *Composições Varias,* 4th ed. (Lisbon, n.d.), pp. 249–50.

45 Duarte, *Leal Conselheiro,* chap. XLVII, pp. 189–99.

46 On this subject, see the dissertation by Baquero Moreno, "Subsídios para o estudo da sociedade medieval portuguesa," pp. 207–10.

47 Ibid., pp. 168–69 ff.

48 *Orden. Affonso,* vol. V, title VIII, art. 1, pp. 37–38.

49 Ibid., vol. V, title XV, arts. 1–2, pp. 49–51; Baquero Moreno, "Subsídios," p. 140.

50 *Orden. Affonso,* vol. II, title XXII, art. 1, p. 195, cited by several authors, the most recent of which is Baquero Moreno, "Subsídios," pp. 145–46.

51 Baquero Moreno, "Subsídios," p. 149.

52 Ibid., p. 155.

53 Ibid., pp. 156–61.

54 José Joaquim Nunes, *Cantigas de Amigo,* I, 93.

55 "Visitação à Egreja . . . 1467," p. 143; "Constituições do Arcebispado de Lisboa," pp. 14, 95; Francisco Inácio dos Santos Cruz, *Da Prostituição na cidade de Lisboa . . .* (Lisbon, 1841), pp. 394–97; *Orden. Affonso,* vol. V, title IX, pp. 37–40, title XIV, pp. 48–49, title VII, pp. 32–35, title VI, pp. 29–32, title XVI, pp. 52–53.

56 *Orden. Affonso,* vol. V, title XVIII, pp. 54–58, title XX, pp. 74–75. See also the examples given by António José Saraiva, in *Historia da Cultura em Portugal,* I, 40–42, on the practical punishment of adultery given by outraged husbands. On the death of Maria Teles, see Fernão Lopes, *Chronica do Senhor Rei D. Fernando,* chap. CI, p. 348.

57 José Joaquim Nunes, *Cantigas de Amigo,* I, 100, 104, 115, among others.

58 Santos Cruz, *Da Prostituição,* pp. 395–97; A. H. de Oliveira Marques, "A Pragmática de 1340," offprint of *Revista da Faculdade de Letras* (Lisbon), 2nd ser., XXII (1956), 18, 30.

59 *Doc. Hist. Evora*, pt. 2, p. 53.

60 *Orden. Affonso*, vol. V, title XXII, pp. 86–89.

61 *Fuero Real de Afonso X*, ed. Alfredo Pimenta, p. 142; see also the odd commentaries in the notes on pp. 427–30 of this source.

62 Vol. V, title XVII, pp. 53–54.

63 *Canc. Bibl. Nac.*, VI, 28–29, no. 1253; 44, no. 1266; 45, no. 1267; 60–61, no. 1279; 308–9, no. 1505; 346, no. 1530. There is also the possibility that many songs of love may actually reflect affection between two men.

64 For example, II, 142–46; IV, 7, 158–60, 161–66, and 264–65.

65 *Chronica de El-Rei D. Pedro I* (Lisbon, 1895), chap. VIII, p. 39.

CHAPTER 6 : WORK

1 *Orden. Affonso*, vol. I, title LXIII, p. 360.

2 On the categories of rural laborers, see Henrique da Gama Barros, *História da Administração Pública em Portugal nos séculos XIII a XV*, 2nd ed., III (Lisbon, 1946); Alexandre Herculano, *História de Portugal*, 8th ed., VII–VIII (Lisbon, n.d.); as well as the various articles in the *Dicionário de História de Portugal*, where the principal bibliography is given.

3 My *Introdução a História da Agricultura em Portugal: A questão cerealífera durante a Idade Média* (Lisbon, 1962), pp. 98–103, discusses forms of land ownership and taxation.

4 On the corvée and on military service, see the general works, such those by Gama Barros and Herculano, and the articles in the *Dicionário de História de Portugal*.

5 Law on price control in João Pedro Ribeiro, *Dissertações Chronologicas e Criticas sobre a Historia e Jurisprudencia Ecclesiastica e Civil de Portugal*, 2nd ed., III, pt. 2 (Lisbon, 1857), pp. 66–67.

6 See especially Gama Barros, *História da Administração Pública*, III, 15 ff. Several historians have referred to the matter of choosing one's work, and to labor conditions in general.

7 *Doc. Hist. Evora*, pt. 1, p. 164, pt. 2, pp. 97–103; *Orden. Affonso*, vol. I, title XXVIII, pp. 181–84, title LXVIII, p. 411; António Cruz, *Os Mesteres do Pôrto: Subsidios para a História das Antigas Corporações dos Ofícios Mecânicos*, I (Oporto, 1943), 2; Marcelo Caetano, "A antiga organização dos mesteres da cidade de Lisboa," pref. to *As Corporações dos Ofícios Mecânicos: Subsidios para a sua história*, by Franz Paul de Almeida Langhans, I (Lisbon, 1943), p. xxxiv.

8 *Doc. Hist. Evora*, pt. 2, pp. 159–61.

9 A. Sousa Gomes, *Carpinteiros da Ribeira das Naus* (Coimbra, 1931), pp. 73–74, 85–86, and 107–8; Gérard Pradalié, "Lisbonne, de la Reconquête à la fin du XIIIᵉ siècle" (unpubl. diss., Faculté des Lettres et des Sciences Humaines, Toulouse, 1961), pp. 100–101; João Manuel Esteves Pereira,

A Industria Portugueza (seculos XII a XIX) com uma introducção sobre as corporações operarias em Portugal (Lisbon, 1900), p. xvi; João Brandão, *Tratado da Majestade, Grandeza e Abastança da Cidade de Lisboa* . . . (Lisbon, 1923), pp. 57, 205 ff.; António Lopes de Carvalho, *Os Mesteres de Guimarãis* (Barcelos, 1939–44), I, 67–68; António Cruz, *Os Mesteres do Pôrto*, pp. lxvi, lxviii; A. H. de Oliveira Marques, "Estratificação económico-social de uma vila portuguesa da Idade Média," offprint of *Ocidente*, LXV (1963), 75.

10 J. M. Esteves Pereira, *A Industria Portugueza*, p. xvi. In Guimarães there was a street of the Shoemakers (R. Sapateira) in 1167 (A. L. de Carvalho, *Os Mesteres de Guimarãis*, III, 194).

11 *Tratado . . . da Cidade de Lisboa*, p. 83.

12 Ibid., p. 84, n. 222.

13 *Doc. Hist. Evora.*, pt. 1, p. 193.

14 Based on the numbers furnished by João Brandão, *Tratado . . . da Cidade de Lisboa*.

15 *Doc. Hist. Evora*, pt. 1, pp. 147–48.

16 See Chapters 4 and 7 of this book.

17 António Cruz, *Os Mesteres do Pôrto*, p. xxii.

18 A. Sousa Gomes, *Carpinteiros da Ribeira das Naus*, pp. 47–108 passim.

19 Ibid., pp. 47–105 passim.

20 *Doc. Hist. Evora*, pt. 1, pp. 138–41, 144–45; António Cruz, *Os Mesteres do Pôrto*, pp. lxvi–lxx.

21 Marcelo Caetano, "A antiga organização dos mesteres da cidade de Lisboa," pp. xiii, 372–77.

22 *Doc. Hist. Evora*, pt. 2, p. 154.

23 Calculations based on the Price Schedule of 1480 in *Livro Vermelho de D. Affonso V* (Ineditos de Historia Portugueza, III [Lisbon, 1793], pp. 512 ff.).

24 Ibid.

25 Fortunato de Almeida, *Historia da Igreja em Portugal*, II (Coimbra, 1912), 493–97.

26 Ibid., p. 496; Gama Barros, *História da Administração Pública*, III, 112–15; *Fuero Real de Afonso X, o Sabio: Versão portuguesa do século XIII*, ed. Alfredo Pimenta (Lisbon, 1946), p. 344.

27 *Doc. Hist. Evora*, pt. 1, p. 129.

28 Ibid., pp. 130–31.

29 Oliveira Marques, *Agricultura em Portugal*, chap. VII.

30 *Orden. Affonso*, vol. I, titles I–LXX; Virgínia Rau, *A Casa dos Contos* (Coimbra, 1951); Gama Barros, *História da Administração Pública*, III, 199–250.

31 *Livro Vermelho de D. Affonso V*, pp. 507–9.

32 Rau, *A Casa dos Contos*, pp. 33, 34, 48, 240–41.

CHAPTER 7 : FAITH

1 "Visitação do Arcebispado de Lisboa (século XV)," *Revista Archeologica e Historica,* II (1888), 15, n. 11; "Visitação à Egreja de S. João do Mocharro d'Obidos por D. Jorge da Costa, em 14 de Fevereiro de 1467," ibid., I (1887), 122; Damião de Góis, *Chronica do Prinçipe Dom Ioam,* ed. A. J. Gonçalves Guimarães (Coimbra, 1905), chap. II, pp. 4–5.

2 Damião de Góis, *Chronica do Prinçipe Dom Ioam,* chap. II, p. 5.

3 "Visitação à Egreja de S. João do Mocharro d'Obidos por D. João, bispo de Çafim, em nome do arcebispo de Lisboa, aos 2 de junho de 1473," *Rev. Archeol. e Hist.,* I (1887), 169, n. 7; Rui de Pina, *Chronica do Senhor Rey D. Duarte,* Ineditos de Historia Portugueza, I (Lisbon, 1790), chap. IX, p. 99.

4 Pierre David, "O Pontifical de Braga no séc. XII, com notas sobre um Pontifical de Santa Cruz de Coimbra, da mesma data," *Liturgia,* I (August–October 1947), 137, supplement to *Mensageiro de S. Bento,* XVI, no. 8.

5 "Visitação à Egreja . . . 1467," p. 126; Fortunato de Almeida, *Historia da Igreja em Portugal* (Coimbra, 1910–12), II, 497.

6 Rui Fernandes, "Descripção do terreno em roda da cidade de Lamego duas leguas," in *Ineditos de Historia Portugueza,* 2nd ed., V (Lisbon, 1926), 586.

7 Augustin Fliche, Christine Thouzellier, and Yvonne Azais, *La Chretienté romaine (1198–1274),* vol. X of *Histoire de l'Eglise depuis ses origines jusqu'à nos jours,* ed. Augustin Fliche and Victor Martin (Paris, 1950), pp. 200–201.

8 "Visitação à Egreja . . . 1467," pp. 122–24; Eduardo Freire de Oliveira, ed., *Elementos para a Historia do Municipio de Lisboa* (Lisbon, 1882–85), I, 279; Mário Martins, "O Penitencial de Martim Pérez, em Medievo-Português," *Lusitania Sacra,* II (1957), 101; *Chronica do Condestabre de Portugal Dom Nuno Alvarez Pereira,* ed. Mendes dos Remédios (Coimbra, 1911), chap. LXXX, pp. 206–7.

9 Mário Martins, "O Penitencial de Martim Pérez," pp. 57–59, 82, 85, 92–99, 103–9.

10 Gomes Eanes de Zurara, *Chronica do Conde Dom Duarte de Menezes,* Ineditos de Historia Portugueza, III (Lisbon, 1793), chap. LXVIII, p. 184; Fortunato de Almeida, *Historia da Igreja em Portugal,* II, 485.

11 *Chronica do Condestabre,* chap. LXXX, pp. 206–7; António Garcia Ribeiro de Vasconcelos, *Evolução do culto de Dona Isabel de Aragão esposa do rei lavrador Dom Denis de Portugal (a Rainha Santa),* I (Coimbra, 1894), p. 8, n. 1; Duarte, *Leal Conselheiro,* ed. Joseph M. Piel (Lisbon, 1942), chap. XCVI, p. 354, chap. XCVII, pp. 355–57; Gomes Eanes de Zurara, *Cronica da Tomada de Ceuta por El-Rei D. João I,* ed. Francisco Maria Esteves Pereira (Lisbon, 1915), chap. XXXVII, p. 117, chap. XLVI, p. 142.

12 Zurara, *Cronica da Tomada de Ceuta,* chap. XXIV, p. 75; Rui de Pina, *Chronica do Senhor Rey D. Affonso V,* Ineditos de Historia Portugueza,

I (Lisbon, 1790), chap. CXXV, pp. 432–33; *Chronica do Condestabre,* chap. LXXX, p. 207; Mário Martins, "O Penitencial de Martim Perez," p. 101; Fortunato de Almeida, *Historia da Igreja em Portugal,* I, 577.

13 Mário Martins, *Peregrinações e Livros de Milagres na nossa Idade Média,* 2nd ed. (Lisbon, 1957), pp. 41 ff.; Avelino de Jesus da Costa, "A Virgem Maria Padroeira de Portugal na Idade Média," offprint of *Lusitania Sacra,* II (1957), 21 ff.; José Joaquim Nunes, *Cantigas de Amigo dos Trovadores Galego-Portugueses,* I (Coimbra, 1928), p. 27, n. 1; *Chronica do Condestabre,* chap. LI, p. 126; Rui de Pina, *Chronica d'El-Rey D. João II,* Ineditos de Historia Portugueza, II (Lisbon, 1792), chap. XVI, p. 54; Rui de Pina, *Chronica do Senhor Rey D. Affonso V,* chap. CXLVIII, p. 495.

14 Rui de Pina, *Chronica do Senhor Rey D. Affonso V,* chap. CLVII, p. 517; *Chronica do Condestabre,* chap. LIV, p. 133.

15 Nevertheless, in Évora in the thirteenth century, there must have been at least some ten citizens who had made the journey to Jerusalem and formed a brotherhood (see p. 226 of this book).

16 Mário Martins, *Peregrinações,* pp. 30 ff., 147 ff., 161 ff.

17 Ibid., pp. 53 ff.; Pierre David, "Festas e usos litúrgicos de Braga segundo manuscritos do século XII," *Mensageiro de S. Bento,* XV (July–August 1946), 160–62.

18 The bibliography is vast. See only as examples Fliche, Thouzellier, and Azais, *La Chretienté romaine;* or Johan Huizinga, *The Waning of the Middle Ages,* trans. F. Hopman (London, 1924). Among the Portuguese writers, see António José Saraiva, *História da Cultura em Portugal,* I (Lisbon, 1950), 654 ff.

19 Avelino Costa, "A Virgem Maria Padroeira," pp. 7–13, 30 ff.; idem, *Origem e evolução do culto de Nossa Senhora da Conceição em Portugal: Catálogo da Exposição Documental* (Braga, 1964); Mário Martins, *Peregrinações,* p. 92; Fortunato de Almeida, *Historia da Igreja em Portugal,* II, 475–76; Miguel de Oliveira and Moreira das Neves, *A Padroeira de Portugal: Notas e Documentos* (Lisbon, 1940), pp. 15–16, 18.

20 E. Freire de Oliveira, *Elementos,* I, 420, n. 4.

21 Fortunato de Almeida, *Historia da Igreja em Portugal,* II, 480.

22 *Doc. Hist. Evora,* pt. 2, pp. 159–61. The several quotations in the text are from Alexandre Herculano, *O Monge de Cister, ou a Epocha de D. João I,* 20th ed., II (Lisbon, n.d.), 83 ff.

23 Fortunato de Almeida, *Historia da Igreja em Portugal,* II, 479.

24 E. Freire de Oliveira, *Elementos,* I, 277–79.

25 Fortunato de Almeida, *Historia da Igreja em Portugal,* II, 480.

26 Zurara, *Crónica da Tomada de Ceuta,* chap. XLI, p. 127.

27 In the mid-fifteenth century in Óbidos, one paid, for one mass, an alqueire of wheat, or two alqueires of *segunda* (millet, barley, or rye), or one almude of wine, or half an alqueire of olive oil ("Visitação à Egreja ... 1473," pp. 170–71).

28 Pierre David, "Curso de instituições eclesiásticas medievais, II: A Liturgia," *Revista Portuguesa de História,* II (1943), 611; idem, "O Pontifical de Braga no séc. XII," *Liturgia,* I (July 1947), 105, supplement to *Mensageiro de S. Bento,* XVI, no 7; idem, "Le Missal de Mateus: Notes historiques et liturgiques," offprint of *Biblos,* XX (1944), 327; Duarte, *Leal Conselheiro,* chap. XCVI, pp. 351–55; António Garcia Ribeiro de Vasconcelos, "Notas litúrgico-bracarenses," in *Acta do Congresso Litúrgico Nacional Romano-Bracarense* (Braga, 1928), p. 222.

29 Pierre David, "A diocese de Lisboa seguiu o costume litúrgico de Salisbury?" *Liturgia,* I (April 1947), 54–56, supplement to *Mensageiro de S. Bento,* XVI, no. 4; António de Vasconcelos, "Notas litúrgico-bracarenses," p. 202.

30 Duarte, *Leal Conselheiro,* chap. XCVI, pp. 351–55.

31 Fortunato de Almeida, *Historia da Igreja em Portugal,* II, 473; José Augusto Ferreira, "O Rito Bracarense e o seu Breviário no aspecto historico," in *Acta do Congresso Litúrgico Nacional,* p. 59; Herbert Norris, *Church Vestments* (London, 1949); J. Quicherat, *Histoire du costume en France depuis les temps les plus reculés jusqu'à la fin du XVIIIe siècle* (Paris, 1875), pp. 168 ff.

32 Norris, *Church Vestments,* pp. 157–64, 172; Fortunato de Almeida, *Historia da Igreja em Portugal,* II, 455.

33 "Constituições do Arcebispado de Lisboa decretadas por D. João Esteves d'Azambuja (1402–1414)," *Rev. Archeol. e Hist.,* I (1887), 28–29.

34 Ibid., p. 28.

35 Fortunato de Almeida, *Historia da Igreja em Portugal,* II, 428–30.

36 Henrique da Gama Barros, *História da Administração Pública em Portugal nos Séculos XII a XV,* 2nd ed., III (Lisbon, 1946), 108.

37 "Constituições do Arcebispado de Lisboa," pp. 14, 95; Mário Martins, "O Penitencial de Martim Pérez," p. 101; "Visitação à Egreja . . . 1473," pp. 171–72; "Visitação à Egreja . . . 1467," pp. 139, 142; "Visitação do Arcebispado de Lisbon," p. 51.

38 This subject cannot be treated here in the manner it deserves, because we do not have sufficient data to know the degree of clericalism or anticlericalism among the Portuguese in the Middle Ages. See, however, ballad no. 812 of the *Canc. Bibl. Nac.* (IV, 202–3), where the Augustinians and Cistercians are criticized. On the recruiting and culture of the clergy, see Fortunato de Almeida, *Historia da Igreja em Portugal,* II, 64, 107, 158, 171.

39 Gérard Pradalié, "Lisbonne, de la Reconquête a la fin du XIIIe siècle" (unpubl. diss., Faculté des Lettres et des Sciences Humaines, Toulouse, 1961), pp. 102–3. On the brotherhoods, see also Braamcamp Freire, "Compromisso de Confraria em 1346," *Archivo Historico Portuguez,* I (1903), 349–55. On the founding of hospitals by brotherhoods, see especially Fernando da Silva Correia, *Origem e Formação das Misericórdias Portuguesas: Estudos sôbre a História da Assistência* (Lisbon, 1944).

40 BNL, Ilum. 61 ("Livro de Orações"), fols. 72v ff.; Fortunato de Almeida, *Historia da Igreja em Portugal*, II, 490.

41 *Doc. Hist. Evora*, pt. 1, pp. 38-39.

42 Mário Martins, "O Penitencial de Martim Perez," pp. 99-100; "Constituições do Arcebispado de Lisboa," pp. 14, 94-95; see also Fortunato de Almeida, *Historia da Igreja em Portugal*, II, 305-10. On witchcraft and magic, see also Alexandre Herculano, "Crenças Populares Portuguesas ou Superstições Populares," in *Opúsculos*, 3rd ed., IX (Lisbon, n.d.), 153-80.

43 E. Freire de Oliveira, *Elementos*, I, 273-76.

44 *Orden. Affonso*, vol. I, title XXVI, p. 165, vol. II, title VII, p. 95, vol. V, title I, pp. 2-5, vol. V, title XCIX, pp. 353-55; Fortunato de Almeida, *Historia da Igreja em Portugal*, II, 303-4, 311.

45 *Orden. Affonso*, vol. V, title XXVII, p. 98.

CHAPTER 8 : CULTURE

1 See pp. 207-8 of this book.

2 Throughout this chapter, I have followed, as a basic source, António José Saraiva, *História da Cultura em Portugal*, I (Lisbon, 1950).

3 Henry Carter, "A Fourteenth-Century Latin-Old Portuguese Verb Dictionary," offprint of *Romance Philology*, VI (November 1952-February 1953).

4 Inéditos de História Portuguesa, 2nd ed., IV (Lisbon, 1925), chap. CIII, p. 351.

5 Hermann Keussen, *Die Matrikel der Universität Köln*, 2nd ed., I (Bonn, 1928), pp. 82, 141, 182, and 539, lists the following names: Fr. Vasco Gil, Franciscan, enrolled in 1396, in Theology; Fr. Fernando of Lisbon, Dominican, on the same date and in the same faculty; Fr. João of Santa Justa, Dominican, also in Theology, in 1410; Fr. Fernando, Dominican, in 1416; Fernando de Lucena and Vasco de Lucena, both in 1450, enrolled in Arts.

6 Carolina Michaëlis de Vasconcelos, "Mestre Giraldo e os seus tratados de alveitaria e cetraria," offprint of *Revista Lusitana*, XIII (1910), 149-432. On the bibliography referring to books of this nature, see, in addition to the *História da Cultura em Portugal* by António José Saraiva, Maria Adelaide Valle Cintra, *Bibliografia de Textos Medievais Portugueses* (Lisbon, 1960).

7 *Chronica do Condestabre de Portugal Dom Nuno Alvarez Pereira*, ed. Mendes dos Remédios (Coimbra, 1911), chap. IV, p. 9.

8 Francisco Marques de Sousa Viterbo, "A livraria real especialmente no reinado de D. Manuel," offprint of *Historia e Memorias da Academia Real das Sciencias de Lisboa*, n.s., Classe de Sciencias Moraes, IX (1901), pt. 1, p. 3.

9 *Livro da Ensinança de bem cavalgar toda sela*, ed. Joseph M. Piel (Lisbon, 1944), pp. 120-21.

10 Ibid., pp. 118 ff.

11 José Leite de Vasconcelos, *Fabulario Português: Manuscrito do sec. XV* (Lisbon, 1906) , p. 100 (first published in *Revista Lusitana,* VIII [1903–5], 9–151, and IX [1906], 5–109) .

12 This portrays an ideal type of peasant, of course. It would be interesting to see if systematic studies based on documents confirmed it or denied it.

13 See n. 12.

14 See Chapter 4 of this book, especially p. 151.

CHAPTER 9 : AMUSEMENTS

1 Sílvio Lima, "O Desporto e a Experiência na Idade-Média," in *Desporto, jôgo e arte* (Oporto, 1938) , p. 153; also idem, *Ensaios sôbre o desporto* (Lisbon, 1937) , pp. 10, 59–62.

2 Gomes Eanes de Zurara, *Crónica da Tomada de Ceuta por El-Rei D. João I,* ed. Francisco Maria Esteves Pereira (Lisbon, 1915) , chap. XXII, p. 68.

3 Fernão Lopes, *Chronica do Senhor Rei D. Fernando,* Inéditos de História Portuguesa, 2nd ed., IV (Lisbon, 1925) , chap. XCVIII, p. 338.

4 Ibid., Prologue, pp. 124–25.

5 Zurara, *Crónica da Tomada de Ceuta,* chap. XXII, p. 69.

6 Carolina Michaëlis de Vasconcelos, "Mestre Giraldo e os seus tratados de alveitaria e cetraria," offprint of *Revista Lusitana,* XIII (1910) , 198.

7 Fernão Lopes, *Chronica do Senhor Rei D. Fernando,* Prologue, p. 125.

8 A. de Sousa e Silva Costa Lobo, *Historia da Sociedade em Portugal no seculo XV* (Lisbon, 1903) , pp. 79, 81.

9 Ibid., pp. 78–80, 85.

10 João Pedro Ribeiro, *Dissertações Chronologicas e Criticas sobre a Historia e Jurisprudencia Ecclesiastica e Civil de Portugal,* 2nd ed., III, pt. 2 (Lisbon, 1857) , pp. 69–70.

11 Carolina Michaëlis de Vasconcelos, "Mestre Giraldo," p. 151; *Livro de Falcoaria de Pero Menino,* ed. Manuel Rodrigues Lapa (Coimbra, 1931) , p. 1; Fernão Lopes, *Chronica do Senhor Rei D. Fernando,* Prologue, pp. 124–25.

12 Manuel Rodrigues Lapa, "Livros de Falcoaria," fasc. 3–4 of *Boletim de Filologia,* I (1933) , 215–16.

13 Carolina Michaëlis de Vasconcelos, "Mestre Giraldo," p. 201.

14 José Joaquim Nunes, *Cantigas de Amigo dos Trovadores Galego-Portugueses,* I (Coimbra, 1928) , 30.

15 *Doc. Hist. Evora,* pt. 2, p. 49.

16 Gabriel Pereira, *As Caçadas,* Estudos Eborenses, no. 29, pt. 2 (Évora, 1893) , p. 11.

17 Zurara, *Crónica da Tomada de Ceuta,* chap. XXIII, p. 73.

18 Rui de Pina, *Chronica do Senhor Rey D. Affonso V,* Ineditos de Historia Portugueza, I (Lisbon, 1790) , chap. CXXXI, p. 443; João I, *Livro da Montaria,* ed. Francisco Maria Esteves Pereira (Coimbra, 1918) , pt. 1, chap. IV, p. 26.

19 Rui de Pina, *Chronica do Senhor Rey D. Affonso V*, chap. CXXXI, p. 443.

20 Joseph M. Piel edition (Lisbon, 1944), pp. 113–14.

21 Rui de Pina, *Chronica do Senhor Rey D. Affonso V*, chap. CXXXI, p. 443; idem, *Chronica d'El-Rey D. João II*, Ineditos de Historia Portugueza, II (Lisbon, 1792), chap. XVI, p. 54, chap. XXI, p. 71, chap. XLIV, p. 112, chap. XLVII, p. 125.

22 José Joaquim Nunes, *Cantigas de Amigo*, I, 29; Henrique da Gama Barros, *História da Administração Publica em Portugal nos Séculos XII a XV*, 2nd ed., III (Lisbon, 1946), 367–68; Manuel Paulo Merêa, *Portucale*, XIII, 97–98; João I, *Livro da Montaria*, pt. 1, chap. II, p. 8.

23 João I, *Livro da Montaria*, pt. 1, chap. II, p. 13; Duarte, *Livro da Ensinança de bem cavalgar toda sela*, pp. 6–8; Zurara, *Crónica da Tomada de Ceuta*, chap. XV, p. 49; Fernão Lopes, *Chronica do Senhor Rei D. Fernando*, Prologue, p. 123, chap. XCVIII, p. 338.

24 João I, *Livro da Montaria*, pt. 1, chap. II, p. 12; Duarte, *Livro da Ensinança*, p. 8.

25 *Livro da Ensinança*, pp. 122–24.

26 Ibid., pp. 118 ff.; João I, *Livro da Montaria*, pt. 1, chap. II, p. 9.

27 Duarte, *Livro da Ensinança*, pp. 118 ff.; João I, *Livro da Montaria*, pt. 1, chap. II, pp. 10–12.

28 João I, *Livro da Montaria*, pt. 1, chap. II, p. 8; *Provas*, vol. I, bk. III, p. 292.

29 *Orden. Affonso*, vol. V, title XLI, pp. 148–51; Arnaldo Gama, *A ultima dona de S. Nicolau: Episodio da historia do Porto no seculo XV*, 2nd ed. (Lisbon, 1899), p. 406, n. XX; Rui de Pina, *Chronica d'El-Rey D. João II*, chap. XL, p. 102. See an excellent reconstruction of a gambling house in Alexandre Herculano, *O Monge de Cister, ou a Epocha de D. João I*. 20th ed., I (Lisbon, n.d.), 147 ff.

30 *Canc. Bibl. Nac.*, VI, 109, no. 1325.

31 *Orden. Affonso*, vol. V, title XL, pp. 146–47, title XLI, pp. 148–51; "Constituições do Arcebispado de Lisboa decretadas por D. João Esteves d'Azambuja (1402–1414)," *Revista Archeologica e Historica*, I (1887), 96; Teófilo Braga, *O Povo Portuguez nos seus costumes, crenças e tradições*, I (Lisbon, 1885), 346–49. In the identification of games, the *Diciónario da Lingua Portuguesa* by Morais e Silva and the *Grande Enciclopédia Portuguesa-Brasileira* were also helpful.

32 Teófilo Braga, *O Povo Portuguez*, I, 346–49.

33 See especially António José Saraiva, *Historia da Cultura em Portugal*, I (Lisbon, 1950), which gives the principal bibliography.

34 António José Saraiva, *Historia da Cultura em Portugal*; João de Freitas Branco, *História da Música Portuguesa* (Lisbon, 1959), pp. 21–24. In a 1339 document in the ANTT on the functions of the corregidores (Forais Antigos, m. 10, no. 7, fol. 54), Goliards and *goulães* (who were closely related to Goliards) are mentioned.

35 António José Saraiva, *Historia da Cultura em Portugal*, I, 69; on the fools, see Francisco Marques de Sousa Viterbo, "Curiosidades Históricas e artísticas, XV: Bobos reais," *O Instituto*, LXVI (January 1919), 58–61.

36 Chap. XXX, p. 93.

37 João I, *Livro da Montaria*, pt. 1, chap. II, pp. 10–12; Duarte, *Livro da Ensinança*, pp. 118 ff.; *Provas*, vol. VI, pt. II, pp. 8, 10.

38 Rui de Pina, *Chronica d'El-Ray D. João II*, chap. XLVI, p. 117; Baron of Rosmital, "Viagem em Portugal," in João Baptista de Castro, *Mappa de Portugal antigo e moderno*, 3rd ed., IV (Lisbon, 1870), 51.

39 José Joaquim Nunes, *Cantigas de Amigo*, I, 18–20, II, 235, no. 258.

40 Ibid., I, 142.

41 Ibid., I, 148–53; Teófilo Braga, *O Povo Portuguez*, I, 405; *Canc. Bibl. Nac.*, VI, 98–99, no. 1314, 99–100, no. 1315, 100, no. 1316, 282–83, no. 1479; Freitas Branco, *História da Música Portuguesa*, pp. 23, 29; Solange Corbin, "L'Office de la Conception de la Vierge: Á propos d'un manuscrit du XVème siécle du monastère dominicain d'Aveiro, Portugal," *Bulletin des études portugaises et de l'Institut français au Portugal*, n.s., XIII (1949), 118. A codex of the BNL (Ilum. 61, "Livro de Orações" by F. André Dias) which dates from 1435 lists the principal instruments used, among them, organs, drums, horns, anafis, guitars, lutes, and Moorish rebecks, or *arrabis* (fol. 3).

42 Solange Corbin, *Essai sur la musique religieuse portugaise au moyen age (1100–1385)* (Paris, 1952), pp. 385–86; Freitas Branco, *História da Música Portuguesa*, pp. 28–29; João I, *Livro da Montaria*, pt. 1, chap. III, p. 19.

43 Francisco Marques de Sousa Viterbo, *Subsidios para a Historia da Musica em Portugal*, 2nd ed. (Coimbra, 1932), pp. 3–4 ff.; idem, "A cultura intellectual de D. Affonso V," in *Archivo Historico Portuguez*, II (1904), 261; Rui de Pina, *Chronica do Senhor Rey D. Affonso V*, chap. CCXIII, p. 609.

44 Solange Corbin, "Fêtes portugaises," *Bulletin Hispanique*, XLIX, no. 2 (1947), 210–13.

45 See a good reconstruction of the May festival in Herculano, *O Monge de Cister*, chap. IV, pp. 66 ff.

46 Conde de Sabugosa, *Embrechados*, 3rd ed. (Lisbon, 1921), pp. 14–16; Fernão Lopes, *Chronica do Senhor Rei D. Fernando*, chap. CLXVII, p. 488; *Provas*, vol. VI, bk. II, p. 8, vol. I, bk. III, pp. 340–41; *Doc. Hist. Evora*, pt. 2, pp. 76, 81, 145, 239–40.

47 Zurara, *Crónica da Tomada de Ceuta*, chap. XXIII, p. 72; Rui de Pina, *Chronica d'El-Ray D. João II*, chap. XLIV, p. 112, chap. XLVII, pp. 126–27.

48 Rui de Pina, *Chronica d'El-Rey D. João II*, chap. XLIV, p. 113; idem, *Chronica do Senhor Rey D. Affonso V*, chap. CXXXI, p. 443.

49 Fernão Lopes, *Chronica de El-Rei D. Pedro I* (Lisbon, 1895), chap. XIV, pp. 56–57; Zurara, *Crónica da Tomada de Ceuta*, chap. VIII, pp. 24–26.

50 Damião de Góis, *Chronica do Prinçipe Dom Ioam,* ed. A. J. Gonçalves Guimarães (Coimbra, 1905), chap. I, p. 4; *Doc. Hist. Evora,* pt. 2, p. 239.

51 *Doc. Hist. Evora,* pt. 2, p. 240.

52 Mário Martins, "Representações teatrais em Lisboa no ano de 1451," *Brotéria,* LXXI, no. 5 (1960), 425–30.

53 *Provas,* vol. I, bk. III, pp. 337–47.

CHAPTER 10 : DEATH

1 *Leal Conselheiro,* ed. Joseph M. Piel (Lisbon, 1942), chap. I, pp. 11–12.

2 Gomes Eanes de Zurara, *Crónica da Tomada de Ceuta por El-Rei D. João I,* ed. Francisco Maria Esteves Pereira (Lisbon, 1915), chap. XXXVIII, p. 121.

3 *Leal Conselheiro,* chap. I, pp. 11–12.

4 Ibid.

5 Based on the "Livros de Linhagens" (printed in *Portugaliae Monumenta Historica: Scriptores,* I [Lisbon, 1856; 2nd ed., Lisbon, 1969]), which seem to have recorded only the legitimate children who survived to a marriageable age.

6 António Garcia Ribeiro de Vasconcelos, *Evolução do culto de Dona Isabel de Aragão . . .,* I (Coimbra, 1894), 42–44.

7 "Visitação à Egreja de S. João do Mocharro d'Obidos por D. Jorge da Costa, em 14 de Fevereiro de 1467," *Revista Archeologica e Historica,* I (1887), 152; "Visitação do Arcebispado de Lisboa (século XV)," ibid., II (1888), 28.

8 Fortunato de Almeida, *Historia da Igreja em Portugal,* II (Coimbra, 1912), 492; Eduardo Freire de Oliveira, ed., *Elementos para a Historia do Municipio de Lisboa,* XVII (Lisbon, 1911), 299–300.

9 Teófilo Braga, *O Povo Portuguez nos seus costumes, crenças e tradiçoes,* I (Lisbon, 1885), 186–87.

10 Ibid., pp. 188, 190–91.

11 "Visitação à Egreja de S. João do Mocharro d'Obidos por D. João, Bispo de Çafim, em Nome do Arcebispo de Lisboa, aos 2 de Junho de 1473," *Rev. Archeol. e Hist.,* I (1887), 170.

12 João Baptista de Castro, *Mappa de Portugal antigo e moderno,* 3rd ed., I (Lisbon, 1870), 276–77; Teófilo Braga, *O Povo Portuguez,* I, 198–200; Freire de Oliveira, *Elementos,* I, 276; *Doc. Hist. Evora,* pt. 1, p. 153.

13 Freire de Oliveira, *Elementos,* I, 307; Rui de Pina, *Chronica do Senhor Rey D. Duarte,* Ineditos de Historia Portugueza, I (Lisbon, 1790), chap. I, pp. 74, 75; idem, *Chronica d'El-Rei D. João II,* Ineditos de Historia Portugueza, II (Lisbon, 1792), chap. L, pp. 134–35, chap. LII, p. 141; Baron of Rosmital, "Viagem em Portugal," in J. Baptista de Castro, *Mappa de Portugal,* IV, 53–54.

14 Teófilo Braga, *O Povo Portuguez,* I, 195–200.

15 Ibid., pp. 208–9, 219; Rosmital, "Viagem em Portugal," pp. 53–54.

16 Fernão Lopes, *Chronica do Senhor Rei D. Fernando,* Inéditos de História Portuguesa, 2nd ed., IV (Lisbon, 1925), chap. CLXXII, p. 499; Rui de Pina, *Chronica do Senhor Rey D. Affonso V,* Ineditos de Historia Portugueza, I (Lisbon, 1790), chap. CCXII, p. 607.

17 *Chronica do Condestabre de Portugal Dom Nuno Alvarez Pereira,* ed. Mendes dos Remédios (Coimbra, 1911), chap. XV, p. 39.

18 "Visitação à Egreja . . . 1467," pp. 140–41; "Visitação do Arcebispado de Lisboa," p. 16; Teófilo Braga, *O Povo Portuguez,* I, 208.

19 See Teófilo Braga, *O Povo Portuguez,* I, 219 ff.

20 Rui de Pina, *Chronica d'El-Rei D. João II,* chap. XXXII, p. 83, chap. L, p. 136; idem. *Chronica do Senhor Rey D. Affonso V,* chap. CCVII, pp. 595–96.

21 Fernão Lopes, *Chronica do Senhor Rei D. Fernando,* chap. XXXIV, p. 193, chap. CL, p. 451.

22 Fernão Lopes, *Crónica de D. João I* (Oporto, 1945–49), vol. I, chap. VII, p. 15; Rui de Pina, *Chronica do Senhor Rey D. Duarte,* chap. II, p. 78; idem, *Chronica d'El-Rei D. João II,* chap. I, pp. 9–10, chap. XIV, p. 52.

23 Rui de Pina, *Chronica do Senhor Rey D. Affonso V,* chap. CXXXVII, p. 457.

24 Rui de Pina, *Chronica do Senhor Rey D. Duarte,* chap. II, p. 78; J. Baptista de Castro, *Mappa de Portugal,* I, 276–77.

25 Rui de Pina, *Chronica do Senhor Rey D. Duarte,* chap. VII, p. 93; idem, *Chronica d'El-Rei D. João II,* chap. LIV, pp. 142–43.

26 Teófilo Braga, *O Povo Portuguez,* I, 203–4.

CRITICAL BIBLIOGRAPHY

CHAPTER 1 : THE TABLE

Neither medieval nor modern Portuguese nutrition has been studied in depth. In the licentiate degree dissertation that I presented to the Faculdade de Letras of Lisbon in 1956, entitled "A Sociedade em Portugal nos Séculos XII a XIV: Subsídios para a sua História," I sketched an analysis of medieval nutrition, which is summarized or corrected here, and which has already been broached again in my article, "A Pragmática de 1340," an offprint of the *Revista da Faculdade de Letras* (Lisbon), 2nd ser., XXII, no. 2 (1956). Again, in the book *Introdução à História da Agricultura em Portugal: A questão cerealífera durante a Idade Média* (Lisbon, 1962; 2nd ed., Lisbon, 1968), I studied the production and consumption of bread and grains used for making bread.

In an article entitled "A medicina no *Cancioneiro de Garcia de Resende*," in *Arquivos de História da Medicina Portuguesa*, n.s., XI–XII (1920–21), Maximiano Lemos collected all the clues on food which appear in the ballads of the cancioneiro. João Manuel Esteves Pereira, in his little book *A Industria Agraria: Apontamentos para a historia das industrias portuguezas, seculos XII a XIX* (Lisbon, 1895), also studies in detail the consumption of fruits and vegetables during the Portuguese Middle Ages.

For comparison with the corresponding situation abroad, one can refer to Max von Boehn, *La Moda* (Barcelona, 1928–29), vol. I; to Henry Hamilton, *History of the Homeland* (London, 1946); and to the informative little book by F. Funck-Brentano, *La Société au moyen age* (Paris, 1937). An interesting article by Marianne Mulon, "Recettes médiévales," was recently published in the French review *Annales*, XIX (September–October 1964), 933–37. The many monographs on daily life in other European countries are also very useful.

There are several kinds of sources. The principal information can be found in the chronicles and in other literary texts. The most important chronicles to consult are Fernão Lopes' *Crónicas de D. Pedro I, D. Fernando,* and *D. João I,* and Garcia de Resende's *Crónica de D. João II.* Valuable information can be found in the *Ordenaçoens do Senhor Rey D. Affonso V,* vols. I–V (Coimbra, 1792); in the *Dissertações Chronologicas e Criticas sobre a His-*

toria e Jurisprudencia Ecclesiastica e Civil de Portugal by João Pedro Ribeiro, 2nd ed. (Lisbon, 1859–96), vol. III; in the "Inventários e Contas da Casa de D. Dinis (1278–1282)," published in *Arquivo Histórico Português,* X (1916), 41–59; in the *Leal Conselheiro* by King Duarte (I used the edition of Joseph M. Piel [Lisbon, 1942]); in the *Livro da Montaria* by King João I, ed. Francisco Maria Esteves Pereira (Coimbra, 1918); in the *Provas da História Genealógica da Casa Real Portuguesa,* ed. António Caetano de Sousa, 2nd ed. (Coimbra, 1946–54), vol. I, bk. III; in the *Documentos Historicos da Cidade de Evora,* ed. Gabriel Pereira (Évora, 1885–91), pt. 1; and in the *Elucidario das Palavras, Termos, e Frases que em Portugal antiguamente se usarão, e que hoje regularmente se ignorão* by Joaquim de Santa Rosa de Viterbo, vols. I and II (Lisbon, 1798–99).

Among the unpublished sources, the priceless cookbook from the sixteenth century was edited by Maria José da Gama Lobo Salema in her dissertation, "Tratado de Cozinha, Século XVI (MS. I-E-33 da BN de Nápoles)," (Faculdade de Letras, Lisbon, 1956). This same cookbook was later edited by António Gomes Filho, independently of the work by Maria José Salema, in *Um Tratado da Cozinha Portuguêsa do seculo XV* (Rio de Janeiro, 1963). The "Livro do Almoxarife Régio do Pescado," relative to the court of Afonso V, is in the Arquivo Nacional da Torre do Tombo (Lisbon), Fundo Antigo, bundle 156, no. 1. Among the Alcobacense codices of the Biblioteca Nacional in Lisbon, no. 208, "Livro dos Usos da Ordem de Cister," deserves emphasis.

CHAPTER 2 : DRESS

There is no general history of medieval Portuguese clothing. The article by Quirino da Fonseca, "Nótulas sobre o vestuário em Portugal na Idade Média," in *Memórias da Academia das Sciências de Lisboa: Classe de Letras,* I (1935), 227–55, is limited to presenting a list of terms for dress and materials, without documented references for the identifications proposed, many of which are wrong. The work is practically unusable. More exact, with passages transcribed from the sources, is the article by Henrique Lopes de Mendonça, "Achegas para um vocabulario de indumentaria arcaica," in *O Archeologo Português,* XXVIII (1927–29), 60–142; however, the long list of terms presented relates as much to modern times as to the Middle Ages, and the meaning of each word is not explained.

Consequently, it becomes necessary to refer to foreign manuals as guides for the framing of terms and for comparisons. Among the many works existing on the subject, I would like to call attention to the following books: J. C. Flügel, *The Psychology of Clothes,* 3rd ed. (London, 1950); F. Kiener, *Le Vêtement, la mode et l'homme: Essai d'interpretation psychologique* (Paris, 1959); and Henry Harald Hansen, *Klaededragtens Kavalkade* (Copenhagen, 1954; I used the German translation by Wolfheinrich von der Mülbe, *Knaurs Kostümbuch: Die Kostümgeschichte aller Zeiten,* Munich / Zurich, 1956), a summarized but suggestive work in which economic, social, esthetic, and cultural conditions are not forgotten. The small manual by Frithjof van Thienen, *Acht eeuwen westeuropees costuum* (Zeist, 1961; I utilized the French translation by Marcel Autresoux, *Huit siècles de costume*, Marabout Université, no. 6, Verviers, 1961) also presents a good overall view. Histories of the clothing of the various countries whose styles might have influenced the Portuguese are indispensable. For Spain, refer to the good manual by Carmen Bernis Madrazo, *Indumentaria Medieval Española* (Madrid, 1956). For France, in addition to J. Quicherat's classic, *Histoire du costume en France depuis les temps les plus reculés jusqu'à la fin du XVIIIe siècle* (Paris, 1875), see the well-documented study by Joan Evans, *Dress in Mediaeval France* (Oxford, 1952). For Burgundy, the basic book is the very accurate work by Michèle Beaulieu and Jeanne Baylé, *Le Costume en Bourgogne de Philippe le Hardi à la mort de Charles le Téméraire (1364–1477)* (Paris, 1956). The *Cahiers CIBA*, published in Basel beginning in February 1946, include some generally well-written monographs containing bibliographies. See, among others, L. G. Deruisseau, *Les Modes de la Renaissance italienne* (II, no. 20, November, 1948); A. Latour, *Le Gant* (III, no. 27, January, 1950); M. Braun-Ronsdorf, *Le Mouchoir* (IV, no. 41, May, 1952); and R. Flury-von Bültzingslöwen, *La Chemise* (no. 71, August, 1957). The little volume by Jacques Ruppert, *L'Antiquité et le Moyen Age,* vol. I of *Le Costume* (Paris, 1957), is also useful. And many other books could be mentioned.

In an analysis of medieval Portuguese dress, it is necessary to examine, in the first place, the iconographic sources: sculpture (especially the reclining statues), painting (pictures, illuminations, frescoes), and the decorative arts. There still is no corpus of these sources. One must refer to the general histories of art and to the many monographs published on the subject. Among the most important may be cited Reinaldo dos Santos, *Os primitivos portugueses,* 2nd ed. (Lisbon, 1957); Aarão de Lacerda, *História da Arte em Portugal* (Oporto, 1942–47), vol. I; João Barreira, *Arte Portuguesa: Pintura* (Lisbon, n.d.) ; by the same author, *Arquitectura e Escultura* (Lisbon, n.d.); the six volumes published in the *Inventário Artístico de Portugal* (Lisbon, 1943–59), covering the districts of Portalegre, Santarém, Coimbra, Leiria, and the southern zone of Aveiro, as well as the city of Coimbra; Manuel Monteiro, *A Escultura Românica em Portugal* (Oporto, 1938); Reinaldo dos Santos, *O Românico em Portugal* (Lisbon, 1955); and the magnificent illustrations in the *História da Literatura Portuguesa Ilustrada,* ed. Albino Forjaz de Sampaio, vol. I (Lisbon, 1929). Fascicle no. 10 in the series of *Boletim da Direcção Geral dos Edifícios e Monumentos Nacionais* (1937), entitled *Frescos,* was dedicated to the medieval frescoes. Among the unpublished sources, I used the "Comentário ao Apocalipse de Lorvão" (c. 3, e. 3, p. 8, no. 160), the "Testamento Velho de Lorvão" (c. 3, e. 3, p. 6, no. 106), the "Livro da Sagrada Escritura de Lorvão" (c. 3, e. 3, p. 6, no. 105), the "Psaltério de Lorvão" (e. 3, p. 6, no. 95), and the "Livro de Horas de Duarte" (e. 3, p. 7, no. 140), all of which are in the Arquivo Nacional da Torre do Tombo (Lisbon); and the Códice Alcobacense no. 376, in the

Biblioteca Nacional of Lisbon. Examples of medieval clothing could be cited from numerous other codices scattered throughout Portugal.

References to items of clothing in the documentary sources are found in literary texts, in legislative documents, and elsewhere. Although references to dress can be found in practically all the chronicles and other literary texts, the principal literary sources are the following: *Cancioneiro da Biblioteca Nacional,* ed. Elza Paxeco Machado and José Pedro Machado, vols. I–VIII (Lisbon, 1949–64); *Cancioneiro da Ajuda,* ed. Marques Braga, vol. I (Lisbon, 1945); *Cantigas de Santa Maria de Afonso X, o Sábio,* ed. Manuel Rodrigues Lapa (Lisbon, 1933); *Cancioneiro Geral de Garcia de Resende,* ed. A. J. Gonçalves Guimarães, vols. I–V (Coimbra, 1910–15); Fernão Lopes, *Crónica de D. João I,* vols. I and II (Oporto, 1945–49); João I, *Livro da Montaria,* ed. Francisco Maria Esteves Pereira (Coimbra, 1918); and Duarte, *Livro da Ensinança de bem cavalgar toda sela,* ed. Joseph M. Piel (Lisbon, 1944). The legislative documents include *Ordenaçoens do Senhor Rey D. Affonso V,* vols. I–V (Coimbra, 1792); and *Portugaliae Monumenta Historica: Leges et Consuetudines* (Lisbon, 1856). Other documents yielding information about clothing are "Livro dos Bens de D. João de Portel," in *Archivo Historico Portuguez,* IV (1906); João Pedro Ribeiro, *Dissertações Chronologicas e Criticas sobre a Historia e Jurisprudencia Ecclesiastica e Civil de Portugal,* 2nd ed. (Lisbon, 1857–96), vol. III; *Documentos Historicos da Cidade de Evora,* ed. Gabriel Pereira, pts. 1–3 (Évora, 1885–91); *Provas da História Genealógica da Casa Real Portuguesa,* ed. António Caetano de Sousa, 2nd ed., 12 vols. (Coimbra, 1946–54); and António Cruz, *Os Mesteres do Pôrto: Subsídios para a História das Antigas Corporações dos Ofícios Mecánicos* (Oporto, 1943).

Using the data furnished by the cancioneiros, Teófilo Braga, in *O Povo Portuguez nos seus costumes, crenças e tradições,* vol. I (Lisbon, 1885), made the first attempt at characterizing the pieces of medieval dress (twelfth century through the fifteenth). Two subsequent studies have dealt with the same subject: my article "A Pragmática de 1340," published as an offprint of *Revista da Faculdade de Letras* (Lisbon), 2nd ser., XXII, no. 2 (1956), which was extracted, with some modifications, from my dissertation, "A Sociedade em Portugal nos séculos XII a XIV: Subsídios para a sua História" (Faculdade de Letras, Lisbon, 1956); and the dissertation by Maria Otília Simões Martins, "Elementos para o estudo do vestuário nos séculos XIII–XIV e XV" (Faculdade de Letras, Lisbon, 1959).

On fabrics, aside from the information and identifications to be found in the bibliography that has already been cited, see the following basic studies by Carlos Bastos: *O Comércio e a Indústria Têxtil em Portugal* (Oporto, 1950); *Subsídios para a História da Arte Ornamental dos Tecidos* (Oporto, 1954); and *Indústria e Arte Têxtil* (Oporto, 1960). The works by Bastos carry on the catalogue-monographs by Sebastião Pessanha: *Um Nucleo de Tecidos: Catalogo da Collecção do Auctor,* vols. I–II (Lisbon, 1918–19); "Tecidos medievais Portugueses?" *Terra Portuguesa,* III, nos. 29–30 (1918),

81–82; "Os primeiros tecidos portuguezes," *Contemporanea*, III (January 1923), 40–42; and "Tecidos medievais," *Terra Portuguesa*, V, no. 38 (1924), 20–21. On the textile articles existing in museums today, see the Museu Machado de Castro, Lisbon, *Catálogo-Guia: Secção de Tecidos, Bordados, Tapeçarias e Tapetes* (Coimbra, 1943). For comparison with Spanish textiles, see, for example, Monasterio de las Huelgas, Burgos, *Guia Turistica* (Madrid, 1961).

In *A Barba em Portugal* (Lisbon, 1925), José Leite de Vasconcelos has sketched the history of fashions in hairstyles, moustaches, and beards, but the historical and iconographic sources on which he based his discussion are extremely scant, at least for the medieval period.

The meaning of the terms *garvaia* or *granaia* has already been studied by several philologists, from Carolina Michaëlis de Vasconcelos, "Guarvaya: König Sancho I als Dichter eines Mädchenliedes," in the "Randglossen zum Altportugiesischen Liederbuch," *Zeitschrift für Romanische Philologie*, XXVIII (1904), 392–94, to Elza Paxeco, "Guaruaya," *Revista de Portugal*, XIV (January 1949), 21–23. On the so-called "pelote" of João I, see Alfredo Guimarães, "O Pelote de El-Rei D. João da Boa-Memoria," in *Um Retrato de Nuno Gonçalves e outros Estudos*, Estudos do Museu Alberto Sampaio, vol. II (Oporto, 1944), 65–85.

CHAPTER 3 : THE HOUSE

No work is devoted solely to the medieval Portuguese house. The person interested in the subject has to avail himself of geographic and even ethnographic studies, which give him some assistance by using contemporary evidence. Among these can be cited the excellent syntheses by Orlando Ribeiro: *Portugal, o Mediterrâneo e o Atlântico: Estudo Geográfico*, Universitas, no. 5 (Coimbra, n.d.; 2nd ed., Lisbon, 1963), and *Geografia e Civilização: Temas Portugueses* (Lisbon, 1961).

Two historians from the beginning of this century were concerned, although only marginally, with the general characteristics of the medieval house. They were Alberto Sampaio, in "As Villas do Norte de Portugal" (1st complete ed. in the periodical *Portugalia*, I [1902]; republished in the author's *Estudos Históricos e Económicos*, vol. I [Oporto, 1923], 3–254), and A. de Sousa e Silva Costa Lobo, *Historia da Sociedade em Portugal no seculo XV* (Lisbon, 1903). Some information of interest is found in a conference offered by Raul Lino and published in French (translated by León Bourdon) with the title *L'Evolution de l'architecture domestique au Portugal: Essai* (Lisbon, 1937). In a recent dissertation, the French student Gérard Pradalié supplied fundamental data based on archival sources about the urban house in the twelfth and thirteenth centuries ("Lisbonne, de la Reconquête a la fin du XIIIᵉ siècle" [unpubl. diss., Faculté des Lettres et des Sciences Humaines, Toulouse, 1961]).

Outside of these few works, the entire study of the Portuguese medieval house must rest on the sources, whether manuscripts, or printed, or archeological. I limited this study to the last two.

João Brandão, *Tratado da Majestade, Grandeza e Abastança da Cidade de Lisboa, na 2.ª Metade do Século XVI: Estatística de Lisboa de 1552* (Lisbon, 1923), and Cristovão Rodrigues de Oliveira, *Summario em que brevemente se contem algumas cousas (assi ecclesiasticas como seculares) que ha na cidade de Lisboa*, ed. Augusto Vieira da Silva, 3rd ed. (Lisbon, 1928; 1st ed., 1555), although from the middle of the sixteenth century, provide the essential picture at least for the century immediately preceding. The famous "Livro das Fortalezas" by Duarte Darmas (see *Reprodução anotada do Livro das Fortalezas de Duarte Darmas*, ed. João de Almeida [Lisbon, 1943]) contains drawings and the plans of the principal frontier castles in the beginning of the sixteenth century. Recourse to the artistic and archeological inventories is indispensable, particularly those like *Inventário Artístico de Portugal*, published by the Academia Nacional de Belas Artes, of which the following volumes have already appeared: vol. I—*Distrito de Portalegre*, by Luís Keil (Lisbon, 1943); vol. II—*Cidade de Coimbra*, by Vergílio Correia and A. Nogueira Gonçalves (Lisbon, 1947); vol. III—*Distrito de Santarém*, by Gustavo de Matos Sequeira (Lisbon, 1949); vol. IV—*Distrito de Coimbra*, by Vergílio Correia and A. Nogueira Gonçalves (Lisbon, 1952); vol. V—*Distrito de Leiria*, by Gustavo de Matos Sequeira (Lisbon, 1955); and vol. VI—*Distrito de Aveiro: Zona-Sul*, by A. Nogueira Gonçalves (Lisbon, 1959). Valuable information is also furnished by the volumes of the *Guia de Portugal*, published by the Biblioteca Nacional of Lisbon (vol. I—*Generalidades: Lisboa e Arredores*, ed. Raúl Proença [Lisbon, 1923]; vol. II—*Extremadura, Alentejo, Algarve*, ed. Raúl Proença [Lisbon, 1927]; vol. III—*Beira Litoral, Beira Baixa, Beira Alta* [Lisbon, 1944]; vol. IV—*Entre Douro e Minho*, ed. Sant'Ana Dionísio, pt. I, *Douro Litoral* [Lisbon, 1965], pt. II, *Minho* [Lisbon, 1965]; vol. V—*Trás-os-Montes e Alto Douro*, ed. Sant'Ana Dionísio, pt. I, *Vila Real, Chaves e Barroso* [Lisbon, 1969], pt. II, *Lamego, Bragança e Miranda* [Lisbon, 1970]).

There is also no basic work, however brief, on medieval Portuguese manor houses and palaces of the type exemplified in the study by Adriano de Gusmão, "Solares Barrocos da Região de Basto: Ensaio de Pesquisa Artística," published as an offprint of *XVI Congrès international d'histoire de l'art*, vol. II (Lisbon, 1954). Nevertheless, some monographs relating directly or indirectly to the royal and seigniorial palaces do exist. Among the principal ones are Augusto Vieira da Silva, *O Castelo da S. Jorge em Lisboa: Estudo histórico-descritivo*, 2nd ed. (Lisbon 1937), especially important for the information on the Royal Palace of Alcáçova; Ernesto Korrodi, *Estudos de Reconstrucção sobre o Castello de Leiria* (Zurich, 1898), still useful in spite of the many artistic errors; Raul Lino, *Quatro Palavras sobre os Paços Reais da Vila de Sintra* (Lisbon, 1948); Jorge Larcher, "O Castelo de Sesimbra: Sua história e um subsídio importante para a sua reconstrução," fasc. 4 of *Petrus Nonius*, II (Lisbon, 1940), 267–74; and Rogério de Azevedo, *O Paço dos*

Duques de Guimarães: Preâmbulo à Memória do Projecto de Restauro (Oporto, 1942), corrected in detail by the pamphlet of Alfredo Pimenta, *A Propósito do Paço dos Duques em Guimarães*, Estudos Históricos, XIX (Guimarães, 1942). The consultation of the various fascicles of the *Boletim da Direcção Geral dos Edifícios e Monumentos Nacionais* is indispensable because of the photographs and plans which they contain; historical introductions of interest are also sometimes added.

Monographs on cities and monuments, when scientific and well documented, are also useful. This is the case with the work by Túlio Espanca, *Évora: Guia Histórico-Artístico* (Évora, 1949).

For the study of internal compartmentation, there are two excellent sources: the measurements of the buildings of the palace of Sintra, published by Gabriel Pereira in the *Documentos Historicos da Cidade de Evora*, pt. 3 (Évora, 1891), p. 35; and King Duarte's testimony in the *Leal Conselheiro* (ed. Joseph M. Piel [Lisbon, 1942]). Also consult the descriptions by foreigners, as that of the secretary of Cardinal Alexandrino, who visited Portugal toward the end of the sixteenth century (see Alexandre Herculano, *Opúsculos*, VI [Lisbon, n.d.], 81 ff.).

A complete study of Portuguese medieval furniture is still to be written. The attempt by Alfredo Guimarães and Albano Sardoeira, *Mobiliário artístico português: Elementos para a sua história*, was actually limited to an inventory, in which the Middle Ages occupied a minimal place, and was, moreover, concerned only with the regions of Lamego (fasc. I, Oporto, 1942) and Guimarães (fasc. II, Oporto, 1935; Sardoeira no longer was a collaborator in this volume). The only scientific works that I know of on furniture, both of them restricted to specific types, are Augusto Cardoso Pinto, *Cadeiras Portuguesas* (Lisbon, 1952), and J. F. da Silva Nascimento, *Leitos e Camilhas Portugueses: Subsídios para o seu estudo* (Lisbon, 1950), the latter, however, being a weak study. Alfredo Guimarães studied the importance of leather coverings in his article "Couros policromados de Córdova," in his collection *Um Retrato de Nuno Gonçalves e outros Estudos*, Estudos do Museu Alberto Sampaio, vol. II (Oporto, 1944), 45–58.

Even here, therefore, direct consultation of the sources is necessary. As a start, one may read the various chronicles, although they furnish little information. Most of the relevant documents have been gathered in the following collections: *Provas da História Genealógica da Casa Real Portuguesa*, ed. António Caetano de Sousa, 2nd ed., 12 vols. (Coimbra, 1946–54), especially vol. I, bks. I–III; the *Portugaliae Monumenta Historica: Diplomata et Chartae* (Lisbon, 1867); João Pedro Ribeiro, *Dissertações Chronologicas e Criticas sobre a Historia e Jurisprudencia Ecclesiastica e Civil de Portugal*, 2nd ed., vols. I–V (Lisbon, 1857–96); the "Inventários e Contas da Casa de D. Dinis (1278–1282)," published in *Arquivo Historico Português*, X, (1916), 41–59; the *Descobrimentos Portugueses: Documentos para a sua História*, ed. João Martins da Silva Marques, vol. I and supplement (Lisbon, 1944–45); F. João da Póvoa, et al., "Memórias sôltas e inventário do oratório de S.

Clemente das Penhas e do mosteiro de N. S.ª da Conceição de Matozinhos dos seculos XIV e XV," ed. A. de Magalhães Basto, fasc. I of *Boletim Cultural da Câmara Municipal do Porto,* vol. III (Oporto, 1940); and even the valuable *Elucidario das Palavras, Termos, e Frases que em Portugal antiguamente se usarão, e que hoje regularmente se ignorão* by Joaquim de Santa Rosa de Viterbo, 2 vols. (Lisbon, 1798–99; 3rd ed., Oporto, 1962–66). A large number of the facts to be found in these and other sources were assembled in my unpublished licentiate dissertation, "A Sociedade em Portugal nos séculos XII a XIV: Subsídios para a sua Historia" (Faculdade de Letras, Lisbon, 1956), vol. II.

The forms of rental or ownership of houses was studied in its essence by Henrique da Gama Barros in the monumental *História da Administração Pública em Portugal nos séculos XII a XV,* 2nd ed., vol. VII (Lisbon, 1949), which draws the bulk of its information from the *Ordenaçoens do Senhor Rey D. Affonso V,* vol. IV (Coimbra, 1792). In my licentiate dissertation, I also dealt with this question, using the information contained in the *Documentos da Biblioteca Nacional Relativos a Lisboa,* 1st ser.: *Séculos XII a XV* (Lisbon, 1935).

CHAPTER 4 : HYGIENE AND HEALTH

There is no history of hygiene in Portugal. The work of Fernando da Silva Correia, "Esbôço da História da Higiene em Portugal," offprint of *Portugal Sanitário* (Lisbon, 1938), is only an amalgamation of facts on the history of medicine or on the history of attendance (the pamphlet is unusable for citation, as the pages are not numbered). Consequently, the scholar must go directly to the sources or utilize what little information is collected in histories of medicine, which will be indicated further on. Among published sources we may cite the work of Eduardo Freire de Oliveira, *Elementos para a Historia do Municipio de Lisboa* (Lisbon, 1882–85), especially vol. I (consultation of the *Índice dos Elementos . . .,* vols. I–II [Lisbon, 1942], is useful, although this is quite deficient); the *Provas da História Genealógica da Casa Real Portuguesa,* ed. António Caetano de Sousa, 2nd ed. (Coimbra, 1946–54), especially vol. I, bks. I–III; the *Documentos Historicos da Cidade de Evora,* ed. Gabriel Pereira, pts. 1–3 (Évora, 1885–91) ; and numerous data scattered here and there in the collections of documents and legislation, in chronicles, and in the cancioneiros. The chapter "Nul bain pendant mille ans" in the book by Manuel Gonçalves Cerejeira, *A Idade Média* (Coimbra, 1936), pp. 92–101, deserves mention although it is full of inaccuracies and exaggerations.

There are more than a dozen secondary studies with the title "História da Medicina em Portugal," but none can be considered up-to-date and in conformity with the demands of modern historiography. The only one that truly represents a work of original research and still deserves confidence is by Maximiano Lemos, *Historia da Medicina em Portugal: Doutrinas e Instituições,* vols. I–II (Lisbon, 1899). A convenient summary is that by Augusto da Silva Carvalho, *Historia da Medicina Portuguesa* (Lisbon, 1929). More complete, including aspects of medical philosophy and science, is the chapter by Joaquim de Carvalho, "Cultura filosófica e scientífica," in *História de Portugal*, ed. Damião Peres, IV (Barcelos, 1932), 475–528.

A comprehensive bibliography of Portuguese medical history, including manuscript sources, is collected in Augusto da Silva Carvalho's "Medicina: A literatura médica até ao fim do sec. XVI," in the *História da Literatura Portuguesa Ilustrada*, ed. Albino Forjaz de Sampaio, III (Lisbon, 1932), 64–78, brought up to date in the pamphlet by Luis da Pina, "História da História da Medicina em Portugal," offprint of *Imprensa Médica*, no. XX (March 1956).

A systematic collection of all the data on medicine existing in printed sources was begun by Maximiano Lemos, "A medicina no *Cancioneiro de Garcia de Resende*," *Arquivos de História da Medicina Portuguesa*, n.s., XI–XII (1920–21), and by João da Meira, "Os gafos do Nobiliário," ibid., n.s., III (1912), 194–96. One aspect of the superstitions accompanying the therapeutics of the period and the relationship between medicine and astrology is treated in a curious and well-documented essay by Francisco Adolfo Coelho, "Os Dias Egypcios," published in the *Revista Archeologica e Historica*, I (1887), 65–70.

The most reliable study of medieval epidemics is still that by Antonio da Cunha Vieira de Meireles, *Memorias de Epidemologia Portugueza* (Coimbra, 1866), corrected in some details by João de Meira, "A peste de 1384, e as diversas palavras empregadas para designar o bubão pestilencial," *Archivos de Historia da Medicina Portugueza*, n.s., II (1911), 179–92, and "Da peste de 1415 e da palavra 'trama' significando 'bubão pestilencial,'" ibid., n.s., III (1912), 178–82. The *Regimento proueytoso contra ha pestenença*—a very rare book first published about 1498, and reissued in 1899 (ed. Luciano Cordeiro), 1961 (ed. Fernando da Silva Correia), and 1962 (Oporto, in a facsimile)— contains data of major interest for the study of therapeutics and of medicine in general.

Particular aspects of the history of medicine were studied in the following monographs by Augusto da Silva Carvalho, almost always well documented and structured: "Historia da estomatologia: Doentes, dentistas e odontólogos," in *Revista Portuguesa de Estomatologia*, nos. 1–6 (July 1934–June 1936); *Historia da lepra em Portugal* (Oporto, 1932); "Historia da Oftalmologia Portuguesa até ao fim do século XVII" (Lisbon, 1940), offprint of the *Boletim da Sociedade Portuguesa de Oftalmologia*, II (1940); *Historia da Urologia em Portugal até ao Meiado do Seculo XIX* (Lisbon, 1925); and "Subsidios para a historia das parteiras portuguesas," *A Medicina Contemporânea*, 3rd ser., July–August 1931.

Certain diseases and the causes of the deaths of kings and princes have also merited the attention of modern doctors. As an example, the studies by Fernando da Silva Correia may be mentioned: "A causa da morte da Infanta Santa Joana: Uma história clínica do sec. XV," offprint of *A Medicina Con-*

temporânea, LX, nos. 24–28 (1942), and *A História Clínica d'El-Rei D. João II* (Lisbon, 1942).

Biographies of and documentary information on Portuguese physicians in the Middle Ages are provided by Pedro de Azevedo, "Físicos e cirurgiões do tempo de D. Afonso IV," *Arq. Hist. Med. Port.*, n.s., III (1912), 3–11; by João de Meira, "Se Pedro Amarello foi medico do Conde D. Henrique e de D. Afonso Henriques," ibid., II (1911), 157–64; and by Egas Moniz, "O Papa João XXI," offprint of *Biblos*, VI, nos. 1–2 (1930), 1–17. The principal sources of information on this subject, however, are a series of articles by Francisco Marques de Sousa Viterbo: "Medicos da Familia Real Portugueza: Apontamentos para a Historia da Medicina em Portugal" (pt. 1), *Jornal da Sociedade das Sciencias Medicas de Lisboa* (1892–93); "Noticia sobre alguns medicos portuguezes ou que exerceram a clinica em Portugal: Subsidios para a Historia da Medicina Portugueza" (pt. 2), *Jorn. Soc. Scien. Med. Lisboa* (1894); ibid. (pt. 3), *Jorn. Soc. Scien. Med. Lisboa* (1895); ibid. (pt. 4), *Jorn. Soc. Scien. Med. Lisboa* (1896–97); ibid. (pt. 5), *Arq. Hist. Med. Port.*, n.s., V (1914).

On the history of pharmacy, the fundamental works are still two nineteenth-century studies by Pedro José da Silva, both of which are based on documentary sources and which even today are not surpassed in their information: *Ensino da Pharmacia em Portugal e nas principaes nações da Europa* (Lisbon, 1866), and *Principaes factos da pharmacia Portugueza nos seculos passados* (Lisbon, 1868). A convenient compilation, in chronological order, of the legislation dealing with pharmacy is by Manuel das Dores Telo da Fonseca, *História da Farmácia Portuguesa através da sua legislação*, vols. I–III (Oporto, 1935–41).

Public assistance in the medieval period has been relatively well analyzed. The fundamental works are by Vítor Ribeiro, "Historia da Beneficencia Publica em Portugal," offprint of *O Instituto*, XLVIII–LIV (1901–7), and by Fernando da Silva Correia, *Origem e Formação das Misericórdias Portuguêsas: Estudos sôbre a História da Assistência* (Lisbon, 1944), in spite of the disorganized and inaccurate exposition of the latter. Angelo Ribeiro gives a systematic and convenient summary in "Assistência," in *História de Portugal*, ed. Damião Peres, IV (Barcelos, 1932), 531–70.

There are some monographs on the hospitals of the Middle Ages. Fernando da Silva Correia wrote "Os Hospitais medievais portugueses," offprint of *A Medicina Contemporânea*, LXI, nos. 11–13 and 15 (1943); "Hospitais pré-quinhentistas portugueses: A lição da História," offprint of *Imprensa Médica*, IX, nos. 23–24 (1943); and "Os Velhos Hospitais da Lisboa Antiga," offprint of *Revista Municipal*, II, no. 10 (1942). *Esparsos: Arqueologia, Etnografia, Bibliografia e História* by José Maria António Nogueira (Coimbra, 1934), pp. 75–125, contains useful, first-hand information on the medieval hospitals of Lisbon; the work was first published in successive numbers of the *Jornal do Commercio* in 1865. Francisco Marques de Sousa Viterbo published unedited documents in "Noticia historica e documental de alguns hospitais do tempo de D. Afonso V e D. João II," in the *Archivos de Historia da Medicina* (1895).

The devotion of Nossa Senhora de Roc-Amadour (of the "Reclamador," as she was called in the Middle Ages) and hospital aid under her protection has been treated by José Júlio Gonçalves Coelho in a monograph, a little old and in need of corrections, but still the best work on the subject: "Nôtre-Dame de Roc-Amadour en Portugal (son culte–hôpitaux et hôtelleries): Mémoire historique," offprint of the *Bulletin de la Société scientifique, historique et archéologique de la Corrèze* (Brive, 1912).

CHAPTER 5 : AFFECTION

A history of love in Portugal, whether for the medieval or the modern era, is nonexistent. There is not even an attempt at analyzing philosophic and literary conventions in the genre of the famous book by Denis de Rougemont, *L'Amour et l'Occident* (Paris, 1939; 3rd ed., Paris, 1962), which was published in English as *Love in the Western World*, trans. Montgomery Belgion (New York, 1940). Rougemont's book is helpful, although its ideas need to be related to the Galaico-Portuguese troubadour lyric. The brief works that carry suggestive but deceptive titles—such as Luis Chaves, *O Amor Português* (Lisbon, 1922), or Magnus Bergström, *O Amor e a saudade em Portugal: Conferência* (Lisbon, 1930)—are no more than sketches, in which, furthermore, the Middle Ages occupies very few pages, with historical and scientific accuracy diluted by folklore and ethnology.

Two books, however, must be mentioned immediately, even though the problem of love is not their primary concern: the one by José Joaquim Nunes, vol. I (*Introdução*) of the *Cantigas de Amigo dos Trovadores Galego-Portugueses* (Coimbra, 1928; text in vol. II, Coimbra, 1926), in which the study of many aspects of daily life is based on an analysis of the ballads; and the other by António José Saraiva, the *História da Cultura em Portugal*, vol. I (Lisbon, 1950), an often successful synthesis.

Here, as in the other chapters, recourse to the sources is necessary. Among the legislative texts one may consult the *Ordenações do Senhor Rey D. Affonso V*, vols. I–V (Coimbra, 1792); the *Ordenações do Senhor Rey D. Manuel*, IV–V (Coimbra, 1797); and the *Fuero Real de Afonso X, o Sábio: Versão Portuguesa do Século XIII*, ed. Alfredo Pimenta (Lisbon, 1946). The most important narrative sources are the chronicles by Fernão Lopes. In the *Leal Conselheiro* (see the edition by Joseph M. Piel [Lisbon, 1942]), Duarte furnishes valuable information. The *Amadis de Gaula* is fundamental reading for the study of actual and idealized emotional practices, at least among the nobility; see the complete text in any of the Spanish editions, including the one in the series Tesoro de Autores Ilustres, LXIII–LXVI (Barcelona, 1847–48), or the edition by Pascual de Gayangos, in the series Biblioteca de Autores Españoles (Madrid, 1857). References of interest, especially for the study of marriage, can also be found in the religious texts; see the following, all in *Revista Archeologica e Historica*: "Visitação do Arcebispado de Lisboa (século XV)," II (1888), 8–16, 22–32; "Visitação à Egreja de S. João do Mocharro d'Obidos por D. Jorge da Costa, em 14 de Fevereiro de 1467," I (1887), 119–27, 137–44, 152–56; and "Constituições do Arcebispado de Lisboa decretadas por D. João Esteves d'Azambuja (1402–1414)," I (1887), 10–15, 28–31, 60–64, 77–79, 94–96, 108–9. The *Provas da História Genealógica da Casa Real Portuguesa*, ed. António Caetano de Sousa, 2nd ed. (Coimbra, 1946–54), as well as the *Documentos Historicos da Cidade de Evora*, ed. Gabriel Pereira (Évora, 1885–91), should also be consulted. The most important sources, however, are the cancioneiros, especially the *Cantigas de Amigo* (see the edition by José Joaquim Nunes, which has already been cited). The *Cancioneiro Geral de Garcia de Resende* also contains important information. For the *cantigas de escárnio e mal-dizer* (songs of derision), consult the *Cancioneiro da Biblioteca Nacional*, ed. Elza Paxeco Machado and José Pedro Machado (Lisbon, 1949–64), especially vol. VI.

The juridical studies on paternal power, filiation, marital laws, divorce, and so on include valuable material. The following works by Manuel Paulo Merêa may be consulted: "Notas sobre o poder paternal no direito hispânico ocidental: Em torno do § CCVI do Foro de Cuenca," offprint of the *Anuario de Historia del Derecho Espanol*, XVIII (Madrid, 1947), republished in *Estudos de Direito Hispânico Medieval*, II (Coimbra, 1953), 83–112; "Nótulas Histórico-Jurídicas, II: Sobre a adopção no século XII," *Boletim da Faculdade de Direito* (Coimbra), XXXI (1955), 372–76; "Perfilhação," *Revista Portuguesa de Filologia*, VII (1956); "Da minha gaveta (Silva Histórico-Jurídica), II: Sinopse histórica da adopção (perfilhamento)," *Boletim da Faculdade de Direito* (Coimbra), XXXII (1956), 182–94; *Evolução dos regimes matrimoniais: Contribuições para a História do Direito Português*, vols. I–II (Coimbra, 1913); "Sobre o Casamento de Juras," *Boletim da Faculdade de Direito* (Coimbra), XIV (1937–38), 12–20, republished in idem, *Novos Estudos de História do Direito* (Barcelos, 1937), 131–38; "Mulher recabdada," *Revista da Universidade de Coimbra* (Miscelânea de Estudos em honra de D. Carolina Michaëlis de Vasconcelos), XI (1933), republished in *Novos Estudos de História do Direito*, pp. 75–82; "Um problema filológico-jurídico: A palavra 'arras,'" *Boletim de Filologia*, IV (1937), republished in *Novos Estudos de História do Direito*, pp. 139–49; "Em torno do Casamento de Juras," in *Estudos de Direito Hispânico Medieval*, I (Coimbra, 1952), 151–71. The erudite pioneer work of Frederico Francisco de la Figanière on the various kinds of dowries in the introduction to the *Memorias das Rainhas de Portugal: D. Theresa–Santa Isabel* (Lisbon, 1859), pp. xiii–xxxi, deserves to be mentioned. Guilherme Braga da Cruz also supplies interesting material in his article "Algumas considerações sobre a 'Perfiliatio,'" offprint of the *Boletim da Faculdade de Direito* (Coimbra), XIV (1938).

For the study of marriage in medieval Portugal the basic work is still the book by Alexandre Herculano, *Estudos sobre o Casamento Civil: Por ocasião do Opusculo do sr. Visconde de Seabra sobre este assumpto,* 5th ed. (Lisbon, n.d.). More erudite in its use of detail from the sources and in its juridical comparisons, though not affecting the main hypotheses of Herculano, is the work by Luís Cabral de Moncada, "O Casamento em Portugal na Idade Media," *Boletim da Faculdade de Direito* (Coimbra), VII, nos. 61–65 (1921–22), republished in *Estudos de História do Direito,* I (Coimbra, 1948), 37–82.

Contemporary morality has been treated with historical accuracy by Humberto Carlos Baquero Moreno in a licentiate dissertation entitled "Subsídios para o Estudo da Sociedade Medieval Portuguesa: Moralidade e Costumes" (Faculdade de Letras, Lisbon, 1961). The history of prostitution has not yet been written, in spite of the various works that have appeared on this subject or on related topics. Only Francisco Inácio dos Santos Cruz, *Da Prostituição na cidade de Lisboa* . . . (Lisbon, 1841), can be consulted to some advantage. In the article that I wrote, "A Pragmática de 1340," offprint of the *Revista da Faculdade de Letras* (Lisbon), 2nd ser., XXII, no. 2 (1956), there are references to prostitution in the fourteenth century.

For its suggestions and hypotheses, it is worthwhile to consult the book by G. Rattray Taylor, *Sex in History,* 2nd ed. (London, 1959).

CHAPTER 6 : WORK

The problem of occupations has been broached especially from the point of view of the corporative organization. The erudite studies by Franz Paul de Almeida Langhans may be noted *(As Corporações dos Ofícios Mecânicos: Subsídios para a sua história* [Lisbon, 1943], and *A Casa dos Vinte e Quatro de Lisboa: Subsídios para a sua história* [Lisbon, 1948]). In addition, there are the excellent syntheses by Marcelo Caetano ("A antiga organização dos mesteres da cidade de Lisboa," preface to *As Corporações dos Ofícios Mecânicos,* I, xi–lxxv, and "A Administração municipal de Lisboa durante a 1.ª dinastia (1179–1383)," offprint of *Revista da Faculdade de Direito* [Lisbon] VII–VIII [1951], this last, however, dealing only incidentally with the problems relating to occupations). But, with the obvious exception of the last-named work, these deal little with the Middle Ages, precisely because the corporative organization did not develop before the sixteenth century. Research on the period previous to this led to the promising results of Gérard Pradalié in "Lisbonne, de la Reconquête à la fin du XIIIe siècle" (unpubl. diss., Faculté des Lettres et des Sciences Humaines, Toulouse, 1961), and of Maria Teresa Campos Rodrigues in "Aspectos da Administração Municipal de Lisboa no século XV," *Revista Municipal,* nos. 101–9 (1964–66). But neither of these monographs is solely, or even predominantly, preoccupied with the problems of work.

Three principal studies deal with the artisans of specific cities. For the city of Oporto, there is the scholarly work by António Cruz, though it does not examine as they deserve to be examined the medieval sources in the archives in Oporto: *Os Mesteres do Pôrto: Subsídios para a História das Antigas Corporações dos Ofícios Mecânicos* (Oporto, 1943), vol. I (the only one published). Certain historical questions about the master craftsmen of Coimbra were dealt with by José Pinto Loureiro in a monograph based on original sources: "Casa dos Vinte e Quatro de Coimbra: Elementos para a sua história," offprint of *Arquivo Coimbrão*, III–IV (1937). From the expository and documentary chaos of the seven volumes by António Lopes de Carvalho, *Os Mesteres de Guimarãis* (Barcelos, 1939–44), it is still possible to glean some useful information about the craftsmen of Guimarães in the Middle Ages.

A short, almost forgotten work by João Manuel Esteves Pereira, *A Industria Portugueza (seculos XII a XIX) com uma introducção sobre as corporações operarias em Portugal* (Lisbon, 1900), records some primary data and contains information and suggestions of some utility even today.

As the foregoing suggests, the most important studies on medieval vocations have dealt with the craftsman. On the condition of the peasant, the work by Henrique da Gama Barros, *História da Administração Pública em Portugal nos séculos XII a XV*, 2nd ed., vol. III (Lisbon, 1946), has not yet been superseded. In my *Introdução à História da Agricultura em Portugal: A questão cerealífera durante a Idade Média*, 2nd ed. (Lisbon, 1968), I dealt with some marginal aspects of this problem.

The civil servant has not been examined by anyone after Gama Barros, in the aforementioned work. Virgínia Rau, however, in *A Casa dos Contos* (Coimbra, 1951), has considered the personnel of the Exchequer. Several years ago, Manuel Gonçalves Cerejeira published an interesting article on the economic situation of the professors of the studium generale entitled "Notas históricas sobre os ordenados dos lentes da Universidade," in *Boletim da Faculdade de Direito* (Coimbra), IX, nos. 81–90 (1925–26). It also behooves the scholar to consult António José Saraiva on this subject, in his *História da Cultura em Portugal,* vol. I (Lisbon, 1950).

Though the sources have much of interest to offer on the topic of work, they continue to await someone's thorough investigation: this is the case with the *Documentos Historicos da Cidade de Evora*, ed. Gabriel Pereira, pts. 1–3 (Évora, 1885–91); with the short study by A. Sousa Gomes, *Carpinteiros da Ribeira das Naus* (Coimbra, 1931); and with many other documentary collections, chronicles, and other published documents. In addition, the works by João Brandão *(Tratado da Majestade, Grandeza e Abastança da Cidade de Lisboa, na 2.ª Metade do Século XVI: Estatística de Lisboa de 1552* [Lisbon, 1923]) and Cristóvão Rodrigues de Oliveira *(Summario em que brevemente se contem algumas cousas [assi eclesiasticas como seculares] que ha na cidade de Lisboa,* ed. Augusto Vieira da Silva, 3rd ed. [Lisbon, 1938]) allow one to compare the medieval situation with that of the sixteenth century.

In my licentiate dissertation, "A Sociedade em Portugal nos séculos XII a XIV: Subsídios para a sua História" (Faculdade de Letras, Lisbon, 1956), I dealt with some problems relating to salaries and prices. On this subject, it is always necessary to consult A. de Sousa e Silva Costa Lobo, *Historia da Sociedade em Portugal no seculo XV* (Lisbon, 1903).

CHAPTER 7 : FAITH

The only history of the Portuguese Church is that by Fortunato de Almeida, *Historia da Igreja em Portugal,* of which vols. I and II (Coimbra, 1910–12), are concerned with the Middle Ages. An erudite work based on primary sources, it is less trustworthy in the problematic and in value judgments, which are almost always oriented apologetically. Moreover, the book lacks a comprehensive view and does not consider events and norms as they applied to the ordinary man; a "History of the Church," however, cannot be a "History of Religious Sentiment," which is still to be written.

The *História da Igreja em Portugal* by Miguel de Oliveira is no more than a manual (although quite praiseworthy) in which the conclusions of Fortunato de Almeida are generally summarized.

For comparison with Christianity in other countries, one may consult any good history of the Church. The best is perhaps the monumental work edited by Augustin Fliche and Victor Martin, *Histoire de l'Église depuis ses origines jusqu'à nos jours* (Paris, 1940–64). Volumes IV–XV, each with a different author, concern the Middle Ages.

For a study of penances and of the frequency of sins, see Mário Martins, "O Penitencial de Martim Pérez, em Medievo-Português," *Lusitania Sacra,* II (1957), 57–110.

Certain aspects of religious devotion have already been the subjects of useful monographs. These include Mário Martins, *Peregrinações e Livros de Milagres na nossa Idade Média,* 2nd ed. (Lisbon, 1957); Avelino de Jesus da Costa, "A Virgem Maria Padroeira de Portugal na Idade Média," offprint of *Lusitania Sacra,* II (1957); and idem, *Origem e Evolução do Culto de Nossa Senhora da Conceição em Portugal: Catálogo da Exposição Documental* (Braga, 1964). Much weaker is the study by Miguel de Oliveira and Moreira das Neves, *A Padroeira de Portugal: Notas e Documentos* (Lisbon, 1940).

Accurate biographies of saints or of other figures of the Church are rare. Among them, the erudite work by António Garcia Ribeiro de Vasconcelos, *Evolução do culto de Dona Isabel de Aragão esposa do rei lavrador Dom Denis de Portugal (a Rainha Santa),* vols. I–II (Coimbra, 1894), is important for the medieval period.

The liturgy has been given particular attention by Pierre David, António Garcia Ribeiro de Vasconcelos, and José Augusto Ferreira. By the first are some fundamental articles, particularly "Curso de Instituições eclesiásticas medievais, II: A liturgia," *Revista Portuguesa de História,* II (1943), 607–15; "O Pontifical de Braga no séc. XII, com notas sobre um Pontifical de Santa Cruz de Coimbra, da mesma data," *Liturgia,* I (June–October 1947), supplement to *Mensageiro de S. Bento,* XVI, nos. 6–8; *Le Missal de Mateus: Notes historiques et liturgiques,* offprint of *Biblos,* XX (1944); "A diocese de Lisboa seguiu o costume litúrgico de Salisbury?" *Liturgia,* I (April 1947), 54–58, supplement to *Mensageiro de S. Bento,* XVI, no. 4; "Festas e usos litúrgicos de Braga segundo manuscritos do século XII," *Mensageiro de S. Bento,* XV

(July–August 1946), 155–62. António de Vasconcelos published "Notas litúrgico-bracarenses" in *Acta do Congresso Litúrgico Nacional Romano-Bracarense* (Braga, 1928), pp. 177–255, in addition to various other articles. Finally, the most significant of José Augusto Ferreira's articles is "O Rito Bracarense e o seu breviário no aspecto histórico," in the aforementioned *Acta*, pp. 41–63.

Church Vestments (London, 1949), by Herbert Norris, is a trustworthy guide to religious dress.

Once again, recourse to the sources is indispensable. The various chronicles by Fernão Lopes, Gomes Eanes de Zurara, and Rui de Pina furnish all kinds of information; and Duarte's *Leal Conselheiro* cannot be overlooked. The cancioneiros also contribute to our knowledge of the religiosity of the period. Visitations and episcopal constitutions are very important, for they display an undisguised picture of daily life. On the Middle Ages see the following: "Visitação do Arcebispado de Lisboa (seculo XV)," *Revista Archeologica e Historica*, II (1888); "Visitação à Egreja de S. João do Mocharro d'Obidos por D. Jorge da Costa, em 14 de Fevereiro de 1467," ibid., I (1887); "Visitação à Egreja de S. João do Mocharro d'Obidos por D. João, bispo de Çafim, em nome do arcebispo de Lisboa, aos 2 de junho de 1473," ibid., I (1887); "Constituições do Arcebispado de Lisboa decretadas por D. João Esteves d'Azambuja (1402–1414)," ibid., I (1887).

Documentary collections such as the *Elementos para a Historia do Municipio de Lisboa*, ed. Eduardo Freire de Oliveira (Lisbon, 1882–85), vol. I, or the *Documentos Historicos da Cidade de Evora*, ed. Gabriel Pereira (Évora, 1885–91), require attention. The Afonsine and Manueline *Ordenações* similarly contain much data of interest.

Certain aspects of witchcraft, magic, and the persistence of paganism were broached by Alexandre Herculano in a short article, "Crenças Populares Portuguesas ou Superstições Populares," in *Opúsculos*, 3rd ed., IX (*Littera-tura*, I) (Lisbon, n.d.), 153–80; the article was initially published in *Panorama* in 1840. Teófilo Braga, in *O Povo Portuguez nos seus costumes, crenças e tradições*, 2 vols. (Lisbon, 1885), also comments on this subject, with an impressive amount of data, but also with too much play of imagination. José Leite de Vasconcelos, in *Etnografia Portuguesa Tentame de sistematização*, vols. I–IV (Lisbon, 1933–58), provides a more recent study of medieval superstitions, as well as of customs and traditions.

CHAPTER 8 : CULTURE

Culture is one of the few aspects of medieval Portuguese society on which we have satisfactory monographs and comprehensive studies. António José Saraiva, with his monumental *História da Cultura em Portugal* (Lisbon, 1950–52), vols. I and II (for the Middle Ages), filled a void; the work is one of singular scientific probity, with especially bold economic and social hypotheses. Far beyond the defects which the study naturally bears as a pioneer work, often requiring simultaneous examination and synthesis, this book represents a true landmark in Portuguese historiography. António José Saraiva's work is completed in matters of detail by Manuel Rodrigues Lapa, *Lições de Literatura Portuguesa: Época Medieval*, 4th ed. (Coimbra, 1956); and by José Joaquim Nunes, vol. I (*Introdução*) of *Cantigas de Amigo dos Trovadores Galego-Portugueses* (Coimbra, 1928), among others.

The numerous series of books on hunting, veterinary science, falconry, etc., are registered in the useful guide by Maria Adelaide Valle Cintra, *Bibliografia de textos medievais portugueses* (Lisbon, 1960).

CHAPTER 9 : AMUSEMENTS

Again, there is no manual nor series of monographs on the various diversions of the Middle Ages. Sílvio Lima left us some essays, interesting for their ideas, but limited in extent and in documentary foundation: they are *Ensaios sôbre o desporto* (Lisbon, 1937); and *Desporto, jôgo e arte* (Oporto, 1938), especially the essay entitled "O Desporto e a Experiência na Idade Média." Teófilo Braga, in the valuable work *O Povo Portuguez em seus costumes, crenças e tradições*, vols. I–II (Lisbon, 1885), furnishes a great deal of information on games, dances, and popular songs. Some introductions and prefaces to editions of texts contain comments on sports and the amusements of the medieval period. This is the case of Carolina Michaëlis de Vasconcelos, "Mestre Giraldo e os seus tratados de alveitaria e cetraria," offprint of *Revista Lusitana*, XIII (1910), 149–432; Manuel Rodrigues Lapa, *Livro de Falcoaria de Pero Menino* (Coimbra, 1931); idem, "Livros de falcoaria," fasc. 3–4 of *Boletim de Filologia*, I (1933), 199–234; José Joaquim Nunes, vol. I (*Introdução*) of *Cantigas de Amigo dos Trovadores Galego-Portugueses* (Coimbra, 1928). On games, see still further Fortunato de Almeida, *Historia de Portugal*, III (Coimbra, 1926), 289 ff.

The principal sources are the *Livro da Montaria* by João I, ed. Francisco Maria Esteves Pereira (Coimbra, 1918); Duarte's *Livro da Ensinança de bem cavalgar toda sela*, ed. Joseph M. Piel (Lisbon, 1944); the various chronicles by Fernão Lopes, Gomes Eanes de Zurara, Rui de Pina, Garcia de Resende, and Damião de Góis; the Afonsine Ordinances (*Ordenaçoens do Senhor Rey D. Affonso V*, vols. I–V [Coimbra, 1792]); the cancioneiros, both from the earliest times as well as the one by Garcia de Resende; the narratives in the *Provas da História Genealógica da Casa Real Portuguesa*, ed. António Caetano de Sousa, 2nd ed. (Coimbra, 1946–54), vol. I, bk. III, and vol. VI, pt. II; and the *Documentos Historicos da Cidade de Evora*, ed. Gabriel Pereira, pts. 1–3 (Évora, 1885–91).

Gabriel Pereira devoted a short study to the hunts which would be worth continuing and expanding: *As Caçadas*, Estudos Eborenses, no. 29, pts. 1–2 (Évora, 1892–93). In addition to that, it is necessary to consult A. de Sousa e Silva Costa Lobo, *Historia da Sociedade em Portugal no seculo XV* (Lisbon, 1903), for the most complete and accurate analysis of game reserves, density of forests, and the wild animal population.

The *História da Cultura em Portugal* by António José Saraiva, vols. I–II (Lisbon, 1950–52), includes a study of the mentality of the aristocracy and of the clergy, with abundant references to the forms of amusement favored by these classes; particular attention is directed toward the troubadours and minstrels.

On music, consult first of all the excellent manual by João de Freitas Branco, *História da Música Portuguesa* (Lisbon, 1959), which makes available a vast bibliography, including documentary references. The basic book for the study of serious music in the Middle Ages is the monograph by Solange Corbin, *Essai sur la musique réligieuse portugaise au moyen age (1100–1385)* (Paris, 1952), completed by her "L'Office de la Conception de la Vierge: À propos d'un manuscrit du XVème siècle du monastère dominicain d'Aveiro, Portugal," *Bulletin des études portugaises et de l'Institut français au Portugal,* n.s., XIII (1949), 105–66, and by her "Fêtes portugaises," *Bulletin hispanique,* XLIX, no. 2 (1947), 205–18. The documentation collected by Francisco Marques de Sousa Viterbo (*Subsídios para a Historia da Musica em Portugal,* 2nd ed. [Coimbra, 1932]), in addition to that found in some articles by the same author, has not yet been studied thoroughly.

On the bullfights, there is a digression with a certain historical basis by the Conde de Sabugosa in his book *Embrechados,* 3rd ed. (Lisbon, 1921), pp. 13–58.

The medieval Portuguese theatre has up to now been quite neglected. Historians of literature tend to begin their story with Gil Vicente and to repeat generalities based on the drama of other European countries for the period preceding his. Nevertheless, see Mário Martins, "Representações teatrais em Lisboa no ano de 1451," *Brotéria,* LXXI, no. 5 (1960), 422–30. Among the general studies, consult Mário Martins, *Estudos de Literatura Medieval* (Braga, 1956); António José Saraiva and Oscar Lopes, *História da Literatura Portuguesa,* 2nd ed. (Oporto, n.d.); Teófilo Braga, *História do Theatro Portuguez,* vol. I (Oporto, 1870); and Alexandre Herculano, "Origens do theatro moderno: Theatro português até aos fins do seculo XVI" and "Historia do theatro moderno: Theatro hespanhol," both in *Opusculos,* 3rd ed., IX (*Litteratura,* I) (Lisbon, n.d.), 75–84 and 117–52.

CHAPTER 10 : DEATH

No study on life expectancy in medieval Portugal, the manner in which people faced death, and the way of holding funerals and wearing mourning has as yet been written. The books by Vítor Manuel Lopes Dias—*Cemitérios, Jazigos e Sepulturas* (Oporto, 1963), and *Notícia histórica da inumação* (Oporto, 1963)—devote only a few lines to the Middle Ages. Consequently, one must rely almost exclusively on the sources here.

In addition to the various chronicles by Fernão Lopes, Zurara, and Rui de Pina, Duarte's *Leal Conselheiro* and the fifteenth-century visitations and constitutions mentioned in the bibliography for Chapter 7 provide useful information. Freire de Oliveira (*Elementos para a Historia do Municipio de Lisboa* [Lisbon, 1882–85]), Gabriel Pereira (*Documentos Historicos da Cidade de Evora*, pts. 1–3 [Évora, 1885–91]), and João Baptista de Castro (*Mappa de Portugal antigo e moderno*, 3rd ed., vol. I [Lisbon, 1870]) complete the picture.

Among the studies which furnish information, see principally Teófilo Braga, *O Povo Portuguez nos seus costumes, crenças e tradições*, vol. I (Lisbon, 1885); António Garcia Ribeiro de Vasconcelos, *Evolução do culto de Dona Isabel de Aragão esposa do rei lavrador Dom Denis de Portugal (a Rainha Santa)*, vols. I–II (Coimbra, 1894); and Fortunato de Almeida, *Historia da Igreja em Portugal*, vols. I–II (Coimbra, 1910–12).

On tombstones and recumbent statues, we are much better supplied with studies. Among the many monographs and innumerable references scattered throughout all kinds of works, see as examples J. M. Cordeiro de Sousa, "Inscrições Sepulcrais da Sé de Lisboa," in idem, *Colectânea Olisiponense*, 3rd ed., II (Lisbon, 1958), 9–41; and idem, "Os 'jacentes' da Sé de Lisboa e a sua Indumentária," ibid., pp. 43–63.

SOURCES OF ILLUSTRATIONS

Academia das Ciências, Lisbon
Crónica Geral de Espanha
Fig. 27: fols. 186v, 192v, 205
Fig. 77: fol. 182
Fig. 80: fol. 266
Fig. 96 (right): fol. 27

Arquivo Nacional da Torre do Tombo, Lisbon
Commentário ao Apocalipse de Lorvão
Fig. 10 (left): fol. 59; *(right):* fol. 115
Fig. 69: fol. 64
Fig. 72: fol. 207
Fig. 81
Fig. 96 (left): fol. 136
Livro das Aves
Fig. 4: fols. 58v, 29, 41v, 43, 26v, 47v, 28, 17v, 53v, 5, 12, 32v, 45v, 60v, 35
Livro das Fortalezas de Duarte Darmas
Fig. 58: fols. 117v–118
Fig. 59: fols. 52v–53
Fig. 60: fols. 58v–59
Fig. 61: fols. 72v–73
Fig. 62: fols. 43v–44
Fig. 63: fols. 3v–4
Fig. 64: fols. 29v–30
Fig. 65: fol. 1
Fig. 66: fol. 122
Fig. 67: fol. 100
Fig. 68: fols. 116v–117
Fig. 85: fol. 115
Fig. 86: fol. 52
Fig. 87: fol. 64
Livro de Horas de D. Duarte
Fig. 56: fol. 120v

Fig. 75: fol. 310v
Fig. 97: fol. 144v
Fig. 99: fol. 323v
Livro da Sagrada Escritura de Lorvão
Fig. 70: fol. 158v
Missal Antigo de Lorvão
Fig. 83: fol. 1v
Fig. 84: fol. 4v
Fig. 89
Fig. 91: fol. 3
Psaltério de Lorvão
Fig. 20: fols. 98v, 109v, 107
Fig. 95: fol. 107v
Testamento Velho de Lorvão
Fig. 71: fol. 85v
Fig. 88: fol. 130v

Biblioteca da Ajuda, Lisbon
Cancioneiro da Ajuda
Fig. 42: fol. 231
Fig. 94: fols. 171, 111, 151, 109, 113, 119

Biblioteca Nacional, Lisbon
Cód. Alcob. 208
Fig. 93: fol. 32v
Cód. Alcob. 376
Fig. 92: fols. 3–3v
Cód. Alcob. 426
Fig. 90: fols. 251–251v
Ilum. 42
Fig. 3
Fig. 25 (left)
Fig. 57 (right)
Fig. 74
Fig. 78
Fig. 82

332

Inc. 533
  Fig. 5: fol. 19v
  Fig. 25 (right): fol. 69
  Fig. 76: fol. 83
  Fig. 98: fol. 38

British Museum, London
  Royal Ms., 14 E IV
  Fig. 6
  Fig. 79

Landesbibliothek Stuttgart
  Hist. 4.° 141
  Fig. 41

Musée des Beaux-Arts, Dijon
  Fig. 51

Museu Nacional de Arte Antiga, Lisbon
  Fig. 1
  Fig. 2
  Fig. 31
  Fig. 52

Österreichische Nationalbibliothek,
Vienna
  Cod. Vindob. 3270* Philol. 291
    Fig. 57 (left): fol. 1

The line drawings, by Vítor André, are based strictly on paintings, illuminations, and other iconographic sources from the twelfth through the fifteenth centuries.

INDEX

334